WITHDRAWN

The International Theological Library.

EDITED BY

CHARLES A. BRIGGS, D.D., D.LITT.,

Graduate Professor of Theological Encyclopædia and Symbolics, Union Theological Seminary, New York;

AND

THE LATE STEWART D. F. SALMOND, D.D.,

Sometime Principal, and Professor of Systematic Theology and New Testament Exegesis, United Free Church College, Aberdeen.

THE CHRISTIAN DOCTRINE OF GOD.

BY WILLIAM NEWTON CLARKE, D.D.

THE
CHRISTIAN DOCTRINE
OF GOD

BY

WILLIAM NEWTON CLARKE, D.D.
PROFESSOR IN COLGATE UNIVERSITY

NEW YORK
CHARLES SCRIBNER'S SONS
1925

DEUS ACCIPIAT

PREFACE

THE work that was entrusted to me by the General Editors of the International Theological Library was simply the presentation of the conception of God that is characteristic of the Christian religion. I was not sent to search for God, but rather to report as well as I might what the Christian faith testifies concerning him. It has seemed to me that this single commission was enough for me to undertake, and I have attempted nothing more. No report of the literature of the subject will be found upon these pages, nor any quotation of other men's work, nor any controversy. It is the sole endeavour of the book to set forth the Christian doctrine of God for the present day: not the doctrine of the past, or of the future, but the thought of God that we may now entertain if we follow the leading of Jesus Christ the revealer. So far as I have the power, I have sought to be faithful both to the ancient light and to the modern, and I have hoped that my presentation might bear reasonably well the tests of the present time. There are many ways of dealing with the vast and glorious theme, and certainly there must be room for a book that simply aims to show forth the doctrine as Christian faith may receive it now.

I have written in the full conviction that the light which Jesus Christ gives us upon God is the true light, and that God is such a Being as he inspires us to love and trust. Some things we believe about God that have been learned from other sources than his revealing, but we may be sure that of

God's character and relation to our life he has given us the true knowledge. His God and Father is the living God. Of course I know that there are many intelligent minds who cannot receive this, and that many who believe it most devoutly would differ widely from me in the portrayal of that living God. But I can say that I have earnestly sought to make the spirit of the teaching of Jesus determinative of every view of doctrine that is presented here; and while I have nothing to claim for my own work in presentation, I do claim that the substance of that which I present is the heart of the Master's message to the world, and for its own sake is worthy of all acceptation.

It will easily be believed that in so vast a subject the difficulty of satisfactory arrangement is very great. One may almost say that every part of the subject implies every other part, and cannot be treated without it. Accordingly a writer finds himself making use of matters that are yet to be unfolded, and using again what has already been discussed. But since the difficulty resides in the nature of the subject, I have ceased to be anxious about it, and have allowed anticipations and repetitions to come as they will, when the subject-matter brings them. As to the general arrangement that I have adopted, I may say that it is the one that seems to me best suited to the character of the Christian doctrine. It is the order of religion, rather than of philosophy or of science; for I conceive that in religion is found the clearest way to the knowledge of God.

Inasmuch as I have discussed the same subjects in other writings, I have here and there used an earlier expression of my own, without indicating the quotation. In general, the position that is held in this book is the same as that which I have occupied before. But of course a man is no more bound to agree with his earlier self than with any other man, and I have felt myself entirely free to depart from positions that I once held, whenever better light or sounder processes enabled me to do so. The claim of truth is far more compelling than the claim of consistency, and I respond to it with a far more loyal heart.

WILLIAM NEWTON CLARKE.

COLGATE UNIVERSITY, } *January*, 1909.
HAMILTON, NEW YORK. }

CONTENTS

THE
CHRISTIAN DOCTRINE OF GOD

THE CHRISTIAN DOCTRINE
OF GOD

INTRODUCTION

1. THE THEME AND THE TREATMENT

CHRISTIANITY is a doctrine of God and a life in God. It is scarcely more; for its great peculiarity is its proclamation of a work of gracious help from God to man, performed because God is what he is, and all its substance beyond this consists in the unfolding of what it means, in experience and thought, that God is such a Being as Jesus Christ makes known. Christianity is religion with such a God, and Christian theology is the doctrine of such a God, and of that which follows from his being.

It is the purpose of the present volume to present the Christian conception of God, his character and his relations, especially his relations with men. The aim is practical, as becomes a Christian study, and the work is inspired by the hope that to the reader God may become more clearly and truly known. This is a lofty aim, but the endeavour may not be in vain. Certainly we may be sure that the God and Father of Jesus desires to be more clearly and truly known, and our means of acquaintance with him are such that any reverent student may perhaps help his fellows toward such better knowledge.

The title, "The Christian Doctrine of God," is not without ambiguity. In fact, it has been understood in various ways in the history of Christian thought, and it is necessary at the outset to indicate in what sense it is now employed.

Theology has usually assumed that the Christian doctrine

of God is simply identical with the conception, or group of conceptions, that the Bible contains. It has been taken for granted that the Scriptures of the Old and New Testaments yield a single and consistent conception of God, and that this must be accepted by Christianity as its interpretation of the divine Being. If this view were adopted the present task would be to collect and formulate the utterances of the Bible about God, and send forth the summary of these as the Christian doctrine. But in the theological classification that now prevails such analysis and synthesis of the biblical material is the work of biblical theology, and the results of such labour have already been presented in the volumes of the present series that are devoted to that department. But apart from this incidental consideration, the Christian doctrine of God is not co-extensive and identical with the doctrine of God that is brought forth from the Scriptures by the study of biblical theology. The Scriptures bring us the Christian conception, but they bring us much besides, for they preserve the record and influence of much that was left behind in the course of the progressive revelation. It is for us to distinguish things that differ, and use the contents of the Scriptures in loyalty to their historical character. And it is further true that the Christian doctrine does not inherit solely from the Bible. It inherits also from the long course of Christian history; for the Christian mind has been at work upon the thought of God, and the thought of God upon the Christian mind, for almost two thousand years, and the Christian doctrine is the outcome from the entire process. It is not yet completed, nor will it ever be. A true doctrine of God will be always the same and yet ever changing, for the human apprehension of the great reality will be altered from age to age, and each period will require its own forms of thought for the abiding truth. Grounded in the Bible, the Christian doctrine of God has partly been developed since the Bible was written, and has now, as in other ages, to take its form for the present time. Hence the present discussion, while it finds its inspiration and main substance in the sacred writings of Christianity, will not treat the Christian doctrine of God as merely the equivalent of the biblical utterances.

It has sometimes been assumed that at some point in its history the Christian Church has obtained a doctrine of God that may be accepted as sufficient and final. Doctrine expressed in creeds has often been practically regarded thus by those who held allegiance to the creeds; and theology has been expected, if not required, to expound the authorized conceptions. According to the full ecclesiastical view of religion, the Church alone has authority to declare doctrine, and doctrine declared by her is final, even concerning God. Even where there is no such acknowledgment of the sole authority of the Church, many have practically taken as complete and final the doctrine that their own branch of the Church has formulated. Various schools of Christian thought have had their doctrines of God, diverging though with much in common, and each has held to its own, especially to its own peculiarities, as if improvement were not to be expected. But the history of our doctrine is not now to be traced, and there will be no opportunity to select the best from among its various historical forms. Moreover, the Christian doctrine of God is not identical with any statement that has been made in a creed or put forth by an ecclesiastical authority. Claims to that effect will not bear examination, and the theory on which they rest is untenable. Nowhere along the course of the past has the doctrine been completed. The growth of a living thought is never finished, least of all the growth of this greatest of all conceptions. Hence the present treatment will not consist in the selection and unfolding of some doctrine of God that has been proclaimed by church or creed in some past time, or is offered as sufficient now.

It is sometimes thought, again, that the Christian doctrine consists in that which has been common to good Christian belief in all ages. There have been divergences on this side and on that, but the specialties of individuals or groups may be ignored: the Christian doctrine is the doctrine of the central consensus, the persisting view, which Christendom has held in common. But neither is this definition accepted here. True thought concerning God has always been at the heart of the Christian doctrine, but it is not a fact that the consensus, if we could discover it, could be identified with the genuine Christian conception. To the genuine conception the persisting belief has done justice only in part. It has been a growing thought of God, variable with the variableness of the Christian people and their life, influenced by the temporary peculiarities of their mental practice, changing with the extent of their knowledge, impoverished in their times of spiritual decline, and progressively enriched by their long experience. Evidently we cannot expect to identify the common element in all this, and if we could find it we could not call it the Christian doctrine of God.

By the Christian doctrine of God is meant, in the present discussion, the conception of God which Christian faith and thought propose for the present time, in view of the Bible, and of the history, and of all sound knowledge and experience, interpreted in the light of Jesus Christ the Revealer. It is the doctrine concerning which we can say, at the point at which we now stand, that it is true if Jesus Christ does reveal God truly. It is the view of God for which we may fairly claim that Christianity stands responsible, in the presence of such life and knowledge as surround us now. This volume is designed to present if possible the conception of God for which Christianity now stands. It is a doctrine that is grounded in the Christian revelation, developed in history, and now restated once more after many times, in the presence of modern knowledge.

This is the only tenable and the only Christian definition. The Christian view of God comes to us from Jesus Christ, who lifted older conceptions to fresh glory and gave them new power. In him it came from God himself. It was never a fixed and unchangeable deposit of truth, for even if it had been possible to give such a deposit of truth concerning God, neither human language nor human thought was ever capable of receiving and holding it.

The Christian view of God came from Jesus not as finished once for all, but as a living, growing thing. It has lived in Christian experience in various degrees of strength and weakness, clearness and obscurity, always in forms supplied to it by existing life. As it came alive to other ages, so it has come alive to ours, and as alive we must treat it. It claims to be truth, truth in the midst of truth, truth supreme, and like other truth it must be apprehended as men are able. It must now fit in with other truth, just as it fitted in with truth known in other periods. It must now be apprehended as truly, clearly and Christianly as is now possible, and be set in its due place among the other views of reality that this age entertains. In so far as this is done, we shall have the Christian doctrine of God for the present time. It will be Jesus' own doctrine, and the biblical doctrine, and the historical doctrine, brought into the present age. It will be the latest historical form of that conception of God which we owe to Jesus Christ. We shall pass it on to our successors, and it will be their privilege and duty to state it yet again.

The main purpose in this book is to state the Christian doctrine of God—not to prove it, but to present it. The method of this endeavour must correspond to the nature of the enterprise, and a few words about it may be recorded here.

It is necessary first to grasp the thought of God that is given in the life and teaching of Jesus Christ. He it is who gives us the true point of view and the true knowledge. We must endeavour to become acquainted with God in the manner that he commends to us, and to enter into the benefit of such acquaintance. The Christian doctrine holds that God is such a Being as Jesus shows him to be, so that one who knows him thus will never need to make essential revolution in his thought of him. In his own soul and in all his revealing Jesus had to do with the real God, the God who exists, the same forever, and in such a God it is forever safe to believe. The fact that we obtain knowledge about him from other sources besides Jesus makes no difficulty for the Christian faith. There are great fields of fact into which his revelation did not enter, and in which new light is sure to arise as our knowledge grows, extending and enriching our idea of him whom we adore. But the Christian doctrine affirms unwaveringly that the view of God which Jesus gives is forever true, an unalterable verity, changing for us only by being better known. As it is apprehended more worthily, of course it will open again and again in fresh glory, but the new glory will be the old glory better understood. With such a doctrine set before us, it must be our first work to make the central substance of it our own. The revelation of God that has been made in Jesus Christ is the heart of the Christian doctrine of God, in this age as in every other.

Here we have to do with the words of Jesus and the events of his career, which we must interpret with the best wisdom that we can command. But his contribution to the doctrine is not all contained in his written words, or in the records of his life, for in their experience he imparted to living men a living gift that transfigured all their dealings with God, and transfigured even God himself. All this we must understand through historical imagination entering into the life of vanished days, and above all by the discernment of the spiritual eye, the sympathetic perception of the Christian soul. Christian doctrine must be formed from ancient materials by gathering those elements that are spiritually characteristic of Jesus Christ, and building them into a structure that corresponds to their nature. These alone may enter. If anywhere in our biblical material or elsewhere we find a thought that does not agree with the spirit of the testimony of Jesus, it must contribute nothing to our construction of the Christian doctrine. But that rich total of spiritual truth which does accord with him is ours to use.

It may easily be called narrow thus to take a single teaching as the core of our supreme doctrine. So it might be if that teaching were not such as it is, but when we discern its quality the suspicion of narrowness passes away. Jesus does not bring us a doctrine of God, he brings us God. His word is not philosophical, but religious. He does not explain God, but looks into his face, and leads us to do the same. Among the great teachers of the world he is the One who gives us God as a living reality, to be known in actual life. Under his leading we know who God is before we begin to discuss him. It is the glory of the Christian conception of God that it is first of all a religious conception, and it is so noble a religious conception that man can form none nobler or more satisfactory. No authority or hint of Jesus limits us to learning about God from him alone, but no school equal to his for learning this great lesson is known to men, and Christianity is not to be reproached for narrowness because it learns of him.

The first effect of this mighty knowledge of God thrown out into the world of men meets us in the early Christian experience. Here we see how great it is, and perceive its nature more clearly. Beginning from this, we have to deal with the fact that the Christian thought of God has lived through all the Christian period, and been apprehended in many ways. The doctrine of the present day is an outcome from the history, as it must be. In the long development there has been much that is Christian and much that is not, as well as much that is reasonable and much that is not. Here again the Christian selective sense must do its work, just as the rational selective sense performs its function. We are required to judge what is Christian and what is not, to observe what has been disproved, outgrown or transformed by the Christian movement of life, and to gather in what belongs to the true Christian doctrine. We must not, and we need not, cut off the doctrine of the present day from that of the past. What we trace over the threshold of the present age is a genuine progress of unfolding truth. Christian thought in the latest time comes not to destroy but to fulfil. In the history we meet views of God that have been the heart and life of all doctrine, the centre of the divergences, and the glory of all Christian time. If we can make these our own, and cast them into the forms that are truest and most useful now, we shall be no less loyal to the past than to the future in so doing.

By this long road we come with the doctrine to our own time, and endeavour to express the Christian thought of God in the light of the present day. Nearly or remotely, all knowledge has its effect upon the idea that we can hold of God. At every turn we find that the knowledge that is characteristic of the present age is influencing the conception of him. If we complain of this we are wrong: our faith must fairly meet the knowledge of the age, and our present doctrine of God must take account of all truth now known that can bear upon it. We shall find that some ancient conceptions of God are tenable, or possible, no longer, and that some are necessary now that once were not within the reach of thought —so great are the changes that come with change in the extent of knowledge. Yet God is always the same, and the view of his character and relations with men which Jesus imparts is true forever. This is the heart of the Christian doctrine, and this truth must take present form from present conditions, that the old and the new may work as one.

So our task is to construct the doctrine of God that corresponds to the testimony and spirit of Christ, and to the other truth that is known at present. It is an obvious criticism upon this proposal that it leaves much to the judgment of him who undertakes to construct the doctrine. This is true, and one could easily wish for a less exacting method. But this seems to be God's way with the free spirits whom he has gifted with the powers of life—he bids each and all of them turn their faces toward him, and report to one another what they see. Each sees for himself. Yet there need be no fear that any one man will form a doctrine. No one can do that— it is the work of many together. Nothing is a doctrine that has not its roots both in the gift of our Lord and in the experience of his people. Yet one man may do his best to present the doctrine which the revelation of God and the experience of men are commending to the present time. With diffidence and yet with confidence this task must now be undertaken. After the doctrine has been presented, however, there will remain still another task. The question will arise whether the doctrine is tenable; whether facts can be brought forth that have the right to shake our faith in it; whether, after all is said, the world would be justified in rejecting it. This question of course must be considered. We must remember by what kind of evidence a doctrine of God can be supported, and judge whether belief in the God and Father of Jesus Christ is justified or condemned by the sum of what we know.

When we come to the evidence, however, it will be best of all if we find confirmation of the belief in which this book is written, namely, that the Christian doctrine of God, when rightly presented, is gloriously self-commending. If it is not, indeed, it cannot be commended. Proof may be offered in favour of it, but the best ultimate proof is found in what it is. Objections may be brought against it, but it is by the virtue of the doctrine itself that they are to be overcome. Certain it is that the Christian doctrine offers the noblest and most satisfactory thought that was ever offered to the mind and heart of man. It commends itself at once to sound reason, and to that high faculty of faith by which it is given to man to lay hold upon that which is above him. Although the Christian doctrine of God is far from being so obvious that it cannot be doubted, though doubt is possible and even easy, and is suggested by familiar facts, yet the doctrine is so noble in itself, and so normal to all sound thought, and so congruous with a rational interpretation of existence, that mind and heart are justified in accepting it as true. The endeavour of this book is to present the God and Father of the Lord Jesus Christ, in the character which Jesus gives to him, and help the reader to see and feel that he must be the living God.

It will not be surprising that in this endeavour the method is not in any great degree controversial. The limits of space do not allow comparison among the innumerable statements that have been made, or elaborate defence of the judgments

that are accepted.   But apart from this, the best presentation
of the Christian doctrine can scarcely be controversial.   It is
not to the spirit of controversy that the vision of God is assured, or even to the method of argument.   When we see how
Jesus taught men to become acquainted with God, we blush
at the frequent assumption that we can know him through
discussion, sometimes keen and dialectical, sometimes angry.
We shall encounter views of God that we cannot accept: we
may leave them, but we need not stay to slay them.   The
views of him that we accept should be borne in upon our
souls by the tide of a mighty peace, and received in a calmness that has small place for controversy.   The doctrine of
God will fight its own battles, and the best that we can do for
it is to set it forth.

Yet with all our confidence we cannot hope to frame a
doctrine of God that will be free from difficulty, or one that
will relieve any day's life of its common perplexities.   The
subject is too great for that.   In the conception of God is
involved the entire mystery of existence; and that mystery is
not only very broad and deep but very near, manifesting itself
not only in the problems of infinity but in the commonest
affairs of life.   No doctrine will immediately solve the daily
problems that beset all serious minds.   The contradictions
of life are to be harmonized in God as their final unity, but
though we are ever so sure of this, we know that the perfect
harmony is not yet manifest.   We must wait, if for no other
reason, because we are not yet capable of that comprehensive
understanding which discernment will require.   We are still
God's little children.   But there is comfort in the fact that
the Christian belief is not merely an acceptance of conclusions.
Christianity is not ashamed to say that its belief is a grasping
of realities.   The realities are unseen, and we wait for them.
Nevertheless, even now we have more than glimpses of that
supreme reality in which the final solution will be found.   The
vision of God is already clear enough to give us peace, to
sustain us in good endeavour, and to be "the master light of
all our seeing."

2. THE SOURCES

The sources of the Christian doctrine of God lie partly farther back than Christ. We find them not only in the Hebrew faith that cradled the Christian faith, but in the general faith of mankind, and far among the primitive thoughts of men. The chief source we find in him whose mission it was to show us plainly of the Father; for Jesus has imparted to the world a better knowledge of God than any other. His revelation in himself and his spiritual work forms the main substance of the Christian doctrine. We study his contribution farther in the early Christian experience which showed more fully what it was and how great was its value; and we trace the development of the doctrine that sprang from him, as it came from him to us. From these sources we gather our material for judging what, in the light of Jesus the Revealer, God is.

(1) *The Ancient Ethical Conception*

This book does not trace the idea of God from its beginnings. It must suffice to say that the best living conception of God is the growth of ages, and that the experiences from which it took its rise are among the oldest possessions of mankind. As for its origin, the idea of God would seem indebted to primitive observation of the world, and to the primitive experiences of man; to the recognition of external power, and to man's reading of his own life. Back of our searching, however, the idea seems grounded in human nature itself; for religion has never been satisfactorily accounted for by reference to external suggestions, but appears to have its foundation in the nature of the being in whom it exists. The simplest and truest explanation of belief in God is, that it is always the nature of life to take hold upon the realities that it needs for service to its welfare, and that for the human spirit God is one of those realities. Certain it is that from its early days the human race has been believing, however crudely, in a divine power, authority and helpfulness, and has acted upon the belief.

The primitive religious conception entered in due time into fellowship with the primitive ethical conception. At what stage the ethical element came into fruitful union with the religious feeling we shall never know, for it was not an event but a process, and it belonged to a far-off time, from which no records have come down. But through experience of life it gradually came to pass that the divine relation was felt to involve a moral claim, to be fulfilled not only in formalities of religion but in the conduct of life, acceptable to the powers above in proportion as it was right. The ethical conception of God is the thought of him as making such a claim on men because of a moral character that he himself possesses.

Such an ethical conception, it is needless to say, has not belonged to any one religion alone, and has existed in all possible degrees of strength and clearness. Within the field of our knowledge no religion has ever been wholly destitute of the ethical quality. Even the lowest religions have contained some moral counsels and appeals, justified by moral quality attributed to the objects of worship. The range of morals may have been narrow and low, but recognition of a moral claim from above has nowhere been wholly wanting. It is in this that the uplifting power of religion has had its surest sanction. Worship has in itself a certain degree of power to elevate heart and life for the worshipper, but its good influence may be more than matched by unworthiness in its object. When the object of worship is of such character as to require that a man shall do in his life the thing that he holds to be right, worship becomes truly elevating; and when the character is such as to inspire an ever-ascending ideal of what is right, and insist with ever-growing urgency upon loyalty to this rising standard, then religion becomes best and most beneficent. The gradual establishment of belief in a moral God forms a great element in history, which can now be mentioned only in passing. To the presence and value of the moral element in the religions of the world we can only pay thankful tribute. Often it has high quality, and sometimes in a dark atmosphere there flashes out a high moral claim. Doubtless the ethical life of the world has suffered much from religion, but it owes to religion immeasurably more than it has suffered from it. Faulty enough indeed the influence has been, but the ethical life of the world has on the whole been greatly reinforced and purified by its religions.

The ethical conception of God rose highest in the religion of the Hebrew people, and is set forth in the noblest way in the noblest parts of the Old Testament. The prophets were its greatest heralds, but in varying degrees the Law, the Prophets and the Psalms all proclaim it. The tracing of the growth of this high quality in Hebrew doctrine and life, however, lies outside our field. The Hebrew Scriptures were complete when they were placed by parents or teachers in the hands of Jesus, and all their ethical wealth was ready to be taken up into a doctrine that would glorify its glories and remedy its defects. For the present purpose there is need of nothing more than a brief reminder of that ethical conception of God to which the highest souls of Israel had attained.

Christians have always said that the high Hebrew conception of God was due to revelation. Men were not merely discovering God, but God was making himself known to men. This is so largely and richly true that in order to do it justice we must allow to the great word revelation its broadest and most significant use. God's methods in making himself known are sure to be many: it cannot be that he reveals himself only in some single mode. He has revealed himself through individual experience, as when the writer of the fifty-first Psalm learned from his own sense of guilt how little God cared for sacrifice, or Hosea learned God's love through his own experience of love in spite of sin. He has revealed himself through larger experiences, as when through Israel's trouble the seers of the Exile became acquainted with a greater and nearer God than they had known before. He has revealed himself immediately in the communion that holy souls have had with him, and has enabled such souls to tell what they have learned. All this he has done, in accordance with his universal method. That which has gone on elsewhere went on also among the Hebrews, and God was in it: life developed ethics, as it must, and suggested an ethical doctrine of God. There is every reason why Christian students should recognize the natural growth of ethics, and perceive God revealing his own character by that means. Ethics and ethical views of God grew up among the Hebrews upon the true human method, which is the divine method. Some truths about God they learned for themselves, through his providential teaching, and some they received by contribution from other peoples with whom they had to do. Much they learned also through his more direct manifestation of himself to the men of God who of old were moved by his Holy Spirit. Under the one name of revelation we must include all of these processes in which God was becoming known, for all were works of God, who was voluntarily offering himself to human knowledge and fellowship, in one as truly as in another. Among the various methods there is no shadow of inconsistency. If God lives indeed, we may be sure that human life, ordained by him, will reveal him in some measure, and equally sure that as a living Spirit he will show himself to spirits that have vision, as he did to the Hebrew prophets. Back of the ethical conception of God which is recorded in the Old Testament lie both these divine modes of revelation, worthy of God and man.

In the Old Testament God is always intensely personal, and by no means least in the parts in which his moral quality is most strongly emphasized. He always speaks as I, is spoken of as He, and is addressed as Thou, and he always appears as One who stands in real and vital relations with men. To the men whose life the Old Testament records, God was just as living and personal as themselves, and just as capable of communion with them as they were with one another. The fact that he was invisible only threw the relation more into the realm of the spirit; it did not in the least diminish the reality of it in common life. The gradual retirement of early anthropomorphism did not take away the personal quality. The prophets had as vivid a sense as any men ever had of the living God.

Concerning the character of God the Old Testament is not of one voice throughout, but its highest thought attributes goodness to him in high and glorious degree. To him holiness belongs. Holiness, our comprehensive term for all that is most impressive and glorious in the perfect Goodness, seems at first to have denoted that which belongs to God, or is divine, in distinction from what is human; but before the Old Testament had borne its whole message holiness had come to denote what is morally pure and exacting, in contrast to evil of every kind. There is no defining of holiness, but the word assigns to God all that makes his presence glorious in itself and searching to men. For it is important to note that God's great goodness appears not as an abstraction, but always in concrete and practical relations. It is toward men that his face is turned. He is the righteous God; and righteousness is a quality that belongs to personal relations. His character is such that he must do right toward men and demand right from them. His righteousness is both terrible and gracious, for it sets him against all wrong and evil, and makes him a Being upon whom the strongest and simplest confidence may take hold. It appears both in strictness and in faithfulness, in severity and in grace; for in the Old Testament God's righteousness includes both of these. In a word God is worthy to be adored, trusted and obeyed. Above all, he is such a Being, and so related to men, that it is the supreme duty of men to do his will. This is the underlying principle in the entire fact and method of divine Law for men. The reason and method of the divine will are not brought out in their glory as they are by Jesus, and the blessedness of the divine way of life is not made so plain;

but the rightful sovereignty of the will of God is proclaimed in the Old Testament as the essential fact in life. The absolute moral supremacy of God is a lesson that stood waiting to be taken up and established forever in the teaching of Jesus.

Israel stands, in the Old Testament, as the group of men to whom God has specially bound himself. At first Israel has to do with a national deity, but gradually the God of Israel passes over into the God of all; yet Israel never ceases to be the people that stands in special relation to him. The covenant of the national God becomes a covenant of the universal God; though his relation to other men comes also into sight.

To Israel he stands related through his Law, for he has been pleased to lay upon this people great and clear requirements. Men are here under special obligation to God: they owe him duty, and are bound by his commands, for his Law brings divine instruction, and carries divine authority. In this way what lies deep in his heart and character is set forth as standard and guide for them. Sin against his will thus revealed is sin against himself, which he may punish or forgive. But the prophets know that it is not only within the sphere of explicit law that his requirement moves. They rise to condemn unrighteousness and unworthy life of every kind, not merely on the ground that God has forbidden it, but on the ground that it is wrong and men know it to be wrong. They appeal to conscience and common knowledge, and insist upon God's demand that men live up to what they know, and do that which they understand to be right and worthy. Prophets simplify a claim of God which in law has been felt to be complicated, and hold forth his demand for whatsoever is pure in personal life and right between man and man, as well as for all that is reverent and obedient toward himself. The best that men know how to do is represented as the way by which they are to advance toward fulfilment of God's own standard.

In the Old Testament God is often represented as extremely

severe toward the sinful. We find language which, taken by itself, would make him appear to delight in punishing, and to be satisfied in the doom of those who disobey him. In a similar spirit the institutions of the Old Testament represent him as a God who withdraws himself from the sinful, separated, dwelling apart in a holy place, and approachable only through priestly meditation. One would think that to ordinary men he must have been more terrible than attractive. But this is the waning element. As revelation advances and grows clearer he appears more and more as a God who desires not the death of the wicked, and who welcomes the penitent to his fellowship. He does not delight in punishment. He is interested in men for their good, and is satisfied only when they are right. This is the waxing view of God, the more characteristic view, which becomes more and more impressive as the true light draws on.

To Israel, and, in the end, to all men, God is thus related through love. With Israel he has his covenant, in which his gracious character is especially manifest. Gracious he is, and merciful. He is patient, long-suffering and full of compassion. He delights to pardon. He desires not the death of the wicked, but that he turn from his evil way and live. So far as he is offended by his people's sins, he is ready at any moment for his anger to be turned away. In the established system of sacrifices he is believed to have provided means for the people's expression of their penitence for sin, as well as of their gratitude and consecration; but his forgiving grace is his own, and is not purchased by their offerings. He desires not sacrifice, but a broken spirit. The later prophets and psalmists perceive that not toward Israel alone is God thus gracious, but that the same heart of love flows out toward all the world. God is so truly good that he can be trusted never to forget, or to abandon his purpose, or to be indifferent to sin, or to deal unworthily with men. Thus accompanying that holiness which the Old Testament sets forth is that supreme excellence which the New Testament discovers more richly, under the name of love.

To Israel, and to all men, God stands related, again, through the experiences of life. In law, in prophecy and in history, the Old Testament illustrates the activity of God in human affairs and his moral interest in the doings of men. His requirement is not partial or special but searches through the whole of life. His watchful interest constitutes what Christian doctrine has called a Providence, in which his purpose is that men shall be taught the lessons of his character and will. The history of Israel is interpreted as one long course of probation and education, in which God is seeking to make his character known and lead men to give due reverence and obedience to him. Prophets and prophetic historians are never weary of reiterating that good comes to Israel when Israel is faithful to God and his righteousness, and calamity is the sure result of infidelity to him. The prophets, indeed, expound the ethical conception of God far more profoundly, variously and practically than does the Law. But the relation of God to the continuous life of men is not always plain or easy to be understood; and the Old Testament records the perplexity which is inevitable in a world so compounded of good and evil as this world is. How the wrongs and inequalities of life and the manifold sorrows of the world are to be understood in view of the righteousness and grace of God is a mystery, and sometimes a heart-breaking mystery, to prophets and poets. But the goodness is never given up, even if it is momentarily obscured. The devout spirit holds it fast, and labours to solve the problem in the light of it. The temper in which even the most agonized inquiry is made is well represented by the prayer, "Righteous art thou, O Jehovah, when I contend with thee, yet would I plead the cause with thee: wherefore doth the way of the wicked prosper?" (Jer. xii. 1.) Exceptions to this reverent confidence are but slight, and out of the inquiry comes the conviction that God has a gracious purpose in the troubles that have been so perplexing.

The God thus ethically conceived is the God of nature, the creator of the world, the Lord of providence. Late in the course of thought concerning him was brought forth that great psalm of creation which stands at the front of the Hebrew Scriptures (Gen. i.). He is the creator of all things and the giver of human life. The movements of nature in the world are results of his immediate activity. His high character makes him terrible as well as glorious to men, for toward wickedness he stands as judge and punisher. Yet "the fear of the Lord" is no mere dread; it is a solemn and reverent regard to his righteousness.

The ancient ethical conception of God runs through all antiquity, but nowhere else does it stand out in forms so clear and practical as in the highest utterances of the Old Testament. Even here, however, it is not complete, or satisfactorily carried to its applications. Inferior conceptions of God exist beside it, brought over from early religion and not yet banished by the higher truth. It must never be forgotten that along with the ancient ethical conception, the Old Testament preserves many more primitive conceptions that cannot be reconciled with it. He is sometimes shown as capricious, revengeful, unreasonable, cruel; and we have to own that now and then Moses appears at better advantage than he. Even at the best he is still far too much conceived of as a God of partialism, bound to a nation. (Christianity has suffered beyond expression from the conscientious endeavour to attribute to the God of the New Testament all the passions and doings of the God of the Old.) Moreover, we find the faults that are inseparable from a legal system in religion, such as was in full force late in the Old Testament period. Under such a system God appears as One who is satisfied when men obey specific commands, and expects them to deserve his favour by such obedience—an error that Jesus had to meet and set aside. But in spite of such defective views of God, which could only retard the reception of nobler thought, the ethical conception is present in power in the Old Testament, and constitutes the crown and glory of the Hebrew religion. Here shines out the thought of God as moral character, rightly claiming to dominate the life of man. That the manifestations of moral sway that are attributed to him are often below the best is but a natural fact of history, of slight importance in comparison with the sublime belief in an ethical God that runs increasingly through the Old Testament as a living power.

(2) *The Testimony of Jesus*

The Christian doctrine takes its name from Jesus, the Son of God, known as the Christ, and from him it derives its character.

Jesus quietly appeared among the Jewish people and uttered his word concerning God and man. It is a striking fact that he did not come proposing a new doctrine of God. or announce the need of a revolution in the knowledge of him that had been received from the fathers. As a Jew he was born to a conception of God, and he never rejected his inheritance. He lived the life of a devout Hebrew, looking to God in the spirit of the religion of the prophets. We know how he condemned the abuses of the old religion, which in his day was a religion partly of the prophets and partly of the law; and yet he never stood as a rejecter of the doctrine of God which the ancient religion had bequeathed. He began where he found himself, and used what he had received. Nevertheless, it is a fact that he brought in a new religion, and did for the doctrine of God more than any other has ever done or can do. He enlarged, enriched, spiritualized the conception of God, and freed it from perversions that were injurious to religion; and at the same time he brought it into actual life in its new simplicity and glory, and helped men to live by it, as no one else has ever done. He has given a richer doctrine of God, and inspired and illustrated a better practice of God, than the world has known elsewhere.

This certainly is a most remarkable combination—a vast improvement in the highest of human conceptions, introduced not in theory merely but in actual life, and yet introduced without profession of revolutionary intent, and without strong emphasis upon any additions to thought already held. One thing is clear—the conception of God that came to Jesus out of the past was so sound and true that he could accept it and use it as the basis of his own doctrine. He was able to take up the best doctrine that he found in the holy writings and worthiest life of his people, and carry it to a still higher use. Such an acceptance bore witness to it. The contribution of the past is approved by being taken up into the nobler doctrine of the future.

Of course this does not mean that Jesus approved and appropriated all that is said of God in those Scriptures that lay in his hands. He did not deliver to us all that the Old Testament says of God as Christian testimony. To suppose that he did has been one of the most hurtful errors in Christian teaching. When he condemned the spirit ascribed to Elijah in calling fire from heaven to destroy his enemies, he condemned the spirit ascribed to God in supposing that he would send fire from heaven for such a purpose at Elijah's call (Lk. ix. 51–56). When he said, "Love your enemies, that ye may be sons of your Father who is in heaven" (Mt. v. 45–46), he made many of the old conceptions of God impossible. For in the Old Testament there are recorded many conceptions of God, ranging from low to high. There is much there that falls far below Jesus' level, and loyalty to him requires that we distinguish it from that which corresponds to his high spirit. Nevertheless, it is true that the increasing revelation of the Old Testament leads directly on to Jesus and is crowned by his utterance. He, the truest of revealers, accepted and appropriated the noblest conception of God that the old faith had known, and initiated the Christian doctrine at the summit of the old belief. We do not find him quoting inferior statements of the old Scriptures concerning God. Whatever fell below the height at which he began formed no part of his doctrine; but whatever from the ancient source was in harmony with the spirit of his mission he made his own and transmitted as his own to us.

In this true sense Christianity was the heir of Hebraism in

its doctrine of God.   But it must be added that the ancient
ethical conception of God that thus came into Christianity
was not altogether a specialty of Hebraism.   Confidence in a
God who is felt to be worthy of confidence is of the very substance of religious life, and in the history of religion a God
actually worthy of confidence has many a time been discerned and trusted.   God has not left himself without witness, and has in some measure become known for what he
really is.   Worthy conceptions of his character have not been
confined to Israel.   So when Jesus took his stand upon the
doctrine of the prophets, he gave his sanction not only to the
Hebrew revelation at its best, but to all doctrine of a worthy
God that human faith has ever attained.   He set the crown
of his approval upon the process that has formed an ethical
doctrine of God, wherever it has gone on.   In bearing witness
to the eternal goodness he bore witness to the value of every
recognition of the eternal goodness that has ever been made.
He showed that all high moral conceptions of God have been
right—imperfect indeed, yet real visions of the truth.   It was
the Hebrew race that contributed the conceptions that stood
ready to be adopted into the Christian faith, but in accepting
them Jesus put himself in connection not with Hebraism only,
but with the entire history of religion, and set the seal of
honour upon that moral element which has been the best
element in all the religions of the world.

Coming to the testimony of Jesus, we discover that the
doctrine of God that he gives us is a religious doctrine: that
is to say, it presents God in relations with men, and in those
relations which are learned and experienced in the life of religion.   His teaching gives us this, and nothing more—a
practical doctrine of God as men have to do with him.   Jesus
knew God in human life, and proclaimed him as a living
reality there, but into other fields of thought concerning
God he did not enter.

In modern times it is easy to imagine that the doctrine
of God must necessarily be largely metaphysical.   Philo-

sophical speculation has had a large place in the history of theology, with the result that the current doctrine of God contains a large element that originated in that quarter. At present also all thought concerning the doctrine of God is influenced silently or otherwise by suggestions from physical science, and influence that begins there easily passes over into the field of philosophy. So it happens that all inquiry concerning God is affected now by considerations that arise outside the field of religion. Questions of a metaphysical nature are always with us, and seem indispensable. A practical conception of God must have a metaphysical one, we may think, for its basis. How can we even pray to him, we may ask, until we have rational evidence that our doctrine of him is tenable? how make any practical use of his existence, unless we can build our use on valid reasonings? Modern methods of thought are answerable for much of this, but theology must bear part of the responsibility, for it has often made metaphysical grounds seem indispensable even to the simplest Christian faith.

Theology must discuss God in metaphysical light, but it is important to know that not in such discussing did the Christian doctrine of God originate. The Scriptures that Jesus read entered but very slightly into any field of thought concerning God except the practical and religious. The character of the narrative of creation at the beginning of Genesis illustrates the fact. Creatorship is there announced, but not in the interest of philosophical thought or construction of doctrine. It is announced in the interest of religion, for the illuminating of relations in which men stand to God. So the Old Testament throughout is not a book of philosophy or doctrine: it is a book of religion, in which God appears in his relations with men, that they may live with him and with one another as they ought. It is needless to say that the law is practical, or that it is religious, although its idea of religion is not the highest. The prophets did not philosophize or argue—they adored, trusted and loved; they bore "the burden of the Lord" in their messages to men; they rebuked, threatened and consoled in view of the reality of the living God.

What is true of the doctrine that Jesus found is true of the doctrine that he gave forth. Theology has much metaphysical doctrine of God, but it is remarkable how little of it has come from any words of Jesus. It is not too much to say that concerning God he is exclusively a religious teacher. Of course it is easy to adjust his words to metaphysical settings, and read philosophical meanings into them, and suppose that they embody doctrines that have been modernly developed, but the words themselves are of another kind. They are simply words of real life and practice. If they sound metaphysical, the context turns them to religious use. The synoptical Gospels contain very little that requires even such help from a context, for the synoptical teaching obviously moves in the practical and religious realm. The baptismal formula illustrates the point as well as anything: if we attribute this to Jesus, still it is the practical Trinity, object of practical faith and devotion, to which the passage bears witness, and not the metaphysical doctrine of which historical theology has been so full. If we attribute to him all that the Fourth Gospel quotes as from his lips the case is still essentially the same, for in these utterances the intent is to serve religion: there is a deep mystical tone in the voice that speaks, but nothing concerning God is offered as a contribution to metaphysics or abstract thought, or even as an explanation of some mystery of his being. In fact, if one were to read only the words of Jesus, unaffected by theological development, he would scarcely have any metaphysical doctrine of God at all. He would have a vivid and powerful conception of him, but it would live and move and have its being in the atmosphere of religion.

This quality in the teaching of Jesus must be placed at the very front of our inquiry. From Jesus our Master we must accept a religious and practical doctrine of God, for that is what he offers us. According to him, the religious element comes first: our Master has taught us religion, not philosophy: hence the Christian doctrine starts from recognition of God in his relations with men, and from experience of men in their relations with God. It is a doctrine not of speculation but of life. Of course the metaphysical element must enter into it in due time, and speculative thought, which is a legitimate thing, must do its work, but the primary element, with which speculation itself must deal, is religious. If this is news, it is good news.

Another fact must influence the whole discussion, namely, that the thought of Jesus concerning God is necessarily expressed in terms belonging to the time in which he spoke. He spoke of God not to men who inherited the traditions of Christian thought, or even to trained thinkers of the first century, but to plain men of his time, Jews with the Old Testament in their heart and memory, who were beginning to respond to his own uplifting influence. Forms of thought that belong to later times we shall not find in his utterances. If his doctrine is to be fitted into structures of later thought, the work must be done later: we shall not find it done by him. This seems very little to say, and yet the saying it is not superfluous. It means that every Christian age must cast the substance of his teaching into forms that correspond to its own knowledge and modes of life. He gives us no formula of doctrine concerning God: he gives a living knowledge of him, which we must plant as a living thing in the soil of our own times.

In perfect harmony with these facts is the teaching of Jesus as to the manner in which knowledge of God is to be obtained. It is true that we have no formal lesson from him on this subject, and yet he has given us clear teaching, of the utmost value. With him knowledge of God is not school-knowledge, it is life-knowledge; not information, but acquaintance. The practical and religious idea is still at the front. God is not to be known by reasoning out doctrines of him, but by living with him in the spirit which his character calls for. A man is to know God as a child knows his parents, by experience. Information is valuable, but will

never make God known as he is. Doctrine is helpful, but
to know the doctrine of God, however correctly, is not to
know God. Concerning his own acquaintance with God,
Jesus uttered the profound saying, "Neither knoweth
any one the Father, save the Son, and he to whom
the Son wills to reveal him" (Lk. x. 22). His own knowledge is that of a Son, who knows the Father through
the intercourse which sonship opens. It is a knowledge
founded in spiritual kinship, and built up in the experience of filial life. Of the same nature, it is implied, all
genuine knowledge of God must be. "He to whom the Son
wills to reveal him" can be no other than he to whom the
Son can reveal him, the one who is responding to that grace
which will lead him into the filial life, where God is known as
Father by his child. According to Jesus, God is to be known
not by theory but by practice, not through mental investigation but through spiritual trust and fellowship. Only a son
can know the Father.

This is good news, for it opens knowledge of God to all
who are ready to receive it. This accords with Jesus'
appreciation of the attitude of little children, and shows why
that which is hidden from the wise and intelligent may be
revealed to babes.

When we come to the direct testimony of Jesus concerning
God, we find it summed up in his own attitude and action.
In no text is it summarized, and the total of his words would
not express it, taken apart from his life. What he thought of
God is represented by what he did in view of him. He assumed God as real, recognized him in a definite character
and relation to himself, acted upon his reality, and showed
men what it would mean for them to do the same. He
taught by living, assuring men of their liberty to live with
God as he did, and showing them what such life would
mean.

The points involved in this course of practical teaching are
the essential points in his religious conception of God. Some

of them may be drawn out in order; and yet the formality of such treatment of his living thought almost calls for apology.

It is very little to say that the existence of God was with Jesus unquestioningly assumed. To think of him as interested in the classic arguments for the existence of God is quite impossible. The case in the Old Testament is essentially the same; over against idolatry prophets endeavour to impress the reality of the living God upon the minds of men, but no one argues that God exists. As for Jesus, he stood at the summit of confidence. To him God was real, and there was never need to bring convincement to his mind or satisfaction to his heart by way of evidence.

Just as simple and unartificial was his assumption of the oneness of God. To Jesus monotheism needed no proof. His thought of God was such as to allow no place for more than one. He assumed that the God whom he trusted was the only God, as a man assumes the air that he breathes or the ground beneath his feet. To him the God of nature and the God of the soul were one. He identified the God of nature and the Father of his disciples: "The fowls of the heaven, . . . your heavenly Father feedeth them." "If God so clothe the grass of the field, will he not much more clothe you?" (Mt. vi. 26–29) He was always drawing from nature illustrations for the life of the soul. The oneness of God is the ground of his method in the parables, where one divine process is represented as going on, in the material world and in the inner life of man. The body of his teaching justifies us in picturing Jesus as observing the manifold beauty and power of nature around him, and attributing it all to the God in whom his soul had spiritual peace.

To Jesus the oneness of God was as real in the moral realm as in the natural. The fact of moral evil, the great divisive and perplexing element in life, was to him a terrible reality, yet it suggested to him no dualism. Great as sin was, he did not regard the world as divided between two equal lords, or suspect that the presence of sin proved his Father not to be actually over all. Rather, to him the fact that God is over all was what made sin so horrible. The parables of recovery recorded in the fifteenth chapter of Luke show how he regarded sinful men in their relation to God. According to that great revealing passage, he knew no division of God's world by sin: sin destroyed no sovereignty of God, and took no man out of his field into a region where he belonged to another. Sinful men were still God's own, their sinful life was still lived under responsibility to him, and when they came to repentance he welcomed them as his own returning to himself. Moral dualism of good and evil now existing, Jesus well knew; but of moral dualism as really dividing the realm of existence and limiting the sovereignty of the good God, he had no knowledge.

Jesus taught that oneness of God which is implied in the personal nature of religion. For him the life of religion was life in personal fellowship with the living God; and from the nature of the case, if such life is open to one, it is open to all. Personal religion is universal religion. Accordingly he always gave the impression that the God who was God to him might in the same spirit be God to any man. It was his mission to bring men out of moral alienation into such life with God as he was living. In the experience of a normal relation to God he did not expect his own life to be peculiar, for he was calling men on every side to come and share it. When he said, "Come unto me, all ye that labour and are heavy-laden, and I will give you rest" (Mt. xi. 28), he was proclaiming God as one and the same to himself and all others; for the unfolding of the invitation was, "Take my yoke upon you, and learn of me, for I am meek and lowly in heart, and ye shall find rest unto your souls," and the promise gave assurance that, by taking the position before God that he himself was holding, any weary soul might find rest. The same God would be the same to all who bowed before him, and would give the same rest to any weary soul that sought it in humility and obedience. This practical identity of God to all who acknowledge him in reverence and trust is one of the most precious lessons of Jesus for the world, for in this dwells the secret of universal religion, sufficient to bless and satisfy mankind.

It is difficult to emphasize strongly enough what Jesus says of God's attitude toward the sinful. Religion has often taught that between the good and the bad there is a great gulf fixed; that the good must show their disapproval by holding aloof from the bad, and the greater the goodness the clearer and more condemnatory must be the separation. As we have seen, the Old Testament contains this teaching, but with a better doctrine rising above it. Jesus detracts nothing from the intensity of the Old Testament's condemnation of sin. Instead of that, he detaches sin from formal and ceremonial connections, and reveals it in its true place in the heart and life. It appears as a personal matter and a real, a dreadful quality in character and in act. No influence has ever been so powerful in condemning sin as the influence of Jesus. But as to the attitude of God toward the sinful, he gives currency and power to that better doctrine which was already present in the Scriptures. With him, there is "joy in heaven over one sinner that repenteth" (Lk. xv. 7): scribes and Pharisees may murmur, but he is glad when the wicked forsake their way, and so is God; however it may be on earth, there is joy in heaven. Not only so, but God, like himself, seeks to bring the sinful home. Jesus absolutely reverses the idea that God holds himself aloof from sinners, and reveals him as the generous, helpful, forgiving God, who is always seeking to save men from the evil that he hates. The superiority and aloofness of the religious, which was supposed to be an imitation of God, was a strong argument for despair to those who were regarded as sinful, but Jesus wakened hope in such by showing them that God loved them. He made them feel that his own sympathetic endeavour to bring them home was a true expression of God himself. His principle was that the good will do good to the evil, and God most of all, since he is the best. Sinful souls may imagine that to run away from God is the only safety, but he encourages them to run into God, their refuge and strong tower, their Saviour. Loving kindness toward the sinful is the very heart of the God whom he makes known. This was not a new teaching, but it was a teaching never yet brought to fulness and power, and as a gift to the world it is entirely right to call it Jesus' own. The most truly Christian doctrine of God is that which does best justice to this matchless revelation. A sinful world could never have devised it or discovered it, and does not even yet believe it, nor do even Christians yet accept it with all that it means, but it is to be welcomed as the utterance of One who knew God as a Son knows a Father.

There was great revealing also in the teaching of Jesus as to what it is that pleases God. The idea was abroad among his contemporaries that what God desired was obedience to his Law, which Israel possessed, and that he expected men to deserve his favour by doing the things that he had prescribed. Of course the Law with its institutions was largely an external thing, as a law must be; hence it was understood that God required strict attention to external obedience, and was pleased with scrupulous conformity to his commandments. Thus conscience became self-judgment respecting a thousand particulars, and into religion there entered a thousand unreligious acts. Even wherein the demands of God's Law were more ethical, the legal idea led men to think that they were to deserve his favour by their virtue. All this was natural, for a system of law in religion is necessarily a system of merits, and implies that its God is One who can be satisfied by the meritorious fulfilling of a law. But Jesus gave a very different impression as to the thing that is pleasing to God. His God is not a God of legalism at all. His will for men cannot be embodied in commandments, nor is obedience to commandments the thing with which he can be satisfied. The God of Jesus is the God of reality and spiritual life. He wants sons, men so like him in character and love that their own hearts will impel them to the life that he delights in. He seeks not obedience to a law but response to a God. He is to be pleased not by specific conformity but by intelligent loyalty, and accepts men not when they have kept his commandments but when they accept him as their God. His favour cannot be earned by merit, but it is gained by acceptance of his fellowship, to which he graciously summons all. He is a God who calls for trust in his love, unity with his holiness and loyalty to himself, all in the genuine heart and the real life.

It was in this most particularly that Jesus proclaimed a new religion. He called men away from religion without to religion within, from religion of forms to religion of reality, from reliance upon merits to trust in God. He thus reveals a God whose demand is the demand of his own character, whose service is perfect freedom, and whose grace is the hope of his creation. All this is in sharpest contrast to the religion of law in the midst of which Jesus lived. It is true indeed that the prophets were forerunners of such a religion, but that only reminds us that Jesus was successor and heir to the religion of the prophets, and not to that of the Law. With Jesus first this religion of spiritual reality and freedom came to its place and power, and by him first it was firmly grounded in the character of God. He it was who taught the world that the living God is the God of such religion.

In perfect harmony with this teaching, Jesus sets forth the relation in which God and men stand to each other, and in which it is right that they should live. We are struck at once when we approach him by the fact that his idea of this relation is extremely simple and intelligible. The mysterious elements in the relation of human and divine are not prominent in his discourse. If we follow his thought in simplicity of spirit we shall find the relation difficult indeed because it is morally exacting, but not perplexing through obscurity. The name that Jesus gives to God in relation to men is as simple and natural as it is great and rich in revelation. His favourite name for God is Father. Not only is it true that his own relation to God was filial, but also that into the filial relation and life he called men, offering it to them as their own. This conception was by no means peculiar to Jesus, nor was it new when he took it up, but it is the most characteristic of all thoughts respecting God that appear in his teaching, and the one under which, more than any other, the others must be gathered. It is true that there has been much perplexity over the meaning of this name when applied to God, and the discussions of it have not always been free from bitterness. But if we simply take the teaching of Jesus as it stands, and bring in no perplexing elements from without, there will be no difficulty in perceiving what the name Father meant to him, and the name will be found to constitute a worthy heart for a doctrine of God.

Here again we meet the fact that his teaching moves on the practical plane, and leaves abstractions aside. Nowhere does he tell, or hint, how God came to be Father to men, or to himself. He treats the relation of Fatherhood in God simply as existing, and as a fact of which men may avail themselves. He exhibits it as open to their use, and tells them how they may live in accordance with the claim that it makes and the privilege that it offers. He treats it as he might treat any other present reality into which men may enter and find it enriching their life and fulfilling their destiny.

A reader cannot fail to notice that Jesus treats the human life that corresponds to God's Fatherhood as one that ought to be existing in full force and beneficence. The relation of sons is not a special creation: when men live rightly they live in accordance with it. The filial life that is described in the Sermon on the Mount is the life in which man finds his true place and fulfils his nature. For it he was made. This element in the teaching is helpful in defining our conception of God as Father, for it indicates and assumes that God regards men as his own. The human parent regards the child as his own, for the good reason that he is his own. The relation is one of fact, recognized in affection and in life. This element of real belonging, so familiar and so beneficent in the human family, Jesus assumes as underlying all manifestations of the divine Fatherhood toward men. Whatever the reason may be, God considers human beings as his own, on him dependent, to him responsible, to him by nature responsive. We may inquire how this came to pass, and when we do so we shall naturally ground it in the creative relation and the kinship of spirit with spirit. God is the source of men's existence, and they bear his spiritual likeness; whence it is most natural that they should be found dependent upon God, responsible to him, and by nature adapted to respond to his holiness and grace. This explanation we find reasonable. But Jesus nowhere brings it out. He takes the relation as he finds it, and shows men how God regards them as his own, and teaches them how to fulfil the relation on their side. Some men have become aware of the relation and begun to act upon it, and some have not, but on the side of God, and in deepest reality, it belongs to them all, since he looks upon them as his own.

According to Jesus, the fatherly relation of God is a relation of love, care and discipline, all corresponding to that parental proprietorship which is always implied, and to the holy character which belongs to God forever.

The element of love lies in the nature of the case. Parenthood implies love, and the God whom Jesus knows is One to whom love belongs. If we imagine the Being into whose face Jesus looked, and try to interpret the name Father as applied to him, the element of love will be the first to reach our hearts. And the love which we attribute to God will of course be coloured in our thought by the character which Jesus has helped us to behold in him. It will be a faithful, pure and holy affection, desirous of doing the highest and worthiest good to its objects, hating evil and leading into right. All worthy severity will be as normal to it as all worthy tenderness. Such love will work itself out in just such action as Jesus attributes to God as Father. It appears, he says, in faithful and watchful care; "your Father knoweth that ye have need of all these things" (Mt. vi. 32). It appears no less in holy strictness and discipline, requiring in his children conformity to his own spirit of holy conduct; "if ye forgive not men their trespasses, neither will your Father forgive your trespasses" (vi. 14). And in such a relation there is of course on the side of God complete and cordial accessibility for his children; "pray to thy Father" (vi. 6). In his paternal character God tenderly loves the human children who rightfully belong to him, he attends to their necessities in an unforgetful providence, he trains them in likeness to his own character, and he is freely open to their approaches in trustful prayer. His Fatherhood is as holy as it is sweet, as strict as it is tender, and the best possible good comes to men when they meet it with a filial loyalty that corresponds to its divine nobility.

The true response to the Fatherhood of God includes the acceptance of his will as the best possible good. This was the constant attitude of Jesus himself: he accepted the will of God, not only in submission but in aspiration—not only as a will to be wrought upon him, but as a will to be accomplished by him. When he said in Gethsemane, "Thy will be done" (Mt. xxvi. 42), he proposed not only to endure the will of God, but to rise and do it. Such response to the Father he enjoined upon all the children. Since the Father is perfect, the child must aspire to be perfect. So good is he that his will is worthy to be accepted by all his children as their own. This representation of God places him and men in the noblest relation that can be conceived, since it brings all his moral excellence to bear upon human life with genuine uplifting power.

Side by side with divine Fatherhood, in the discourse of Jesus, stands the Kingdom of God. If we were to say that he spoke of God as king, we should speak in too modern a manner; but the kingdom of God was often upon his lips. This was inevitable if he was to speak at all to the people among whom he was born, for the idea and expectation of the kingdom of God was part of their very life. There is room for question as to how far his use of the familiar phrase coincided with the common use of his day and how far it departed from it; yet the contribution that he made to the conception of God by means of this phrase is largely independent of any such ambiguity as this question may imply.

Students of the Gospels are divided as to whether Jesus conceived of the kingdom of God in the Jewish manner, as a kingdom to be established in this world immediately, in methods corresponding to the apocalyptic hopes, or whether for him the idea was wholly spiritual and the kingdom consisted in the moral dominion of God over the hearts and lives of men. The latter view has been the more common, but many students think that the former is properly contained in the records. Of course it is partly a question of historical criticism, seeking to know what he actually said. Probably it cannot be claimed that the question of Jesus' mental picture of the kingdom of God has yet been finally answered. But his mental picture of the God of the kingdom is more ascertainable. Whether we study his own words, or examine the conception of God that he handed on to those who learned of him, we find a God whose kingship is so merged in the Fatherhood as to be no longer of the ancient earthly kind. He represents the relation with God into which men are brought as a family relation, rather than a governmental or official one. The dominion of God over men that he pictures and commends is a dominion of the divine worthiness over the human life. If it is true that the apocalyptic description of the coming kingdom is really found in the language of Jesus in the Gospels, even then the thought which the apocalyptic language represents is only a passing form, and the abiding substance in his conception of the kingdom is the moral and spiritual reign of God over human life. It is not surprising that in the Epistles, and in the Fourth Gospel, the phrase "kingdom of God" almost disappears, while God as Father stands out in clearest light. It is true that some elements of the Jewish conception of the kingdom have long survived, in the advent-hope and its kindred thoughts. Nevertheless, the fact remains that Jesus himself contributed an understanding of the prayer "Thy kingdom come" so spiritual and practical as in the main to banish the ancient idea of a temporal kingdom, and bring in confidence in the spiritual reign of God.

God reigning in his beneficent holiness and grace is the God whom Jesus commends to the loyalty and confidence of men.   This reign, or dominion, or control, according to him, is God's by right, and men are justly bound to do it honour. God is their rightful Lord and Judge.   His claim of obedience is upon them.   His will is that which they ought to do, and he requires them to do it.   All this, which is commonly associated with royal authority and the kingdom of God, enters into Jesus' thought and teaching, and yet there is nothing in this whole range of ideas that does not fall within the field of Fatherhood as he portrays it.   Here Jesus far surpasses those who were before him.   What others pictured under the form of an outward institution, he set forth as belonging to a natural relation.   The right, the righteousness, the seriousness, the strictness, the urgency, the control, which had been associated with the ruling of a king, Jesus gathers in, along with proprietorship and love and care and discipline, under the relation of a Father.   Regal authority he transforms into parental authority, which makes its own appeal because it is not arbitrary but natural, not special but essential to the relation in which God and men exist.   The Gospels do not contain the idea that God as king demands the loyalty of men as subjects, but they are full of the idea that God as Father claims the loyalty of men as his children.   With Jesus the sovereignty of God is undiminished, but is transfigured by the light of the Fatherhood shining through.

If we imagine that this change detracts from the seriousness of the relation in which men stand to God we have not understood the Master.   The holiness of God is scarcely mentioned in direct terms in the Gospels, but is the underlying fact in all that Jesus said.   It is always both implied and apparent that God is all-pure, that sin is contrary to his nature and his will, and that to him men in their sinfulness are responsible. Above all others Jesus has made God known as the enemy of sin in the world. Above all others he has taught how terrible a thing it is to cast in one's lot with sin and identify one's self with its destiny, and all because God is what he is. His reproofs of selfishness, insincerity, heartlessness, falseness before God and wrong toward men, are unparalleled in their severity. His warnings of doom to those who persist in evil have burned themselves into the memory and convictions of Christendom; and the reproofs and warnings are all grounded in the character of God and the relations of men to him. The holiness of the Father is as terrible to an evil will as it is glorious and lovely to the loyal heart.

If we ask what elements in Jesus' conception of God are most characteristically his own, the question is not so easily answerable in terms of doctrine as in terms of life. In thought, he did not add so very much to what was known of God. He unfolded the highest that Hebrew faith had reached, and did not radically alter it. This is to say that the heart of his testimony is one with what has been known, dimly or clearly, in the general religious life of mankind. All religion has been prophetic of his God, and has caught glimpses of him. Nevertheless the testimony of Jesus concerning God has its clear characteristic elements, making it unique.

1. From the conception of God he throws off all that is not ethical. With him character enters into all, and all conceptions that do not have it for their life are dead. Therefore all formalities and externalities drop away, and all satisfaction of God in acts non-moral vanishes. It is impossible to think of the God and Father of Jesus as pleased with service offered to himself in outward forms in which the inner life has no expression. He is a God whom men must know as moral through and through.

2. As to character, he attributes to God all that the human heart and judgment can approve, and encourages men to attribute to him nothing else. In a plain and reasonable sense, his God is all-good and all-worthy. His goodness is of such nature that all human goodness points up to it, and all goodness that men may ever be able to conceive may be gathered about it in perfect harmony. He clarified, simplified and harmonized the idea of perfect goodness, and planted it, under the name of God, in the soil of human life.

3. He presents God in the closest and most beneficent relations with men. He knows no distant God, no God unapproachable. His God is at hand to all, holding himself aloof from none, loving and seeking the sinful. He is the Father of men, who embraces them in his love, searches them with his judgments, hates their sins, is accessible to their prayers, watches over their life, and is at the disposal of all who desire his grace. Their life is the sphere in which he desires to be manifest.

4. To crown all, he presents God as the supreme ideal, the goal of human faith and hope; for he reveals him as the Father, sonship to whom is fulfilment of human nature and destiny. Above all human dreams and endeavours he shows God the eternal Goodness, revealed there not as a glory forever separate from man, but as a glory into which man may enter; and he offers as the inspiring guide of life the amazing word, "Ye shall be perfect, even as your Father who is in heaven is perfect" (Mt. v. 48).

5. This high lesson Jesus has brought home to men in two ways. On the one hand he has taught that what God was to him in his own life, God would be to any man. On the other hand he has made the impression that the high goodness of purity and love that appeared in Jesus himself was the truest representation of God that has ever appeared in this world of men, and was an adequate expression of God in human life. This twofold teaching is the most effective manifestation of God that was ever made.

That which we name the Lord's Prayer gathers up in practical effect the testimony of Jesus concerning God:

"Our Father, who art God,
    Be thou revered,
    Be thou supreme.
    Thy purpose and thy pleasure be fulfilled,
  As with thyself, so among men.

"Father, provide for thy children:
    Daily give us bread.
  Father, forgive thy children:
    For we have forgiven those who did us wrong.

"Father, protect thy children:
    Bring us not into peril of sinning,
    But deliver us from the evil power."

(3) *The Early Christian Experience*

Out of the life and death of Jesus, recorded in the Gospels, came that great result which we call Christianity, and that peculiar development in life which we call the Christian experience. The whole story of the Christian experience in any age has never been told, but the latter half of our New Testament gives us some clear glimpses into the Christian experience of the first generations after Christ. Though we long for greater fulness of portrayal, still we see, in the light of reality, what that new life meant to the men who lived it.

The early Christian experience was a new life in God. To Gentiles it was in great measure life in a new God; and to Jews it was life in a God partly new, known in new light and fulness, and with attention to qualities dimly known before. It was new life in God, in which Jesus Christ was revealer, introducer, helper, inspiration, guide. It was new life in Christ; but it could not have been that if it had not been new life in God. The truth constitutive of the new experience was, that God so loved the world as to be in Christ its Saviour (John iii. 16). Fundamental in this truth was the relation of God to his world; and the dominant fact was that that relation was of such nature as to be truly expressed in the gift of his Son to mankind and the work of grace that Jesus had performed. In that early experience God appears as all-pure, condemning evil, and as all-gracious, loving men, and seeking to put away the evil that he condemns. Men are his, and he acknowledges them, and seeks to bring them spiritually to himself.

It still remains true, as in the teaching of the Master, that emphasis falls first of all upon the practical aspect of the conception of God. God appears in relations with men. Metaphysical aspects of his being are scarcely in sight, while his character, his attitude of heart toward men, and his action for their welfare, are at the front. The God of those who had learned of Jesus was like the God of Jesus himself, a God at hand, in closest relations with men, and known in his intimate work of redemption and saving help. The doctrine of God is still a doctrine of religion. Within the New Testament we have indeed the beginning of Christian theology, and find views of God that move within the field of metaphysics. Yet in the apostolic writings theology has scarcely at all become self-conscious, and the metaphysical touches are all in the interest of religious faith and life. The modern theological mind has found in the New Testament far more theology, strictly so-called, than is really there, and needs to recognize more simply the vast excess of religion over theology in the sacred books.

To some extent we may be able to put ourselves in the place of the Christians of the first age. Suddenly there had risen before them the most splendid Figure that has ever been present to the thought and faith of men, the Christ of the Epistles. It is not to be supposed indeed that to the body of the Christian people that figure was so distinct and glorious as it was to Paul and his companions in leadership, but certainly here they all obtained their inspiration and newness of life. The Christ of the Epistles is the Jesus of the Gospels raised to the glory of God in the unseen world, radiant with

the beauty of holiness and love that had shone in his life
and death, revealing in the eternal Godhead all the loveliness,
adorableness and redemptive grace that had been manifested
in himself, and standing forth as medium and representative
of the divine salvation that was making all things new. If
we were among the early Christians we should be aware,
through this vision of newly-revealed reality, of a new sense
of God: this perhaps would be the greatest new thing of all.
If we were of the Gentiles, it would be a sense of God as one
only God, holy and gracious: and this would be not only a
new sense of God, but almost a sense of a new God. If we
were of Jewish training, the God proclaimed by the prophets
would now appear in new glory through his revelation of himself in Christ. In Christ we should behold him: looking upon
Christ we should discern his character and heart revealed.
With a glad surprise we should find ourselves living our daily
life in God and Christ, as in an atmosphere of invigorating
purity and love. We should recognize God as the living One,
alone, over all, and ourselves as mysteriously precious to his
heart; God as holy, awful, righteous, and ourselves as sinful,
unworthy, unresponsive; yet God as reconciling men to himself in Christ, and ourselves as receiving the reconciliation by
his gracious help; God as our Father, and ourselves as entering in Christ into the life and lot as his children; God as
making life new, and our own life as taken up into his renewing grace and made forever worth living. The early Christian
gift received was this marvellous uplifting of life; and the
secret of the great uplifting was that God was acting out in
Christ his own heart and character, and offering himself as
the saving Friend that he really was. Between God and
Christ, in the contemplation of this life, there was no contrast
or rivalry. God was in Christ and Christ was in God.
Each implied the other, and from either or from both was the
gift received. Christ was unspeakably precious because
the glory of God was seen in his face, and God was unspeakably precious because in the beloved Christ he stood revealed. Christ was Saviour because he brought salvation

from the heart of God, and God was Saviour because in Christ
he had found his way to the heart of men.

In a word, life was made worth living by the relation in
which God now stood to the Christian. The relation specially
emphasized was that of Father. Life was splendid and invigorating because it was the life of a child of God. It was
not by accident that, as we have said, the kingly aspect of
God's relation retired from prominence. The kingdom of
God, inherited in idea from Hebrew sources, retired mainly
into the future, and became an eschatological conception,
while the fatherly relation of God took its place in the world
of present experience. This change was a natural result of
the influence of Jesus, and a necessary consequence of that
personal quality in religion which he promoted. National
religion would move on to the ideal of a kingdom with God
as king, but personal religion to the ideal of a family with God
as Father. So it is a mark of true progress in religion that
Christians think less of being subjects of God's reign, and
glory in being his sons in Christ Jesus. If the New Testament had made the divine kingship as prominent as did the
Old, it would not have been "the New Testament of our Lord
and Saviour Jesus Christ."

The ethical conception of God, existent in all religions,
powerful in Hebraism and highest in the teaching of Jesus,
comes in the early Christian experience to manifold practical
application. Here men are learning what it is to live under
the inspiration of the divine character. The ethical claim
is enforced by the character of God and their relation to him.
"Be ye holy, for I am holy" (Lev. xx. 7: 1 Pet. i. 17) was
spoken of old, but appears now with new fulness of meaning.
In children of God, all holy and worthy living is a matter of
unquestionable duty, and is destined to become a matter of
unconquerable nature. The forms of holiness and virtue are
numberless in real life, but in them all the problem is simply
how to act as true children of God. The children should be
like the Father, and the likeness to him for which they hope
must be attained through his grace and their own endeavour.

The glory of God's character draws them on because it is their own ideal, and the love that makes him a Saviour enlists his children in all works of love and helpfulness. This is the position of God in the inspiring and forming of the Christian life.

In the New Testament the ethical demand is wrought out in the various forms of duty, personal and social. As of old, so now more largely and intelligently, the ordinary duties of life come under the sanction of religion, and are at once more clearly defined and more strongly enforced by association with the character of God. To all right living the knowledge of God in Christ brings both motive and guidance. The extent to which this enlightening and inspiring went in the early Christian life is of course indicated only in part by the writings that survive from the period. It is certain that to the Christians God appeared as the sun of righteousness, for the illumining of all conduct.

The severity of God and the seriousness of dealings with him by no means disappear in the early Christian experience. That he is holy with a holiness that condemns all sin and makes dealings with him dreadful for those who identify themselves with evil, is a thought that is always present, as in the teaching of the Master. The holy love that desires to save is only another aspect of the character that hates evil and can approve no choice of it. Soft and easy conceptions of God, unexacting, destitute of moral vigour, have absolutely no place in our records of the early Christian experience. But, of course, since the Christian gift is gracious, curative, sanctifying, the severer aspect in God, though always recognized, is secondary in the Christian conception.

It could not be expected that Jesus' own conception of God would be received at once in its fulness, and enter unmixed into the Christian life. It fell into the midst of inherited ideas. The first Christians received from Jesus, but they received also from the past. The Hebrew Christians retained their old Scriptures, and the Gentile converts accepted them, as bearing divine testimony concerning God in all their parts; and the Hebrew Scriptures contain much that accords with the testimony of Jesus about God, and much that does not. Moreover, only by perpetual, universal and unhindered miracle could Gentile ideas, long inherited, have been prevented from influencing the actual thought of the Christian people concerning God. Hence by necessity the early experience embodied mixed conceptions. The wonder is not that the first Christians fell short of the simplicity and spirituality of Jesus in thinking of God: the wonder is that his gift came home to them with a power so transforming, and gave rise to an experience of God so truly Christian.

As to the range and scope of early Christian thought concerning God, he naturally was contemplated chiefly within the relation that Christian men sustained to him. It is there that his Saviourhood was manifest, his Fatherhood was experienced, and his ethical appeal was felt in its power. The God of our early Christian records is God revealed in Christ and known in Christian life. Of course, this would be so, and it would not have been strange if no other view had been given us. But we have more. The writers of the New Testament contemplate God in his relations with the general humanity, though mainly in connection with his gracious work in Christ. It is assumed, as in the Old Testament, that God is active and self-expressing in the order of nature, and that the world brings a real revelation of him: so Paul affirms in his declaration of universal responsibility and sin, at the beginning of his epistle to the Romans (i. 18–19). But the universality of God's relation to mankind, while it is recognized, is still complicated with recognition of the special privileges of Israel. The Jewish people are represented as highly and exclusively privileged, God being to them what he was to no others. After the large grace of God in Christ had appeared this ancient difference could not fail to be the subject of inquiry. In such discussion of it as is recorded God is set forth as the one God of all mankind, holding a real and rightful sovereignty over all, entitled to do with them as he judges best. Over them all, as Paul concludes, he exercises a gracious intent, not an indifferent sway, and both desires and designs their good. In the chapters of the Epistle to the Romans which treat of this matter (ix.-xi.) Paul very briefly sketches his outline of the events in which, as he conceives, the universal grace of God will be vindicated against the charge of partialism. The scheme is indicated in few words, but the doctrine is that God who is over all the world rules it all in the spirit that is manifested in Christ, Gentiles as well as Jews having been always included in his gracious counsel. Paul represents that his grace in Christ is equally free to all men, because God himself is one, and stands in one relation to all humanity (Rom. iii. 29-30). Nevertheless, the universality of this relation has not yet worked itself entirely free from the inherited influence of Jewish partialism.

The early Christian experience depended upon no philosophical doctrine of the relation of God to the world. No such doctrine do we find in our records. The Hebrew idea of the presence of God in nature still lived, but finds little expression beyond the synoptical Gospels. It is not in the Epistles that we read, "Consider the lilies of the field, how they grow" (Mt. vi. 28). A design of God in the events of life is joyfully affirmed, and what we are wont to call Providence is recognized as a great reality. God is not far away. To those who love him, all things work together for good. He gives a peace that passeth understanding. He is the God of all consolation, and the God of hope. He is the rightful Lord and righteous Judge of men, from whose just governance no one can escape. The doctrine of the Logos in the thought of the age implied a distant God, transcendent in the sense of superior and separate, communicating with the world through intermediaries. But in the Fourth Gospel, where the Logos is introduced (i. 1-18), there is nothing of this intended, for here the Logos is not an intermediary, but a mode or manifestation of God himself. God himself is in touch with his world. Throughout the New Testament God is conceived as free and independent in his relation to the world, not in bondage to the order of nature, but able to act at his own volition in human affairs.

The early Christian experience contained the elements out of which was formed the doctrine of the Trinity. The Christian heart knew God as he had been known of old, only now more clearly through that great expression of his being which the new gospel made. It was indebted for this fresh manifestation of God to Jesus, who had already begun that marvellous work, continued till now, of creating the conviction that God was like him and in him was truly expressed. And it was indebted again to that glorious interior life, wherein God was found inhabiting the human spirit and transforming men into his own likeness. God, God in Christ, God in men; Father, Son, Spirit; these were the forms that the thought of God assumed under the interpretation which the new experience gave it. The developing of this testimony into a doctrine came later in the course of Christian thought, and at present it is necessary only to exhibit the facts of experience out of which the doctrine sprang. God was thrice known, and known in three positions, or relations, in the dealings of the soul with him. In the days of the New Testament these three positions of God were vividly discerned, with that free spiritual energy which belongs to a great new experience, and the Christian heart was busy with adoring and appropriating the God who was thus known. The three experiences of God were all essential to the new life, and all equally essential, and there was no other that took rank with them. So they stood out by themselves. But in the recognition of them in the first days there was no speculation, and no suggestion of a theory of the hidden Godhead. The enumeration of them only told what God was to those who were living the new life. It was all practical, experimental, religious, like all else that was characteristic of the primitive Christian faith.

Thus the gift that was offered by Jesus was received and put to use in the early Christian experience—imperfectly no doubt, and yet in vital power. Jesus offered God in life, and in life he was received. Christianity was first an experience, and an experience of God, by which, since God was both

Lord and Saviour, all human living was transformed. God was the sun in heaven that made the new spiritual day. In course of time the sun and its light would be investigated; but what made the brightness of the day was the shining of the sun, not the investigation or its results, and it was the brightness of the day that suggested the inquiry. The doctrine of God that appears within the New Testament is chiefly the perception in human life of the divine Being for whose fellowship man was made. The perfect Father, revealed by Christ as Saviour from sin, known in the communion of the Holy Spirit, governing all life in the counsel of wise love, this is the God in whom all live and move and have their being, and with whom his children who are reconciled in Christ live in filial unity.

(4) *The Historical Development*

The conception of God that Jesus made alive went forth to live in the world of men, and how inspiring and helpful it was, the story of the first Christian generations shows. God the righteous and gracious One, the sum of all known good, Father and Saviour to men—these visions of the eternal reality entered into life to remain there as transforming forces. However imperfectly it has been apprehended, Jesus' own conception of God has been ever since in the world, and its presence has made an ever-widening circle of light and warmth.

Since the gracious gift must follow the fortunes of human affairs, the Christian doctrine of God has had its development. An unchanging deposit of truth is an impossibility. All conceptions that go out among men are thought upon, and thereby altered. Since thought is eager and unresting, no conclusion reached can remain a conclusion merely, for every conclusion becomes in turn a premise, helpful in reaching other conclusions. Moreover, all practical and religious conceptions go forth to be acted upon, and the manner in which they are acted upon reacts upon the manner in which they are held. Thus both in thought and in practice the Christian conception of God was destined to development. It necessarily became an historical doctrine, living and growing with human life, passing through the vicissitudes in form and substance that constitute history in thought. The story of this development is not now to be rehearsed, but it is necessary to remind ourselves of some of the main elements that have entered into the process.

The Christian doctrine of God has received its development under many influences. First the thought of God that Jesus offered was received as men could receive it, and became effective in the great experience that constituted Christianity. In the process it became blended with other thoughts concerning God, inherited, or acquired from other sources: it was never alone. In the resulting combinations, it was subjected to the various intellectual methods of successive ages, combined with various intellectual conceptions, and interpreted in the light of many kinds of religious experience. It was affected and altered in various ways by the reaction upon it of organization, of institutions, and of religious practices. Other ideas in Theology had their influence upon it, and theological controversy modified it in incalculable ways. From age to age new knowledge, new scientific methods, and new interpretations of the world have had their effect upon it. And the entire movement has proceeded in a moral world, where the strength and weakness of human character could not fail to be influential upon the quality of all high ideas. Plainly these unavoidable influences, so various and so strong, must have given a genuine history to the doctrine of God among Christians. A doctrine unalterable there could not be, but there has been a developing doctrine. Plainly also the development must have been partly normal and partly abnormal. Some of the contributing influences have been helpful and some harmful to a true knowledge of God as Jesus reveals him, but none of them could be escaped. Through such a course the doctrine was compelled to pass, being in the world. The seed of God was cast into the human soil, and met such fortunes as were inevitable. The doctrine of God has always been a divine light in the world, but a light dimmed by human obscurities.

A little more must be said of the process. The first Christians were Jews, and necessarily took the idea of God that their Master gave them into union with such conceptions of him as they already possessed. These conceptions, inherited and acquired, were partly spiritual and lofty, and partly legalistic and unspiritual. Jesus immensely elevated the Jewish idea of God for his disciples, but it was not in human nature that their idea should at once become perfect and bear perfect fruit. The Christian thought of God soon passed out into the Gentile world, to be a new light and glory there. But it entered the Gentile world through Jewish minds, and in Gentile minds it fell into the midst of conceptions far inferior to the Jewish; and anti-Christian views of God could not fail to be influential in the thinking of Gentile Christians. When Christianity outwardly conquered the Empire, it received into itself a vast amount of slightly altered paganism, and turned to the long and perilous work of assimilating hostile elements that were found upon its field. In all this we find the clear presage of a mixed and imperfect doctrine.

Moreover, according to Jesus the way to know God is first and chiefly through trust and love and the experience of the loyal life. But it was inevitable that, when men had turned to thinking about the God whom they loved and honoured, they should attach excessive importance to the intellectual method of knowing him, and esteem a deposit of doctrine above a germinant life. It was certain too that a church would arise, and be accorded an authority in interpreting truth such as the Master's method would give to no one whatever, and that the church's conception of God would be regarded as the Master's own. It was inevitable that the Christian ideas should be subjected to the metaphysical methods of thought that ancient Greece had bequeathed to the early centuries, and that that which Jesus put forth in simplicity should be analyzed and reconstructed in a manner quite unlike that in which the new faith began. It was inevitable that there should thus be formed a Christian mode of thinking that was not altogether Christian, which in turn would fashion the idea of God somewhat after its own likeness. It was inevitable that theological discussions and theories should modify the idea of God, and that forms of doctrine on other points, once accepted, should tend to bring the conception of God into harmony with themselves. It was inevitable that the intellectual conception of God should be narrow when the range of knowledge was narrow and claim new largeness when knowledge took on new breadth, and that the conservatism which attaches to sacred things should often resist the broadening of the thought, and bring on controversy when worthier conceptions were seeking a welcome. It was inevitable that the question whether the doctrine of God could live with new knowledge should be recurring from time to time, that needless modifications should be proposed by progressive thought, and that cautious faith should insist upon keeping the doctrine too small for the expanding universe. These are not risks and perils of some particular time: they belong in various forms to all Christian ages.

These are the resistances: the persistent and positive force has been the Christian experience, which has never become extinct, and has always, in spite of all defects, tended to be protective of the true thought of God. The clear and strong doctrine of Jesus has lived on and done its work of blessing. Experience of God as Father to the soul and as Saviour in Christ has always been alive, imperfect but genuine. The gift of sincerity and Christian intention in the making of doctrine has never been absent. Much that became harmful by outliving its day was wholesome and helpful in its season. Much that may seem to us unworthy of the faith, and even false to it, was in its time a real expression of the faith. But the main point is that Jesus' own representation of God, as all-good and worthy of all trust and obedience, has never passed out of sight or lost its power. The definition of what is good has been faulty, and misconceptions of the divine goodness, grace and authority have been both perplexing and misleading; yet the conception of divine goodness, worthy of all loyalty and confidence, has been the waxing light through the Christian period—waxing unevenly, yet brightening toward the perfect day. This is the glory of the Christian doctrine, and it is the good side of the errors and misjudgments of God in the Christian history that they have generally been errors and misjudgments concerning this beneficent truth. Goodness, holiness, love, have been misconceived, saviourhood has been misinterpreted, and the beauty and the moral claim have often been misunderstood or misapplied. But the perfect goodness of God has been steadily believed and gloried in: though known so imperfectly, it has not been unknown, or unprized. This high conception has held its way through history, now blending with one kind of thought and knowledge and now with another, shadowed now by this defect and now by that, adjusted now well and now ill with other truth, but never ignored or omitted. As ages passed it has entered as a living force into the thought of each successive time, and learned, imperfectly yet really, to live with all that is vital in human experience. The doctrine of the all-good God has changed from age to age as the idea of the good has changed, but it has remained alive, and acted as a moral power. The doctrine of the good God in vital relations with men, the Father who counts them his own, the Saviour who seeks their welfare, the Lord who governs them in righteousness and wisdom—this doctrine has utilized and outlived many inadequate interpretations, metaphysical and practical, and come down to our day bearing the essential moral quality which it bore at first.

This brief account of the historical development introduces the question in what sense and degree this development should serve as a source of the Christian doctrine of God in the present day.

Evidently not as providing at some point of the course a

sufficient and final statement. What we have seen of the process is sufficient evidence of this. Finality has never been reached, nor, in conceptions of God, is it attainable. What is man, at any given hour of history, that he should know all that is to be known of God? and what is any generation, that it should formulate a final doctrine concerning him? No age is bound by the conclusions of another, or is at liberty to take them as final and exclusive of further thought. Each generation must know God for itself as it may, in the light of its own knowledge of other realities and of the cumulative experience of mankind. The truth that has been embodied in former expressions must be considered again in view of larger knowledge, and errors and inadequacies must be eliminated, if that may be. The doctrine of each present day must take forms that are alive for the men of that day, and must be in a true sense their own work, wrought out of the materials that revelation and experience provide. Accordingly, as we do not expect now to frame a doctrine that will need no revision hereafter, so we do not receive as final any statement of the past.

We believe in the guidance of the divine Spirit upon the Christian people: it might be thought therefore that we must regard the latest form of thought concerning God as God's own immediate testimony to himself, to be received without question as sufficient to the present time. But the guidance of the Holy Spirit upon the Christian people is a guidance upon people who think for themselves and are daily learning through experience. It does not offer a finished product, but always brings something to be wrought upon with all diligence by the best powers of man. The historical process brings to our generation material for analytical and reconstructive labour. Its contribution of doctrine concerning God must be criticised in Christian light, that we may discover the Christian element in Christian doctrine, and be prepared to do it honour. In the records of the past we find much that has done honourable service and lived out its day, and much that might better have been left out of Christian thought, while as the persisting and dominant force we find that vital experience of God of which Christ is the inspiration. Out of this mixed material bequeathed to us we have to select what is abidingly Christian, and bring it into combination with the truest and best that is known to-day, and set the Christian thought of God as a living thought among the other thoughts of the time.

That is to say, the present doctrine of God must represent the present stage in the long historical development. It must be the next doctrine after that of yesterday, and the prelude to a better doctrine to-morrow. It is to-day's form of the one persisting Christian truth. It is something to obtain as clear a view as this of our task when we undertake to set forth the doctrine for to-day.

In this light the historical development becomes to us a source of doctrine, by bringing to us the permanent and the temporary elements in thought concerning God, that we may disentangle them and place them respectively where they belong. We must follow the exacting method that is indicated at the beginning of our study. The Christian doctrine for to-day must be found by learning as truly as we may the central conception of God as Jesus gave it, by observing what forms, worthy and unworthy, it has received in its historical development, by separating it as far as possible from contradictory conceptions that have become blended with it, and by giving it form that corresponds in some good degree to the living thought and experience of our time.

Like the original voice of Jesus, the historical development bears witness that the central element in the doctrine of God is the moral and religious. That is the persisting element. Not the divine power but the divine character is at the front. Not the philosophy of his nature but the love and righteousness of God is the primary fact in the doctrine. When we question the long development as a source of doctrine, this is its reply, that for to-day as for all the yesterdays there must be an ethical and religious doctrine of God. This Jesus gave, and this the ages have vindicated as the necessary doctrine. God in relations with men, touching them with a moral claim and redemptive helpfulness, covering all their life with his requirement and embracing it all in his paternal love—this is the vision that Jesus opened, and all the darkness of intervening ages has not hidden it.

History contributes also its mandate, bidding us find for our doctrine of God its place among the thoughts that are now vital among men. By all its successes and all its failures it calls us to this endeavour. It warns us to inquire whether our conception of God can live with the truth that is known now. The true doctrine of God certainly can live with all other truth: can ours? Yet it is not a question of comparing two philosophies of God, one derived from Christian thought and another grounded elsewhere. The question is whether the ethical and religious doctrine of God which Jesus gave us is compatible with the knowledge of existence that we now possess. Large conceptions of general existence have greatly changed since Jesus spoke. Has the change rendered his moral conception of God untenable? The change is indeed great. The world has expanded until it has become the universe. The sum of existence, unimaginably vast, is seen to be held together in a manner unsuspected when the Christian doctrine of God was first conceived. The evolutionary method is recognized as universal, and as providing to all existence a unity not only of method but also of interdependence and solidarity. There is a single whole, moved by forces that appear to dwell within; and man, long regarded as separate and supreme, now stands vitally connected with the whole mass of being. He is indeed invested with the unique dignity of a personal spirit, and yet he seems only an infinitesimal element in the immeasurable whole. In a world thus conceived, new questions arise. In such an order of nature, what place exists for God? Does the observed character of the universe lead us to believe that God is personal? Is the ethical element in life so prominent and dominant as to warrant belief in a God whose chief quality is moral character? Is it credible that man is dear to a power above him, and the object of a faithful care that can be called a providence? May our life still be dignified, consoled and glorified by association with such a Being as Jesus taught us to call "Our Father who art in heaven"? In a word, is there a Father, a God related to us men as the God of Jesus Christ was declared to be?

The Christian doctrine answers these questions in the affirmative. Many judgments that have entered into it in the past may drop away, and much that has seemed essential to it may be dispensed with, but confidence in the Eternal Goodness remains as its very heart. The Christian doctrine has simply moved on into another age with whose thoughts it has to live. It is a mistake to regard its task in the light of a conflict, and suppose that it is called to conquer and silence the thought that is characteristic of the age. It has rather to claim its place and win its welcome with the thought of the new period. Since the doctrine is true at heart, it can live in the modern world. It can enter into union with the truths that are found in the evolutionary view of the universe. It can legitimately proclaim its ethical God and Saviour in the world of modern knowledge. And the form of the Christian doctrine for our day is the form that it takes when it has entered into union with the knowledge of our day. The present Christian doctrine is the doctrine that we owe to Jesus, preserved till now by passing through forms that suited times now past, now wrought into unity with modern knowledge, and applied to life as an undying moral and religious doctrine.

It is still too early for the Christian thought to have established its place fully in fellowship with the new thought of the time. The question of compatibility has had first to be wrought out, and for a time there has been unavoidably an appearance of conflict. But it will be plain by and by that the conflict was only in appearance, and that in this age, as in every other, there is room for a free doctrine of the eternal goodness.

I. GOD

1. CHARACTER

WHEN we have passed beyond the study of our sources and come to the doctrine of God itself, it may seem that to establish the existence of God ought to be our first endeavour. This has been the common practice, and perhaps the custom may seem as necessary as it is venerable. Nevertheless, it is quite contrary to the Christian idea. The Christian doctrine of God does not begin with proof, it begins with the announcement that is made by Christian faith in pursuance of the Christian revelation. Faith does not set out to find an unknown God, or to assure itself that God exists: it has heard his voice, and begins in confidence in his reality. It assumes the existence of God as its first certainty, and then proceeds to learn about him all that can be learned. The Christian doctrine is reached by unfolding the conception of God that is assumed as true by the Christian revelation and experience. When the doctrine has been presented, and it is apparent what manner of God the Christian faith is assuming to exist, it will be time to inquire how far the doctrine thus obtained is commended as true by fitting in with other truth that we have reason for holding. Proof comes at the end, not at the beginning, and bears the nature of confirmation, not of discovery. There may be other ways of approaching the knowledge of God, but the Christian way is the way of recognition rather than of demonstration. Not that God is, but what God is, is the first point in the Christian doctrine. This method is sometimes condemned as unscientific and misleading, but it is neither, and it will be vindicated in the end as best suited to the subject and most helpful to sound knowledge.

Beginning, therefore, with the assumption of God, the Christian doctrine must tell what manner of God he is assumed to be. In approaching this task we are clearly and safely guided by the nature of religion, and especially of the Christian faith. There is only one region in which our work can rightly begin, and that is the region of character. The ancient conception of God which Jesus raised to full glory was an ethical conception. The experience in Christ by which God has become vitally known to the Christian people is an ethical experience, expressive of the character of God and realized in the character of men. The Christian salvation is God's characteristic work, and the Christian doctrine is primarily an account of him as a moral Being, in characteristic relations with other moral beings. In other words, the Christian doctrine of God is first of all a doctrine of the divine character. Here falls the emphasis. It was so in Jesus' own revelation, and in the experience that wrought the marvels of transformation in the early Christian days. Here the strength of the Christian doctrine has always resided, and must always dwell.

This is the same as to say that Christianity does not approach God first as Creator, or as the great First Cause, or as the Almighty. Theological inferences from the facts revealed by natural science do not stand at the front. No form of the doctrine of power is the primary element. Metaphysical considerations do not come first. If character is not made primary in the doctrine of God, the resulting life will be lacking in the Christian quality. If merely philosophical conceptions of God, or conceptions borrowed from the material universe, had been the starting-point, the Christian point of view would never have been reached. If causation, or control, or the reign of law, be made the ruling principle in doctrine-forming, and character comes in only as a kind of afterthought, the resulting doctrine will be comparatively void of power. The Christian thought is loyal to the true light only when it consistently sets character at the front, and exhibits men as face to face with God in moral relations.

So with Moses and the prophets and with Jesus and the apostles we seek to set God forth in the character that he bears.

The Christian doctrine of the character of God is as simple as it is bold and comprehensive. It affirms that when God is seen in the pure Christian light, he is seen as he really is. In Christ, it says, and through his influence, God is truly manifested. He always has been, is, and always will be such a Being as we shall know when we have rightly discerned the Being of whom Jesus is the revealer. It is not meant, of course, that all that has been taught concerning God under the Christian name is true, or that any adequate statement of his nature has ever been made. It is meant that when the entire conception of God has been unified, and harmonized with the thought of Jesus as its centre and keynote, God will be known as he is. The character that Jesus opened to our knowledge is the real character, not to be transformed for us by any future discoveries or experience. It is no temporary or incidental character, borne only in certain relations or revealed only for certain purposes, but is the same from everlasting to everlasting, and the same in his relations with all beings, because the same in himself the eternal God. Though he is variously manifested and known, he changes never, neither adopting nor abandoning any moral trait. Jesus showed him as he essentially and eternally is, so that one who has learned to love the God whom he made known will never need to alter the quality of his affection and adapt himself to a different God. This truth, that God in Christ is the true and only God, has never held its rightful position in Christian thought, but it has never ceased to influence the Christian heart, and it is the theme upon which various doctrines in Christian history have been imperfect variations. It is the central Christian verity, and it is the growing Christian doctrine.

It might seem that it must be a boundless and hopeless task to seek clear conceptions of the character of God. We readily assume that whatever is great must needs be complicated, intricate, and essentially difficult. But it is good to remember that the discernment of character is one of the most familiar of human activities, and one in which we may most reasonably hope to be successful. It is well for us that our labour lies in this field. Ethical judgments are far easier than philosophical solutions. Moreover, we shall be able to correct our suspicion that the divine character must be intricate and obscure. The great is the simple. In its operation there are mysteries that are far beyond our solving, but in itself the character of God is simple and intelligible. We are accustomed to complexity in the derived and imperfect, but here we shall be brought to gaze upon the simplicity that belongs to the original and eternal.

2. PERSONALITY

Before proceeding to unfold the doctrine of the character of God, it is necessary to dwell for a little upon that element of Personality which the Christian experience and doctrine so evidently imply.

The idea of divine personality is as old as religion. In the early days of unsophisticated activity, prayer came into practice because there was no doubt that there was some one there to be spoken to and to respond. Some one was believed in who could hear the confession of sins and forgive them, who could receive thanksgiving and grant new gifts, and who could keep that which was committed to his care. Man has always regarded the divine as similar to the human, and pictured the gods as personal like himself. What was true in early ages has been true in general ever since. Where divine personality has been ignored in theory through pantheistic thought, it has been restored in practice by the incursion of polytheism. The conviction of divine personality is no part of the childishness of mankind. Man has often been scoffed at for thinking that God is like himself, but instead of folly this is a beginning of wisdom. Anthropomorphism has taken many false and misleading forms, but the truth that man bears the likeness of God and God the likeness of man lies at the foundation of all strong religion.

The Christian doctrine implies personality in God in the same manner with all the religions. It deals with the common experiences of dependence, trust and communion with God, and assumes that they are not false and delusive experiences. If they are not, God must be able to meet the praying soul with an intelligent and active response. But the Christian doctrine lays an emphasis of its own upon the divine personality, for it insists beyond all others upon the divine character, and character inheres in personality, and in nothing else. All doctrine of an ethical God is doctrine of a personal God; and one may almost say that the whole of Christianity consists in the unfolding of God's character. Since character is the vital point in the Christian conception of God, God is necessarily conceived as capable of possessing character; and the capacity for character is identical with what we know as personality.

When we turn to our Christian documents, their testimony to the personality of God is perfectly informal and overwhelmingly abundant. In the Old Testament, as we have seen, God speaks as I, is addressed as Thou, and is referred to as He. His personality is taken for granted, after the manner of the ages in which it was unquestioned. Jesus does not proclaim the personality of God, but he assumes it always, for he is always ascribing to God qualities that could not possibly inhere in anything but personal being. The Christian doctrine has always followed the Master in attributing to God not only the name but the powers and actions of a personal Spirit. In the times of the Bible the question of divine personality did not arise, for the metaphysical definition of personality did not yet exist, though the fact was acted upon as consistently as in any age; but if it had arisen we can see how prophets and apostles would have answered it. That God is holy, or that God is love, would have been sufficient evidence that God may be spoken of as He and addressed as Thou. The reasoning is sound. Character implies personality: no personality, no character. Morality inheres in nothing else: right and wrong are possible only to persons. So common knowledge testifies. In forming our Christian doctrine of God we do not so much attribute character to a Person— though we might do this—as we affirm personality as the only possible basis for character.

Now and then some one rises to assert the existence of a moral order without a personal God. Righteousness is affirmed to be characteristic of the natural order and movement of the world, though no mind made it so. Somehow universal nature brings forth justice, and men may expect right to be done and wrong to be punished by the unconscious order of the world. Sometimes benevolence is attributed to the same mindless movement, and sometimes malevolence and cruelty are said to be its traits. But it is unsatisfactory to attribute genuine moral qualities, whether good or bad, to a mindless order. The only soil in which they can grow has no existence there. Our acquaintance with the habits and habitat of right and wrong is too much for such a doctrine, and we are not surprised that it does not attain to a position of lasting power. The only tenable interpretation of character is that which grounds it in the nature and relations of a personal being. If character be attributed to God, he must be a being who is capable of having it, and such a being has the powers that make up personality. The thought has its difficulties, but the necessity of personality as the substratum of character is inexorable, and the difficulties must be met in loyalty to this requirement.

What do we mean when we speak of God as personal? Our answer to this question must be incomplete, but need not be obscure or doubtful, and there is no reason why we should shrink from the definition that we can obtain. We know on what basis of knowledge personality must be defined. Personality is a human gift, known to us only in ourselves and other men. We know that there may be higher personalities than the human, but we are not acquainted with them. We see suggestions of personality in animals below us, but they are not so clear and full as to provide us with personal companionship in that region. We human beings are persons, and from ourselves alone can we define what we indicate by that name. If we say that God is personal, we must mean that in certain respects God is like ourselves. We may own that in these very respects there may be important differences between God and us, and yet we must mean that the likeness in constitution is genuine, and consists in something that is essential in the nature of both. From this assertion we need not shrink, and should not be repelled by any charges of folly. The doctrine that God is like man is the most ancient of all doctrines of God, and is destined to survive, in some form, as long as a doctrine of God is held. It has not to be accounted for: the only question is, in what sense is it true? What likeness between God and men is affirmed when it is said that God is personal? What facts justify us in speaking thus of God?

It is necessary to give some account of personality as it exists in ourselves; and this we will do not by describing it as it may appear at some given moment, but by tracing its genesis and growth.

A human being is born of parents and of a race, and received into a social group and order, where he is acted upon by those who are farther along than himself in the movement toward personality. He himself is not a person at first, but is to become one. If he were not acted upon by others he could never become a person: if he were not spoken to he could never speak: if he were not called out he would never be developed. All human life is social, and personality has no existence except in relations with others. Thus personality implies society, and is absolutely dependent upon it. A person is a member of society, and this fact of social relatedness is a true and abiding element in his personality. As he has received from others, so he stands always bound to others by indestructible ties, and lives his life by social giving and receiving.

When once the human being has begun to exist, life goes on, by combination of mysterious inward impulse and outward influence, and trains the incipient person at once to self-consciousness and self-determination. Probably these two possessions come by simultaneous development. Life trains the growing person to consciousness of himself, and to determination of his own conduct. He comes to a consciousness that is more than a mere being aware of surrounding things: it is an inner sense of being himself, with continuous identity and significance. And he comes to a self-direction which is first instinctive but gradually becomes a rational self-guidance: his action is his own even though in limited degree, being expressive of himself and by himself directed. All the activities of life tend to the formation of a being who is thus self-conscious and self-determining in the relations in which he stands; and in proportion as these powers are developed the human being advances in personality, or becomes a person. A person is a being in relation with others, who is aware of himself and has power of directing his own action. Evidently such personality is an ever-growing thing, never complete, always becoming. Self-consciousness is never perfect, for a human being is never conscious of all that is in him. Self-direction is always limited, for there is much in life that a person does not determine for himself; and the relations of a human being are not all determined by himself, are not fully known to him, and can never be utilized by him to the full possible extent.

From this view of human personality we turn to look upon personality in God. Here at once we meet this difference, that in God we do not trace the genesis of personality. Not in relations do we find it originating, or on them depending. We can say that outside of relations man would not have become a person, but we cannot say the same of God. Of God outside of relations we have no knowledge; and certainly what we know of him within relations is not of a kind to make us conjecture that he depends upon them for his personality. But of God within relations we may speak. In his case, as in ours, relations bring to expression those powers of self-consciousness and self-determination which make up personality. The Christian doctrine uses its terms in a sense that accords with our experience and knowledge when it says that God is a personal being. By this is meant, that God is One who knows himself, or is conscious of himself and the significance of his being; that he is One who directs his own action, making it expressive of the self of which he is conscious; and that he is related to other being, and other being is related to him. A conscious, intelligent, active, related being—this is a person, and such is God. This is the Christian conception.

It is indeed the Christian conception. It is quite superfluous to show that the God and Father of Jesus Christ is thus a self-conscious being who directs his own action, that he knows, loves and acts, that he exercises the powers of a rational mind and does the work of a reasonable will, in relations with other existence. What this modern language expresses is all implied in what Jesus says more simply of God. All Christian thought accepts him as such a Being, and all Christian life proceeds as if such he were. "Pray to thy Father," said Jesus. The Christian faith is faith of one personal being in another. With a conscious mind the worshipper stands face to face.

Thus reaching the idea of personality in God from that of personality in men, we must observe what changes come to the idea in this transference. Of course we drop all such anthropomorphisms as relate to bodily form and aspect, locality and local environment. No longer do we picture or locate God. If we quote the ancient pictorial language, we understand that it is figurative. What is more important, we drop all idea of incompleteness and limitation. We cannot imagine the perfect, but we can to some degree imagine the annihilation of imperfections of which we are aware in ourselves. We have an incomplete self-consciousness, but in God we think of it as complete, or consciousness of all that the self-knowing One contains. We know self-direction, applied to parts of our action, but in God we think of it as unhindered and perfect, governing all that he does. We know relations with other beings, which in our case are partly chosen and partly accepted, whether we will or not, but in God we think of them as appointed by himself, entered and maintained in full independence. In God the elements of personality are carried up to perfection. In tracing the process we have transcended the range of humanity, but not the nature of personality. (The God whom we discover is a personal being in the same sense with us, notwithstanding that his personality rises above ours by the height of perfection.)

Sometimes we are led to fear that we must lose the fact of personality when we rise to the height of God. We are compelled to define personality in terms of our own because we know no other, and in such conditions it is easy to assume that in us the type or ideal of personality must reside. When we look at ourselves, personality seems very closely surrounded by confining lines. Our theories have drawn them too closely, in fact, for until of late we have never recognized the social aspect of personality as one of its elements. Yet we do find human personality a mysteriously bounded and exclusive thing. Each person has his own field of life: if modern psychology suggests weird possibilities of division and overlapping, still the normal experience thus far testifies that persons are ordinarily separate from one another, and one personal consciousness does not take in another's contents. These restrictions are so real to us that we may think they are of the nature of the case, and judge finitude to be of the very essence of personality. So personality in God may seem inconceivable: infinite personality is often said to be a contradiction in terms, since one element in the conception is limited and the other unlimited. Pantheism declares the divine and the personal to be incompatible, and many besides pantheists have difficulty with the personality of God.

But why claim that our personality must be typical? A little acquaintance with human nature should teach us better. Our personality shows no signs of being typical or ideal, the standard for the conception. It is but of yesterday. In every individual it is but just born. In the race it is still growing, and still ungrown. Only in recent times has it been recognized in analytic thought, and it was so long unrecognized partly because it was still so immature. No element in it is perfect, or near perfection. With our self-consciousness so incomplete, our self-determination so interfered with by external forces, and our relations mastering us more than we master them, how can we think that the ideal of all personality is found in this imperfect constitution of ours? The typical personality must be found beyond the limitations that confine our life. It cannot be in us: it must be in some being in whom all the powers that enter into personality exist in perfection of quality, in fulness of degree, and in freedom of action. In this view the opinion that infinity and personality are mutually exclusive loses its convincing power. The limitations that we find so strict and separative are guides for personality to grow by, rather than bounds essential to its perfection. We might imagine that the narrow limits of our life were favourable to that complete self-knowledge and self-mastery which the true type implies—for is not the small more manageable than the great? But it proves otherwise. Any field of intelligent life is too great for us to master altogether, and in proportion as we know ourselves we know that only a perfect spirit can be the type and standard of personal being. Only the perfect can fully know himself, or direct himself, or be master of his relations. The essential powers of personality as we know them even in ourselves are of such kind that they can have their perfection in none but God. So when the Christian doctrine represents God as personal, it means that in him is the perfection of the powers that constitute personality in us; and this surely is no difficult doctrine or obscure. Where indeed should the type of spiritual existence be? in the derived, or the original? in the creature, or the creator? in the child, or the Father?

Thus we do not say something unintelligible when we speak of a personal God. But we have to confess that the greatness of such a God is incomprehensible though not unintelligible, and we must not forget that what we cannot comprehend we cannot fully describe. Since God's personality so far transcends our own, our human descriptive terms are inadequate to set it forth. We must use such language as we have, but we must be mindful of its insufficiency. This trouble goes back even to the simplest matters. We designate a person by a pronoun, and when we speak of God in terms of personality we use the pronoun He. We have no means of doing better, but our word narrows our thought. All personal pronouns take their suggestiveness from human nature and their measurement from human dimensions. This one retains qualities derived from human individuality, in which limitation is an unavoidable element. A word that ordinarily represents a man has no power to represent that infinite greatness, fulness and variety which we must attribute to him who is all in all. Through depending upon the pronoun He we may easily come to think of God as if he corresponded to some single type of personal being; whereby we should do injustice to him and impoverish ourselves. The ancient "plural of majesty," applied to him, if it could be used with a fine poetic largeness, might have its virtues still. But our pronoun is imperfect again, for it is limited even in gender. It is masculine, and suggests only the idea of masculine personality. God is regarded as male: what can he be called but He? Yet this must be wrong, for the ideals of the feminine as well as of the masculine must reside in the being of God. All that is womanly can be traced back to him as truly as all that is manly. All the virtues evoked in all sorts of human beings by the experiences of life are lowly reproductions of good that is eternal in God. All ideals of goodness that have ever inspired humanity are "broken

lights" of his full-orbed perfection, and the powers by which
men have done their various work have all existed in imperfect likeness to his.   He transcends the "He," for to know
the personal God as he is would be to know all personal
powers and excellences in perfection and in unity, infinite
variety being gathered into one.

If we could not thus expand and fill out our conception of
personality, the doctrine of a personal God would be a
restriction upon the range of our thought and the upreach of
our faith.   Such a restriction it is often alleged to be, but it
is not.   On the contrary we find liberty and rest in the thought
that perfect personality requires the largeness of infinity, and
can exist in God alone.   In affirming perfect personality in
God, the present Christian doctrine reaffirms a thought that
has been among its vital elements from the beginning, namely,
"God is a Spirit" (Jn. iv. 24).   The text is sometimes trans-
lated, "God is spirit," as if it were intended for a statement of God's metaphysical nature.   But the context gives
the words a simpler and stronger meaning, for it adds that
because God is a Spirit, "they that worship him must worship
him in spirit and in truth."   The declaration is that God and
man correspond each to the other: man is a spirit, and so is
God: "spirit with Spirit can meet," and only in such meeting
is there genuine worship.   So wherever the human spirit seeks
the divine, the divine may be found, whether in a so-called
sacred place or not; for the divine is indeed a Spirit, that
knows and loves and acts without such limits of time and space
as confine the human.   It would not have been quite the
same to say, "God is a Person, and they that worship him
must bring him genuine personal worship," and yet this poor
paraphrase is not so very far from the meaning of the words.

In this consideration of divine personality it has been assumed that a spiritual anthropomorphism is a true key to
right knowledge of God.   Man is like God, and may learn
of him by knowledge of himself.   This claim is sometimes
condemned as presumptuous, even by men of faith, and many
deny that we have the right to project our own likeness up to

the region where we are looking for our God. Such action, we are told, vitiates our whole endeavour: what but childishness would be so rash? But the condemnation is not valid. Personality is the highest fact that we know in all the realm of being. As to what there really is above us, we are far more likely to find the truth by seeking from the height of the human spirit than by searching in regions that are farther away from the supreme reality. Surely the Highest is to be discovered in the light of the highest that we know. God is to be discovered in the light of man, rather than of nature and the world non-human, and from finite personality we may best ascend, if we wish to think upward to the reality that surpasses all our thoughts. Starting from this human personality of ours, we are able to perceive that the like of it, carried above the human and expanded to infinity, would be a God, adequate to the universe. Without fear, therefore, the Christian faith holds the doctrine of the personal God as true doctrine, to be completed, not superseded, by knowledge yet to come.

Doubtless it is true that the vastness of the thought renders a personal God hard to believe in, and that many will stumble at the difficulty. The virtual infinity of the universe as now conceived is so overwhelming to us as to place beyond our imagining a mind that can comprehend it and control it. This we must not only acknowledge, but claim. It is not a sign of the absence of God, but of his greatness. We do not usually suppose that what lies beyond our imagining cannot exist, and we must let in no influence from so absurd a supposition. No one has ever comprehended the Milky Way, but that is nothing against its reality; and if no one can comprehend the infinite personality, still an infinite Person may exist. Nay, it is inevitable that all the greatest realities should be beyond our comprehension. Any evidence of a mind in the constitution of the world leads us on at once into the incomprehensible, for a mind capable of weaving its own thought into the web of existence is too great for us to comprehend. What we are learning of the world in modern science goes to confirm the reality of an incomprehensible all-embracing mind, in which the powers that we know in ourselves as personal exist in boundless freedom. But it is not through the vastness of the universe that we are to become acquainted with that mind. It is in the life of the soul that we have learned to believe in the will of God, the wisdom of God and the love of God, and it is there that our personality finds its rest in his.

3. GOODNESS

The Christian doctrine of God is first of all a doctrine of character, and the character is perfect goodness. It declares that God, who as a personal spirit possesses character, is completely and absolutely good. This, with what is involved in it and comes forth from it, is really the Christian message to the world.

It is needless to show that this great affirmation has always been characteristic of the Christian doctrine. This was the great word uttered already in the Hebrew Scriptures, as it had been uttered with many perversions in the religions of the world. This was the testimony of Jesus, and this the lesson that made all things new in the early Christian experience. Never before Jesus, however, was the perfect goodness of God proclaimed with clear voice and full rejoicing. In the Old Testament it was announced now and then without reserve, but the confidence was dimmed by frequent questioning. The apparent contradictions against the divine goodness that the life of the world affords rose to trouble souls that sought to trust the higher good. The perplexing facts of life, the prosperity of the wicked, the sufferings of the good, the seeming ruin of the nation that stood for God above the rest, the failure of righteousness to vindicate itself, raised agonizing doubts, and only through hard struggle did the faithful come to confidence in the goodness of God. They would not give it up: if they could have done that they might have understood the world, though with a cheerless understanding.

They would not give it up, and hence their perplexity and anguish. Yet amid the darkness, faith in the goodness of God is on the whole the faith that rules in the Old Testament. Such faith comes gradually more and more to be the guide and rule of life for men. The good God requires men to be good also—this is the key to the ancient law of ethics in its highest forms. The contents of this requirement are not wrought out all at once, of course, and it is equally a matter of course that the contents of the idea of goodness itself were not perceived so truly and fully as to render possible a full application of it to life. But in the Hebrew religion the goodness of God stands as the law of righteousness for men, even long before men have learned how much that law must claim.

Jesus is the first to hold with high understanding and unbroken joy that God is altogether good. He utters no commonplaces on the subject, but he utters the truth and lives the life. His testimony is to the effect that God is perfectly worthy of the simplest and most comprehensive confidence, and his will is worthy to be chosen and done by every soul. Thus he taught, and thus he lived. For him this affirmation was undisturbed by the evil of the world. There is no sign that the problems that afflicted Job and Jeremiah ever troubled him. He knew the evil of the world of men, but it did not darken for him the heaven of his Father. If his own will, as in Gethsemane, needed to bow to that of his Father, still his Father's will was good in his sight, and to bow to it was his privilege, however painful the sacrifice that was involved. With clear discernment of what perfect goodness means, Jesus held through his entire career, with unbroken confidence and joy, that perfect goodness dwells in God. And he held, and taught, that divine goodness is perfect and sufficient law for human goodness, and men must seek to be children of their Father who is in heaven, bearing his character.

When the doctrine of God went forth from Jesus into Christian life and thought, it went as the doctrine of a perfect goodness. As an ethical standard, the goodness of God was taken for immediate use. The old command, "Be ye holy, for I am holy" (Lev. xx. 7), had obtained new fulness of meaning, and was now brought home to application in present life. Moreover, the living sense of the perfect goodness of God appears to have been to the early Christians like a new sun in the heavens, brightening all above and all below. Doubt or question of the divine goodness does not appear on the pages of the New Testament, and, except in the Apocalypse, the facts of life that commonly raise doubt of it do not stand out in such light as to suggest the question. Even there, perplexity is conquered by faith. The Christian glory of love fell upon all in which God was manifest, and his goodness was unquestioned.

The Christian doctrine has always proclaimed that God is good, but has never done full justice to its own testimony. Its affirmation has never varied, and yet it has never been a clear and consistent doctrine of perfect goodness. In this there is nothing strange. The Christian people have been sure that God is good, but have not fully known what goodness means. The doctrine has been clear and earnest in the proclamation of goodness, but unclear and often wrong in the definition of it. This was an inevitable condition, which we must bear in mind if we are to understand the Christian history. The question whether God is good is always present, for the moral mysteries of life never allow it to be forgotten. The Christian faith has always taken the same side of the question, affirming in doctrine, prayer and song that God is good. But the full meaning of goodness is a long lesson to learn, and unavoidably the truth was affirmed long before it was well understood. Christian faith has affirmed the goodness, and attributed to God such attitudes and works as corresponded to its idea of goodness; but these have sometimes been such as almost to rob the joyful tidings of its welcome. The upward struggle in the history of doctrine has been the long endeavour to bring the body of doctrine into harmony with the goodness of God. The endeavour has been only half conscious, for the Church has held its mixed doctrine of goodness, unaware of the moral contradictions. This is the pathetic element in the story of doctrine. But the happy element beside it is that Christian faith has never sought relief from perplexities, whether necessary or needless, by denying or doubting that God is good. It has never sought unity of thought by denying the perfect character. This it has always held fast, even while it was holding doctrines that must afterward be altered by the influence of so high a truth. Even until now the Christian faith is faith in the perfect goodness of God, held despite all difficulties. Something in defence of this high confidence will be said elsewhere: at present it is enough to say that the Christian doctrine has always declared that God is good, and that in the later times it is seeking more intelligently to conform itself to this supreme truth.

By the nature of the case as well as in the light of the history, the statement "God is good" needs definition. What do we mean, and what ought we to mean, by goodness, a term that we use in application both to men and to God?

Of course our conceptions of goodness in character are all derived from our experience of character in men. Human life is our only field of observation, and it is a field in which ideas of good and evil in character inevitably grow up. Moral character belongs to nothing but personality and conduct, and to all that is human it does belong. Life cannot fail to teach lessons about goodness, what it is. It teaches imperfectly, but it teaches, and in the long run it teaches well, so that trustworthy conceptions of goodness come to be abroad.

Life cannot teach except progressively, leading on from thoughts that have been to thoughts that are to be: wherefore our conceptions must be variable, changing with our condition. Objection is sometimes made to our affirming that God is good, on the ground that goodness is not the same to all, so that the statement has no definite meaning. It is quite true that goodness is variously conceived among men. The idea varies with mental development, with social experience and with moral progress. Differences in all these are sure to make difference in the ideal of goodness. But all sound human progress tends to the elevation and purification of this ideal. The existence and progress of a sound ideal of goodness is no dream. The differences, wide as they look, are differences in one idea, and beneath them there is a genuine unity of conception. It is not in vain to look for a deep central agreement as to what is good in human character and conduct. The variations illustrate the unity, rather than destroy it. Goodness can be defined.

Goodness means the same in all moral beings. In different moral beings there will indeed be different degrees of goodness, and different modes of putting it into action, varying with position, relations, degrees of intelligence and grades of character. Various good acts may look so unlike as hardly to show their identity in moral kind. But it never turns out that goodness is essentially one thing to one moral being and another thing to another. It is the same at heart for all. The identity is often concealed by the fact that duty is one thing in one position or relation and another thing in another. Acts that would be wrong for the parent are right for the child, and acts that are wrong for the child are required of the parent, yet no one doubts that goodness is in principle the same for both. In like manner, goodness means the same in God as in man. We need not be misled by the fact that God does and must do much that man may not do, for that makes no difference with the unity of goodness for the two. When we say that God is good, we must mean that God possesses that character which constitutes goodness in men. We can mean nothing else, for if we tried to give them any other meaning the words would convey no genuine thought. This we do mean. This is what the Christian doctrine means when it affirms that God is perfectly good: it attributes to God the character that we men in our long career of moral experience and judgment have learned to consider good and to approve as worthy of moral beings.

The goodness that the Christian doctrine attributes to God is perfect goodness; and that means that to God we assign all the qualities that enter into goodness as we know it among ourselves, and hold that he possesses them in perfect degree and without defect or contradiction. In him, we say, all that we know as good is raised to its highest power, and exists as an unbroken moral consistency. This is the Christian affirmation. Here again we do not apologize for letting our conception of God begin in our knowledge of man. We have no other way of reaching above ourselves, and this way is justified in the end by what we discover.

From this mode of approach to the subject does it follow that in the goodness of God there are no traits that are not included in human goodness? Is there something in the divine goodness that has no place in the goodness that belongs to man? or is the range of virtues essentially the same in both?

As to this, it is plain that if additional virtues do enter into the goodness of God, lying wholly beyond the range of human virtue, we can have no idea of what they are. They are as far beyond our ken as a fourth dimension in space, if such there be. But this also is plain—that if such additional virtues do exist they are not inconsistent with the traits that enter into human goodness. In a God of perfect goodness there are no moral contradictions; and any excellences in him that are hidden from us would certainly appear as excellences if they could be submitted to our moral judgment. Of course it is conceivable that there are kinds of virtue quite unknown to us in our present state but existing in God, which in some future state we may become capable of apprehending. It seems scarcely probable. It seems more probable that the traits that constitute moral excellence are really the same in all beings, and that no greater number of essential virtues is required to make a good God than to make a good man. In God the qualities that render a moral being good exist in perfect fulness and have complete freedom of exercise. In men they are infantile in grade, or juvenile at most, and are growing up through the keenest moral conflict. But the holy war in their favour has this to encourage it, that these qualities which make up human virtues constitute divine perfection also, and that to gain them for one's own is to enter into the fellowship of eternal being.

This view of the relation between human goodness and divine involves two facts with respect to our understanding of the goodness of God. One is that the goodness of God is essentially intelligible to us. Our conception of it is an extension of what we already know. The essential meaning of goodness, or moral excellence, has been brought to light in the experience of human life, and has become settled in our convictions. Goodness in God is no vague and indefinable quality, that may turn out to be one thing or another, or may elude us entirely when we seek to understand it. We are released from all perplexities that come from the belief that God has a standard of his own which we can never hope to understand. The central idea of the morally good has become clear in human life, and is so grounded in the deeps of our moral experience as to be unalterable. Great harm has come to religion and to common life from the idea, expressed or implied, that God has given one standard of goodness to men, but has another for himself. But this is no true part of the Christian doctrine of God, which affirms that goodness is one and the same everywhere, and even in God is essentially intelligible to us.

The other fact, equally unquestionable, is that in the operation of divine goodness there must be much that we do not understand. We say that in God the goodness that we know is raised to its highest power. That means that it will take forms that lie beyond our experience, and perform works that are beyond our understanding. Much of its operation must be to us mysterious. Some of its workings will be plain to our comprehension, but some will require time for their explication, while some we may never in this life be wise enough or good enough to understand. Acting in goodness supreme and infinite, God must be his own interpreter to the inferior knowledge and virtue of men, and his self-interpretation may often seem to them slow and painful. We men have a clear grasp upon the principle of goodness in God, and yet are certain to find that the practice of it is often beyond our comprehension. Like human goodness, and yet beyond it, is the divine.

It is now time to seek for a definition of the inner nature of goodness. What lies at the heart of it? What is it that makes either a man or a God good? The question must be answered in the human light. Abstract discussion helps but little: it is from concrete goodness that a valid definition must be made, and the concrete goodness that we can observe and estimate is human.

Human goodness is expressed and discovered in the social relations that belong to mankind. Without the social fact, or the fact of relations, personality and character could not be developed or put to their proper use. Only in relations is self-revelation made, and only there is true self-knowledge attainable. Hence it is through the actions of men in their relations that the idea of goodness has been developed. There was no other way. As a moral quality governing the will and inspiring the affections, goodness is invisible; and for that reason it had to be discovered and defined in the light of what was done in the relations in which men live.

Defining goodness from human experience we shall say that practical goodness consists in the normal fulfilling of a man's relations, or the fulfilling of them in a manner that accords with their nature at its best; and further, that goodness itself, regarded as an interior fact in the man, consists in the moral qualities by virtue of which he is able, and sure, to give normal fulfilment to his relations. A good man is shown to be good by conduct that does justice to the relations in which he stands, and is good by possession of the moral qualities that bring such conduct forth. A good man is one who does what is right and good toward all with whom he has dealings, including both his God and himself; and that by which he is constituted good is the set of qualities by virtue of which this fitting and worthy conduct comes to pass. It may seem that a definition of goodness ought to be more abstract than this, but this simple and concrete method is the one by which mankind obtained its idea of goodness, and is the most effective method, even yet. It is evident that here we have a clear and firm principle for our definition, whereby goodness has a solid meaning, while yet it is plain that goodness actually existing will be of all degrees, and be judged by an endless variety of standards. This combined firmness and flexibility in the definition commends it as true to the facts with which it deals.

But we can carry our defining further. To some extent we can analyze the goodness that we discover. We can specify the qualities that a man must possess in order to the normal fulfilling of his relations, and thus indicate the constituents of goodness. In order that a man may normally fulfil his relations, three things are necessary; and it is difficult to see what fourth can be added as of the same rank with them.

The first thing needful for worthy fulfilment of relations is discernment of the relations as they are, and of what they require. Every man is aware of some relations in which he stands, and has some good understanding of them, and these are the ones to which he is most likely to do justice. A man's relations to his family, to his neighbours, to the state, to the needy, to the sinful, to himself, to God, require to be perceived somewhat as they are, if he is to fulfil them as their nature demands. He must apprehend them justly enough to see what they require. It is easy to see a sufficient reason why human relations are so poorly fulfilled: if there were no other reason, it is enough that they are so poorly understood. By ignorance, indifference and lack of moral insight it is brought to pass that the relations of life are overlooked, misconceived and sinned against. One thing that a man needs in order to full goodness is a broad, rich, intelligent knowledge of the relations that he has to fulfil, with perception of what they mean and what they require.

A second thing needful we perhaps may name spirituality: it is the primary choice and assertion of the considerations that take hold upon the soul and the higher life. The name may seem inadequate, for it is none too definite, and the quality takes many forms, but the quality itself is distinguishable enough. A parent may feed and clothe his child with perfect judgment, but he must also attend to the child's truthfulness, purity, intelligence and preparation for worthy life, if he is to fulfil his relation of parenthood according to its nature. A community may prize prosperity in business, but it needs also to prize justice and the ideals that make for righteousness. A man may prize his relation to God as a means to his own welfare, but if he is to fulfil it worthily he must prize it also as a means for serving God's purpose in a useful life. The considerations that take hold upon the soul and the higher life include conscience, righteousness, love of purity, interest in the moral ranking of things, longing for supremacy of the best. One who is to fulfil his relations in normal manner must have this quality of spirituality, or dominant high choice and judgment. This will make him high-minded, righteous, helpful to the best, in all relations that he sustains; and only thus can he fulfil them normally, in the manner of a good man.

A third thing needful is unselfishness in the broadest sense, with all that it means. A man cannot do justice to his relations with others if he considers himself alone, or sets his own interests at the front. His neighbour must be to him as himself, and often more, for relations are reciprocal, and only by genuine sharing of interests can they be properly fulfilled. And yet unselfishness is a poor and insufficient name. Beautiful as it is, unselfishness is only a negative thing, and only a positive grace can suitably fulfil the human relations. Unselfishness is only a less perfect name for the grace of helpful love, which is indeed the fulfilling of relations, since it does the thing that is needed, out of a willing heart. It considers not itself, but accepts the call of life to free self-sacrifice, and thus becomes the fulness of life and the crown of perfectness.

If we say that goodness means essentially the same for all who are capable of goodness. we imply that the moral qualities that make a good man are sufficient to make a good God, if they exist in perfection. Certainly we are safe in defining practical goodness in God just as we define it in men. With him also goodness comes to effect in the fulfilling of his relations according to their nature, and goodness in itself consists in the character by virtue of which he normally fulfils them. Doubtless this definition seems cold and external, but that is because the relations themselves are not set forth by it. When we remember what they are, as we shall soon have occasion to do, even this cool definition will glow with spiritual light and warmth, for in the relations of God with other beings are involved all the tragedy and glory of moral existence. The due fulfilment of the relations in which God stands to other being calls for a goodness beyond all that we can describe; and if they prove to have been fulfilled by him in accordance with their highest nature, the fact will show that in himself he is good beyond our farthest thought. All that we can say of the goodness that lies hidden in God's infinity and eternality is, that it is the quality that makes him what he is to us and other beings, and that it consists in the character that fulfils all relations as they ought to be fulfilled.

When we seek to know what this sufficient divine goodness consists in, we must answer the question exactly as we answered it with respect to men; for we are quite justified in saying that the qualities that will make a good moral being will make either a good man or a good God. The character by which a man will do justice to the relations in which he stands is the character by which God will do the same. Any moral being must fulfil his relations by knowing them as they are, and holding a high moral judgment concerning them, and devoting himself to the good of those with whom he has to do. A sound moral understanding of the case, a heart set upon right adjustment of moral values, and a spirit of self-forgetful devotion to others' good, are enough, by way of character, to secure the right and worthy fulfilling of all relations. Even God himself needs no more than this. No relations can be conceived that do not require these qualities, discovered in human goodness, for their proper fulfilment, or that require, in character, anything more. In men these traits exist only in rudimentary degree, but we can imagine them carried to perfection, and then they suffice for God himself.

So our induction from the goodness that we are acquainted with leads us to say that the perfect goodness of God consists in perfect knowledge and understanding of all relations in which he stands to other beings and other beings stand to him, in perfect choice and use of the highest considerations and seeking of the worthiest ends, and in complete unselfish devotion to the good of all. In divine action these qualities will be broken up into endless variety and infinite beauty, and will appear far more glorious than one could guess from the crude and unpoetic language in which we set them forth. This we should expect of anything good enough to be divine. Both in their simplicity and in their boundless possibilities, and in their sure mysteriousness as well, we find confirmation of the claim that these are the true essentials of divine perfection.

We have not named these elements in the goodness of God, but their right names lie just before us, simple and comprehensive, familiar yet inexhaustible. The right discernment and understanding of all relations is Wisdom. The choice and affirmation of the highest considerations is Holiness. The unselfish and self-giving impulse is Love. These qualities may be defined in other terms than have now been used, and we shall soon see what boundless wealth of spiritual meaning their familiar names half cover and half reveal. But however inadequate our names for them may be, these are the true constituents of goodness, human or divine. Wisdom, Holiness and Love are all required to make a good man, and no fourth element can be added on the same plane with them. Even so Wisdom, Holiness and

Love make a good God, and when these are perfect in degree and operation nothing needs be added to make a perfect God. Or if it is not so, and there may be a larger and more complex doctrine of divine perfection at last, still such larger doctrine is not for this world, or for us men in our present limitations. This well-grounded and simple idea of divine perfection is the largest and best to which we can hope to attain. This is the substance of the Christian doctrine of the goodness of God—that is to say, of the character of God, which must next be unfolded by examination of these essential constituents.

But the order in which the three elements in goodness have been presented belongs rather to the human sphere than to the divine. We are accustomed to think of human goodness in view of its origin and development, and it is natural to speak first of the right discernment of the relations which it fulfils. Discernment, estimate, impulse—that is a natural order of presentation in the human field. But our exposition of goodness in God may better follow another method. Here is no origin or development to be considered, but the setting forth of a character. We have no occasion to unfold one element from another, as if we were giving an account of the formation of the character that we portray. The ancient discussion as to the relative rank of attributes in God, and which of them should be considered inclusive of another or comprehensive of the whole, need not occupy us. Two facts only need be influential just now: one is, that in presenting the Christian doctrine we are setting forth a character; the other, that the character has been shown to us in a gospel, or a message, or a characteristic work. As Christian students we are seeking to portray the character of the God and Father of Jesus. Our task is to present as truly as possible the elements that enter into the character, and to exhibit the character in the light, not of independent constructive thought but of the redemption that gives name and quality to the Christian doctrine.

To this end it is best to begin at the heart of the matter.

Instead of saying that the character of God consists of Wisdom, Holiness and Love, we shall do better justice to our task if we invert the order, and say that it consists of Love, Holiness and Wisdom. We are unfolding the Christian doctrine and the Christian doctrine of God begins with Love. It does not undertake to decide whether love or holiness is intrinsically the more important, for that is a question of which we shall largely be relieved by looking into the nature of the two; but as a message, the doctrine that Jesus has given to the world begins with love. With Love, therefore, our discussion shall begin; afterward we will turn our gaze to Holiness, and Wisdom will be best understood in the light of both.

4. LOVE

That God, standing related to other beings, fulfils his relations with them in accordance with the first and supreme demand; that he cares for them; that his thought and interest are not centred in himself, but go out with full sincerity and unselfish devotion to those with whom he has to do: this truth is Alpha and Omega in the Christian doctrine. That doctrine proclaims not a self-centred but an outreaching God. It tells of One who comes forth to other existence, not coolly or calculatingly but with the impulse to which belongs the warmest name that our experience has taught us to give to an affection. That name is love. Within the conception of God as existing in the attitude of love, all that is special and peculiar in Christianity is contained.

There is a passage in the New Testament that has been recognized oftener than any other as expressive of the heart of the Christian message; and it affirms that "God so loved the world that he gave his only-begotten Son, that whosoever believeth in him might not perish but have eternal life" (Jn. iii. 16). Here the emphasis falls upon love. When it is written that "God is love," such honour is given to love as is never given to any other quality in character; and that God is love stands in the New Testament as one of the ultimate utterances of the Christian faith and thought. The entire working-out of the Christian message and experience in the Scriptures is an unfolding of the significance and power of redemptive love in Christ. This prominence of love throughout the Christian system is what we should expect. Various true views of God have been entertained by men, but that God is love has nowhere else been proclaimed as truth and wrought out into a message of grace and help. This is the Christian specialty; and a religion that had such a truth to offer could not set it anywhere but at the front. No wonder that the new song is a song of the love of God.

In seeking to know the nature of divine love we are guided, as elsewhere, by our knowledge of the human. We know that love must be essentially the same in God as in man, or else the word can have no meaning for us. We are familiar with love in human life—a passion and an affection, a longing and a mighty sacrifice, all in one. It is an eager desire, often a craving that seems the most selfish of all things, and it is an unselfish affection, a free outpouring of one's best for another's sake. As these two impulses seem completely opposite to each other, so in experience love is full of contradictions; and yet the hunger and the generosity of love, the craving and the giving, the demanding and the sacrifice, are not so deeply contrasted as they appear. Both are forms of one thing, for both are natural expressions of the high estimate which the heart sets upon the object of its affection. Love prizes its object so highly that it cannot rest without possession, and at the same time so highly that it cannot withhold any service or blessing, any gift or sacrifice. Love does not of necessity imply high moral approbation, for, as all the world knows, it often goes off with heart-breaking intensity to an unworthy object, but it does imply an overwhelming sense of value, with intense choice and eager longing. The selfish side in love is often the greater, but the truer love becomes to its own nature the more thoroughly is it ruled by the unselfish and sacrificing impulse. It is love and love only that understands how it is more blessed to give than to receive. Nevertheless, at no stage in the progress of its sweet unselfishness does love lose its desire for reciprocation, without which it would be but an imperfect thing. Love unreturned has often a marvellous beauty of its own, and love not yet returned may be the secret of high endeavour; but the ideal of love implies equality of affection, each giving all and receiving all.

Though human love contains elements thus practically conflicting, it is not essentially a strife, or a struggle of opposing impulses. The ideal of love is a mighty peace. Love has its own joys; and if they include unspeakable satisfaction in the reciprocity of souls, they include also the gladness of the heart that serves, and the incomparable joy of self-giving for another's sake. All the works of love are joys to love, whether they be hard or easy. Love is beneficence and rests in the peace of beneficence. Love is the daily light of life, a light that shines in calmness. Even its shadows are beautiful, and its radiance is the glory of the world.

From human love we look upward to divine, to find that though we rise to a higher world the principle is the same as in the world below. If we have any doubt about our right to infer what heavenly love is from the best that we know of love on earth, we have only to listen to our Master, who helps us to do this very thing. He has said, "If ye then, being evil, know how to give good gifts to your children, how much more shall your Father who is in heaven give good things to them that ask him" (Mt. vii. 11). From the trustworthiness of parental love, which is as pure and fair an affection as we know, he bids us learn of what nature is the love of God. Human love is Jacob's ladder, with God's angels ascending and descending upon it, and God himself standing above.

God, then, is moved by the well-known desire to impart himself and all good to other beings, and to possess them as his own in spiritual fellowship. This is his love. This is the attitude in which he stands toward other beings who are in relations with him, and it is thus that he fulfils his relations. As in the human case so in the divine, the two-fold desire does not of necessity imply approval on the lover's part. But it does imply high prizing, a great sense of value in the object loved—and it is no cool estimate, but a glowing sense of value on the part of him who loves. The Christian doctrine is that God, related to other beings, cares for them with such love as this; he feels their worth, he longs to do them good, he desires their fellowship in a love that returns his own, he longs to impart himself to them in a mutual affection, and his longing toward them is an impulse to self-sacrifice for their sake, such as human love has learned to know in its holiest experiences. Such love in God, the Christian doctrine affirms, is no special or temporary thing, part of some special scheme of his administration of affairs, but belongs to his eternal nature, which in Jesus Christ has found true expression. In this attitude he stands, because he is what he is.

With this conception of love in mind, we may inquire what the writer meant to affirm when he wrote the unparalleled sentence, "God is love" (1 Jn. iv. 8). Nowhere else does the simple copula bind a noun to the divine name.

At a glance we see that the statement contemplates God in his relations with other beings. Love is a matter of relations and does not exist outside of them, for it implies two, lover and beloved. Even when we speak of self-love, we mean that the self is counted twice, once as loving and once as loved. We know no love except where there are two, and to say that God is love is to place him in thought over against beings who are objects of his love. This natural meaning is the meaning in the context, where the thought moves in the region not of abstractions but of concrete facts. We might think that we must find the writer's meaning in the remote depths of solitary divine existence. Because the word "is" is there, we might think that we must read a description of the essence of the Godhead, an account of what God is in himself, apart from all relations. But in the context the writer offers the God whose love he is affirming as example and inspiration of love to people of the common life, who know one another face to face and must show their love in works of helpfulness. "God is love, and he that abideth in love abideth in God, and God abideth in him. . . . We love, because he first loved us. If a man say, I love God, and hateth his brother, he is a liar" (1 Jn. iv. 16–20). These are words of a seer, but he is not gazing into the depths of God to describe something not revealed in relations or in works: he is rather declaring what he beholds when he gazes into the face of God revealed in Christ. God is revealed in love. Love is so characteristic of him in the characters in which he is best known to men that we do not know him aright except as we discern the love that makes him what he is to us. God is love in act: look at God and you look at love. "God is love" differs little in meaning from "God is lover"; and yet there is a depth and largeness in the phrase that the substitute does not contain. We can scarcely put this larger thought into language of definition, and may well be thankful for the richer and more poetic word that stands upon the sacred page. We may experiment by saying, "God is One whose essential character eternally makes him lover," or, "God has love for the very atmosphere of his life and doing," or, "God is so identified with love that it is his very self." All these mean that we know God as love, and do not rightly know him otherwise. The more truly we know him the more shall we know him in this character. Love is no accident, but an essential in God.

According to the New Testament, the proof and measure of the love of God is the gift of his Son for the world, with all that it implies. Jesus Christ is the gift, and the passion of redemptive love burns in what he was and what he did. The cross of Christ, symbol of redemptive sacrificing, is the symbol of the love of God himself. "God commendeth his own love toward us, in that while we were yet sinners Christ died for us" (Rom. v. 8). The familiar saying that begins with "God so loved the world" (Jn. iii. 16) contains these thoughts: God holds the world dear to himself; he desires possession of the world in the fellowship with himself for which it was created; he cannot bear that it should perish, or be morally corrupted to its ruin; he gives his Son, which is to give himself, that it may not thus perish but may become his own. This is to say, in such terms as we have used before, that God prizes the world, longs to possess it in fellowship, feels toward it the impulse of self-devotion, and freely sacrifices for its sake; and this is the work of love. In the Christian doctrine, God is the Being of whom such love is the natural and true expression.

What does this saying imply as to the extent or breadth of the love that it records? What is the world, which God is said to have loved thus? Doubtless it is mankind, the sum of humanity. "The world" is not something less than this. Here we come upon one of the many illustrations of the oneness of the relation of God to all. God is One and all else is another, and his relation to all that is not himself is one relation, in the sense that it is expressive of one character. "God so loved the world," and loves it all and always. But the fact that it is love adds its touch of definiteness and beauty to our thought of the world-wide relation. The object of this affection is not merely humanity as a total, weighed in the balances of judgment and found valuable. It is humanity regarded as lovable and able to make response to love. But a race that can respond to love is a race of persons. Humanity as a mass cannot love God in return, but human persons can: hence the world that God loves is a world of persons, a race whose members are spiritually akin to God, and therefore dear to him. It is mankind as a whole, but as a whole made up of persons capable of returning love. To this "world," the love of God is both universal and particular. The Christian doctrine not merely affirms the negative truth that God "hateth nothing that he hath made" (Collect Ash Wednesday): it declares that God loves all existence, and is love in his relations with all beings who are capable of loving.

As to the manner in which God's love goes forth in action to men, it is portrayed in the New Testament most worthily of God. Love goes forth freely. Paul, the earliest great expositor of God in Christ, delights to speak of the love of God under the name of Grace. In his representation of it, grace is the characteristic form of the love of God as it appears in the Christian gospel. Grace is the suitable expression, in such a world as this, of the fact that God is love. Grace is helpful love, viewed especially as free and unpurchased. It simply gives. In Paul's field of thought, with its vivid remembrances of a legal system of life, grace stands opposed to works, or meritorious deeds, regarded as claiming to deserve something at the hands of God. It is Paul's joyful conviction that grace, the divine principle, stands opposed to all forms of the idea of merit. In God's gospel, he says, the idea of obtaining the divine favour by righteousness of law, or meritorious doings, has no place. It was never a true idea, and now is revealed the method of grace, or kindness undeserved, by which the infinite goodness freely grants the needful gifts to the unworthy. No question of deserving arises: that is not the principle that rules (Rom. iii. 20, ff: iv. 4-5). The love of God is an affection whose nature is to give, and free grace in Christ is simply the normal utterance of such freely-giving love in such a world as this.

The doctrine of free grace is the Pauline commentary upon the Johannine word that God is love. That word is Johannine, and yet it is Paul who has sung the psalm of love, in the thirteenth chapter of First Corinthians. It is human love divinely inspired and raised to heavenly quality that he has in mind; and yet we may doubt whether he would have sung a song of praise so rich and noble, if his heart had not been praising the love of God himself. Certainly Paul would say from the heart that God's love "suffereth long and is kind, envieth not, vaunteth not itself, seeketh not its own, is not provoked, taketh not account of evil, beareth all things, believeth all things, hopeth all things, endureth all things"

(1 Cor. xiii.). He represents God as dealing in this spirit with sinful and needy men, and his God is a God of such love as this.

The idea of free grace is the idea of independent and original love in God, called out indeed by its objects, but having its source in himself. "He first loved us" (1 Jn. iv. 19). This has always been of the substance of the Christian doctrine. The Christian preaching has been wont to declare that the word "whosoever" corresponds to an open door for all souls that will claim the privilege of faith, and has thereby represented the love of God as one love, simple, straightforward, universal, equal toward all mankind, due to his own nature. But the doctrine of divine love has often been held in inconsistency, blended with conceptions that neutralized much of its power. Sometimes the universal breadth of divine love has even been denied by Christians; and often the simple doctrine of free grace has been robbed of power by ideas that spring from that legalism to which the heart of man is so prone. It may be truly said that the characteristic Christian truth of free grace has always been intended in the Christian doctrine, but it must also be said that it has never fully come to its own, having often been held in bondage by ideas that contradicted its message so worthy of God.

For the injustice that has been done to the love of God in the historical Christian doctrine there may be many reasons, but one deep-lying cause is very evident. Justice has not been done to the truth that love is among the fundamental, essential and eternal elements in the divine nature. This truth has been universally accepted in Christian doctrine, and preaching, prayer and praise have been filled with it, and yet the due effect of it has not been wrought. Love has been treated too much as a special manifestation, due to the will of God and designed for certain purposes, and too little as the true manifestation of his very self.

Such a mistake is not to be wondered at. Truth so great as that of the essential love of God, thrown out into the living and thinking world, could not at once make all its meaning manifest or its power effective. It must come gradually to its place in thought and life. We may remember that it is only on the latest pages of the New Testament that we find that supreme generalization of its spiritual revealing, "God is love." We have no reason to suppose that this great word was ever spoken by the Master: it came as the distilled essence of his revelation in life and death, in word and deed. But we observe how late it came—only after the truth as it is in Jesus had had time to do its work. It came, too, not from among the people, but from the heart of the most mystical and far-seeing Christian of his day. It came as a verdict from experience, reflection and spiritual vision, and it was long in coming forth.

The recording that "God is love" marked an era in Christian understanding. Thoughtlessly we might regard it as the end of an era, but it was the beginning, not the end. That truth, once made current, must needs become a theme of long reflection and inquiry. What does it mean? How much does it imply? What fruit should it yield in practice and what in doctrine? What should it expel from among the thoughts of Christians, and what should it introduce? This truth, which is the specialty and glory of the Christian faith, is the most revolutionary of truths. When once it has taken its place, religion that was not dominated by its quality is something that must be exultantly left behind. It is a germinant doctrine, too, not a stationary one, and its influence must grow while men learn through trustful and adoring communion with the God whom it proclaims. Evidently the gracious revolution that this truth will work must be long on the way. It is not too much to say that centuries must pass before the questions just now mentioned could be thought through.

Accordingly, Christian thought has been busy upon the love of God in all generations, with the success and the inadequacy that always belong to its work. Some of the inadequacies and misconceptions are easily understood. For one thing, the very preciousness of the Christian gospel has

had its influence in limiting the conception of the divine love.
The Christian revelation has been so unique and glorious in
the esteem of Christians that they have been tempted to see
but little of the divine love in anything else. As for all the
rest, this supreme manifestation of love has brought it to pass
that love was regarded as only a minor element in the relations
of God with his creation as a whole, and with the world outside of Christianity. It has been common to say that God
in Christ is love; and by God in Christ was meant God in his
dealings with those who have heard of Christ or are to hear
of him. In his relations with mankind as a whole, and with
the non-Christian parts of it, there was righteousness, there
was inflexible justice, and there was general providential
kindness, but love was reserved for those who saw it in the
face of Christ; in which it was implied that love was so special
an element in God's activity that it could be thus reserved for
a part of his creatures. Because the doctrine or announcement of the divine love was so glorious a specialty of Christianity, it has almost seemed that the love itself must be a
specialty also. Since love was manifested as God's special
means of accomplishing certain results for a certain part of
his creatures, his love itself has been estimated according
to the extent of what it appeared to be accomplishing, or
according to the diameter of the circle of its influence in the
world. Thus the universal free gospel of God has been the
means of teaching to many of his children a partialistic doctrine of his love. It has been accepted as a first postulate in
doctrine that love intended its highest blessing for only a
part of men; and such a view must set limits upon the conception that could be entertained of the love itself. When
the aim and end of love is held to be the benefit of only a part,
the love may indeed be felt to be of deep intensity and power,
heart-winning and heart-breaking to those to whom it is
given, but no such view of the matter assigns to love its place
as eternal and essential in the nature of God. That God is
love is too large a truth for doctrines of partialism in the
divine interest and activity.

Against all such limitations upon the love of God stands the great Christian doctrine, which is Christian as being true if Christ is a true revealer, and true since no other doctrine can be true of the perfect God. The God whom Jesus teaches us to know is one God, who stands in one relation to all that is not himself. There are many single relations involved, but they are all included within this one and influenced by its character. In this one relation God regards all as his own, since he is the source of all; and, doing justice to the relation of a Creator, he cares for all, and desires the highest good of all. Toward all spiritual beings he is truly represented by that love which passeth knowledge in which the Saviour Jesus exhibits him. He desires for himself the spiritual fellowship of all souls, and is impelled to do good to all by free self-giving. It is in love that he fulfils all relations in which he stands, and without love they could not be fulfilled. This is the truth that sums up the teaching of the Christian revelation, and no narrow doctrine of love can be true of the God and Father of Jesus. To interpret his love in view of what we are able to observe in the world is only a partial process that must mislead us; we go far deeper into reality when we dare to interpret what we observe in the world in the light of his love. Instead of judging that the love of God is no greater than we can perceive the gospel to be, we may better say that his gospel is as great as the love of God, and the love of God is as great as God himself. When we learn how much this means, we shall be learning the truth as it is in Jesus.

The full effect of the truth that God is love must be allowed in all statements concerning the relations that he sustains to men. All of them are relations with beings whom he loves. There are none to whom he is indifferent, or whom he regards without that affection which is essential in his character. From the nature of his love we learn that the method of free grace in his gospel was not arbitrarily chosen, or chosen at all, since it represents him as he is, and is the necessary method in all religion that corresponds to the divine reality.

Hence we are sure that free grace, or genuine helpful kindness, has always gone forth from him to men, in such forms as were available. Before its flow can cease, God must be changed; and it is because he can never change that the revelation in Christ is a trustworthy revelation. This is not the whole of the Christian doctrine of God, or the only truth concerning him. With this other truths are blended in harmony. But the Christian doctrine, if it is faithful to the light amidst which it arose, will certainly confirm the confidence of all

> "Who deemed that God was love indeed,
> And love creation's final law,"

for it will discern as the First and the Last a God who cares for all.

5. HOLINESS

When we advance in our contemplation from the Love of God to his Holiness, we take but a short and natural step. Love is that attitude of unselfish and earnest care for all beings in which God fulfils his relations toward them, and Holiness is that devotion to the highest and worthiest elements in moral existence by virtue of which he is able, and certain, to fulfil all relations in the worthiest manner. Love is the gracious attitude or movement of the divine Being toward all other beings, and Holiness is the moral character by which the character of the movement of Love is determined. And when we discern this moral character, it is a glorious, radiant and searching purity, a positive goodness incomparable, which is to all sin and wrong what the sun is to the night.

Like many another idea of high significance, the idea of holiness began in far less significant form. It seems at first to have been the idea of the divine: that was holy which belonged to the god. His possessions were holy because they belonged to him, and certain acts and ceremonies were holy because they had to do with him. So there were holy persons, times and places, so called because they were claimed by him. Customs and practices were holy when they were parts or instruments of his worship. Solemnity, awe and reverence before the god imparted to such objects a peculiar quality: they were pervaded by his atmosphere, and men gave them something of the reverence that they gave to him. What was their own was not holy, but the god and his possessions were gathered in a class apart. If the god was not much superior to men, the word holy had but slight ethical significance; but so far as religion was a deeply serious matter, it grew in depth. That great human experience, the joining of morality and religion, is responsible for the enrichment of the idea of holiness. In the light of it there appears to be one moral standard for human and divine. Men had their moral ideals, such as they were, developed in experience, and goodness had a meaning to them; but now it came to be perceived that goodness belonged to God as well as to men, and the religious obligation bound men not only to ceremonies of worship but also to virtue in common life, and to high character. With this conviction came new light upon the moral difference between God and men. God was better than men. He required men to be right because he was right, good because he was good. In him to whom they were already giving reverence there was character that deserved a better reverence. The awe that had been awakened by deity was now evoked by superior goodness, which called the best in men to action, and condemned and shamed their evil.

This is only a hint of the principle on which a long course of experience proceeded. We may call the enhancing of the idea of divine holiness a natural process, if by that we mean a process natural to a world where God is making himself known. It is a work of God, wrought in accordance with his own nature and that of men, in pursuance of his constant purpose to be known. High quality in God does not come to be believed in, we may be sure, without his knowing it, or apart from his self-revealing will. We may call the process natural or supernatural, according to our use of terms, but for true representation of it we may need something different from the meaning of either, as they are commonly employed.

On the way to the Christian doctrine, the idea of holiness passed through both the stages that have been mentioned. Both are traceable in the Old Testament, but the glory of the Old Testament is the strong revealing of the ethical idea of the divine holiness. "The Lord our God is holy" (Ps. xcix. 9) may indeed have meant at first, "Our God is apart from us, and we must stand in awe before him"; but it came to mean, "Our God is infinitely better than we, in the very character that we know we ought to bear." The outward institutions of the law, centring in a sacred place with holy orders of men and instruments of worship, laid emphasis upon the separateness of God from men and the holiness of whatever belonged especially to him. The prophets, and the more ethical parts of the law, laid their stress upon the high character of God, glorious above, and searching and exacting in human affairs. The psalmists, too, had learned something of the higher holiness, and knew it both in penitence and in exultation. As knowledge of God became truer, his holiness was more and more identified with his moral excellence, offered to men as standard and inspiration of goodness. This was the growing thought in that religious life of the Old Testament which entered most congenially into the teaching of our Lord.

When we come to Jesus, we find him taking up the highest conception of God into the presence of which he was born, and bringing it enriched and enlarged into his own life and teaching. So far as the records testify, holiness was not much upon his lips, but it was always in his thought. Never in the Synoptics, and only once in the Fourth Gospel (Jn. xvii. 11), is he reported to have spoken of God as holy. Nevertheless, what he did was precisely to exhibit God as holy, with searching and uplifting power. And when his influence had gone forth into the world and his followers were viewing God in his

light, they beheld a holy God, unspeakably glorious in goodness, urging his goodness upon men as the standard for their
life. Like all his teaching, his presentation of the divine
holiness was practical, not theoretical: he offers no abstract
doctrine of what holiness consists in, but he does what is
better far, he makes such an impression of the holiness of
God as was never known elsewhere. Indeed, the Christian
gift in relation to the holiness of God is rather an impression
than a doctrine, and only from the impression can the doctrine
be rightly drawn.

Holiness in God appears in two lights, somewhat differing
yet perfectly consistent with each other. In a sinful world it
is natural that the divine holiness should first be thought of
in contrast with the ever-abounding evil. That God is unlike
men, having in him nothing of the evil that is so great in them,
is the first impression when it is said that he is holy. Holiness
is purity, freedom from stain, spotlessness of character.
He stands by himself in human thought and reverence, as
the One in whom whatever is contrasted to perfect good has
no existence. This is the negative aspect of the divine
holiness, which is here the absence of all that ought not to be.
But evidently such a view of God is not complete, or finally
sufficient. Neither doctrine nor love can be content with
telling what God is not, even though the negation be so glorious a one as this. We have not done justice to the idea of
holiness until we have affirmed the presence in God of all
possible goodness of every kind, all moral excellence that can
be conceived, and more if there can be more, in fulness of
degree and perfect freedom of operation. Evil can be absent
from a moral being only through the presence of sufficient
good, and in the holy God every form and mode and part of
character is filled with actual and effective goodness. Instead
of being merely the negation of evil, his holiness is the positive
goodness that renders evil impossible, and is itself complete
and unchangeable.

Probably the popular idea of the holiness of God is the

former of these, rather than the latter. Holiness would commonly be defined as purity, sinlessness, a character without stain. That this is a negative conception, and therefore an incomplete one, is undeniable; but that it is an unworthy or ineffective conception is very far from being true. It is perfectly worthy to think of God as unlike ourselves, as free from our evil, and in profoundest contrast to all that our moral judgment disapproves. This as we have said is a natural first thought about his holiness, and of the two conceptions it is evidently the easier to obtain. As it is a natural first stage, so it is probably a necessary first stage in the thought of moral perfection, conceived in a sinful world. And it is a thought that has promise. If we can clearly think of a Being who has in him absolutely no moral evil, we are far on the way toward thinking of a Being in whom all goodness dwells. It is certain, too, that this negative idea has vast power of appeal to men in whom evil is great and strong. A God in moral contrast to ourselves is a great fact to encounter. To see that God is unlike us in all that we know as wrong is to obtain a vision of working and effective holiness that has value unspeakable. If evil is not in God at all, that means that he and it are opposites, and that with all the force of heart and will he must be against it; and thus through the contrast the holiness comes at once to be counted as a militant fact with which every sinful being must deal. Militant purity is a mighty thing to believe in, and a tremendous thing to live with: it is an infinitely beneficent thing, but none the less is it a serious and solemn fact. Sin stirs the conscience, and teaches the lesson of its own dreadfulness; and when it has been made plain that God has in him absolutely nothing of this which is so horrible in us, it is evident that sin has a tremendous enemy who must be taken into the account. For one who is making evil his own, the purity of God brings rebuke, condemnation, and the certainty of danger. That which is not in God cannot prosper in his world, even as it ought not to prosper anywhere. The original and sovereign purity seals the doom of sin. But it also brings

hope and cheer to all good. If any man has begun to hate
his own evil, he may take courage when he knows that God
has nothing like it in himself. One who welcomes even a
small territory of clean and worthy life in his own being may
rejoice to know that the pure space in his life is like God,
in whom no evil dwells. He who is eager in a strife against
evil of any kind may be the more eager and hopeful when it
appears that in all such striving he is on the Lord's side.

In fact, perhaps it is not too much to say that the more
negative idea of God's holiness, much as it may be criticised
for incompleteness, is the main working idea of holiness in a
sinful world. The purity of God—it is a glorious and
powerful thought, and it is on the stainlessness of the divine
character that the emphasis in popular thoughts of holiness
is likely to rest.

Nevertheless, it is true that a negative description of holiness
is not a complete account of it, and the doctrine of holiness
is at the deepest a doctrine of absolute and perfect moral
excellence. Holiness is not made by omissions, but by realities that fill out character and life. There is in God a character that is the perfection of character: this is the great announcement of the Christian doctrine. And what do we
mean by that?

Here at first look it seems that we can never do more than
stand adoring at the mystery of God, for we know that the
inner being of God is beyond our exploring, and must remain
unsearched. It is the character of God in himself that we
desire to apprehend when we seek to define his holiness;
but of God in himself, apart from such manifestations of him
as are made in his relations with other beings, we can discover nothing. How then shall we tell what his holiness
includes? But we have one way of knowledge here, though
only one. The only way by which we can enter that mysterious realm is the way of our own worthiest conceptions of
what is good. This path will not lead us so far as we might
wish to go in the knowledge of God, but we are sure that it
leads us in the right direction. All that we can clearly say

concerning that perfect inner goodness of God which we call his holiness is, that in it all human ideals of good, of every kind, find their satisfaction and are more than satisfied. All goodness of which human ideals are "broken lights" is there complete. We are always cherishing our ideals of what is right and worthy, and of the character that ought to be. We know they are all imperfect, and therefore we may fear to trust them, and think we must have some other guide in forming our idea of perfect holiness. So we may set out to search for some goodness that lies outside our highest human conceptions of goodness, and suppose that we cannot know God until we have found it. But the effort will be in vain, for we have really no means of imagining the perfect good, except by carrying up toward perfection our living ideas of imperfect good. Jesus never taught us any other way, nor has the Christian doctrine ever proclaimed any goodness in God that was not imperfectly presentable in terms of our best conceptions. There is literally no way into that mysterious region except the way that our nature compels us to travel in. Nor will this way mislead us. The best that we know or can imagine exists in God, and is infinitely bettered there. Human ideals of goodness, when their faults are corrected, their narrowness is enlarged, and their utmost is satisfied, converge in God, and point to the goodness that really lives in him. They lie in various fields of life, and embody various forms of virtue, but the variety only works toward completeness, and in God they all find harmonious fulfilment. His positive holiness includes all worthy character that is known to humanity, in degree never imagined by man: it is of the same kind with human goodness, but in infinite perfection. Our thoughts of goodness are poor and faulty, but they are of noble kinship, for they rise to God himself, and in him is a character that corresponds to them while it rises far above their farthest height.

Here dawns upon us the inconceivable magnitude of holiness in the character of God. What has just been said is enough to show that his holiness is no single form of excellence, no single attribute in a list of divine virtues. Since it fills and satisfies all our ideals of goodness, it must be not so much an attribute as a character. It is no fragment of goodness, no one side of perfection: it includes goodness of every kind, and is perfection. The name holiness, instead of specifying one of God's qualities, sets forth his moral perfection as a whole. God's holiness is nothing less than the sum of his goodness, the glorious fulness of his moral excellence. Yet even language so lofty as this falls short of the descriptive power that would convey the impression of what holiness is. In the mention of it, from the Christian point of understanding, there is suggestion of a radiance, a forthshining glory, all unutterable in human terms, of which we may humbly record our living sense, and to which we can do justice only by lowly and exultant adoration.

Holiness is the moral perfection of God; and its comprehensive character is set in its place in the Christian doctrine by the statement that we have already made concerning his fulfilment of his relations with other beings. It is in holiness, we have said, that he fulfils those relations, or does what they require. They are all included in the beneficent sweep of love, and the fulfilment of them all is dominated by the character of holiness. It is because he is holy that God can do justice to all relations in which he stands, and be toward all what God ought to be. Evidently, to say this is to identify holiness with universal perfection in character. Only to the most comprehensive and perfect goodness could such a position and rank be given. It is right to say that the holiness of God is the moral excellence by virtue of which he worthily fills his part in every relation that he bears to other beings.

Since the holy God is thus fulfilling his relations to other existence, the moral significance of the universe is sufficiently accounted for. Of the universe, we say, for though we are acquainted only with the world, we know that the universe is the real unit, and that one significance must pervade it all. Moral significance in the universe means that intelligent life within the universe is always moral: wherever there are beings possessed of moral powers, there exists a holiness for them to receive as the standard of their moral character. It means also that the career of the universe as a whole is certain to be directed with reference to moral ends. With a God of holiness in all and over all, both these things must be so: life has moral significance to every soul, and existence has moral significance for the universe itself. It is by such administration that the holy God fulfils his relation to the universe as a whole, and to the moral beings whom he has brought to exist within it. To the universal moral significance the holiness of God is the key.

In fulfilling his relation toward men, the holy God does his part by holding forth his own character as the standard for theirs. We may say that in practice his holiness is his morality in dealing with men, or his insistence upon the moral element in life. By virtue of it he places moral meanings at the front, and keeps them there; he deals with men as capable of good and evil, right and wrong; he administers their destiny on moral grounds. This he does, as we shall see more fully in another connection, by his gift of moral nature to men, by perpetual communication between his own spirit and theirs, and by the gradual self-manifestation by which he gradually brings more and more of this great influence into the world. Under his administration it is possible for men also to be holy, and the holy God lays emphasis upon the matters that are essential to the making of holy men. He insists that they too shall set their affection and will where his are set, upon the moral aspect of their life. In all human experience, whether high or low in grade, there is found an element of moral exactingness: there is an inward claim and an upward call. It may be definite or vague, and it may suggest now more and now less of the good that men need to do, for these things depend upon conditions that vary; but the moral exaction is nowhere wholly wanting in the life of men. This element in life is the counterpart of the holiness of God with whom men have to do. It is the claim of his

character upon theirs. Because men are living in the world
of a holy God, therefore it is that their life is framed upon an
ethical plan, and into every day's living there comes something of the reasonable demand of the divine perfection.

This demand, as accords with the comprehensive nature of
divine holiness, applies to every part of human life and action.
It has often been thought that it is in religion that men have
to do with God, wherefore the special rites and ceremonies
of religion have been associated with him, and held sacred
for his name's sake. Because they were thought to be the
link between man and that supreme reality above to which
his moral nature points, they have been cherished and held
in the highest reverence. A better knowledge of the holiness
of God and its claim upon men does not take away the value
of religious acts, but it does deprive them of their uniqueness
as response to the divine claim. The divine perfection includes the ideals of all goodness that is possible to men, and
the demand that it makes is a demand for high moral quality
in every part of life. Its appeal takes hold upon the conscience,
and the conscience judges action and character of every
kind. The holiness of God calls for devotion to the worthiest
ends in everything; for morality belongs to no one department
of life—it is of equal force in all. His claim touches the
intellectual life, and the æsthetic, and the executive, and the
social, just as truly as the religious. If the devotional and
ethical life stands related to his all-dominating holiness, so
does the artistic, the reflective, the constructive, and whatever
other there may be. God commands us in industry and lei-
sure, in pleasure and in pain, as well as in prayer. His
character, held out as standard for ours, demands that among
our neighbours we be honest, righteous, pure, diligent, enter-
prising, helpful; that in the work of the intellect we think
clearly and distinguish the true from the untrue; that in
using our æsthetic faculties we disentangle them from the
appetites and passions, and make them servants of the higher
life; that in all executive work we hold our practical powers
under intelligence and moral judgment, do the best work

possible in its kind, and serve humanity. All this, and more, is urged upon us as duty by the holiness of God, or the all-inclusive goodness which is the type for all sound human character. God is one, and so is our life, and upon the whole of our life falls the comprehensive claim of the comprehensive holiness.

This all-inclusive claim of the divine holiness accords as well with the nature of man as it does with the nature of God. God cannot do otherwise than make it, and man ought not to do otherwise than honour it with obedience. All that God's claim requires is that a man be normal. If a man is his true self, he is right. But the norm of man is found in the soul. In the advancing animal life the soul has mysteriously come forth, the marvellous blossom of consciousness, reason and aspiration, upon the ancient physical stock. It is normal that the flower advance to the fruit of which it is the promise, and the fruit is the character worthy of such a being. But the character that is worthy of a human being is the lowly reproduction of the character of God himself. The normal character for man is identical with the actual character of God—save that the human must always remain within the limits of the human, and can never equal the divine. When that holiness which gives moral significance to life lays hold upon a man, it calls him simply to be himself, and rise to the quality that belongs properly to his nature. There is no goodness in God that is not adapted to call out a similar goodness in man, and there is no worthy possibility in man that has not its counterpart in the holiness of God. Man is himself, fulfilling his nature, when he responds to the holiness of God and takes it for his own.

Such being the conditions, we see at once why the call of divine holiness is so indescribably exacting. How can it be otherwise? There is good reason why the moral judgment should be the most urgent thing with which we have to do, for it is the voice of God, bringing the message which it is life for us to hear and ruin for us to reject, and at the same time it is the voice of our own nature, solemnly confirming the testimony of God. In the quality of holiness, or the eternal good for which even we were made, there is full justification for all the urgency of conscience and divine demand. Here, too, dwells the reason why the universe was so constituted that sin could not prosper: the holy God could not make a universe in which it could. It is here also that the retributive quality in the divine holiness is found, and is intelligible. Holiness rewards the soul that does it loyal service, and brings punishment upon the soul that sets its claim at nought, and all because it could not do otherwise. From the inward necessity in God life is so ordered that in holiness is welfare and in sin is doom. So central is the character of God that whatsoever will not revolve in loyalty around it is a wandering star, for which the blackness of darkness is reserved. The retributive quality in life administered by God needs neither apology nor explanation, when once the relation of perfect goodness to both God and man appears. The goodness that makes God what he is, is all that can make man what he ought to be. In such case there is no need of law or decree to establish a retributive order, for the retributive element in life is a part of the very fact of life with holiness as normal quality.

Holiness is the exigent quality in the being of God, and in his relations with men, and in the very nature of things it is a serious matter to have to do with it. It is a serious matter to live in a moral world, but the seriousness of living in a moral world is concentrated for us in a personal relation, by the fact that we have to do not with an abstract morality but with a holy God. His existence makes seriousness and solemnity characteristic of ours.

But, on the other hand, we are never to think that the divine holiness intends to sadden the universe. It constitutes the glory of existence, both human and divine. That God has in himself in infinite fulness the qualities, by virtue of which he can perfectly fulfil and satisfy all relations in which he has placed himself to other beings; that he bears the character in which all human ideals of goodness are more than realized;

that he is holding forth this character, perfect in itself and
ideal for humanity, as the standard to which he seeks to
bring his creation; that he has wrought the claim of his own
holiness into the structure of his universe, and ordained it to
be a power that makes for righteousness in all life: what
heights and depths of spiritual glory such words as these open
for our contemplation! We cannot fathom the depth of
goodness that is thus described, or exhaust the wealth of
promise that it opens for God's creation.   In such a presence
we can only adore with gladness.   The Christian doctrine
affirms that such a God exists, a God to whom "Holy, Holy,
Holy," is the appropriate address, whose essential holiness
surpasses thought, and whose manifested holiness imparts
solemnity and hope to all spiritual existence.   God's holiness
has two companion-glories, equally to be rejoiced in and
adored: one is that it utterly condemns all choice and love
of evil, and the other that it stands as support and encouragement to every loyal choice of good.   It would be a sad mistake
to think of such a presence chiefly as threatening and saddening.   It is threatening to evil, and saddening to unworthy
hopes and joys, but the eternal holiness is the hope of the
universe, and the enlightening sun to all eyes that discern
what true light is.

There is no other doctrine of God that contains any such
conception of holiness as the Christian doctrine offers.   It is
a daring act for Christian thought and faith to affirm such a
holiness, in the face of all doubts and questions and perplexing
facts, but in so doing it bears a testimony as beneficent as it is
courageous.   What if the entire humanity could firmly
believe in a Being of perfect goodness, from whom all high
human ideals originate and in whom they are more than
realized, who makes good his relation to all intelligent beings
by insisting upon the ethical significance of life, who destines
all goodness to success and all evil to failure, and whose
character claims the loyalty of all who live!   What a light in
darkness such a faith would be!   Such holiness in God sets

the distinction of right and wrong on eternal foundations, justifies and sustains the moral meaning and importance of life, and accounts for the moral element that cannot be eliminated from our thoughts concerning destiny. It makes life serious in every part, and gives assurance that it can never cease to be serious, however long it may continue and in whatever world it may be found. It shows why life is worthy to have been brought forth by God and to be lived by men. It establishes goodness as the determinative fact in all existence, and shows why a worthily aspiring man is not alone, but is entering into the eternal fellowship. The holiness of God is the everlasting glory, in the light of which every reasonable being ought to join in the adoring song, "Holy, Holy, Holy, Lord God of hosts, Heaven and earth are full of thy glory: Glory be to thee, O Lord Most high" (Sanctus of Holy Communion).

6. WISDOM

Wisdom is something that calls for no abstract consideration. It is a practical thing, and is sufficiently known by its works. Its nature is plain enough in human affairs, where it is known as a broad and true understanding, which implies power to form the truest judgment. In personal life, it is good understanding of the relations in which one stands, and of matters with which one has to do. It is higher than knowledge. Knowledge moves in the intellectual realm, wisdom rather in the moral, just because it has to do with those relations which give to life its moral significance. Knowledge may deal with things that have no moral quality, and knowledge is not purposive; but wisdom looks to ends, and would scarcely even have been named if it had not been for that deeper significance which morality imparts to life. A wise man is one who knows not only what things are, but what they mean: he knows, too, how to handle them, and turn them to worthy use. In the fine saying of Tennyson, "Knowledge comes but wisdom lingers," the nature of wisdom is suggested as plainly by a hint as it could be by a definition.

Wisdom, known among men, belongs in perfection to God. In God, so far as we can define it, wisdom is understanding, comprehension, just knowledge of all things in their true significance, together with ability to design the accomplishment of the ends that he proposes. It is that comprehensive grasp upon the meaning of all relations in which he stands, by which God is able to act in view of them and do them justice. It is knowledge of all things as they are, with the intelligence and coördinative power that can use them for ends beyond themselves. With God as with men, wisdom is no mere intellection, and no mere consciousness of things: it moves in the moral realm. If this were not a moral universe, knowledge might suffice; but it is a moral universe, and in God there is wisdom.

Placing this quality in connection with love and holiness as they have been set forth, we may say that God's wisdom is that understanding of all things which enables him to fulfil his relations to other existence. It is the perfect understanding through which he is able to carry into effect his holiness and love. He does not misconceive, and has no illusions. He knows all that holiness demands and love requires, he is conversant with the nature of all beings with whom he has to do, and he knows how to act in view of all. His wisdom is the understanding that makes him master of every situation. A man may know a situation, and understand the elements with which he is dealing, but not be wise to know how his problem may be solved and his purpose accomplished. But God has perfect wisdom. He sees his way through—if we may speak thus after the manner of men—and knows that he is right. He has great works, but no unsolved problems. He knows the end from the beginning, and knows how the end is to be reached.

The Christian doctrine affirms the perfect wisdom of God. All intelligent theism does the same, but the Christian thought is clearest and most positive in its affirmation. The doctrine with which the Christian faith began had this already as an inheritance. In the Old Testament, God is a Being who holds all things in his hands, and who understands all so well as to be able to conduct their existence aright. The exquisite personification in the eighth chapter of the Book of Proverbs represents Wisdom as God's counsellor from the beginning. The fortunes of Israel may seem obscure and perplexing, but they are conducted by One who understands. Over the world there reigns a wisdom that all men may safely trust. There is a controlling and coördinating God. When the life of the individual is considered, this is what gives light amid the mysteries of experience—God understands, and is able in his wisdom to order all aright. Sometimes in the Old Testament the programme of the divine wisdom is assumed to be known; as when it is held, in some of the Psalms, that justice will very soon be visibly done between good and bad, and God will be vindicated at once in the sight of men. But these interpretations of the method of wisdom prove to be only tentative; they are expressions of faith that was intelligent according to its time, but they are not finally true. Such vindication has not been made. Yet whether the operation of wisdom in the world is immediately interpretable or not—and even the trustful heart often finds it beyond the reach of present understanding—the faith of the Old Testament rests always in confidence that God is wise, and wisdom governs all.

In the New Testament, also, the sufficient wisdom of God is assumed as the sufficient foundation of faith. Thus Jesus taught, by word and action. His Father had perfect understanding, and it was not only safe but honourable and glorious to follow the leading of his wisdom. The whole doctrine of the divine wisdom is wrapped up in the words, "Your Father knoweth what things ye have need of, before ye ask him" (Mt. vi. 8). The divine Father knows all situations in which his children find themselves, he understands all that can influence their lives, and he judges truly of all the needs that consequently arise. This comprehensive understanding, too, is not that of an intellect that merely knows; it is the understanding of a Father, whose knowledge is that of a person dealing with persons, and is instinct with sympathy. Comprehending with a sympathetic discernment, he can be trusted concerning all. Still further, this discerning and sympathetic wisdom is no provincial knowledge, but takes in the affairs of all men. No one ever supposed that this rich and helpful word of Jesus applied only to those who first heard it, or to any other special group. When he represented religion as personal, consisting in the relation of the soul to its God as the relation of a child to its father, he gave a promise that was universal, the same for all. If to his little flock he could say, "Your Father knoweth what things ye have need of before ye ask him," he could say the same to all men. A God whose wisdom did not embrace all would not be a wise God for any. The field of his knowledge, insight and sympathy must be as wide as the field of moral existence, and he must know what every soul needs, without petitions ascending from any quarter to inform him. By confidence in such wisdom any soul may rest in certainty that God knows what he is doing, and is competent to direct all affairs.

In the early Christian life, that deep and restful faith in God which proved so great a blessing was in part a confidence in the divine wisdom. Paul perceived that the more profoundly Christ was understood, the greater and more amazing would be the wisdom of God revealed in him. He saw also that in the administration of human affairs in the interest of salvation the wisdom of God was destined to be most gloriously shown. It was not at once apparent in its fulness, for only events yet to come could reveal it; but the very "unsearchableness of his judgments," or mysteriousness of his work, was but an indication of "the depth of the riches both of the wisdom and the knowledge of God" (Rom. xi. 33), which in due season was bound to be manifested in the triumph of grace over sin. In his own time God would vindicate his wisdom in human affairs, and meanwhile glimpses of its glory were the joy and study of trustful hearts.

The Christian doctrine has always declared God's wisdom to be perfect. Between omniscience and wisdom the distinction has not always been drawn with care, but the differentiation has not been necessary for practical purposes. That God knows all and that God understands all are so nearly the same in effect that the need of sharp distinction is not urgent. The Christian belief in divine wisdom has been a conviction that God's understanding of all things is to be trusted as absolutely sufficient by all beings. It accepts the reality of a wisdom that includes intellectual understanding, right moral estimate, sympathetic comprehension and intelligence in control.

The wisdom that is attributed to God must needs be a creative or designing and productive wisdom, as well as a wisdom of control and administration. All comes from God, and in him is all the wisdom that can be needed for making the universe to be what it is and ought to be. Here analogies from human knowing fail us in part, though in part they help us. We are familiar with a theoretical knowledge that is not constructive, an understanding of something once built, that could never have built the thing. Our knowledge of nature is necessarily of this kind. We are familiar also with practical knowledge of situations in which we find ourselves, but which we did not originate, knowledge gained from experience, whereby we learn to adapt ourselves to our relations and turn them to use. But these forms of knowledge are after-products of existence, and are not sufficient for illustration of the wisdom of God. The difference is that from him all has proceeded. All relations in which he stands are of his own ordering. Not only is he wise enough to employ for his own purpose the relations in which he stands, and to fulfil them normally when once they are established: he is wise enough to have established them at first, and to have ordained them in accordance with his own worthy nature. He has brought into existence a universe in which he could express himself, both intellectually and morally. He has created relations that are worthy of him, of innumerable kinds. He has known a universe through and through. He has unfolded the plan of existence, material and spiritual, and understood the vast system of being that he created. The Christian doctrine affirms that he made it worthy of himself, and possessed the wisdom that was necessary to so inconceivable a work. And it adds that in the development and administration of his universe, with all the works and destinies that it includes, he is so wise that his children may safely trust him in all respects and through all duration.

Such a conception of the divine wisdom is an ever-expanding conception, growing greater in proportion as our knowledge of its field of operation is increased. When the Christian doctrine first arose, the realm of known existence was comparatively narrow. It seemed great, indeed, to the men of the time, but, in comparison with our view of the universe, it was so small that we often fancy ourselves at liberty to smile at it. The earth was flat, the sun existed to give it light and seasons, the human race was small and just created, the elements of human nature had not yet been studied out, and what we call science was unknown. It is true that the great mysteries were the same as now, and we must not be high-minded, as if life had glory and pathos first in our time. What we call the problems of existence are present in every personal life, in any age. The field of existence then known was "all" to the men who knew it, even as the field of existence that we know is "all" to us, and brought to them the essential problems of universality. Nevertheless, it is both true and important, that the word "all" was narrow then, and is incomparably broader now; and that with it has grown the conception that we need to entertain of the divine wisdom. The flat earth has become a globe, and the globe a speck in a universe of inconceivable vastness. The human race has become both great and ancient, its varieties perplexing, its life complicated, its moral problems overwhelming, its destinies mysterious. The meaning of existence is a question anxiously discussed not only by philosophers but

by the people everywhere.   To say that all is under the ordering and sway of divine wisdom is to affirm far more than
could possibly be present in thought to any writer of the
Bible, for a wisdom adequate to the world that is known to-
day must be far broader and more various than any that men
of the first century could imagine. To declare that this
world as now known is the product and the field of perfect
wisdom is to make an affirmation that could never have
arisen in full magnitude in any mind of that century; and to
go further and embrace the scope of the universe as now
conceived under the thought of perfect wisdom is to do what
could never be imagined until our age had dawned.

Nevertheless the Christian doctrine affirms to-day what it
affirmed at first. In the larger field it holds what it held in
the smaller. It is still a doctrine of perfect wisdom in God,
all-inclusive, adequate. It still attributes to God that
comprehensive knowledge and sympathetic understanding of
all existence whereby he is forever worthy of the confidence
of all who exist.   Neither the world, nor the material universe,
nor the universe of spiritual life and destiny, it declares, is too
great for him. He understands it all through and through,
as one whole and in its infinity of detail, so perfectly that men
may trust him in everything without a fear. He is so wise
that he has a right to have a universe in existence.

It is evident that the conception of an adequate wisdom
enters congenially into company with the idea of orderly and
continuous operation on the part of God.   Probably this has
never been denied in terms among Christians, and it has often
been affirmed; but the doctrine of the operation of divine
wisdom has of necessity been conditioned by the conception
of the world that was abroad. It is only of late, comparatively,
that the idea of genuine unity and continuity in the universe has begun to do its work.   Before it became influential,
it was natural to think of God's wisdom as manifest in special
operations, in overruling, in correcting, in controlling alien
affairs and irregular movements. In a fragmentary world,

God's interventions and occasional touches were the chief demonstrations of his wisdom. This was never the entire thought, and yet this view of the matter has inevitably been present when the method of the world was so conceived as to suggest it. But the genuine Christian thought welcomes the idea of a genuine universe, conducted by a single method and expressive of one continuous purpose. Hence in this respect the Christian doctrine is conspicuously at home with the modern view of the universe. In the modern light, God in his wisdom appears not as the coördinator of fragments or the repairer of defects in operation: he is the originator and conductor of a scheme of things that has its meaning in itself, and proceeds by forces that he has placed within it. Nothing but a genuine universe, indeed, could give worthy expression to such wisdom as the Christian doctrine ascribes to God. If at the present stage of a career as yet unfinished, meanings have still to be discovered and methods to be justified to human thought, that is nothing strange, and casts no doubt upon the ruling wisdom. In a universe so vast, it will be no wonder if meanings always remain in part for faith to apprehend. But the Christian heart has always been believing in the perfect and all-comprehensive wisdom of God who is the source of all, and now it is permitted to welcome a view of the universe that corresponds to its idea of wisdom. The wisdom that the universe exhibits is single, all-inclusive, constructive, continuous, coördinating, adequate—just as the Christian faith declares the wisdom of God to be. In what manner the divine mind is active in the exercise of such wisdom, we may never know; but we see innumerable relations established, and one continuous wisdom working in fulfilment of them; and Christianity is true both to its ancient doctrine and to the modern light when in the presence of every intelligible fact it answers, "Lo, God is here."

But the Christian doctrine is doing its most characteristic work in this field when it joyfully sets forth the wisdom of God as his adequacy to the work of doing justice to the meaning of his holiness and love. This above all others is the point for

Christian emphasis. He knows what holiness as a motive would do, and what love as a motive would bring forth, and this he knows with perfect understanding, with respect to every complication and contingency that can arise in the affairs of his universe. To do all that holiness and love require in all the various and ever-changing conditions of existence, meeting all occasions as they rise, sacrificing neither love nor holiness, neither hasting nor resting in the work, omitting nothing and doing nothing amiss; to be true God to all existence without fault or failure—this is the work to which the wisdom of God renders him forever adequate. Not only is he the eternal holiness and love, but he is the eternal holiness loving in wisdom. So affirms the Christian doctrine, and so rests the Christian faith.

7. UNITY IN CHARACTER

The elements of character that have now been attributed to God are no scattered and inharmonious elements. They constitute a real unity of character, so clear that we can understand it, and so important that we must not fail to attend to it. This unity constitutes an indispensable element in the Christian doctrine of God, and because it has not been clearly discerned the doctrine has greatly suffered, and religion has suffered with it.

It is easy to assert a perfect unity of character in God, but it has not proved so easy to keep a well-defined unity steadily in view. The trouble is in us. We ascribe to God certain qualities of character, set forth in familiar terms, but when we come to define them we are under the influence of our own limitations, and however large and worthy the terms that we use, our conceptions are sure to become narrowed toward the dimensions of humanity. Naturally, if not inevitably, we bring the perfection of God down toward our own imperfectness; and one result is that the qualities that we attribute to him are not harmonious among themselves.

Virtuous traits as they exist in us are often more or less inconsistent with one another, and it often seems to us, judging somewhat from ourselves, that they must be so in God. The God of the Christian faith has been adored and loved, but now one side of his character and now another has been in sight, different aspects of his being have seemed inconsistent and contradictory, and there has been good reason why the Christian mind should be perplexed. There is trouble when unity and consistency cannot be discerned in the character of him with whom we have to do.

Holiness and love are the great outstanding attributes, and between these there is often felt to be a genuine contrast. In theology the two have often been treated as profoundly unlike each other. Doctrine has proceeded now from holiness and now from love as starting-point, and now toward holiness and now toward love has the soul's attitude in adoration been turned. Now from one and now from the other Christians have felt that they must take the key of their faith and life.

For this apparently there are reasons. Love and holiness make different impressions upon us. Love is winning, we say, and holiness is awe-inspiring. Love gives, and holiness demands. Love sets a major key for life, and holiness a minor. A sinner feels that he may live with love, but must perish in the presence of holiness. Moreover, love is a familiar and cherished element in human affairs, while holiness is regarded as something that comes in exactingly from above: love in fact is human, but holiness is divine. It is not strange that the two have been suspected of being irreconcilable in their very nature, and inharmonious even in God. The religious experience often confirms the impression, for the condemnatory voice of conscience and the joyful song of salvation are so unlike as to suggest that the contrast cannot be reconciled, even in the attributes to which they are deemed to be responsive. It has been thought that law represented God's holiness and gospel his love; and law and gospel have been set in such contrast that law must be satisfied before gospel could exist. So it has been common to hear of conflicting divine attributes, holiness and love disagreeing in their demands, and of plans to bring them into harmony. We hear even of God himself as planning to reconcile them. But though the belief in conflict among divine attributes may have arisen naturally, still it has made great trouble, both in theology and in religion. Nature is against it. The conviction that God is one and harmonious, never divided against himself, cannot be kept down, for there is no satisfactory theism without it. Internal conflict in the perfect Being is incredible. This conviction may be long in winning its way, but no scheme of doctrine that contradicts it has sure lease of life, and as long as internal conflict in God is assumed, there is perplexity for faith and weakness for theology. A truly religious theology will posit an intelligible unity and consistency in the character of God.

One cause of the suspicion of internal conflict in God is that Theology has been too much in bondage to its doctrine of Attributes. The qualities of character and modes of activity that we attribute to God have been analyzed, and treated almost like separate entities. God has often been spoken of almost as if he were composed of attributes, each of which had its special dictation to offer him. Often indeed his character and works have been set forth in terms of what his attributes would demand and do. When the sense of his unity is lost, it is the attributes that are thought to be in conflict; and this is not surprising, when attributes are set apart from the Being who possesses them, and almost personified in themselves.

The method of representing God in terms of attributes corresponded to some stages in the understanding of psychology; but it is doubtful whether it has done more good or harm, and certainly it is not adapted to the present condition of knowledge. It is a formal, scholastic and unfruitful method. We do not study any other character by such means. If we were invited to form a judgment of some great man by analyzing his character into separate attributes and accounting for his actions by them, we should promptly decline, distrusting the method, which is not the method of life. It is God that we wish to know, not his attributes. The practice of collecting and classifying his qualities under this special name has not been favourable to that impression of glorious reality which the living God would desire to make upon us. We discern qualities of character in him, of course, and give them the names that belong to them. But we must not be bound by an artificial method to analyze him into these qualities and then discuss what each of them will lead him to do. There is a better way than this. The Christian view shows us God himself, standing in certain relations to men, and acting on certain principles, or under certain impulses. The impulses and principles spring from within himself, and are expressive of what he is. We give names to them, and to the traits of character which they represent and verify to us. But our best way to know him better is not to search out what his separate attributes must do, but to learn what he himself is doing. We should learn the attributes from God, not God from the attributes. If we can see God himself in the unity of his spiritual work, we shall discern the unity of his character.

If we bring together what the Christian doctrine contains, this unity will be before us.

In God we behold a Being whom we call good; and by this we mean, as we have defined goodness, that he is One who, standing in relations with other beings, fulfils those relations in accordance with their nature. He is all that he ought to be toward other beings—all that they could ask or wish, even if they knew all that could be known—and hence it is certain that he is all that he ought to be in himself. He is good, in perfection. Now, having such a Being as this within our spiritual ken, we look with eagerness to see what this perfection means, and to understand, if we may, what character it is that he expresses by this perfect fulfilling of all relations.

First of all we come upon the great revealing fact that God loves all beings. We find him so related to them that he desires to do them good. To him they are precious. Toward them he is not selfish or self-centred, a God distant and reserved, but One who longs to impart to them himself and his own fellowship, and to have them for his own as children of his heart. He is a self-outpouring friend, ready to do good by all means at his disposal. The great vision of God that the Christian light reveals to us is, that God is love toward all existence, and the most significant fact concerning all existence is, that it is loved by God. We behold him in his attitude toward all that is not himself, and it is an attitude of outgoing affection that seeks the good of all. Since he is the First and the Last, his attitude is taken by himself: it is not forced upon him by any external facts, but is the true representation of what he is, essentially and forever. It is his nature to be the outreaching friend of all existence.

We now look further, to see in what manner God acts for the accomplishment of this desire of love to do good to all. We do not see him in all the relations that he sustains, for many of them lie beyond our sight, and some perhaps lie essentially beyond the range of our experience. But we see him in one relation that has true revealing power. We see him in his relation to ourselves and our fellow-men; and we are moral beings, in dealing with whom he is manifested as he is. We are sure that what the great Lover of other beings is toward our group, he is toward all, and is by virtue of what is essential in himself. When we ask, then, in what kind of action he expresses his love toward men, we find that he acts out his love by insisting always upon the higher, worthier, more spiritual aspect of their life. He has so made them and the world in which they live that nothing but goodness can bring them a prosperous existence. He has so formed their life that experience produces in them moral judgment and gives them moral ideals, and then he insists that to their moral ideals they shall be faithful. He is against all that is abnormal to the rising life of the spirit in them, and is on the side of all that is pure and holy and uplifting. Whenever life develops any new possibility of virtue, he is on the side of that possibility. His call for loyal response to his own goodness is unvarying and inexorable, and his interest in the moral welfare of other beings never dies. The best is what he forever insists upon and promotes. This high moral emphasis is characteristic of God and representative of his real self. In God resides the perfect goodness, shining forth for the guidance of finite beings, claiming their loyalty, defeating their sin, crowning their response to its own demand. God, we say, is holy.

We look once more, for we have beheld a situation that still has its question for us. The First of spiritual beings stands so related to other beings that he is to do toward them all that his own perfect holiness and love suggest. He is to administer their life, and all existence, under these companion-impulses, or on these companion-principles. The undertaking is immeasurably too great for us to comprehend: it is so far beyond us, indeed, that we have to acknowledge that we should not even be able to judge whether or not it was worthily performed. But as for God himself, we learn that he is wise. He is as wise as he is holy or gracious. He knows all things, but he is more than omniscient, which would not be enough: he has that penetrating and sympathetic understanding by which he sees as simple all that we call complex, and is able to guide his action in righteousness and grace. He understands his work, and all the beings upon whom it is performed. His wisdom is an ethical wisdom, not a mere knowledge, and forms an element in his character. He would have no right to undertake what he did not know how to perform, but this he has not done. His wisdom stands as basis for universal and everlasting confidence in him.

Now of the character that is thus portrayed there is this to be said: It is an intelligent and straightforward character, in which contradictions do not appear, either as present facts or as possibilities. Its line of moral movement is direct. The eternal and essential love that ever reigns in God is an infinite desire for universal welfare, and for satisfaction for his heart in such welfare. What shall love do? By what kind of action shall that desire be wrought out and carried toward effect? Surely by action of that which we call holiness. Through expression of the perfect moral excellence of God the perfect love of God is to work out its own satisfaction. There is no other way. If love desires the welfare of beings who are intelligent and moral, that simply means that love desires them to become like the good God and receive the blessing of his fellowship. Love is the great desire that other beings may be holy, and so the demands of holiness upon them are agencies with which love can by no means dispense in seeking what it longs for. There is no way to do the perfect good, except by promoting likeness to the perfect character. There is no final object for love to seek but this, and there is no way for love to obtain its object, except by holding forth the claim and the privilege of holiness. Hence that insistence upon the good, that strictness and sternness by which God opposes evil, that terribleness against wrong, that vision of infinite purity which he unveils for men to see afar, all these are most congenial agencies for love to use in the fulfilling of its desire to bless. And if love and holiness thus combine in forming the perfect character in God, it is completed by addition of the wisdom that understands what is to be done, and cannot be thwarted by the complexities of the undertaking.

We have reached this account of the unity by way of the relations in which God is known to us. This is the only way of approach that we possess, and we need not doubt that it leads us legitimately. But it brings us to the point of the ancient controversy to which we have already alluded. Coming to God through the relations in which we know him, we first meet the fact that he cares for us, and for all; and thus the first truth that we encounter is that God is love. But no sooner have we discovered this than we also discover that his attitude toward us is taken and held in holiness, and that he himself is holy. With two such qualities recognized and adored, the question may arise, upon which of them we ought to place the stronger emphasis. The question has long been discussed, and schools of theology have been formed and types of religion constituted by judgment between the primacy of holiness and the primacy of love; and by the discussion the conception of God has been deprived of much of the clearness and simplicity to which it is entitled. It has also been deprived of much of its power. But the discussion as to the relative rank of love and holiness need not be continued, because such contrasting of the two is not in keeping with their character or helpful to a true doctrine of God, and because as a matter of fact it makes very little difference which side of the question we take. Holiness and love are different aspects of the divine character, but really they are so nearly alike that our God will be essentially the same, whichever we may put first in thought—provided only that we are seeking to know him in spiritual reality, and not in dialectical acuteness. Holiness and love do not need to be brought together and reconciled before they can kiss each other. They are of one spiritual kindred, and by their very nature unite to form one perfect and harmonious character. How naturally the two combine a comparison of their characteristic works will show.

Holiness has always contributed the element of solemnity to the thought of God. It is associated with greatness, majesty, power: in his holiness God is magnificent, impressive, overwhelming, while along with the supremacy and splendour appears the perfect worthiness, the adorable purity, the dominant excellence. In perfect righteousness holiness shines forth. Let one who has been reared under thoughtful Christian influence try to gather into one the impressions that are made by the mention of God as holy. The word stirs sensations that have no parallel. Splendour and solemnity are blended, but most of all holiness means purity, cleanness, the opposite of sin, a realm where evil is not. It implies insistence, strictness, justice, everlasting remembrance of man's responsibility. It sets forward the exacting aspects of moral existence. It recalls man to conscience, and places him in an atmosphere too pure for him to bear. It suggests law and righteousness on God's part, and transgression and guilt on the side of man. It makes God seem unapproachable, while yet it shows that to approach him is the one thing needful. Thus holiness humbles man, and fills his life with seriousness. It sets a ban upon sin, and makes forgiveness look precious, though it may seem to put forgiveness beyond reach. Holiness long ago suggested that God be called a jealous God (Josh. xxiv. 19). In some senses the word is utterly false, for the jealousy that implies meanness can have no place in him; yet jealous he must be in his holiness, in the sense that he brooks no rival in the life of moral beings, since any rival must be infinitely less worthy of their affection and loyalty than himself. Of the evil that wins his creatures away from him to their ruin, it is entirely right to think of him as jealous. In the universe of a holy God there is no safe place for sin.

Somewhat like this is the effect of the divine holiness upon one who thinks of it sincerely, and we are sure that this effect is right. Even if awe before a holy God should sometimes grow to an excess, being alone, still it is an excess upon a wholesome side, which one would not wish to cure except by the worthiest means.

Love contributes the tender and winning element to our thought of God. It is a harder thing to believe in than holiness, in a world misled by moral evil. Conscience, condemning, makes it easier to recognize a holiness that condemns than a love that comes to help; moreover, the heart that loves little has but dim vision for perceiving love. But when love is once clearly discerned and believed in, all things are new. Trust takes the place of dread. "Perfect love casteth out fear" (1 Jn. iv. 18), and even imperfect love makes filial response to God. It beholds a God from whom all good is to be expected, who can be trusted for all patience, forbearance and help that his child may need, and who will never fail the soul that trusts him. But back of all such personal views of his fatherly care, the vision of love is the vision of a God who is Saviour to his creatures involved in sin. When we have heard of divine salvation, it has been proclaimed as the supreme work of love. It is because God is love that we think of him as Saviour, and we call his love the sole reliance of men who need deliverance from evil. Love, we say, is self-sacrifice for the other's good, it delights to give, it is forgiving and forbearing, it waits for nothing but the need, and so the God of love, and he alone, will be the divine Saviour. This vision is indeed the spiritual dawn, the dawn of a day that knows no night, since God is eternal. All existence is now transformed, to the soul that has the vision, for love is not exclusive but goes out to all. All is new when one perceives that the God of love is the only God that lives, on whose bosom the universe is borne.

Somewhat like this is the impression of love. If holiness humbles man, love humbles him also, by the outpouring of good that he does not deserve and the opening of opportunity beyond his highest thoughts. If the sense of love should grow to an excess, that could only mean that our conception of it was partial, and love was not sufficiently interpreted in the light of other truth.

Holiness and love are practically in contrast for us to this extent, that each has its atmosphere, unlike that of the other. But in God they are not in contrast, though they are not identical. God is not two, now holy and now love: he is not holiness here and love there. He does not need to alternate or divide between these two principles. God is one. He is holy, and he is love, always one God. The harmony of holiness and love is the great fact that gives unity and power to the Christian conception of God. The Christian doctrine is not that God has succeeded in harmonizing them, but that in him they are in harmony. It is impossible to frame any acceptable definition of holiness and love that will represent either as capable of acting without the other, or as existing without perfect fellowship of the other in the being of God.

Look first at holiness. If holiness in God is the fulness of his moral excellence, love is included within it. Perfect moral excellence without perfect love is inconceivable. If God is perfect holiness, it is necessarily implied that he is perfect love. Upon this we need not dwell. If again we think of holiness as that sum of qualities by virtue of which God rightly fulfils all relations in which he stands, the case will be equally clear. The right and normal fulfilling of any personal relation is impossible without love, as human experience demonstrates; and as to the supremely important relations that God sustains to other moral beings, nothing less than perfect love can possibly satisfy their demand. So we are not justified in setting love apart as something separate from that goodness of which holiness is the sum. In doing so we should deny the goodness of God, and become unable to conceive of him as God to all with whom he has to do. Love is included in holiness.

As regards love, it cannot be defined without including the quality of holiness. Even imperfect love, such as we know among ourselves, implies at least some genuine virtue and devotion to the higher ends in life. Perfect love implies complete purity and full devotion to those worthiest ends. We say that love is God's desire to impart himself to other beings, with all that the gift will convey. But that desire is perfect only as the gift is perfect. Since the impartation of himself is the gift of the perfect good, the love that would give it is the perfect love, and none other is perfect. We say again that love is God's desire to possess other beings in spiritual fellowship; but here again we must say that the perfectness of the love is measured by the quality of the fellowship that it offers. It is the holiness of the fellowship that makes it so infinitely worth giving and receiving. If the gift were less holy, the love would be less perfect. Holiness is included in love.

If each includes the other, and in its action implies the action of the other; if we cannot adequately define either of the two without using something of the other as an element in our definition; then surely we have no reason to think of holiness and love as contradictory in principle or incompatible in practice.

The harmony may be illustrated and confirmed by another inquiry which is indispensable to the forming of a true doctrine of God. Whether holiness and love are harmonious or not may fairly be tested by inquiring how they will lead God to act toward the human race. Two facts meet us: one that the human race is imperfect, developed only in part, still on its way from its beginning to its end; the other that it is also sinful, having consented to the worse instead of the better, and fallen into sin for which it is blameworthy. We may suspect that concerning the manner in which holiness and love would act toward such a race we can only conjecture, and our guesses will be of little worth. Yet there may be moral certainties that will guide us to conclusions of which we may be reasonably sure.

Holiness in God is the administrator of an inexorable demand. Humanity is a race whose normal advance is from the beastlike to the godlike: its norm is the spirit, and the spirit can prosper only in goodness. Holiness in God, therefore, holds men to that goodness which is their higher life and their only successful life. At least it is to holiness that we naturally attribute this strictness and insistence of God. It has so made the world that clinging to that lower life which ought to be abandoned is ruin. Through conscience, experience and revelation it testifies that there is but one right life. Mankind, weak and undeveloped, has sinfully yielded to the abnormal, and is involved in moral evil, which in its nature is a hopeless thing; and holiness in God, fulfilling his relation to men, stands against this evil, and works against it. It makes the sinner suffer, for it has wrought punishment into the very structure of existence, so making the world that a man reaps as he has sown. In this relation holiness is the emphasis of God upon the difference between good and evil. It holds forth the good, in the form of divine authority, requiring that there be a genuine moral order in which men shall live, and a firm hand administering their destiny. It upholds that constitution of the world which stands as a true expression of God against sin, making no compromise with evil, and dealing with men always in view of the unchangeable moral element.

To all this, what has love to say? In this severer view of the divine relation love joins without objection. Nay, it would propose the same. Love is God's desire to impart all good to men: but it is good for men to live under a holy and righteous order, accountable to God. This therefore love desires. Moreover, to men as they are there is no imparting all good without enforcing the contrast between good and evil, and setting them against all evil, even though it be part of their very selves. All revelation and enforcement of that eternal contrast which it is ruin for men to forget is agreeable to love, for the good that love desires to impart includes the full establishment of the universal righteous order, grounded in the holiness of God. Love delights in the righteous order as profoundly as holiness. It wishes men to know their danger from sin, and to feel the pressure of all warning, reproof and pain by which they may be won away from it. Love, seeking the best for its objects, is content with all that holiness requires, or rather it requires the same.

To the divine love we attribute God's desire to save men from sin. Salvation is the fruit of love: so it appears in the New Testament, and so the Christian faith delights to testify. Love and salvation correspond to each other. Given weakness, and love will desire to help; danger, and it will come to the rescue; sin, and it will seek to save. It is love that makes God the helper of his creatures against the moral evil that holds them in its grasp. Love is the deliverer.

What has holiness to say to the saving of men from sin? Holiness is on the side of such work, just as truly as love. Here it has been sadly misunderstood. Holiness dealing with sin in men has been interpreted as almost equivalent to punitive justice and nothing more. It has actually been

thought that holiness would be content to rest in the condemnation of the sinful, and have no inward difficulty in
leaving them condemned—a dreadful conception of holiness,
and of God. But we mistake if we think the proposal for
salvation could come only from love. It is an incalculable
misfortune that such an idea has ever been abroad, for thereby
injustice has been done to God, the conception of salvation
has been narrowed and weakened, and one of the worthiest
ethical appeals has been robbed of its power. Salvation
springs from God's holiness, just as truly as from his love.

The fact that suggests salvation is the presence of sin,
which is opposite to holiness. Holiness, of course, includes
a sincere and profound opposition to sin. But a sincere and
profound opposition cannot be content without something
done. Our partial and half-hearted hatred of sin is often
satisfied with an inward condemnation that merely condemns,
and sometimes thinks itself satisfied when a sinner suffers
punishment; but perfect holiness will not be content with
such hatred. When God in his holiness finds in existence the
sin that he hates, he desires to abolish it. In God, hatred of
sin and desire to put it away from men must be equal; and
the hatred of sin is no more an expression of his holiness than
the desire to put it away. Perfect holiness must go forth as
an impulse for promotion of its own quality in other beings;
and in a sinful world that is salvation. It is impossible to
think of holiness as content to let sin go on without endeavour
to save men from it. It is equally impossible to think of
holiness as satisfied with inflicting punishment upon sinners.
A God whose holiness was as well satisfied with punishing
sinners as with saving them would not be a holy God at all,
for his so-called holiness could be satisfied without insisting
upon the highest good.

We may learn also from our other definition of holiness.
We have said that holiness is the character by virtue of which
God fulfils his relations with other beings. From the perfectly holy One there goes forth such action as worthily
belongs to the position in which he stands toward others of

every kind. First among the relations that God sustains to men is that of creator, or source and cause of their existence. If he did not exist they would not, and if he had not willed it they would never have lived. Next among his relations come such as that of the great to the small, the strong to the weak, the perfect to the undeveloped, the pure to the impure, the holy to the sinful. These relations are necessarily involved in the very existence of God and men, and neither God nor men can escape from them while the existence of both continues. It is the impulse and nature of holiness to do all that these relations normally suggest. But in them all the normal work for God is helpfulness. It is normal—that is to say, it is right—for the great to be at the service of the small, the strong to help the weak, the perfect to discipline the undeveloped, the pure to cleanse the impure, the holy to save the sinful from their sin. We know that this is the way among men, and all the more must this be the way with God. The good God is so related to weak and sinful men as that the relation itself suggests help from him, to deliver them from their evil. If he left the human race unhelped, he would not be acting normally, or worthily of himself, as the great, the strong, the perfect, the pure, the holy. Back of all relations that can be expressed in terms of character or power lies the absolutely fundamental relation of Creator and creature. In every grade of rational life, one being owes something to another whom he has caused to exist. A God who did nothing to save a sinful race of which he was the Creator we could not revere as holy. He would be ignoring a relation in which he had placed himself, and that would be as impossible to holiness as to love.

If we take any other admissible definition of holiness, the result will be the same. We may accept the definition that holiness is purity asserting itself. Then perfect holiness will assert itself against all moral evil, by all means that are in keeping with its nature. It will condemn all evil, and souls that have cast in their lot with evil will be condemned with the evil that they have made their own. The condemnation that proceeds from holiness does not cause the deprivation and suffering that sin must bring, but it does correspond to it and confirm it, and it lasts as long as the choice of evil continues, whether for an hour or forever. But purity cannot be sufficiently asserted in condemnation, or in punishment. No governmental insistence or severity can do it justice. If the perfect purity asserts itself in a world of moral beings, it will offer itself to them, and urge itself upon them. Any assertion of purity that does not include the eager offering of purity to those who need it is only a technical and outside assertion, never to be mentioned in connection with the holiness of God. If purity asserts itself worthily of God, it offers itself to spiritual beings as the only good, and comes winningly to them with its appeal for their allegiance. Only in proportion as purity has asserted itself invitingly to men is it justified in asserting itself condemningly upon them. Purity that asserts itself imparts itself. And so the self-asserting purity is one in message with the self-asserting love. Holiness desires to save from evil.

Sometimes we are led to look upon men less in their guiltiness than in their imperfectness. We blame our race, but in some lights we pity it even more, and we feel that the pity is right. Sin came into the race in its infancy, before it knew the full significance of what it did. Man at the best is but a little one, with the powers of a universe playing upon him. He is undeveloped even yet, and no high approach to perfection can be expected of him. Present sin has been as much inherited as committed. So man seems to us unfortunate, quite as much as blameworthy, and we think it is pity that he needs, mercy and not judgment, so that only love can do him good. This tenderer judgment is coming in in our own time, partly from better knowledge of humanity, and partly by way of reaction from a judgment that was too one-sided to be just. But the case is still the same. The love of God would go out to such a race as this bearing help, but his holiness would go at his side. Divine goodness fulfilling its relations will be faithful to such a race as this, just as truly as love that has compassion on the needy.

Thus holiness and love come into no conflict in dealing with an imperfect world, or with a sinful world. If holiness claims that the soul is supreme, and calls attention to the highest element in life, love knows that the soul is supreme, appeals to its highest life, and waits for its response to its own advances. If holiness insists upon conformity to the highest moral standard, love knows that nothing else is to be desired. If holiness declares that what stands against its claim must suffer, love knows that this is true and has no word to say against it, but seizes upon suffering as a means to win the soul. And if love desires the welfare of men, their welfare stands in holiness, and holiness is sharer in the desire. If love seeks to save from sin, so does holiness, with an impulse no less eager. If love rejoices over one sinner that repenteth, holiness rejoices too. If love would administer human existence for a good end, holiness could administer it for no other. If holiness is strict, so is love; if love is generous, so is holiness. But it is better to be done with the personifications, and say that God himself is strict and generous at once, and acts equally in holiness and love in both. God is one. God is eternal goodness, loving in wisdom.

If it is true that holiness and love are not inharmonious in their nature, this truth must be allowed its due influence, which will prove most beneficent. Evidently there is henceforth no need of discussing any views or theories in theology that rest upon the assumption that love and holiness need to be reconciled. As soon as the Christian conception of God is held up for illumination, all such theories retire from our field. If the qualities themselves are of one heart and mind, so must be their claims, and there can be no need of bringing them into harmony. If we cannot entirely work out for ourselves the method of their operation, we may remember that we have no need to do so, but may trust all to that perfect wisdom in which the eternal love is working for the ends of holiness. The eternal goodness loving in wisdom may command our perfect confidence.

It is beyond our power to picture to ourselves all that is meant by the one harmonious character of God now indicated. It means too much. Yet the conception is not unclear, and before advancing to other aspects of our doctrine it will be well, even at the cost of repetition, to gather it up as far as possible into a single statement.

Behold a Being in whom every excellence that befits a spirit exists in perfect degree and without contradiction. He is source and sovereign of all other existence, and by virtue of his perfect character is worthily fulfilling all relations that he sustains. He is absolutely devoted to those ends of existence which are worthy of the spirit, namely, to character, purity, truth, righteousness, grace, love, helpfulness. These we see him holding as the motive of his own action, and holding forth for other beings to act upon. We see him exercising firm authority over men, insisting that they live the life of the spirit in purity and high-mindedness, and administering their life in such insistence. He completes the claim of his holiness by the endeavour of his love. Acting toward us men according to his nature, he counts us his own, he loves us and longs to impart himself to us in holy fellowship and possess us in the same; he withholds nothing of patience, effort and self-sacrifice to satisfy his love and holiness through moral union of men with himself. Thus he acts, and thus exists. The impression that we receive of him is solemn, searching, awe-inspiring; we are not worthy to stand before him: yet it is also winning, cheering, uplifting; he wishes us to stand before him. He embraces us in holy love, and cleanses us by gracious holiness. In goodness he is all that we can desire or think, and more. He is the same to all, and the same forever. He is worthy of the perfect and everlasting love of all beings; worthy to be trusted, to be held in loyalty, to be obeyed in the doing of his will and the fulfilment of his purpose. It is the thing most of all to be desired that all intelligent beings may take their place in fellowship with him, conforming to his holiness and satisfying his love.

Such a God is beyond the reach of human comprehension, but not of such acquaintance as the Christian method contemplates. The Christian knowledge of God is not a complete understanding, it is a practical and religious acquaintance; and to this the character of God yields itself perfectly. Jesus is our example here. We can know God as Jesus knew him in personal life. We know him in his holiness, and in his love. We know him but slightly and afar, and can never know him altogether, but we are assured that as we go on to know him better we shall simply be gazing deeper into spiritual perfection. That he seems ever greater to us as we go on is no barrier to acquaintance with him in the fellowship of a worthy life. The Christian doctrine of God and the Christian method of knowing God go perfectly together.

There is no need to show that the existence of such a God is the most glorious and beneficent fact that could be proclaimed. The meaning of it is, that goodness lies back of all existence. Eternal goodness loving in wisdom is the source and fount of all. This is the Christian doctrine, always held. As to what the doctrine may imply, and how it should be unfolded, Christians have differed widely, but from the beginning till now all have held that God is the source of all, and that he is the perfect goodness, love and wisdom. This all creeds proclaim, and all Christian preaching daily reiterates. Doubtless there must remain much to be brought forth from the abundance of a truth so great, and if Christian faith proceeds to bring forth that which still remains undeveloped, it will be acting upon its own traditions; for it has always been held that all purifying and exalting of the Christian ideal of God is simply approximation to the truth concerning the God who lives.

To affirm this doctrine is not to prove it, and it is not to be expected that all men will receive it because it has been uttered even by so revealing a messenger as Jesus Christ. Real belief of such a doctrine is a great and difficult thing. It is difficult because the belief is so exacting: it is difficult also because in the world that we observe there are so many facts that are hard to reconcile with it. There are many who are sure that we can never establish the claim that God is perfect goodness loving in wisdom, and that this is his world. Christianity, however, does not begin with attempt at demonstration. Its convictions are experimental and spiritual, and it has the courage of its convictions. It affirms its doctrine, on the ground of its confidence in divine self-revealing and trustworthy human experience. But it is well understood that the doctrine must be compared with other truth, and Christian faith freely offers it for such comparison. If it is not true, let facts reveal its weakness. But the Christian faith offers its doctrine of eternal goodness loving in wisdom, as the truest and best interpretation of existence: not as an academic thesis, but as a reasonable view of existing things, to be tested by mind and heart, by thought and life, and by comparison with truth in every quarter. It does not ask for such judgment as can be passed in an hour, but it is confident that the long process of experience and comparison will confirm its confidence in the perfect God.

II. GOD AND MEN

1. CREATOR

THE Christian method must be followed in the unfolding of the Christian doctrine, and according to that method the doctrine of God is religious before it is philosophical. Philosophy may look first at universal being, and search for signs of God in pervading methods and principles, but Christianity looks first at humanity and experience, and seeks God in life and personal relations. In the study of Theism we might inquire in what sense it is possible to believe in God, and wait for the conclusion before beginning to believe; but Christian study discovers God in human faith and life, and begins there the construction of its doctrine. It is thus that Jesus the Master has led his disciples. If we employ his method we shall know our God in life, with a knowledge that consists in acquaintance, and then explore the wider fields in which he is to be found.

Under this influence from Jesus Christ as teacher and revealer, the doctrine concerning God and Men is here made to precede the doctrine concerning God and the Universe. We undertake to utilize the Christian light and follow the Christian order. We have already found that the Christian doctrine of God is at heart a doctrine of character: we do not wonder, therefore, that the Christian influence leads us to consider him first in those relations in which character is the controlling fact. Only in his dealings with intelligent and moral beings can the God of character reveal himself at the highest. There is higher revelation in his dwelling with the humble than in his filling space. If we are to know God as he appears in Christ, we must attend first to the relations with moral beings in which he is most adequately expressed. We need in due time to form as clear notions as we may of God in the universe, but we shall learn most about him nearer home, in his relations with ourselves. In fact it is only in the field of spiritual relations and works, which is the human field, that the Christian doctrine of God, strictly so-called, is to be found: here is the Christian centre and specialty, where God manifests himself to men. At every stage of its life Christian thought has passed beyond this original simplicity to consider the larger problems of existence, and so it must always do. Nevertheless, it is our privilege to know God first at home, and to carry out to wider fields a conception of him that has been formed in the experiences of spiritual life.

Therefore next, after studying the character of God, we proceed to consider God in relations with men. With what shall we begin? Several such relations are to be considered, but there is no doubt as to which of them should be considered first. We must begin with the one that is most fundamental and comprehensive; and the first fact concerning God and men together is, that the existence of men is due to God. He is the original, and they are products of his will and work. The primary relation is the one that holds between Creator and creatures. There is no other that lies back of this, except in the thought and purpose of God, and within this all other relations are embraced. This therefore is first to be considered.

The general problem of the nature and method of creation does not meet us here, for we are now concerned only with the relation between God and men. Elsewhere, but not here, the larger question must be considered. The fact affirmed in any doctrine of creatorship is that God is the source of other existence; and the fact now before us is that God is the source or origin or cause of the existence of mankind. It is because of the will and action of the self-conscious and self-determining God that the human race exists. Other inquiries concerning creation may wait, for this is all that we need at present.

The Christian doctrine has always held that man is the creature of God. All Theism of high grade holds the same, and so do the religions generally. There are many ways of conceiving the manner of creation, some of them low and fanciful and some high and spiritual, but the origin of mankind in the divine will and act is common property in the thought of the race. In all pictorial representations of the human beginning, however crude they may be, this first belief finds expression; for it is a universal conviction that humanity is not independent in its existence, but owes its origin to a higher power. The crudeness of the picturing of this power and its working may be disregarded, for it detracts nothing from the strength of the belief. Far above other faiths the Hebrew and Christian faiths ascend, in that they have made prominent the infinite intelligence of the Creator, and the moral element in the creative work. They affirm that a good God created mankind, for a good end, and sustains toward men the conscious relation of a good Creator, dealing with that to which he has given existence. The element of goodness in the Creator has always been at the front in the Christian doctrine, which ever identifies the Creator of mankind with that good God and Saviour who is known in Christ. No other faith compares at all with the Christian in the clearness and force with which the connection between the origin of man and the goodness of God is affirmed. Christianity is sure that the race owes its existence to a good Being.

Very prominent in the Christian doctrine is the statement that God created man in his own likeness. This conception is not peculiar to the doctrine of the Bible, for in any case where an intelligent creator is supposed to exist it is necessarily implied that man, who is also intelligent, bears resemblance to him. Even the myths of savages affirm this. But in Hebrew and Christian faith the idea has meant more than elsewhere, in proportion as the conception of the Creator was more full of meaning. In the first chapter of Genesis (26–27) the thought of the writer seems to be that God created man in his own likeness in respect of capacity for dominion over that which was below him in the order of existence; for the likeness of man to God is mentioned in connection with the dominion that is assigned him over the animal world. Dominion over lower life of course implies that man is above it, as God is. It implies intelligence and will, making authority and efficiency possible; and in this the writer's idea of man's likeness to God seems to have consisted. Of personality this is no metaphysical account, but it is a very true practical representation. With his range of thought, the writer could scarcely have found a more effective way to represent that intelligent, self-centred and controlling quality in which man surpasses all other living beings on earth, and rises into the likeness of the Creator and Lord of all. The likeness of God in man here consists in that to which we, with our different vocabulary, give the name of personality. Resemblance to God as holy is not included under the name. There is no hint in the Scriptures that the likeness of God was understood to have been lost through sin. In the Epistle of James (iii. 9) it is mentioned as a badge of human dignity and worth, a fact in human nature that ought to protect a man from contempt and cursing on the part of his fellows. The point is simply that man resembles God in the possession of the powers that constitute an intelligent and active being.

Mention of the divine likeness in man is not frequent in the Bible, but the idea is everywhere present as the formative idea in religion. The idea is present in all religions, expressed or implied, but most of all in the Christian faith. If there were no spiritual likeness between God and man, there could be no such thing in religion as a vitalizing reality. If the likeness were not believed to be real, the very idea of religion could not exist; and if the belief were only an illusion, religion would be an illusion also. But since he bears the likeness of God in personal quality, man stands as one who may commune with God if God is willing, and rise to life

in spiritual fellowship with him.   Likeness to God is seen to
constitute man's greatness if we look downward for comparison with what is below him, and no less if we look upward to
the One who alone is above him.)

Mankind was created as a race.   Whatever may be its
duration and extent, the racial existence of humanity is due
to God.   He meant it to be a race, self-propagating and continuous.   The manner of its origin, whatever it may have
been, makes no difference here.   As to the manner, the word
creation is sometimes objected to when God's relation to the
beginning is in view, because it has long been associated with
a single method of production, which in many minds is conceived as mechanical.   But there is no proper objection to the
word, for it implies nothing mechanical in the method, and
in fact tells nothing as to the mode of operation.   It declares
only that God by his own will and action gave existence to the
human race.   If we are ever to know in what manner this
was done, we must learn it from such facts as may lie within
our reach.   It has long been believed that God created a
single pair, unconnected with other living creatures, to be
parents of the coming race.   But it is now to be accepted on
sufficient evidence that he brought mankind into existence
by long and gradual process, so ordering his world that
animal life and experience should develop those powers of
intelligence and will by possession of which man came at
length to bear God's likeness.   Like every other great thing
in the world, humanity is the outcome of a growth.   Once
the powers of a spirit existed in their typical perfection in God,
but elsewhere only in promise and prospect, beginning to be
developed through life, but not yet human;   later there was
incipient man, barely human, becoming gradually more
human as experience gave him higher training;   to-day man
exists in various degrees of likeness to him who is above him,
and is truly a spirit, still advancing in the development of
those powers of personality which he possesses in common
with God.   This long course has gone on according to the
will and wisdom of him who is wonderful in counsel and

excellent in working, and is a far more wonderful creative work than an instantaneous act would be. By this process God has created the human race.

We can say in these few words that God created mankind, and we may well be thrilled with wonder and bow in adoration when we think of what it means. But the mere statement by no means shows the place of creation in the doctrine of God. The relation between Creator and creature has profound meanings, and meanings which it is necessary that the creature should grasp, if he is to have true knowledge of his Creator. The statement, "God created man," is not understood until into it is read all the meaning that the separate words should bear. It must mean all that God means, and all that man signifies, and all that is implied in creation.

When we speak of God as Creator, we speak of that Being of perfect love, holiness and wisdom, whose character has already been set forth. God is perfect character, acting. He is the eternal goodness loving in wisdom, worthy of the perfect confidence of all beings that exist or can exist. When we speak of man, we speak of the intelligent and moral being who bears the likeness of God. He came up from stock that did not bear the divine likeness, but he bears it now, and is therefore capable of life in fellowship with God; capable also of life out of that fellowship, in sin against his own endowments and destinies and against his God. His racial career, measured by generations, has already been long and still stretches on into the future. The moral element never departs from his life, and the weight of responsibility and destiny is upon him. When we speak of the creation of man, we mean that this God, with this character, has brought into existence this race, with these qualities, experiences and possibilities. To a race brought forth from below, he has gradually imparted his own qualities of personal and responsible being. The existence of this race is due solely to the will and working of the God whom in Jesus Christ we have begun to know. This we mean when we say that God created man.

When we inquire concerning the relation between Creator and creature, we are asking how this character in God leads him to feel and act toward this race with its qualities and conditions of existence, and, accordingly, how man should feel and act toward this God to whom he owes his being. Of course the former point is decisive of the latter, for God is first. It is the doctrine of God that we are seeking to unfold. So our question means, What, to such a God, is involved in a creative relation to such a race? and how does the eternal goodness fulfil this relation?

The range and extent of the question deserve a word of further exposition. The question contemplates the race in all its variety and through its entire duration. We are not asking how God is related to men after they have fallen into sin, or how he is related to some single part of humanity: not how he is related to Jews or Gentiles, Christians, Turks or infidels, the privileged or the unprivileged. Our question is, how is the divine Being related to anything and everything that is human, when the human has been created by the divine? how, from the time when first there was a human being, on to the time when all destinies of the human shall have been wrought out? This is the field of our questioning. We might limit it to some fragment of this field of life, but the limitation would defeat the inquiry. We can answer any such subordinate question only in the light of the comprehensive one.

It is often felt that this inquiry is beyond our rights, God being so far above us that we are not entitled to discuss his ways. But the objection does not hold. Our judgment as to the meaning and outlook of our own life depends upon the significance that we attach to this creative relation. We cannot be forbidden to inquire concerning a significance so important to ourselves. It has also been said that this inquiry is beyond our power; for what can we know of what creatorship means to God? But neither does this objection hold.

Ethical relations are intelligible to ethical beings, and such are we. Our understanding may be imperfect, but we are not without power to discern the moral significance of a creative relation. To deny our ability to do this is to distrust our moral nature in all its work.

It has often been felt that reverence for God as independent and supreme requires us to deny that he can owe any attention or care to any race, even though he has brought it into existence. That he owes nothing to any one whatever, but is absolutely independent in determining what his relations shall mean to him, has been held to be a first postulate concerning God. According to this view his own will, not responding to anything inherent in the nature of our relation to him, has been regarded as solely decisive of his action toward us men. But this we cannot hold. Not thus does morality work— and to God we ascribe perfection in morality. All that we know of mutual relations, and of goodness, teaches us that the giving of life carries obligations with it. Parents are creators, in a limited and mediate fashion, and all experience bears witness that the giving of life binds the giver to do good to the recipient of the gift. To produce life and acknowledge no obligation to it is to fall below the average of human virtue. Shall we say that what is thus plainly true of men as moral beings is true of God also? Why not? We may hesitate, because we should thus deny the absolute independence of God. But the reason is not good. If God by his independent will has placed himself within certain relations, the necessary effect of those relations is not to be judged inconsistent with his independence. We may hesitate also because it may seem incredible that God should be under obligations, and especially to beings far below him. But this is part of a mistaken idea of sovereignty, which a worthier conception of God makes us outgrow. After all, we need not hesitate. It is a simple and obvious fact in morals among men that the giving of life brings responsibility, and we cannot make God an exception to so obvious a principle. It is no part of due reverence to exempt him from the claims of high morality.

If we say that he does not acknowledge or feel those claims, we imply that he does not possess the highest morality. When we call God the perfect Being, we imply that moral obligations belong to him, and will by him be worthily fulfilled. There is sufficient reason why we must say that a Creator ought to take care of that which he has created, and there is no good reason against it.

Yet it is not necessary to lay emphasis on the idea of obligation. It is enough to ask how the perfect character will lead its possessor to stand toward a race of his own creating. This question we can answer, and we must not imagine that we cannot. The eternal goodness loving in wisdom will not leave such a race alone. He cannot possibly regard it as anything else than a race that exists because of him, for that is what it is. Toward it he will be the good God. By no possibility can we conceive of him as holding an attitude of indifference or neglect toward a race that he has brought into being. One who brought forth a race by long and patient process, only to forget it, or leave its destiny uninfluenced for good, would be justly regarded as unworthy to be a creator. In judging thus we need not wait until we know exactly what a faithful creator ought to do for the race that he has created. What a creator ought to do is the same as what a good creator will be moved to do; and whether we know just what this is or not, we must ascribe it to God, since we hold that he is perfect. One who brings intelligent beings into a moral and responsible existence which they did not seek may fairly be expected to act toward them according to goodness, and be to them a faithful creator. If we hold the Christian conception of God, we must look in his relation to men as men for evidence that he is morally faithful to his creative office.

This is no new or modern statement. The Christian doctrine has always affirmed that the God of absolute perfection is Creator of the human race, and that he is never unfaithful to himself. The idea that he rightly fulfils all relations in which he stands is as old as the high ethical conception of the Deity, and has always been implied in the

Christian proclamation. How much it means has not been fully seen; but the doctrine itself, that the perfect God, always faithful to himself, stands in the relation of creatorship toward humanity, has always been held, not only in thought but also in faith. Something of the meaning still remains to be developed, but not as a new element in Christian doctrine. This is one of the points at which the historical development of the Christian doctrine of God has still to be carried on.

The meaning of the creative relation has to be considered in view of the extent, variety and duration of the race. When we speak of God as Creator to mankind, of course we mean the whole of mankind. Only just now are we beginning to see, and not even yet to feel, how ancient humanity is, and by what course it has come up to its present state. We now think of the race as coming up through unmeasured ages of lower life, and slowly becoming human; as human at length in all its parts, but human in all degrees of advancement; as living to-day in all grades of humanness. To be fully and perfectly human is to be developed in soul and living in fellowship with God; and we know mankind as loyal in some degree to the life that leads to this human destiny, but far more as sinning against it, against itself and against its God. When we look upon the human race, a vast mystery of glory and horror meets our gaze. Then whoever gives voice to the Christian doctrine proclaims that over against this race stands and has always stood the eternal goodness loving in wisdom, doing toward it the work of a faithful Creator. Our fathers said this, and so must their children say, if they are Christians. Our fathers said it in view of the humanity that they had in mind, but we must say it in view of the larger humanity that is known to us. The idea of a faithful Creator is as much a part of the Christian doctrine now as it was when the readers of the First Epistle of Peter were bidden commit their souls in well-doing unto a faithful Creator (iv. 19).

Not only the doctrine of a faithful Creator, but the practical effect of it, has been truly stated by Christians from of old.

It has been said for ages in Christian Apologetics that a good God, if he exists, will certainly communicate with his human creatures in the realm of their spiritual life. He will not be a God apart, he will reveal himself. So he will. Nothing can be more certain. That is the shortest of inferences from his goodness. That the good God will be to men a communicating God is as surely true as anything that we can say of him.

Our assurance of this is enhanced by what the Christian doctrine affirms concerning the likeness between God and men. Man was created in the image of God. The two are not aliens to each other, and the community is in the very nature. God is a Spirit, and so is man, and therefore "Spirit with spirit can meet." Man is created receptive of God, capable of communion with him, and of entertaining him, so to speak, as the guest of the soul. Since this rests upon a fact in creation, it is true not of some specially-trained parts of the race alone, but of man as man, and in his measure of every man, so far as the essentials of humanity exist in him. Man is of such nature that the spiritual impression of God can be made upon him. In his degree, every man is capable of receiving such divine impression; and human nature is such that at its highest the very fulness of God can be expressed in it. The ancient and wide-spread belief in incarnation is genuine testimony to the human sense of kinship to God; and the testimony bears witness to the truth. Therefore the human race as a race has always stood ready by its constitution to receive communication from God. The confidence that he will be a communicating God which is raised by his own nature is confirmed by the nature of the race that he has formed for communication with himself.

As soon as we have taken into account the greatness and antiquity of the race, and the manner of its growth, it is plain that we must enlarge the familiar estimate of the amount of communication that may be expected from the good God. The Christian argument has affirmed that from such a God we might expect the revelation that is recorded in the Old and New Testaments and completed in Jesus Christ. This Christian communication from God has been regarded as a communication to all mankind; but we must remember that this estimate of it was made when the human race was considered but small and of recent origin. It is the fact too that in Christian thinking about human relations with God the race has generally retained pretty nearly the dimensions that were in mind when the Bible was written. Dealings of God with Abraham and with Israel have been regarded as dealings with mankind, and the relation of primitive Chinese or African humanity to God has scarcely been taken into mind at all. But this is no longer tolerable. When we speak of mankind in relation to God we must mean the whole of it. We cannot affirm that the revelation from God that the Bible records was given to mankind. Ages of human existence passed before it came at all, and thus far it has reached only a minor portion of the living race. This rich and glorious revelation was indeed to be expected from the good God, but such a God as it reveals would surely begin earlier with a created race, and do something for it all. The self-communication of a faithful Creator who is the eternal goodness loving in wisdom will begin farther back and be universal. That which he has done in Christ can be nothing else than the culmination of a work of God as God upon man as man. God has always been in communication with all spirits of the human race. So the Christian doctrine has always affirmed, for it has always borne testimony to the true light that lighteth every man (Jn. i. 9).

The doctrine here involved is not strictly that of the divine Immanence, which must be considered elsewhere. It is the doctrine of the will of God in the structure and operation of human nature. God is the author of the scheme of life. It is he who brought it to pass that man advances from the life of the beast to the life of the spirit. The life that moves from the animal to the spiritual realm is of his giving and of his designing. The soul dawning in man is his self-impartation, and it is by his will that human nature has its proper destiny in godlikeness. Now the very fact that the Creator has made man thus is enough to hold Creator and creature together in a relation deep and strong. It is enough to ensure interest of Creator in creature, and to establish responsibility of creature to Creator. Not by chance has man a destiny and life a meaning: it is the gift of God. Man is normally the upward-moving creature, who owes himself to God, and can prosper only by rising to God: to God therefore must his eyes be turned, and all that represents God to him must have authority for his soul.

Not only thus in his constitution, but in the structure of his life, is the touch of God laid upon man. It is by the friendly wisdom of God that human experience is framed to teach the lessons of duty. No man is alone. The relations of life are social, and therefore necessarily moral. They imply mutual duties, which experience gradually brings to light and makes impressive. In them it is always possible to do right and wrong. Out of the fact of duty grows the sense of duty, which is no illusion but a true knowledge, though needing instruction still. The fact of duty is God's appointment, and the sense of duty is God's gift. God is the source of conscience. All moral judgment is an imperfect reproduction of his perfect judgment. All duty, even though it seem limited to narrow circles of human relation, is taught to man at the bidding of the will of God; and in being amenable to his conscience, whether in matters great or small, man is amenable to God who gave it. He cannot learn all duty in a lifetime or in a lifetime become faithful to all that he has learned; but duty is the "daughter of the voice of God," and in the life that he has created ethical, God is holding man to responsibility, and urging upon him the claims of his own goodness. And the claims of duty that are thus pressed home are claims for conformity to God's character of love and holiness. Life is a school for helpfulness, unselfishness, recognition of the claim of the other. Through various experiences God is leading on step by step to the possibility of a reign of love over life. Both the self-prizing and the self-giving impulses are trained by the common experience. Life, rightly followed as a teacher, commends and commands the virtues of self-control, enterprise, courage, manliness, affection, unselfishness, usefulness. Life is always calling attention to its own moral aspects. Primary lessons are first, and higher lessons quickly follow, and the teaching never ceases. The real teacher is always God, whether he is discerned or not. All the way upward from the lowest human stage this is true, that God is gradually bearing in upon the growing humanity the claims of the eternal goodness. At any moment it may be said to any human being, "The best in you is God in you," for by the best in the man God is represented, and is calling him on to better. This is the manner and spirit of God's communication with his created race, and in such work we may truly say that he is the eternal goodness loving in wisdom. This is work worthy of a faithful Creator.

It is plain that this communicating of God with humanity begins from the earliest human times. It ought, for if God could not bring up little children he would have no right to be a Father. We do not honour him when we doubt whether he can thus condescend to human infancy and weakness. It is plain also that this communicating is as wide as humanity. It is not dependent upon time or place, or upon religious conditions. The relation exists in Christian and pagan realms alike. God as God is always in contact with man as man, and therefore with every man, and is represented to each man by that man's best, which is God's own gift and comes with his authority. And the relation of God to man that is thus enacted is not one of hard severity and unloving intention. Judgment with condemnation is not its end in view. It does not contemplate man primarily as on trial. Instead, it regards him as a growing creature who is to be trained by life, disciplined and developed by experience, and brought up toward that for which he was created. Perhaps indeed it might even more truly be said that as a spiritual being man is still in the creative hands of God, and God is still making him:

the creative process, which is an unfolding and training of the spirit, is still in progress. In whichever way the creative work is pictured, the Creator's intent toward man is kindly and helpful, and severity is not an end but a means, a help to purposes worthy of the faithful God.

Evidence of such a relation of Creator to creature may be thought to be wanting, and hesitation about believing in it should not surprise us. There are many reasons why we are slow to believe in it. A sinful race, whose habits of thought we all inherit, is certain to misconceive a perfect God, and to err concerning him by putting him too far away, not seeing how near it is his holy nature to come. We have little experience in really holding the idea of an indwelling God, whose living voice is heard in all significant expressions of the world. We have long conceived of him more or less as transcendent in the sense of distant, or at least as so superior as to be practically afar. We have thought of him as speaking from heaven, and as communicating through messengers, till we can scarcely recognize so intimate a presence as this Christian doctrine implies. We are influenced too by long inheritance of the idea that all teaching of God must needs be perfect and on the highest plane—an idea suggested by reverence, but by a reverence that misses some of God's chief glories. The inherited conception of human depravity shuts out the thought that God can have been always in communication with the human spirit in all stages of its being. Taking our type of thought from the Jewish tabernacle, not from the Word that tabernacled among us, we think that sin must shut God away: he cannot be in communication with a race so evil, and a race so evil could learn nothing from such a God. And then we look about the world, with our crude estimates of good and evil and our readiness to judge men whom we do not know, and ask where are the signs that God has been teaching anything to mankind. Whatever of better things men have possessed or learned by experience we ascribe to nature or the common lot. We set it outside the field of

God's influence, and think of him mainly as passing judgment upon it. Thus do we miss the point.

Nevertheless the faithful Creator does his work. The teaching of life to men is teaching of God. Men themselves may attribute it to secondary sources—to conscience, which they take to be ultimate; to experience, which they do not trace beyond itself; to good influences among themselves, or to nature in general. But it is not rightly understood until it is perceived to be teaching of God the faithful Creator. The voice of conscience, the growth of moral standards, the fine didactic power of common experience, are all from him. Still more, he has access as the living Spirit to the spirits that bear his likeness, and in the secret heart he brings suggestion and inspiration to the man who is receptive of such gifts. It is true that the effect of such influence is far from perfect, for there are many reasons why moral teaching is received by men only in part, and often only in distorted form. Unformed minds can learn but little, and minds astray will learn amiss. Yet moral teaching, and religious teaching also, have come to mankind from the common life, and not in vain. In some degree or other men have always had sense of duty and knowledge of right and wrong, and have looked upward in the spirit of religion. Virtue has always been existent in the race, society has not broken up for want of goodness to hold it together, mutual influence has often supported the things for which conscience and religion stand, and religion in spite of all its evils has nowhere failed to bring some uplifting. Men have always known better than they were doing. It has always been possible for them, following their best, to live in some fellowship with God—a fellowship imperfect enough indeed, but such as the faithful Creator would recognize as not in vain. In some poor degree they have done this; for all following of the better part is just so far fellowship with God, and the better part has been followed in some degree in every day of human experience. The degree indeed has been sadly imperfect. That inexcusable missing or losing of God which Paul attributes to the Gentile world in the first chapter of Romans has been all too real; but it necessarily implies what Paul asserts, namely, that God is so in communication with all men that his influence can be missed, or can be utilized for the highest good.

It is within this primal creative relation that all other relations between God and men are by the nature of the case included. This needs no proof, for it cannot be otherwise. In the light of this original relation all human affairs are to be interpreted, for human affairs must always be within the domain of him who gave the human race its existence. In view of such creatorship, mankind has always to do with the most serious and gracious of beings. All men are living in closest relation to him whose goodness is perfect, the God who is worthy to create. There is much to prevent men from perceiving that they stand related to such a Creator as this, and it is no wonder that many doubt it, and some deny. Yet in proportion as men learn to know things as they are, seeing with the spiritual vision, they find their life to be the gift of such a God, and their destinies to be administered by the giver of their life. In all the relations that are hereafter to be considered, God the Creator stands in perfect character, often misunderstood by his creatures, but administering their life worthily of himself.

Broad as these statements are, they are less broad than the reality. We have spoken only of the human race, for with that alone we are acquainted, but we no longer have a right to think of God as related only to life upon our planet. We must remember the greatness of the universe. It is most improbable that intelligent life is confined to the race of which we are members. It is true that here we must speak without direct evidence, but we can confidently say that the balance of probability is vastly in favour of more life, essentially similar to our own. Concerning it the Christian thought is that wherever spiritual life exists, God is its Creator, and stands toward it in the relation in which he stands to us, his human creatures. Anywhere in his universe, he who has brought spirits into life is to them a faithful Creator, and all relations that they sustain to him are included within this one relation which is original and unchangeable. The Giver of life is the righteous Lord and friend of life.

We thus carry our thought of the Creator in relations with spirits beyond the world in which we live. We must also carry it beyond the time-limits within which our visible existence is confined. It does not fall within the scope of the present work to set forth the evidences of human immortality, or even to discuss at all that greatest and most fascinating of human facts. But it is a proper part of the definition of man that he is lifted by his spiritual kinship to his Creator into a life that transcends the limits of this present world. The spirits that God has created differ from the stones that he has made, for they partake in the spiritual nature of God himself. There is many a question about that larger life that we cannot answer, and before the inconceivable vastness of the fact and the issues that it involves our imagination halts; nevertheless, the fact holds us to itself, and we lose sight of it at our peril. That what is human is deathless is involved in the Christian faith. In considering the relations of man to his God, we do them the deepest injustice if we look upon them as limited to the brief and unfinished life that this world witnesses. They are relations of a larger life. To God himself also we do deep injustice if we dream that we can interpret him as the God of this life only. God is permanent, and so is man, and it is as a permanent being that man stands related to his God. We pray, and alas we sin, not as mortals, but as immortals. So we must add this to our thought about Creatorship and what it means—that to all the human souls that exist or will exist, beyond this mortal life, God stands and will always stand in the relation of a Creator, and all that Creatorship involves is true. Forever do men belong to God, and are bound to exercise their life in loyalty to the divine Friend who gave it; and forever is God toward them, as now, a faithful Creator, fulfilling this primal relation in fidelity to them and to himself. This permanence of the relations between God and men enters into the very warp and woof of the Christian doctrine, and is to be understood as assumed at every point in the present exposition.

2. FATHER

In that testimony of Jesus which is the vital source of the Christian doctrine, God is represented, as we have seen, under the name of Father. The conception did not originate with Jesus, or in the Bible, for it is very ancient and wide-spread, appearing, more or less intelligently grasped, in various religions. The thought was present in the Old Testament, and familiar among the people to whom Jesus spoke. But Jesus gave it a central position, by teaching his disciples to address God as Father when they prayed. In no other way could he have given it a more central place or proposed for it a wider influence. But neither doctrine nor faith has done full justice to the Master's teaching here, and the conception of God as Father has been far less influential than he thus proposed to make it. If the Christian people had learned really to think of God as they address him in the Lord's Prayer, Christian history would have been more truly Christian.

It was a great advance when the relation of God to men was represented thus by a natural human relation, and no longer by an institution. Human institutions have naturally been taken for illustration here, and kingship oftenest of all, but it fails, as they all do, at a vital point. No human royalty rests upon a creative relation. A king is a man among men, with no inherent superiority, raised by agreement or by power to a position of command. His relation to the others is that of an equal, accidentally elevated. All human kings and kingships are of this kind; and when we come to think of God they serve but imperfectly for illustration. Kingship does illustrate some aspects of that divine relation which we are seeking to understand, but not the heart of it. It is a great gain when we turn to that natural relation which involves the gift of life. The relation of parent to child comes

nearer than anything else in this world to illustrating the
fundamental relation of God to men, and it was a true revealing word, illumining the whole field, that Jesus uttered when
he bade men call God Father.

We have already noted that Jesus' account of God as
Father is practical, not speculative. He takes no pains to
tell in what the fatherhood is grounded: he shows what it is
to the soul that enters into it. He gave God's fatherhood as
a rest to the soul and an inspiration and guidance to the life.
With him, God is Father in that he has toward men the love
and fidelity that we know best in parents: he considers us his
own and offers himself to us, he holds us dear and prizes our
love, he is available to us in our needs as a parent is to children.
He is our greater likeness also, as the father is the child's:
somehow we so resemble him that we must seek to resemble
him more. We are so like him in nature that it is our normal
life to be like him in his richest graces. This is the Fatherhood in its practical form.

But though Jesus says no more than this, there is more
implied. If God regards men as his own and feels thus
paternally toward them, there is a reason for it: the relation
is not constructed or invented, but rests on fact, and the fact
is not far to seek. In the thought of the people to whom
Jesus spoke, the creation of man in God's likeness was believed in. In their Scriptures God was known as Creator,
and man as made in his image. But the creative relation and
the parental are profoundly alike. Human parenthood implies the gift of life, so far as that is possible to any but God,
and this gift of life is the ground of that natural proprietorship,
so to call it, in which the child is the parent's own. Moreover,
there is something to be learned from this, that at first the
child has no idea that he owes his life to his parents; to him
fatherhood and motherhood mean simply the love and care
and trustworthy providence of these two persons greater than
himself who are watching over him; but to the parents
meanwhile the tender and joyous fact is that they have given

the child his being, so that he is their very own, mysteriously a part of their very selves. To the child parenthood means brooding love and faithful discipline: to the parents it means all this, with the thrilling fact of life-giving as the secret of all other meanings that it may bear.

It is under suggestion from human parenthood that Jesus bids us call God Father, and we must understand the name accordingly. Jesus would have us know that the heavenly fatherhood is like the earthly, the divine is like the human. The feeling of fatherhood is due in God, as it is in men, to the fact of fatherhood: here also the love and care, the providence and discipline, have the life-giving as the fact from which they spring. The divine fatherhood is the tenderer name for the creatorship. Human beings are held to God's heart as his own because they are his own, since he gave them their existence. He must think of the entire intelligent world, bearing his likeness through his own will and action, as a father regards his children. "Forasmuch as we are the offspring of God," God knows it, and looks upon us as what we are. Creation naturally contemplates what we may well call a family life, a life of spiritual unity and fellowship between God and created spirits, and that rich fulfilment of fatherhood which Jesus bade his friends accept is simply the fulfilment of the ideal of human existence. But as in the human case, the Father is aware of the relation long before the children suspect that it exists, and knows why men are his own long before they begin to understand it. God rejoices in the sense of life-giving, while men only know that they are alive.

This is not the whole Christian doctrine of the Fatherhood of God, but this is the starting-point of it all. It cannot be otherwise. If God, knowing himself as Creator, desired to represent to men in some more expressive form the relation of creatorship, certainly the name that he would teach to them must be Father. Since creatorship is the primary fact, it is impossible to interpret fatherhood in God apart from it. The conjunction is too natural and true to be escaped. God must feel toward the human race as toward his own spiritual offspring and kin. That he does feel so, the Christian doctrine has always affirmed—not always consistently, or in the spirit of freedom, and yet really. Theology has sometimes felt constrained to deny it in terms, but has always affirmed it in fact, even though too faintly. Creative love and redemptive love have never been held to be radically distinguishable, and that is the whole matter. God brought a race into being, he loved it as his own, he sought to save it from its evil, he made himself known as Father when he showed it the God to whom it must return. This is a universal fatherhood in God, grounded in the primary creative relation and wrought out in the work of saving grace.

Certainly in the parable of the Prodigal Son (Lk. xv. 11–32) Jesus intended to set forth such a relation as this. In the parable the natural relation of father and son was never altered, though on one side it was forgotten—for of course it never can be altered. The son belonged to the father all the time, and the father never forgot it, though the son put it out of mind. When the son had had enough of the miseries of the far country, it was to his own home that he returned, and to his own father. The event that Jesus illustrated by the parable was the repenting of a group of sinful men and women; and this he characterized as a home-coming to God. He was offering no theory of human relations with God, but was illustrating the truth as he knew it, and showing what man is to God, even in his sinfulness. God is rightly represented by father and man by son. And the elder brother also was a son.

The parable itself, however, is enough to show that conscious fatherhood is not necessarily accompanied by conscious sonship, or worthy fatherhood by worthy sonship. Here is a good father and a bad son, a conscious father and a son forgetful of the relation. If the parable told the truth about the publicans and sinners who were coming home, God as Father had had in them children unfaithful to their filial rank until that day. That creatorship means fatherhood does not imply that creaturehood means ideal sonship. Good fatherhood with bad sonship is so well known in this world that there ought to be no difficulty in perceiving that the same may exist in the relation between God and men. Human sonship to God is practically unknown in its significance to the most of men, and where it is not unknown it is sinned against. The Father of the great family is a perfect father, but the children are not ideal children. The family idea and relation, so to call it, is always present in the heart of God, but is not realized in the life of men. "I have nourished and brought up children and they have rebelled against me" (Isa. i. 2).

\ But the realizing of the fact of sonship is all that is necessary for realizing the idea of creation and the fulfilling of God's thought for mankind. God has given existence to a race of beings that bear his likeness. He is the perfect God, worthy to be Father in the fullest sense to all creatures. If all these should live as true sons to him as Father, each one of them would be fulfilling the type of his being and the idea of God in creating him. Nothing more than this can God intend or desire for intelligent creatures, for this is utmost good. A perfect son of God would be simply a perfect man, in whom the creative idea had come to fulfilment. A manifestation of the sons of God in the true and full significance of their relation to their Father would be an exhibition of the original intent in the creation of mankind.

Now the Christian doctrine affirms that in Christ God is thus completing his creative work upon men. Through the work and influence of Jesus Christ the ideal of sonship comes to fulfilment, and the Fatherhood, in its truest meaning, becomes a matter of experience. To as many as received him he gave the right to become children of God in actual life, or granted free entrance into the relations of the divine family (Jn. i. 12). The Christian life is distinctly the filial life, in which God is Father and man is loyal, aspiring and obedient child. It is this that makes the Christian life to be the ideal human life, the best life that there is, the crown of living. Its failures are failures to attain success in the life of sonship, and its successes are advances in doing justice to God as Father.

This practical aspect of the divine Fatherhood is of course the one that is most prominent in the New Testament. Here sonship is no theoretical thing: it is a fact experienced, and God as Father is discovered in the life of the soul. If we begin at the Gospels, we find Jesus the Son of God knowing the Father in the experiences of a human life: he looks to God with filial confidence, and devotes himself to the doing of the Father's will. He teaches his friends what God as Father is to them, and how they are to live as his children. Farther on, when the Christian gift has become embodied in a wide experience, the glory is that the Christian people find themselves looking to God as Father and rejoicing to know themselves his sons. The statement that the Christian life is the filial life is a perfectly fair generalization of the contents of the Epistles. The sense of God's fatherhood came in with the new life in Christ, and with Christ and his salvation the experience of it was associated. Sonship in the family of God appears as so fresh and vivid an experience as to seem virtually new. It is not surprising that it was sometimes accounted a wholly new gift of God, belonging solely to that Christian life in which it was now experienced.

The manner of entering upon the filial life with God is represented in the New Testament in two ways. Sometimes it is by a new birth that one becomes a child of God, and sometimes it is by an adoption. In the Pauline writings the adoption is more frequently mentioned, and in the Johannine the birth. It is plain that either of these expressions may fairly describe the entrance upon a new life. God may be said to have begotten children, imparting a new spiritual life wherein men are in filial fellowship with him, or to have adopted children, taking for his own men who were alien from the life of his holy spiritual kindred. One may think of himself as a born child of God through the birth of the Spirit, or as an adopted child of God through the free act of grace.

A grateful heart may interpret the experience by saying, "God regenerated me by his own act," or, "God took me into his family." Either is a true saying, in which the experience is well described. But evidently both are not literal descriptions of the process, for they are inconsistent with each other. If either picture of introduction to the family is urged as literally correct, the other is ruled out. A born child of God cannot have been adopted by him, and an adopted child of God was not born into the family. Adoption and birth are mutually exclusive. This incompatibility makes no trouble, however, if we are not more literal than we need to be. But the presence of this pair of terms makes it certain that the New Testament does not give us a literal and only correct description of the manner of entering filial life. Both descriptions are figurative, and both are useful, but neither of them is exclusive, and the experience might be set forth in yet other ways. In fact, apart from connection with fatherhood, it is represented now as a deliverance, now as a creation, and now as a resurrection.

If we look at the filial life as the New Testament here and there portrays it, we shall see it as a life in which the Fatherhood of God is attaining to the satisfaction of its own desires for men. The ideal, "I will be to him a Father, and he shall be to me a son" (2 Sam. vii. 14), is coming somewhat to be realized. "Ye received not the spirit of bondage, again unto fear; but ye received the spirit of adoption, whereby we cry, Abba, Father" (Rom. viii. 15). This fine enlightening stroke of the apostle Paul portrays God as One who wants no slavish fear in his presence, but would have his child look confidingly and joyfully into his eyes. Here is included all that freedom and trustfulness which Jesus encouraged in the Sermon on the Mount. The life in Christ is a life in the spirit of adoption, or of family fellowship, in contrast to life in a spirit of bondage, or slavishness, in which fear is an abiding element. Father and child are on terms of friendliness: the child stands in awe, but is not afraid: all slavish shrinking before God is past. The servility of legalism has given way to the freedom of filial love. It is implied, of course, that the Father's superiority has no shadow of pride, over-sensitiveness or jealousy, no dignity easily offended, no impatience or quick temper. Calm, just and gracious is the Father; he is not easily angered, and does not readily "take things amiss" with men. "With him is no lust of Godhead: he hath no hand to bow beneath, and no foot that thou shouldst kiss it." We have received the spirit of adoption. Father is the name of our God.

Within this relation of Fatherhood moves that rich and inspiring communion with God which is characteristic of the Christian life. It is a communion that rests on community in character, aims and interests. The child is to be like the Father, and has begun to be so. "That ye may be children of your Father who is in heaven" (Mt. v. 45) is the loftiest expression of the Christian aim, and growth in likeness to the Father and in power to express his character in life is the upward movement in which Christian progress consists. "Beloved, now are we the children of God, and it hath not yet been manifested what we shall be, but we know that . . . we shall be like him" (1 Jn. iii. 2). Child is to be like Father—that is the glorious hope, and the fulfilment of the hope has already begun. God therefore has in the world men who spiritually resemble him, even though only in partial and childish fashion. With them he communes, and they with him. They live in his fellowship, draw inspiration from his grace, have his will for their ideal, and represent their Father in the world. Men around them do not know God as Father in such a life: these men are not of the world, in that they live above it, in the spirit of the family of God.

It is not surprising that this Christian sonship, so contrasted with the experience of average men, should have been taken to correspond to a Fatherhood all its own, quite distinct from that creative Fatherhood of which we have spoken. It has often been thus understood. Nevertheless, all difficulty about the difference is done away when we have

learned that this high spiritual fellowship is simply the fulfilment of that creative relation in which God and his creatures
stand.   This, a son of God, is what from of old he meant by
man.   In gathering Christians to his family, he is only
finishing them as creatures, completing his design in giving
them existence.   He was always creatively their Father, and
now he enjoys that Fatherhood over them which creation
always contemplated.

There is only one Fatherhood in God, and that is grounded
in his creatorship and his character.   There is only one sonship for men, and that is their relation to the good Creator
who counts them his own and loves them with a faithful
parental love.   But though God is always Father, and
though the creative parenthood can never be abolished, still
man, born to be son, may be out of his Father's spiritual life.
He may be ignorant of his Father, or he may be rebellious,
hostile, wilfully astray from him.   A lost man is a child lost
out of his right place in the family of God.   Sonship is completed only in filial love and living.   When one enters upon
such living, he may seem to himself to be entering upon sonship—and so, on his own part, he is.   Before him lies the
filial life for which he was created; but all the holy love and
life to which Christ leads or can ever lead a man will bring
him only to full possession of his birthright as a born son of
the eternal Father.   The birthright he was selling for nought,
but his Father has brought him to his place.   Here in harmony may end the long discussion about the Fatherhood of
God, whether it is natural or spiritual, originating in creation
or in redemption, belonging to all or only to those who are in
Christ.   There is no need of its continuing.   God is always
Father, and man is always son; but the relation may be realized in full, or only in part, or not at all on man's side; and
this makes the difference.

We have said that God's creatorship is the primary relation
of God to other being, within which all other relations move.
We have now said that the Fatherhood is the tenderer name

for the creatorship, when intelligent and moral beings are in the field of view. It follows then that within the Fatherhood of God all his other relations to men are included, and from it they take their character. God in relation to men is first of all the One who called them into being, who considers them his own, and who loves them with the holy affection which is his character. This is to be said before anything else is said concerning the relations between God and men. If there are other moral beings, the same is true of them, whatever their grade of life or their character—God has given them their life, and holds them in the affection of a paternal heart. They also, in whatever world, may say "Father" when they pray, and know that they were created for filial life with God. The range of God's Fatherhood is as wide as the range of intelligent existence.

It follows that the prayer that Jesus taught to his disciples, beginning with "Our Father who art in heaven," is open to the use of all who may desire to use it. It is the human prayer. Parents do right when they teach it to little children. It is right to offer it in the great congregation. The truth is that every one who sincerely prays assumes, just so far, the attitude of a child in the presence of the heavenly Father, and is entitled to call him by the paternal name. But there is one fact that must not be overlooked. One who claims God as his Father makes not only a claim but a promise. The speaking of the name amounts to an oath of allegiance. Whoever calls God Father should understand that he thereby pledges himself to be toward God a loyal child. A relation so rich in moral meaning must not be accepted on one side only. There is much loose and thoughtless talk about the Fatherhood of God that would be stilled at once if this thought came in with power. To claim benefit of the Fatherhood and refuse the loyal sonship is to trifle with God and man. Within the Fatherhood all the works of divine grace and holiness are wrought, and within the sonship all worthy works of men are to be done. Like the father in the matchless parable, God has sons who are astray and sons who have come home.

For his sons who are at home he can do what can never be done for sons who are astray, and those who are minded to claim his paternal blessing must be at home to receive it. Even now they are not forgotten, but only at home can they live the blessed life of sonship. And only there, in the family fellowship, can the Lord's prayer mean all that the Lord intended it to mean.

Indeed, it must never be forgotten that the doctrine of God creates the practical doctrine of man, and in this work the Fatherhood is the vital point. Whether they know it or not, men are to one another what their relation to God makes them to be. In more than a poetic sense, Fatherhood in God implies brotherhood among men. All men have not only a common source of their being, but a common spiritual paternity embracing them and giving its own significance to their life. The relation that they all bear to the authority and love of God their Father binds them together in a higher type of social fellowship than anything else in their life can produce. In a true sense they are brothers—brothers in origin, brothers in destiny, brothers as children of the Highest. All the significance of the Fatherhood of God tends to make men more to one another, and to help them fulfil their relations in a righteous and loving fellowship. It is best for all interests in human life that men should learn to know themselves children of the one Father. This one fact, well learned and well applied, would be a true guide in all social ethics, and would bring in that kingdom of God which is the life of the family of God.

The doctrine of divine paternity, thus broadly interpreted, applies equally well to life in its individual aspects, and in its social. The doctrine of God's comprehensive relation to men always suits the case in hand, whatever it may be. There have been ages of individualism, when religion seemed to be almost entirely a matter between God and the single soul. Then of course the believer's joy and hope stood in his personal sonship to the perfect Father, and the Father's will was the child's law. The later view of life, influenced by more recent experience, gives more prominence to the social element. Individualism does not suffice. The problems of living together on a world-wide scale are thrust upon us; economic issues are found to be decisive of spiritual destinies; the value of a man is a point not only in discussion but in warfare; questions of righteousness appeal to all men's conscience; humanity suffering needlessly cries out for help; education and opportunity are found to be as necessary as light and air; there is need of liberty in knowledge and inquiry; and these matters, once deemed secular, are felt to belong within the circle of religion. Upon the old individualistic basis they might not belong there, but the modern feeling is right in insisting that they do. Certainly these are real aspects of the ordering of the family of God. We misjudge him if we think that he cares only about the individual welfare of his children; he knows how they treat one another, and is interested in the character of the life they live together. He cares whether they live as brothers. Since God is a Father, all these questions of personal value, of righteousness, of liberty and of opportunity concern interests that are precious in his sight. Under him, it is the human way for men to live in mutual reverence and brotherly regard. Thus the Fatherhood brings the questions of social equity and fellowship into the field of religion. If we are to render to God the things that are God's, we must render to his children the things that are his children's. To serve his children is to serve him, and thus the Fatherhood ushers in mercy and truth, righteousness and peace, to be the inspiration of the common life.

3. SOVEREIGN

It is natural to think that the Creator will govern that which he has created. When it appears that creatorship bears the richer meaning of fatherhood, the supremacy of the Creator who is Father is more intelligible and certain still. When in him the perfect character is discerned, the certainty of a genuine governance of God is reinforced by his worthiness. Thus in various ways the sovereignty of God over his universe is urged upon us as a fact that we cannot doubt, and we do not wonder that it has been a very prominent element in Christian thought. It has been far more prominent than the fatherhood, and has been at once a theme of faith and reverence and a subject of keen discussion. It meets us here in our presentation of the Christian doctrine, and we must inquire what we ought to mean when we speak of God as Sovereign, and what place the doctrine of his sovereignty should hold in our thoughts.

Sovereignty is a relation: it implies two. It is not an abstract reality lying back of all relations in which they are grounded, although it has sometimes been represented so. We do not form doctrine concerning God outside of all relations, existing in himself alone, for we have no means of doing so. All the sovereignty of which we have knowledge is the relation between God and that which he rules. The divine transcendence in which such sovereignty is grounded is assumed in all doctrine concerning practical relations.

A complete doctrine of divine sovereignty would have to do with the relation of God to all other existence. His control must be as wide as the universe, and under the title of sovereignty we might treat of his governance over existence of every kind. But we must notice now that it is only in his relations with men that the sovereignty of God is a topic of vital interest in religion, or in theology. In what manner God's will is related to the material universe, and how he controls it, it would be interesting to know; but religion is not directly concerned in that inquiry, and theology can gain from it nothing more than light upon a secondary question. If it should appear that God's will is done there in a manner perfectly absolute and arbitrary, the fact would raise no vital question in religion or theology. Only when sovereignty touches upon the activities and destinies of men does it become a matter that we cannot leave alone. Sovereignty is an extremely impressive word, and when it is applied to human affairs we feel the need of knowing what it means, for its meaning measures the significance of our life. It may be so conceived as to quicken and support our best activities, or to repress or even destroy our sense of freedom and responsibility. Thus in the human circle the nature of God's sovereignty is a vital matter, but speculations about it beyond the field of our own relations do not concern us deeply. The touch of sovereignty upon our own souls is what concerns us.

As to God's sovereignty over men, we are justified in regarding it as a relation that moves within the creative relation, which is the fatherly; and this is a most important fact about it. It is a paternal sovereignty. It is often assumed, indeed, that this order should be inverted, and that the divine sovereignty is the circle within which creatorship and fatherhood should be understood to move. We speak of a sovereignty that corresponds to the relation between God and his creatures; others, of a relation between God and his creatures that corresponds to his sovereignty. This is the view that regards sovereignty as equivalent to determinative authority and power, lying back of all relations. According to it, the sovereign God, entitled to all control, determined in his sovereignty that he would create mankind and be a Father to certain men, whom he selected to be his children.

But as long as we follow the leading of Jesus, our doctrine will not seek to discover and interpret God's pre-creative decisions. He has offered us no help in that endeavour. We may follow our logic into that region, but our logic will not find clear knowledge enough to work upon. The region is too far beyond our ken. The sole supremacy of God is of course the solid fact with which we have to do, but on the question how he must exercise it in the creating of a race of men, we may well hesitate to affirm. But we need not affirm, for affirmation lies equally beyond our necessities and our reach. The sovereignty of God with which religion and the Christian doctrine are concerned is that which he exercises within his creation, over the men whom he has made in his own likeness. It is the practical sovereignty of God over men, or of the Creator over his intelligent creatures. It is the Lordship of the good Father. Because he is and has the right to be the source of all, therefore he governs all. A bad creator would have no right to sovereignty over his work; but God is at once our source and our type, the One from whom we sprang, and to whom it is our normal destiny to rise. He therefore is our rightful Sovereign, and his sovereignty is grounded in the true Father's right and power to govern his spiritual offspring. This is the way along which the Christian doctrine leads us to approach the sovereignty of God.

The sovereignty may be better understood if we inquire what is the end in view, or what the Sovereign designs to accomplish. To this the answer must be that the end in view in the sovereignty of God is the doing of God's will. This is the Christian testimony, from every point of view, and a joyful testimony it is. So good is he, and so excellent is his will, that it is the most desirable of all possible things that his will may be done in perfect measure. The will of God is often a matter for philosophic contemplation, which may be without feeling; but whenever it is the object of loyal regard, it appears as the best thing in all the worlds. The ninety-sixth Psalm sings out the unspeakable joy that the psalmist has in contemplating the blessedness of the reign of God. When he reigns, the world is established that it cannot be moved. It is well that the heavens rejoice and the earth be glad, that the sea roar, and the fulness thereof, and that all the trees of the wood sing for joy before him in his sovereign presence. When his will is done the best is done, and the doing of his will is the object of his sovereignty.

What will of God do we mean, however, when we say that the doing of God's will is the end in view in his sovereignty? The language is ambiguous, and by the ambiguity, often unnoticed, the discussion of sovereignty and the thoughts of the Christian people about it have been much embarrassed.

The word does not tell its own story. By the will of God is sometimes meant the volition, determination, decree of God, and sometimes his choice, preference, desire, requirement. It may mean that God decides and settles certain things, determining that they shall come to pass, or that God approves certain things, and enjoins them upon his creatures to be done. The statement that was just now made may mean that God's sovereignty has for its object the bringing into fact of that which he has determined to be done, or the doing of that which he desires and requires to be done; that in his sovereignty God brings to pass the execution of his decrees, or that he seeks the fulfilment of the moral desires that accord with his character. We may be thinking of an arbitrary will (in no bad sense) which is to be brought into effect by himself in his sovereignty, or of an ethical will that is to be done by men under his sovereignty; or we may think of his sovereignty as including something of both these elements. What is the sovereignty of which the Christian doctrine makes affirmation? Do we mean that God is working out the fulfilling of his appointments, or of his requirements? of his decrees, or of his desires? Which is the Christian view of the sovereignty that he exercises?

Since sovereignty is not an abstraction but a relation, we must understand it, naturally, in the light of what we know of the beings who are concerned. We must interpret it in view of the nature of God and man. The good God and Father will certainly stand as Sovereign over men in a manner accordant with his own nature, and with the nature that he has given to them. A method of sovereignty that suits some parts of his creation is not adapted to others, and we may rely upon God to exercise over men a sovereignty that corresponds to the nature of men, not of plants, or of planets. Father will be true to the nature of children, and to his own. When we say this, our attention is directed to a quality in the nature of both that gives light upon the manner in which we should think of his sovereignty.

A fixed point in all, Christian doctrine is the freedom of

God. Personality, creatorship, righteousness, grace, all imply it. All types of Christian thinking involve it. Predestinarian doctrine in every form asserts it strenuously and without reserve. Such doctrine has sometimes been made so consistent as to deny that any one else but God is free, but to him has always been attributed perfect liberty of choice and action. In making his unchangeable determinations of all that is to come to pass, and in so controlling natural events and human actions that these appointments of his shall all be realized, he has been regarded as absolutely free, able to appoint as he will, to choose as he will, and to accomplish as he will. Predestinarian doctrine affirms freedom absolute and unmodified, and proclaims it with perfect confidence, but it is the freedom of God. On the other hand, doctrine of an opposing type not only leaves the freedom of God unchallenged, but affirms it as a prime certainty. It has rested its opposition to predestinarian doctrine upon the claim that freedom, so far from belonging to God alone, is an indispensable element in the life of any spiritual being, whether God or man. God would not be God without it, and in men, who are created in the likeness of God, a genuine moral liberty is as essential as it is in God himself. God, who is the perfect type of freedom, has given freedom to his human creatures as their characteristic possession, and in them it is inalienable. He who gave it may surely be trusted not to take it away or put dishonour upon it.

Thus freedom is a fixed point in all theology, but the Christian doctrine has been interpreted in predestinarian style or in the opposite, according as freedom has been insisted upon as belonging to God, or to God and men. In this contrast it certainly appears that the opposition has the better case. If we know anything about ourselves we know that such freedom as supports responsibility and gives moral meaning to life is a part of our human outfit. Mystery hangs about our freedom, and certainly we cannot claim that it is ideally complete, yet we always assume it in real life, and cannot live without assuming it. We know, too, whence our freedom came: it is a part of God's gift in constituting our life, and the ideal of it, as of all our essential powers, exists in him forever. So freedom belongs to both; and when we inquire into the nature of God's sovereignty, we are constrained to call it a sovereignty of the free God over beings to whom he has granted freedom in likeness to his own. It is a sovereignty of an Actor over actors, of a Will over wills. All questions about it are to be answered in the light of this fact. It is certain that we cannot answer all the questions that we may ask, but to this central fact in the nature of the Ruler and the ruled we must always be faithful. We have to acknowledge a sovereignty that treats men as what they are, and does justice to the freedom that belongs to responsible spiritual life.

We may try to follow this principle out, and conceive of a sovereignty of a free God over free men, or of a divine will over human wills. If we try to conceive a sovereignty over beings who act, it will not be natural to think of one that consists in predetermining their actions. That kind of control is not congruous with the active, free, responsible nature of God and man. It is claimed indeed that God's predestination does not interfere with the freedom of man; but the claim has never been satisfactorily vindicated as credible. A sovereignty that cancels liberty is not the sovereignty of God over men. The will of God that is to be done cannot be a strict foreordaining will. But on the other hand we can well understand a sovereignty that seeks the doing by men of the ethical will of God and the bringing about of the moral results in which he takes delight. It is this ethical will that is so demonstrably glorious and good for all creation. The will of God that is to be done as the end of the divine sovereignty is that good and acceptable and perfect will of God which men can do by acting out their nature, and the doing of which is their glory and their hope. What men are to do in pursuance of the fact that God is sovereign over them is not to yield their wills to his irresistible determinations, but to yield their wills to his unalterable moral standard, and be

true subjects of the authority that belongs to his eternal
goodness.   This is what we mean when we call God by the
worthy name of Lord.   We may think that we ought to mean
something very different when we call him Sovereign, but
we cannot show that he expects it of us.   So far as the claim
of his sovereignty on human thought or action is concerned,
God is to us men the King of Goodness, whose will we are to
do.

There is more to be said, however, for this, true as it is,
does not exhaust the meaning of the sovereignty that we
must attribute to God.   We have not told all that his sovereignty includes when we have spoken of his right to lay
requirements on the human will.   If this had been the whole,
sovereignty could never have loomed as large as it has in the
field of thought.   Sovereignty of another kind is upon us all.
The truth remains that we men are in the hands of God, the
Creator, Father and Governor of our life.   His sovereignty
over us includes a power of control that naturally belongs to
him and the right to hold and use that power.   We deal with
it in this, that it is ours to acknowledge the sovereign God as
entitled to appoint and establish the conditions of our life.
Independently of us he has formed and maintained the world
in which we live, and determined the influences by which we
as men should be affected.   He has made our life in general
to be such as it is, and has thus provided the school in which
human character is to be developed.   Having given us freedom in his own likeness, he has prepared the field in which
it is to work.   Over these matters it is not possible in the
nature of the case that we should have any control, and it is
for us to acknowledge that they lie within the field of the
sovereignty of God.

It is here that the mysteriousness of our life so often per-
plexes and baffles us.   Sometimes it breaks our hearts.   The
truth is that the world in which God in his sovereignty has
placed us is a very strange and perplexing world.   Often we
fail to see that it is adapted to his purpose or to our good.

Sometimes we suspect that we are in the hands of chance, tossed about by blind forces, and sometimes that we are in the hands of arbitrary power that deprives us of all control. It is out of this sense of human insufficiency and helplessness, when coupled with a submissive recognition of the perfect supremacy of God, that belief in absolute predestination has come. We should not regard that belief as a peculiarity of Christians, or as originating in divine revelation. The facts that suggest it are world-wide, and all religions have had to deal with them. What is known in the Christian world as Calvinism represents a vast element in human thinking, and is simply one of the human interpretations of the mystery of life. For very many that doctrine has helped to give stability to life, and has afforded rest from one class of the human perplexities. But as we have just seen, the doctrine of predestination does not accord with the nature of the human soul, which was framed to be trained through the exercise of freedom. No more than the doctrine of mere chance, at the opposite extreme, does it solve the problem. There is a sovereignty of God in life, but it is not a sovereignty that works by unchangeable decrees and foreordains all that men are to do. Perhaps this is the simplest of all the explanations of the universal mystery, but it is too simple to satisfy the facts.

We can make no full solution, and yet we can do something toward describing this aspect of divine sovereignty. It is enough to say that we are in the hands of God, whose sovereignty is exercised in establishing the conditions of our life. To do this is his right because he is the giver of our life, and because he is worthy to take care of that which he has given. This indeed is a necessary part of his creative work—to place us, his creatures, in the world which he has created. In creating his world, in fact, he brought us forth, and the life that we find mysterious is the life in which he saw fit to train us for higher existence. He understands it, if we do not. So we accept our lot and portion as from him. We acknowledge, though often through tears, that his sovereign power and right have placed us where we are, and subjected us to the influences that are upon us. We do not claim to understand our lot, but we trust him who appointed it. Because we believe that God is worthy to be the Sovereign of our affairs, we accept our life with confidence, and gladly subject ourselves to that moral sovereignty which holds us to the doing of his will.

We may ask whether sovereignty, thus conceived, represents any advance upon the relation of Father, or of Creator. It is evident that such sovereignty comes naturally and worthily out of that Creatorship which is Fatherhood, or rather is a genuine part of it. These different names, though quite distinguishable in definition, really cover one field and are closely alike in meaning. The perfect character lies back of all, making sure the right of God to be Creator, and to be Father to his creatures. The character that justifies him in being Creator entitles him also to be Sovereign over all that he creates. The Sovereignty develops, as we shall see, into Moral Government and Providence, while the perfect Fatherhood becomes a Saviourhood when men are in need. In truth the relation of God to us is but one, though for us it may take many forms and bear many names. The good God is Creator, Creator is Father, Father is Sovereign, and the sovereignty is the authority of the good Father over his children. There is no reason why we should labour to keep these characters wholly separate; or rather, if we are to understand them, it is necessary that we let them flow together. God is but one in all of them. Just as the modern psychology makes of the mind not a group of separate faculties but a unit working in many ways, so the right doctrine represents God not as an aggregate of attributes or relations, but as one Being, a Spirit, who fills many relations and sends his infinite energy forth in many works. So no one of these relations is independent of the others: all of them, rather, are forms of that one comprehensive relation in which God who gave us our life stands to us who owe our life to him.

4. MORAL GOVERNOR

God has to do with men as moral actors, and exercises over them in that character a moral government. The name is an old one, but it is a misfortune that we have not a better, for the mention of a government almost inevitably brings human governments to mind, and we think of God as ruling after the manner of men. In some stages of life human governments have been helpfully employed for illustration of the divine, but at best they are imperfect and misleading illustrations. Much harm has come from depending too much upon them, and the day of their usefulness for the illustrative purpose is now past. God's government is the only one of its kind, since it is grounded in his nature and his relations to men, to neither of which any parallel exists. So we may wish that our thoughts about it were not so likely to be coloured by institutions that differ from it more deeply than they resemble it. Yet to call God a Moral Governor is right, and Moral Government is a good name for one relation between him and men.

Of course any government of God over men moves within the sphere of his creatorship. It means that the Giver of moral life administers that life in accordance with its nature, and thus fulfils his relation to that which he has created. This again, as we have seen, is the same as to say that the government of God moves within the sphere of his fatherhood. Moral government is the Creator's jurisdiction over his creatures, or the Father's discipline over his children. It is no relation between aliens, it is a family relation. The children may not know it to be such, but when they come to see their life either in the Christian light or in the true light of nature they find it out.

The moral government of God is absolutely universal, extending to all moral beings, whether of the human race or not. However many living spirits there may be or have been within the universe, we cannot imagine more than one administration of their spiritual life. Since the one God acts always from his own unchangeable character, we are sure that he has only one principle of moral administration, forever and everywhere. Forms and modes will differ, but the field is the universe, and the period is the entire duration of life, and one God rules the whole upon one ethical principle. Moral government is single, and universal. This is the meaning of monotheism, and this is the teaching of Christianity.

At present we are concerned with only one world, but in considering this we need the lesson of universality. The moral government of God over men is single, and universal: it is as broad as humanity, and the same for all human beings. Within humanity there are differences but no fundamental distinctions, and all men are one in their relation to God their moral governor. This the Christian doctrine has always affirmed, but not always perceiving how true it is. It has always been held that all men are under such government of God, and yet current views of moral government have rendered the belief partly ineffective. It has been common to associate moral government with special parts or features of human experience, rather than with the whole. Christian teachers have often seemed to assume that it could not exist without a degree of intelligence concerning God that most men do not possess; and it has been associated with the presence of legislation, or of clear revealing light, from God. Since distinct revelation was supposed to be thus implied, the strong and effective everyday operations of God with men have been thought of as practically confined to the biblical field. The law of Moses has been regarded as the divine law for mankind, and even called the moral law of God. It has been understood how under the Christian light moral government could be a strong and vital reality, but it has not been so plain how it could be the same without that light. Thus it has come to pass that moral government was preached as an intelligible reality for the privileged among men, but as a somewhat mysterious if not doubtful reality for the un-privileged.

But no such limitation or division is valid. We must not suppose that special revelation, or divine statute, or large knowledge of God, is necessary for genuine moral government of God over men. If there exists anything that is worthy of that name, all men alike are under it. If that is the case, it cannot require anything that only a part of men possess. It must be grounded on the human side not in special conditions of any kind, but in human nature itself. Any law of God for all mankind must be either proclaimed to all or written in the nature of all. But no law has been proclaimed to all. The Mosaic law was never imposed upon all men, and the obligation that comes with the Christian light has not yet gone forth upon all humanity. The only law from God for all men is written in their nature as men: if this does not hold them to him by a valid bond, then nothing does. Only upon that which is natural to God and men can universal moral government be founded, and that which is natural to God and men is a sufficient foundation for moral government. The actual moral government of God implies as necessary to itself nothing more than that God and men exist, with their respective natures and in their mutual relations. It takes various forms in various conditions of life, but the government itself is simply the natural result of the actual relation between such a Being as God and such beings as men. God and men existing, it follows, and is the same for all. Narrower definitions have been possible in days of narrower conceptions of existence, but the time for them is past, never to return.

In the light of God and man, therefore, the moral government must be defined. As to the nature of God, all that has been said of him should now be in mind. The fact before us is that men stand in moral relation with their Creator, Father and rightful Lord, the God altogether good, worthy of all their reverence, love and loyalty. He in whom all goodness dwells complete has rightful authority over them. He is One, the same to all, and is unchangeable in perfection. He is the source of all spiritual ideals that can ever dawn upon the sight of men. His perfect character is on the side of all that resembles it, and against all that contradicts it. And his creatorship and goodness together give him sole and perfect right to be the moral governor over created spirits. This is the Christian view of the Being whose nature determines the nature of moral government.

From the nature of God as throwing light upon moral government, we turn to the nature of man. Certainly the moral administration through which destinies are wrought out must be adapted to the constitution and life of the beings who are under it. In order to conceive rightly of God's moral government, we must conceive rightly of men, what they are, whence they came, whither they go, and how their proper destiny may be attained.

The nature of human life must of course be described in terms of present knowledge. From an origin in animal life, the human race has advanced, and is still advancing, by growth of the soul. Mental powers have been developed from lower to higher grade, and are still gaining in largeness and force. Personality has been attained, and is always receiving enrichment from experience. Relations that cannot be sustained without developing moral meanings have developed the moral life. Conscience has become an abiding reality. Religion has become a constant element in life, and capacity for religion has grown as ages passed. Man is ever becoming more fully man, by the development of that growing element in him which bears the likeness of God. The older view of humanity was that God created a being in his own likeness at a stroke: the newer view is that he brings a being to his own likeness by a process, through gradual development of his powers. Life is God's workshop for the creation of the soul.

In saying this we are not obliged to give a psychological account of the soul and what it consists in. We may leave science to take its time in solving the problems of human nature, for our present interpretation of life is not dependent upon the result.   Whether the deep questions as to the nature of the soul are ever answered or not, the facts that define the moral government of God are the same.   In man there is an element that survives from below, and an element that has gradually entered in the higher stages of life.   He is a complex being, with one part developed on the basis of another, the spiritual on the basis of the animal.   In the present life the two elements are not to be disentangled and separated: neither is to abolish the other: but they need to be adjusted to each other, and trained to such action as is normal to the whole man.   What kind of life is normal to this complex being, it is easy to see.   His proper type is not behind him, but before; not beneath, but above.   It is his proper destiny to make more and more of his higher powers, and let his whole life be controlled by them.   It was once normal for him, that is for his ancestors, to be ruled by powers and passions that are characteristic of the lower world from which he came; but when a soul has been born in him such domination is normal no longer.   The lower powers still exist, but now that the soul has come they are bound to take a secondary place, and yield the supremacy to the new and higher element.   The soul struggles for supremacy, and for life worthy of its rank—this is the human career and conflict. And all the highest possibilities of the soul, even to the height of well-balanced and perfect virtue, are included in that which it is normal for life to bring forth.

These are the conditions of the moral government of God. God altogether good has given existence to a race of men in whom the highest possibilities have been planted, but planted in the midst of elements that must be outgrown and left behind as the higher life develops.   When we say that God is moral governor over such a race, we affirm such facts as these: that the endowments of the race are expressions of God's will concerning it; that the normal destiny of men is of God's choice and appointment; that he is seeking for man the fulfilment of the promise of his nature, and is requiring it of him; that in dealing with moral meanings in his life man is dealing with God as well as with nature and himself; and that from God's moral administration of his life he can no more escape than from his own nature. We imply that in his moral governance God is seeking the end that he sought in creation, and carrying his creative work toward completion. The character that is normal to the growing human spirit is no other than the character of God himself, in finite measure; wherefore God is on the side of the spirit in its great struggle with that which is below it, and that growth and enthronement of the soul which is normal to human nature is the object of his endeavour. He gave moral meaning to life when he gave mankind its endowments, and that meaning he is seeking to realize. Thus his moral administration is intended to promote the good of the governed in the highest sense, for it insists upon the worthiest choice, the supremacy of the spirit, and the training of men to the divine likeness.

We have said that a law of God is written in the nature of man, clear and comprehensive enough to justify a moral government on the basis of it. What law or requirement of God is thus written in human nature? Some may doubt whether so clear and comprehensive a requirement, made known to men in their nature, can be found. The difficulty is due to the long failure to recognize God as the communicating God, always in touch with the spirits that he has created. Placing God mainly outside the natural order of life, and thinking that he can communicate with men only by special and supernatural action, we have assumed that there was no genuine law from him unless it was proclaimed, certified and recorded. If there was no messenger there was no message: if there was no legislation, there seemed to be no law. Yet even while picturing the matter thus, we have insisted that all men are somehow under natural obligation and responsibility to God, the truth of nature being too strong for our narrow definitions. God is the communicating God, the world is his organ, what life teaches he teaches, duty is his requirement, conscience is his voice, and all life involves responsibility to him.

What then is the law of God written in human nature? It is that a man must be loyal to his better part, and do the best that he knows. The normal life, or the only life in which he can prosper and be himself, is the life that does honour to the soul as supreme in the complex constitution of man. Nature itself calls for loyal honour to the higher life. If this is refused, nature sees to it that man relapses toward that from which he came, and loses his proper destiny. Of course this broad demand of nature includes innumerable specific requirements. It prohibits the dominance of the sensual life over the soul, and demands all that makes up high character. Whatsoever things are true, honourable, righteous, pure, lovely and of good report, if there be any virtue and if there be any praise, all these are required of man by the normal law of his being. In personal and in social life, in work and play, in secular transactions and in the life of religion, nature requires that he keep his body under, that he subordinate the secondary part of himself to the primary, that he set his affections on things that are above, that he help his soul to its due supremacy. If he does this, he acts out his true nature: if not, he is false to his real self. And this law of nature is the law of God who is the source of nature. God who created man created him thus, and created him thus in love. The infinite goodness calls him to do justice to his higher self, and all the divine authority is in the call. This is enough to constitute a moral government of God over all men, of every age and place, in whom are found the higher and the lower life.

Implied in this broad demand that a man be loyal to his higher part are two principles, or methods, that belong to moral government. One is the demand that a man shall do the good that he knows. The other is the principle that a man shall reap as he has sown.

As to the first of these principles: God desires the right and good for men, and therefore requires the right and good from men; and it follows that whatever is known by them as right and good is required of them as duty. The claim is universal and incessant that a man shall do the thing that he knows to be good and right. There is no need of written law or special revelation to make this an effective claim. It is written in life and spoken by conscience. Men understand it variously according to their intelligence and character, but the law itself, that a man must do his ethical best, is the law of humanity, which may be disobeyed, but from whose authority there is no escape. Its force is not dependent upon large knowledge of God or of the moral proprieties of life. It was present as soon as a soul knew good from evil, and from that moment it was the law of God himself who had written it in human nature. Life is ethical from the start, and the ethical authority within is the authority of God.

As to the second of these principles: life has a vindicative or retributory power, imparted to it by the Creator. It is so ordained that the good and right works to the doer's advantage, and the wrong and evil to his disadvantage—advantage in the sense that corresponds to the meaning of moral government. It is not that gain and loss in the ordinary human sense are sure to follow from doing well and ill, though this sometimes occurs: it is that in the sense that is suggested by the meaning of moral government, good always and everywhere brings forth good and evil evil, so that man reaps as he has sown. Retribution is twofold in its fruitage, insuring harvests from good and evil seed, but it is single in its principle, and unvarying in its certainty. The harvest is not always recognized, but it is sure. "Say ye to the righteous that it shall be well with him. Woe unto the wicked! it shall be ill with him" (Is. iii. 10–11). That which ought to be shall be, in the way of retribution. This is of the very nature of moral government, and this order has been wrought in by God to the conditions of life.

Apart from religious doctrine it is often acknowledged that the order of existence is righteous, educative and retributive: the universe, we are told is ethical, and holds its denizens to moral living, and brings the consequences. The Christian doctrine agrees to this, but insists upon telling how it came to be so. It is not content with affirming a moral universe: it affirms a moral God and governor. He who created us made our life moral, and taught us of right and wrong by methods of his own; he made his own voice to sound within us, and stands in perpetual communication with the souls that he has made; the authority of duty is his authority, and all suggestions of virtue are from him. He is so expressed in the very structure and method of life that no deed of good or evil can fall outside the circle of his government.

We have said that God's moral government is over all men, at all stages of their existence; but of course this does not mean that it is of equal significance to all. The communicating God is in touch with all, but in some parts of humanity his self-communication has proceeded much farther than in others. The natural voice of God in the soul, of which no spiritual being is destitute, has been both interpreted and supplemented by further expressions of his will. With all increase of knowledge and opportunity, and all growth of conscience, and all self-manifestation of the Father, the moral government grows more full of meaning to its subjects. It was once an administration over spiritual children, mere babes in life, but it becomes an administration over spirits advancing toward maturity, capable of larger response to the eternal goodness loving in wisdom. With such advance life grows more glorious, and more serious. It is a great thing to be in touch with the communicating God, whose touch constitutes a moral government, and the more he communicates, the greater a thing it is to live with him. In Christ he speaks more richly than elsewhere: in Christ therefore men have to deal with higher glories and greater responsibilities. Moral government means more to a well-enlightened Christian than to any one else. All life is great, but life here is greatest, and its moral significance is at the full.

It is easy to see what sin is, under such a moral government as this. For each person the soul is the real man, and yet each person has a lower nature, that may prove to be a support to the soul or a drag upon it. The soul ought to grow up to goodness and fellowship with God, which is the normal destiny, and the man ought to help it grow. If the soul is prevented from moving on to this proper destiny, moral evil will exist. There will be sin, which is moral evil made one's own, if the man takes sides against his soul, and chooses that which will injure it and keep it in unworthy life. For him moral evil consists in the depression of his moral powers from their primacy, the captivating of his higher nature by his lower, and sin consists in his own action toward that end. For the human being contains in himself what ought to be the coming man and the going man, and he may cast in his lot with either; and sin consists in blocking the progress of the coming man whose life is in fellowship with God, and keeping in power the man that ought to go, whose affinities are downward.

It is easy also to see how in such a system of life sin could enter. The process is illustrated in the career of every human individual. The child comes into life unconscious of its lot, but bringing an inheritance from the past. In its inheritance it has lower passions and better possibilities, a complex nature not well balanced and not easily carried true. At first the child is blameless in giving freedom to inferior passions with which it was born. But there comes a time, mysterious and fateful, when intelligence and choice have entered, and what we call the age of responsibility has dawned. That which was innocent in infantile action is sinful now, and there is real virtue now in good action that once was colourless. Mystery covers the change, but the fact is plain. It is normal to leave behind the unworthier part of one's inheritance and advance to a better moral life;

it is abnormal for the lower to hold over and rule where the higher is due; and this abnormal is wrong, when once it is responsibly chosen. It is sin to help the inferior outlive its day and retain a dominion which now belongs to the better part. At first the sin may be but slightly blameworthy, but as it becomes a more characteristic thing it grows more guilty. It may even come to pass that the whole man is given over to the sinful choice and practice whereby his best is subjected to his worst, and his high spiritual possibilities are wrecked.

The race is like the individual, for this, too, began with an inheritance from lower life, while higher powers were dawning within it. Within the animal the godlike grew, and is growing still. Man with these double powers was still a unit, able to throw the weight of his choice and effort toward either side. As the soul in the race grew up, what was once innocent became abnormal and wrong, and the prevailing choice of mankind did not repel the evil but encouraged it. Humanity has often helped its own rising soul, and is partly arrayed in its favour, but it has terribly beaten its own soul down beneath unworthy choices, and kept alive and strong its own inferior part. This is moral evil on a race-wide scale, and on the part of intelligent actors in such choice and working this is sin. This does not mean that sin consists altogether in animal passions, in lust and beastliness and the dominion of the body. These things have indeed survived in excess, and done immeasurable harm to the humanity that ought long ago to have become superior to them. But there is more than this. Since the soul came, the old passion of self-will, developed and strengthened by the long struggle for existence, is not the normal guide and governor. The soul's crown of glory is unselfishness and love and helpfulness, and by these life ought to be inspired. A race that refuses these higher gifts and clings to the self-willed and selfish life is a sinful race. It is bound to be increasingly sinful, for self-will, taking hold upon the higher powers, can work such havoc as life upon the lower plane could never suffer, corrupting the noblest possibilities and spoiling the coming man.

In view of the long history, there is no need to show what harm selfish passion must do in the social life of the race. Selfishness is against nature for the soul, hurtful to the neighbour, destructive of the social order, and thus repugnant against all forms of duty and welfare. When selfishness enters, sin enters, and enters to remain.

What has now been given is purely a natural account of sin. If a natural account of sin cannot be given, no explanation or doctrine of it can be satisfactory; and so we may well welcome a reasonable representation of the natural possibility. But the Christian doctrine adds that all sin is sin against God. Christians have sometimes said that all sin is against God alone, but that is untenable; sins against men are among the most familiar things in the world. But in the Christian light it appears that all wrong deeds are done within a personal relation to God in which all other relations are included. As God is over all, so all is under God. There is no action that is not included under the relation of men to him. Out of his nature came the law written in ours, that the soul, capable of godlikeness, must be the supreme end in life. Any life in which the normal balance is inverted is condemned by God. "The exceeding sinfulness of sin" is apparent by the light of nature, but is glaringly plain in view of God. Eternal goodness loving in wisdom desires the good of all beings, and has appointed for their life a moral order and quality through which alone their good can be obtained. Offence against that order and quality is sin against him. It is thus intelligible that all sin falls under his moral government. Whatever holds the soul down from its normal ascent to godlikeness is resisting and defying God, and he knows it, and is against it forever.

We cannot but wonder that there should be sin in the world of such a God. We can trace the way by which it entered, but the wonder is that the door was open. We may never be able to solve the problem, and certainly we should never talk as if we were easy masters of it, or it were a simple matter. All our thinking about God goes on in a world which this mystery overhangs. Our task is, not to clear the sky, but to obtain the clearest vision that we can beneath a sky thus clouded. Our Christian doctrine proclaims a God of perfect goodness, ruling in a world in which sin is present. That sin is abnormal in the world where the soul lives is just as evident as that sin is abnormal in the world of God. The existing world is the world both of God and of the soul, and in such a realm of life moral government must deal with sin as with an abnormal fact.

The feeling of God against sin is spoken of in the Scriptures as his wrath, or anger. Of course we do not understand this to be a rage, but a holy passion; and we cannot fail to judge that a holy passion against sin is quite worthy of God, and even a necessary expression of his character. If we had reason to believe that God was cool and comfortable about the evil that is defying his will and devouring his children, we should cease to call him Father. We do him no wrong when we attribute to him a holy passion against sin, but rather praise him for feeling as he ought. Yet his anger, we should remember, is not directed against persons, except just so far as they are positively identified with the evil that he hates; and even so, his anger at a person, whom by his nature he loves, is different from his anger at an evil quality, which by his nature he hates. In either case this anger is not of such character as to need appeasement, or to be capable of it. As a holy passion against evil it cannot be appeased, even as it ought not; and when it glows against persons, it only needs that the occasion for it be removed, in order to cease by its own worthy nature.

If we inquire as to the traits of divine character that are expressed in God's moral government, we shall find his government like himself. When we say that God administers the moral life of men, his name bears its full meaning, too rich for words. But in considering this government over persons we are reminded especially of the Righteousness of God, which the Christian doctrine has always recognized as dominant here.

Righteousness is sometimes spoken of as if it were something existent in God himself, apart from what he has to do with other beings. In one sense, so it is. The character that makes him righteous is an independent and eternal character; but righteousness itself is a matter of relations, not an abstract quality. One person cannot be righteous alone, though he may be such a person that he is sure to be righteous as soon as he has to do with another. The righteousness of God is his moral reliability. It is his trustworthiness in the field of moral action. Or, in a word, the name covers all that is meant by the large truth that God is the eternal Right. We adore him as the eternal Life, and as the eternal Love, but as the eternal Right he is equally glorious and adorable. In him all right is grounded, and from him the force of it has come forth to us men. What we name his righteousness is the attitude and work of God as the eternal Right, in his relations with other beings.

We need to make full recognition of the fact that righteousness is a matter of relations, and of relations between persons. We often speak of the righteousness of God as dealing with sin; but we should do better justice if we thought of it as dealing with sinners. This change in point of view is almost indispensable if righteousness is to be correctly understood. It is with good and evil men, and men of mingled good and evil, that righteousness deals in moral government. Moral quality, good and evil, stands before God to be estimated, but the righteousness of God does its work in his dealings with the persons who have good and evil in them, and are responsible in all degrees for their acts and character. God the eternal right has created persons, has constituted the conditions of their life, is exercising moral government over them, and is sure to deal with them in perfect rightness, according to what they are, and do toward them what ought to be done by him: this is the meaning of his righteousness.

It is in this light that we should view the retributive aspects of righteousness. The familiar association between righteousness and retribution is a sound one, but it is both sound and clear only when righteousness is interpreted in the personal manner. Retribution is an element in God's moral government, because it is right: that is, it is right that corresponding consequences to the doer should follow the doing of right and wrong. The reliability of God stands fast for every soul that loves and seeks the better part, and for every soul that does evil. We are accustomed to say that righteousness ensures the punishment of sin; but we should be nearer the truth if we said that it ensures the punishment of sinful persons, in the precise proportion in which they ought to receive it; and by the same definition we should cover the certainty that due return of good will come to the soul that has done the good. Righteousness moves between God and men, and it is upon men that its necessary punitive and beneficent work is wrought. The work is wrought because it ought to be. The righteous retributive law is to be trusted, and no one may either hope or fear that the righteousness of God will fail.

Righteousness in God is often defined almost as if retribution were its only work, and that too with the punitive aspect at the front. But when we identify it with the idea of God as the eternal right, all such defining appears far too narrow. Prominent in the necessary meaning of the eternal right is perfect fairness. Righteousness is fairness, and God is righteous. In his government of men he is absolutely faithful to all demands of fair dealing, In his judgment he never exacts too little, and he never expects too much. Not more than it is fair to ask does he demand of any one, and not less than is right does he require. He makes all fair allowance for human weakness and ignorance, and for all circumstances that have reasonable claim to be considered in the judgment that should be passed upon a man. He estimates men and all their works in perfect justice, in view of all that ought to be taken into the account. "The judgment of God is according to truth" (Rom. ii. 2), without fictitious demands, without unreal standards, without overlooking of anything that belongs to the case.

There are some views of God in his relation to men that vanish away when this vision of righteousness is seen. Sometimes it is said that God requires perfect obedience from every soul and requires it now, and holds all men condemned because they lack it—and this because he is a righteous God. Sometimes it is held that righteousness compels God's judgment upon men to proceed in absolute strictness, knowing no such thing as allowance for human weakness: allowance, it is thought, may perhaps be made by mercy, but is impossible to righteousness—and so the attributes are in conflict. Sometimes it is represented that in the sight of righteousness every sin against God is an infinite sin deserving infinite punishment, because God himself is infinite. Sometimes it is argued that because God is righteous all sin must be punished, even though the sinner be forgiven. But all these views rest upon conceptions of righteousness that Christ never taught us or could teach. The righteous God judges by the standards that are applicable to the case in hand, and by no others. He insists upon all that may fairly be expected, but upon nothing more. He makes all just allowance for ignorance and moral feebleness—and even our common speech bears witness that there is such a thing as just allowance. He knows things by their right names, and passes no arbitrary judgments. Just for the reason that his justice is thus fair to human weakness, is his claim for all attainable good the more incontestable and his punishment the more to be approved. Righteousness includes magnanimity, for magnanimity is right and its opposite is wrong; and God is the most magnanimous of beings. The largest and most generous ideals of fair dealing that have grown up among men are most like him. All the more impressive and searching therefore is his insistence upon the right and good, and all the more solemn is the fact of his moral government.

Far back of the working operation of moral government does the relation of righteousness to moral government appear. It is involved in the very constitution of the order in which spirits have their life.   It implies the creation of an order in which a fair and wholesome moral government can be conducted.   Righteousness in God implies the ordaining of a natural healthfulness in the order of human life.   An order in which sin could exist might be quite defensible, but an order in which sin was unwarned and unreproved could not.   A world in which men must necessarily descend in the moral scale but could never rise could not be defended as the world of a righteous God.   The righteousness of our God and Father is vindicated by what he has done.   The healthful element, or element of moral hygiene, in the order of our world, is evident as soon as we look with discerning eyes. It has been overlooked, and sometimes denied, because Christians have often interpreted the world so much more in the light of sin than of God.   The moral healthfulness of much that enters into human life ought never to have been unnoticed.   That life throughout the broad world has brought forth all the virtues of the present day as well as all the vices, is a sure sign of an indwelling wholesomeness, not altogether overcome by evil.   Life is properly a school of love and helpfulness, and its work has not been wholly thwarted.   Life is educative: both joy and sorrow are teachers, and suffering is one of the greatest of schoolmasters.   Punishment is disciplinary: suffering earned by sin has been a strong means of winning men away from sin—a means only partially successful, as we know, yet one that bears witness to the wisdom and righteousness of him who implanted it in life.   The common experience of the race through long ages has developed the soul up to its present standing and ability. Through that experience God has gotten as good a world as he now has; and all our knowledge of the dreadfulness of sin must not blind us to the fact that the state of mankind still bears witness to a fine wholesomeness in the conditions of its existence.   All this illustrates the righteousness of God; for a God who was to conduct a moral administration over men could righteously place them only where a moral administration was possible on terms that were fair to them.

In the same direction the Christian idea of righteousness leads us another step. If a race in ignorance and moral weakness has fallen into sin, ever so guiltily, and a faithful Creator is its moral governor, it is safe to be sure that divine help against the evil will be forthcoming. Righteousness will suggest it, as well as love. God's moral government is an administration opposed to sin: but an administration opposed to sin in its work upon spiritual beings will not leave sin unopposed in the field of their life. That would not be right; and the honourable plea recorded in the prayer of Abraham, "Shall not the Judge of all the earth do right?" (Gen. xviii. 25), may be just as fitly offered here. A right moral government must contain not only an element of healthfulness in its natural order, but if there is need of it, an element of salvation. It is right for the strong to help the weak, and for the faithful Creator to deliver his creatures from evil. We wrong God's righteousness if we think of it as only condemnatory and punitive. Even before Christ, the Old Testament includes his graciousness within it. That God is a Saviour in spite of his righteousness is what Christians have often said, but that God is a Saviour because of his righteousness, as well as because of his love, is what prophets and apostles have declared. In the Scriptures it appears, just as our best thought of him would expect, that his own righteousness impels him to establish righteousness in the world where it is lacking, and that he is faithful and righteous to pardon and purify sinful men when they confess their sins (1 Jn. i. 9). All this is as it should be, for it is right that God should be a Saviour, and a world in which sin was left unopposed in possession of the field could not be defended as the world of a righteous God. Of him as Saviour we must speak elsewhere: here it is sufficient to note that salvation, or deliverance of men from sin, is a true part of the moral administration of human life by God.

In these statements it has been implied that the intent of God's moral government is gracious toward men, and he is administering their life for their good. This has always been held in the Christian doctrine, though not always with full consistency. That the moral administration of life was gracious toward some of the living has never been doubted by Christians, and it has often been felt that in some manner the government of God must be gracious toward all men; but very rarely has the idea of a universal kind intent been clearly and rationally fitted into a place among the thoughts of the Christian people. Often it has been held that graciousness in God is a matter of decree or determination rather than of nature; and from that starting-point it is impossible to reach the vision of a gracious moral government over all. Often it has been held that the gracious intent of moral government was manifest in the historical Christ alone, from which it was inferred that God was nothing but a Judge to those who had never heard of Christ. But the moral government of which we are speaking is the administration of the life of all mankind. We have to think of the good God whom Christ has made known to us, and to judge of his attitude toward all his human creatures. Of course it is impossible for that God to be governing men otherwise than for their good. Under the Father of Jesus human life has been lived from the beginning and will be lived forever. The Christian doctrine is that his moral government of all men is meant in kindness and adapted to their welfare. His gift of life to the race is a blessing, not a curse, and his governance of men is his means of fulfilling his gracious creative purpose.

5. PROVIDENCE

Equally with Sovereignty and Moral Government, Providence is a part of the relation between God and men. Doubtless the doctrine of providence includes the idea of control and direction over natural forces, as we call them, and the turning of non-spiritual things to spiritual use; but God's administration would not be called providence, or considered in theology, if spiritual beings were not influenced by its operation. The significance of providence resides in God's relation not to things but to persons. The moon can serve providence only by serving life. Discernible in human life there is a natural order, and there is a spiritual order; or in other words there is a spiritual meaning and purpose that cannot be sufficiently set forth in terms of the natural order. The doctrine of providence is the affirmation of that spiritual significance in the world, and of God's directing will and wisdom in giving it effect.

Such a doctrine lies closely side by side with the doctrine of moral government, and perhaps might well be treated as a part of it. Yet the two are not the same. We think of God in moral government as having to do with the souls of men, with reference to their character, their responsibility and their destiny; while in providence we think of his purpose concerning men, and the events and occurrences through which his purpose is to be wrought out. Roughly, one may be called the administration of human character and destiny, and the other the administration of human affairs. Providence may be defined as that comprehensive care by which God brings all things into the service of his spiritual purpose.

The idea of providence is no specialty of Christian faith, for some such doctrine has been held wherever there was belief in God, or in gods. No people have ever believed in the divine without having some belief in a divine administration of human affairs. The belief has necessarily varied in character, according to the conceptions that were held of God. Polytheism implies a miscellaneous and contradictory kind of providence: only monotheism has place for a broad and consistent doctrine. Even under monotheism there is room for large variation in the idea, for the sole God may be conceived in various relations to men and their affairs. A history of Christian conceptions of providence, if it could be written in full, would be a strangely mixed record of human faith and feebleness, of the noblest thoughts and the crudest misjudgments. But the Christian faith in providence has always been a living thing, and in all ages has been the keynote of confidence and hope. Providence, indeed, is more a theme of faith than of doctrine, and the faith may be much clearer than the doctrine. Faith in God does much of its beneficent work by being faith in the providence of God.

The abiding element in the Christian faith in providence is the confidence that God cares for men, and is administering the events of time and the affairs of the world for their good. Two classical expressions give the central idea in its permanent forms. One relates to the more special field of responsive spiritual life—"We know that all things work together for good to them that love God" (Rom. viii. 28): the other to the entire order in which men live—"Of him, and through him, and unto him, are all things" (Rom. xi. 36). This one theme of confidence in God's effective gracious purpose has run through the whole song of Christian faith. Evidently it is a theme capable of innumerable variations, and almost all possible variations it has received. But the main variations result from difference regarding one point in the relation of God to the world in which his providence is observed.

It is evident that the idea of providence must vary with the idea that is entertained of the manner in which God is related to the world. It will be one thing if he is regarded chiefly as above and beyond the world and acting upon it from without, and another if he is thought of as indwelling in the world and acting through its operations. This difference, which will often meet us in our study, is a deep and influential one, and the doctrine of providence lies directly in the field of its influence. It is an ancient difference, too, for both ideas of God have run through all religious thinking, from days far back of the Christian era, and have largely controlled the conception of his providential work.

We must speak hereafter of the Transcendence and Immanence of God. At present it must suffice to note that it has been natural for men to think of God as outside the world and acting upon it mainly from without. We ourselves act upon things about us, and not from within the things, and when God is conceived as influencing visible affairs it is easy to picture divine action after the likeness of human in this respect. Human institutions foster the same tendency, for God is represented as a king, and human kingship has been suggestive of a dignity that shows itself in aloofness. When God is conceived as holy, this world may seem unworthy of his presence, and he may be placed above it, in some higher and purer realm. The stronger the sense of sin becomes, the more does this world seem no place for his abode. But such separation brings great consequences. When God and the world are thus set apart from each other, it follows that the order of the world and the action of God seem to be two things. The course of the world will be under his governance, of course, since he is God, but his most characteristic operation is not in the natural order, it is in action of another class, which becomes known as the supernatural. His favourite work is not only superior to nature, but distinct and different from it, and breaks through nature when it comes. When he appears most like himself, the ordinary course of the world gives way for his entrance. "He bowed the heavens and came down" (2 Sam. xxii. 10).

With God thus conceived as outside the world, the doctrine of providence becomes a doctrine of divine interposition and interference. Special action of God strikes through the order of nature, and providence is a divine practice of intervening in human affairs. This is an ancient doctrine, and it is no wonder that it persistently holds a place in religion. Reverence loves to think that God is highly exalted, and yet is at hand concretely and livingly, ready to strike in at any moment for protection of precious interests and promotion of his own will. With such a view of providence, intervention may be expected at any hour in behalf of those for whom he cares, or against his enemies, and any event that seems specially significant may readily be attributed to such an intervention. Such doctrine of providence is a doctrine of divine occasionalism rather than of steady divine operation, but the occasions are ever arising, and God is at hand. Faith beholds him ever ready, and believing souls look with a most helpful confidence upon the Friend who will never leave them nor forsake them or neglect the interests of his own kingdom. Thus the doctrine is a strong support amid the perplexities of life. It is liable to abuse, as the history of fanatical faith illustrates a thousand times, but it is a doctrine of great practical power.

Through the greater part of Christian time God has been regarded mainly as above the world and operating upon it from without by supernatural action. He is still so regarded by most Christians, though by none with full consistency. That mode of thought is one of the common inheritances from ancient human life. In Christian life it has been supported by the Old Testament, where God was sometimes pictured as sitting in the heavens, looking down upon the earth, descending upon the clouds to intervene in the affairs of men, manifesting himself in events that have no place in nature. It is true that he appears also as nearer to men than this, and the more abiding relation is identical with the one that Jesus dwelt upon; but the more external picture took strong hold upon popular faith, and came over into the popular Christianity. There it has remained. The doctrine of providence has accordingly been very largely a doctrine of supernatural interventions. Special events have been singled out and called providential: Christians have often talked of providences: the God of providence has been the intervening and often the overruling God, who accomplishes by interposition what was otherwise impossible. The providential purpose, being the will of God, has been accounted to be continuous, not fragmentary; and yet God's providential work has been identified very largely with what is special and occasional.

A providence of interventions is naturally understood to be intended for reward and punishment, and for vindication of God. It has constantly been held that providence was protective of the good and destructive of the wicked. In Old Testament times, when the future life was in the background, faith in God took the form of confidence that the present life would witness the full manifestation of his justice; wherefore it was expected that very soon the wicked would receive their punishment and the righteous their vindication and reward. So some of the Psalms most earnestly predict, counting upon a providence that will immediately illustrate God's righteousness. This idea of God's way with men has never died, and still quotes the authority of the Psalms in its favour. Providence has been looked to to punish sin, or at least to expose the sinner, and to treat the good as they deserve. It has been confidently relied upon to annihilate danger for the good and protect them from physical injury, while the occurrence of harm to the wicked was called the punitive work of God, supernaturally wrought in the midst of a natural order that was leaving sin unpunished. So, as by the friends of Job, calamity has been interpreted as proof of guilt, and prosperity as a sign of divine approval, to the very sad disordering of ethical convictions. A similar view has been taken of the important historical crises in which the kingdom of God and the cause of righteousness have been furthered. Solemn indeed are these crises, and impressive to every soul that distinguishes good and evil. With reverence men gaze upon them, especially when they are far enough away for their significance and effect to be appreciated. Surely, men say, this is our God: it must be he, because he comes in so marvellous a manner.

These forms of doctrine concerning providence are sincere and reverent endeavours to interpret life as under a providence of interventions, but they do not satisfy the hope that has been built upon them. It does not prove to be true that occurrences can be relied upon to accord with the character of those whom they affect. Taking the world through, one man is not safer than another from lightning or disease, except as intelligent precaution renders him so. Both the equalities and the inequalities of life refuse to be classified in terms of moral character. Many a heart has been well-nigh broken in coming to the point of making the acknowledgment, but at last it has to be acknowledged that the doctrine of a protective and punitive providence does not correspond to the facts of life. Nothing but the most flagrant injustice is the result if we attempt to explain the misfortunes of life as punitive. The theory does not work. Virtue is no safeguard against sickness, fire and flood, or many another form of trouble, nor does wickedness bring them on. If we have found a case that seems perfectly to prove the doctrine, the next hour may bring us one that just as clearly disproves it. Nor do the crises in history prove on the whole convincing. Sometimes a crisis sets the human movement forward, but sometimes another sets it back. The oft-quoted destruction of the Spanish Armada through a combination of storm and human folly promoted human progress, by preserving from inter-ference the quality by virtue of which England has been useful to later time. The murder of Abraham Lincoln set human progress back, by throwing a task of vast importance into hands less wise and competent. Thus to define provi-dence in terms of divine intervention is to involve ourselves in deep perplexity. If some have found it heart-breaking to abandon such a view of life, more will find it heart-breaking to cling to it and meet the consequences to their faith.

So it is with all doctrines that assume a God mainly outside the world, affecting it by interposition. They have awakened faith, and brought God near to the heart at critical moments, and sustained reverence and gratitude; but they have failed to give a permanently satisfying account of life, and are cer-tain to bring a sad sense of their insufficiency. They have served a useful purpose in the time when they could be calmly held, but they must yield when their day is past. It is often feared that the sense of a living providence must depart when this view of God gives place to another. Parodoxically, and pathetically, Christians often seem afraid that the doctrine which really brings God nearest will destroy the vivid and trustful recognition of his presence. But we may hope that, on the contrary, the change will introduce a doctrine that will better stand the test of life.

Our understanding of providence will undergo an intelligible change if we think of God as nearer to his world. This manner of thought has long been coming in. Of course it is not new, for the Bible abundantly contains it, but it has been partially put out of sight by the other doctrine, and is now returning to its own. God is more and more regarded as dwelling and working in the world itself, and the natural order as his way of operation. The common method of the world is the method of God—not the only method of which he is capable, but the method that he is now employing. The relation of God to his world must be more fully discussed elsewhere: it is enough here to speak of it in the terms just now employed. God acts within the order of the world, the doings of the soul and the movement of history, and has the will and wisdom to make of the whole a system that serves his ends. We do not say by preference that he interferes or intervenes in human events, because we judge that he is in the course of events already. The communicating God is in touch with human spirits, and the coördinating God has his touch upon human events. He is more manifest in one part of the course of events than in another, but there is no need that he interrupt the order of things, or break through into our world, for the order is already his, and in our world he is at work. But we must not forget that the indwelling God is a God indwelling, not a mere equivalent of the forces of the world. Pantheism can have no providence, for in order to a providence there must be a living and intelligent God. What makes God's work in the world a providence is, that the God who works in all things has wisdom and power to coördinate the course of nature and life into a system that is his own and serves his will. He is greater than nature and greater than men. He is greater than the world, and the universe, or there would be no providence at all. He is the master, the meaning-giver, the mysterious controller, the worker-out of a purpose that makes a unity of the whole. His providence is the coördinating control of the indwelling God, giving to the course of life the significance that corresponds to his presence and purpose.

It is nothing against this that in speaking thus we say more than we can explain. We cannot expound separate events and tell what each means, or show how divine and human work together. The mystery will never be gone from life. But though we cannot wholly explain the providence of an indwelling God, certain true and important things about it may be said.

The providence of the indwelling God is the administration of life on the principle that all life has spiritual meaning and value. God, acting in the forces and methods of the world in which life is lived, and in the methods and principles of spiritual existence, influences and directs the life of men in view of the spiritual significance of their being. This is the kind of providence that is attributed to God in the Scriptures, and especially in the teaching of Jesus the Master.

This doctrine puts providence in its right place among the relations between God and men. With moral government it is almost identical. In providence the principles of moral government are applied to life. Providence is the operation of "that power, not ourselves, which makes for righteousness," which power is God—not some impersonal energy, but the eternal character and will. In providence the divine demand for the right and good is applied and illustrated, the retributive principle is wrought out in the spiritual field, and the training of souls which moral government implies is carried on. It is evident also that providence is scarcely more than a form of fatherhood. So Jesus says, with matchless beauty, teaching the children that they are under the Father's providential care. Providence is the Father's practical administration of the life that he has produced: it is paternal, directed to the ends for which existence was given to moral beings.

The providence of the indwelling God is continuous, not fragmentary. Not in occasional appearance does it consist: not in descent from heaven, or special deliverances for his children, or strokes of lightning that kill the wicked, or storms that scatter forces of evil. It does not consist in interruptions of the order of nature. It is always at work, operat-

ing in the forces that give life a continuous significance. It
includes the startling crises, but it includes also the quiet
working of the forces by which they are brought about. It
means that God is in all life, and in all life is working. Shall
we say that God is as patient as nature? or that nature is as
patient as God?—or rather that the patience of nature is but
a partial expression of the patience of God?

The providence of the indwelling God is over all. A
providence of interpositions might serve the ends of favouritism, and the doctrine of it might be the faithful servant of a
doctrine of partialism in God. So indeed it has often been.
Providence has often been interpreted as a special divine care
over a certain favoured part of humanity. But the providence
of an indwelling God can scarcely be devoted in any manner
to promoting the special interests of a part. Such a providence must be as impartial in its range as the light of the sun.
If God is acting in the natural and spiritual forces that
affect mankind, he is acting there upon all, and for all, who
are included in mankind. Such a providence concerns them
all: he "maketh his sun to rise, and sendeth rain," everywhere
alike. Nay, it must extend, as the method of God, to all
spiritual beings who have ever lived. A different set of conditions may exist in another world, but the administration of
the life of spiritual beings in view of its spiritual significance
and value must continue, as long as the life itself continues.

The providence of the indwelling God implies the usefulness of the natural order for spiritual purposes, and turns
natural experiences to spiritual account. The life of the
human being in its present mode is one, a single life, with its
material and its spiritual aspects. Filled with a sense of the
importance of the spiritual, the ethical, the religious, we
might think that this must constitute a life by itself, to which
alone the interest of God would be given. Earnest souls
have sometimes tried to act as if this were so, labouring to
keep their hearts fixed exclusively upon that spiritual element
in which alone they thought that God could be concerned.
The mingling of the material and spiritual in personal life

does bring difficulties to the doctrine of providence. It is easy to believe in the care of God over the life of the soul, and to think of him as acting upon it, since it moves in the realm of freedom, which is the most significant realm, both to us and to him. But the natural order of the world appears less free, or not free at all, and it seems another world. There events come one out of another by an irresponsible unfolding. What deep meaning, we ask, can there be in physical events? How can God turn them to spiritual use? and how can there be a genuine providence, in which the seemingly self-acting system of natural causation is included?

The doctrine of an interventional providence admits that natural events can be made to serve spiritual uses, but tends to imply that they require special divine interposition to make them do so. Nature must be interrupted or over-ruled, or turned to account: God can make it serviceable, but it is not so in itself: apart from his overruling, the natural order of life is something that opposes rather than helps the spiritual purpose of God and meaning of life. This comes of setting God too far outside of his world: his world is made void of inherent spiritual value—a thing that cannot be done without in the end discrediting God himself. But the providence of the indwelling God is a providence that works through all agencies and relations with which men are concerned. What else indeed should be expected from the providence of the God who is the source of all? In his world, life is really one, and all elements that compose it can be woven into the purpose of serving the highest end. Any of them may be misused, but all are adapted to the one design. This doctrine of providence corresponds entirely to what we know of life, for we find our spiritual advantage a thousand times in physical contingencies that display in themselves no moral quality. That means that God in his providential wisdom knows how to make a whole out of what seem to be but scattered parts. He is in all and through all and over all, and has so constituted the world that he can use its various movements for his moral end.

Providence of an indwelling God of course implies all that is meant by sovereignty, in God himself. How much this means, we have already seen that our definitions may fail to tell; but it certainly includes a mysterious power to guide both natural and voluntary forces to the fulfilment of his own ends. These ends are spiritual, and holy; and the doctrine of providence implies that the God of the purpose is adequate to the fulfilment. It affirms a purpose in the general movement of human life, in which God is greater than man: something is sought and will be gained which is not of man's choosing but of God's. Here we are led beyond our power to explain, as we are in all doctrines of the relation between God and men, for we are led to assert a power of God to use free actors for the accomplishing of his own will. Somehow he must be guiding them from above their freedom, directing them in a mysterious control of which they are unaware, and that does not destroy their responsibility in what they do. It is certain that the world must look very differently from God's point of view and from ours, and it is from his point of view that it consistently appears as a world governed by providence. All doctrine of providence implies the superiority of God and his ability to exercise a spiritual control that we cannot explain. His power works upon a higher plane than that of human freedom, and mysteriously controls free beings for their good; and this beneficent power is so inwrought to the creation of the world and man that God exercises it through the methods that are normal to his created works.

Nevertheless, although we refuse to define providence as a divine occasionalism breaking through a regular order, we meet the question whether it consists exclusively in God's operation in the natural order of the world. Is this all? or does providence involve the working of a higher order also, congenial to God, which now and then appears amidst the operations of the method that is familiar to us? Does providence include supernatural occurrences as well as natural? We meet this question in the conviction that in providence we contemplate a God too great to be fully expressed in the natural order of this world as we understand that order. There is more in him than nature can express, and it may well be that he desires to manifest more of himself than can thus be represented. Works transcending this world's order would be incredible if nature were the whole, but there is an outreaching and communicating God, for whose fulness nature offers only an inadequate language. Since there is such a God, it is in harmony with reason that his creatures may now and then hear among them a voice that is not of this world. If we think of God as limited by any necessity to his actual method, we shall not be thinking of him as really God. We call man a free agent, but much more a free agent is he from whom the type of man's freedom came.

It is here, in the study of providence, that we properly meet the question whether God works miracles in his world. This is a question that is greatly clarified by being considered in its proper context, which is not usually done. The context is human. The question of miracles is usually put forward as a question of the relation of God to the order of nature; but it is a question that has no interest, or even existence, outside the human field. It is not a doctrine of Christianity or of any other religion that in his relations with the universe as a whole, or apart from the affairs of men, God is accustomed to depart from the order of nature. Where men are not concerned, miracles are not attributed to him. They are never assumed to have occurred in the geologic ages. Creative acts of universal scope are of course attributed to God, but not to these is the name miracles given. It is only within the human circle that miracles have any interest, or are ever believed to have been wrought. The question about miracles is simply whether in his dealing with men, for the sake of his providential purpose, God sometimes departs from the order of nature. The question is limited still further, for miracles properly have place only in the material world. It is true that we often speak of the miracle of regeneration, or of spiritual gifts, but such speaking is loose and popular, and the word miracle is inaccurately employed. According to universal Christian agreement, the field of inward spiritual operation is open to God, but his action there, free and direct though it is, is not among the acts to which the name of miracles is given. The communion of the Holy Spirit is divine and direct, but is not called miraculous.

Thus the question of miracles relates on the one hand to external nature, and on the other to the spiritual dealings of God with men. It is whether for the sake of his practical purpose for men, or for some of them, God sometimes subordinates the order of nature to his higher end, and does something for which it does not provide.

It is to be noticed that in making our inquiry in this form we use the word miracle in its proper sense. In the present condition of inquiry it is our duty to use the word clearly, and to mean what we say. Ambiguous and evasive definitions we must abandon. It is not surprising that they have had their day of acceptance, but the time has come for clearing the field of them. It is scarcely necessary to say that a miracle cannot be defined as simply a wonder: that was never a definition, or anything more than a description of an effect. The most natural things are wonderful when they are unusual or unknown. Nor can we define a miracle as an act of power, for we know that power is evidenced more in nature than in miracles. Neither are we defining when we say that a miracle is a sign: that does not tell what it is, but what it means. It is more important to note that miracles are often treated in discussion as if they were acts performed by the use of some natural force not understood at the time, though liable to be discovered afterward. Healings, for example, which were regarded as miraculous when they occurred, are said to have been performed by the use of natural powers unknown to the beholders, unknown perhaps to the healer, but afterwards included in human knowledge.

But it ought long ago to have been noticed, and must certainly be acknowledged now, that this solution denies the miraculous element in such events entirely, and defends the miracles in question by explaining them away. The explanation expressly affirms that the events are natural, and have been accounted miraculous only because of human ignorance. If this is all, there are no miracles. Doubtless we can fairly account for some works recorded as miracles on this principle; but just as far as we can do so, it is our duty and privilege to withdraw them from our class of supernatural events, to welcome them into the order of nature, and to adjust our idea of miracles accordingly. When we speak of a miracle, we have no right to mean anything but a direct act of God in the material realm, outside the course of nature. This we do mean in our present inquiry. But we do not inquire whether such acts are performed in the general administration of the universe: we inquire whether God sometimes performs them in the course of his providence over men. He acts upon men through what we call the natural order of the world: does he also act upon them through departure from that order?

When the question of miracles is thus put where it belongs, as a question about God's method in providence, it appears in its true light in reference to religion. In religion it is not a vital question. It is of vital importance that we should know the moral will of God and enter his fellowship and be loyal to his purpose, but it is not necessary that we be able to describe the relation of his action to the order of nature. It is enough to say that the matters that are supremely important to the soul are not of this kind. If God operates in his world by miracle or if he does not, the spiritual realities are the same. In either case he is the living God, and the significance of his being to ours cannot be changed.

There is another reason, however, why the recognition of miracles cannot be of vital importance to the soul. There is no way to identify any occurrence as miraculous, except by evidence, which must consist in testimony, and human judgment. Whether any past event which has been so regarded was really miraculous must be judged by each for himself, in the best light that he can obtain. The days are past when a thousand natural events could be regarded as miraculous simply because they were wonderful. Since miracles came to be considered more thoughtfully, it has been recognized that our belief in them must rest first upon our conviction that they are possible, and then upon convincing evidence that they have occurred. Accordingly it has been customary to cite the witnesses and marshal the evidence. The occurring of miracles has thus been included among the things that we cannot be sure of except through the testimony of our fellows. But nothing can be indispensable to the soul before God, to which the massing of human testimony is indispensable. The certainties that are the food of eternal life, which alone are essential to religion, are certainties in themselves, of which man can become sure for himself through fellowship with God.

It is still to be added that there is nothing in the nature of miracles that can attest spiritual truth. The most that is claimed for them in the way of attestation is that they attest the messengers of God, and give us confidence that their messages come to us by divine authority. But it is coming to be felt, and rightly, that the message does not derive authority from the messenger, but rather the messenger from the message, and that the appeal of God is made through his truth. The witness that God bears to his own spiritual work for men is borne in the realm of the spirit. And so we say on the whole that the question of miracles is of interest in our study of the providence of God, but is not of vital importance in religion, which rests on firmer foundations than that of miracle-working power.

Belief in miracles as a part of the divine administration of the world is much older than Christianity, and much more widespread. Without defining them, all antiquity believed in miracles, and the belief is still a vital one in great parts of mankind. At first it was an instinctive confidence in the ability of the divine power to strike into human affairs with independent action. There was no theory of nature or natural order to occasion perplexity: it was enough that God could act anywhere at any moment, and his unseen power could surprise men with supernatural help or harm. It was in this stage of knowledge that belief in miracles came to be a part of the common stock of belief the world over. But when God came to be conceived more intelligently as a living Lord and Judge, miracles became more significant; and it was in view of the reign of God, not of mere power, that the Christian belief in miracles became so strong an element in life and doctrine.

Unlike other faiths that hold to miracles, Christianity has lived on into the very midst of the scientific stage of thought, which indeed it has been an important agent in bringing on. The resulting situation is peculiar and difficult. It is a striking fact that the Christian religion has come into the modern age with no very general break in its belief in miracles. In the Roman Catholic Church it is held that direct interventions of divine power are of daily and hourly occurrence, largely through intercession of the saints. Protestants oftener speak of the age of miracles as past—not because they are impossible now, but because for some good reason it was the will of God that they should cease. Not all think so, however, and in the rank and file of protestantism there are multitudes who would be ready to acknowledge miracles at any hour. There are many to whom miracles appear to be the glory of the world: in the past they are the very sign and evidence of God, and it is hoped that still more splendid supernatural interventions may vindicate him in the future. The genuineness of the miracles recorded in the Bible is generally maintained. Apologists often admit that some of them might be dispensed with and the faith stand firm, but it is usually held that without the greatest of them there could be no Christianity—often, that there could be no salvation for any one.

Bringing such belief as this, Christianity has come under the influences of the scientific age. It has come to the period of definitions, when belief in the wonderful, or even in the supernatural, however sincere, is not enough to make a satisfactory doctrine, and the idea of the miraculous must find its place among other ideas. It has brought its belief to a time when the order of nature is regarded as a constant order, and the continuity of causation is accepted as an axiom. The modern conception of the unity of the world does not favour the belief in special interferences with its order; and at the same time the study of religious history shows how far belief in miracles is from being proof of their reality. Thus Christianity has come under various influences that tend to disintegrate its old belief. Nevertheless, the sense of the preciousness of the miraculous has not departed. The old religious joy in the presence of a wonder-working God persists, and is associated with much that is best in Christian feeling.

But whatever the feeling of Christians about it may be, the doctrine of miracles is more and more being superseded by the doctrine of the indwelling God. As long as God was conceived mainly as reigning elsewhere and communicating with men only by special revelation, it was natural to think of him as shown to men by extraordinary action. Such belief was the clearest form of belief in an active living God. If the Almighty was beyond the world, he must break in. The idea was not only natural, but practically essential to strong religion, as long as God was in some sense localized outside. But he is localized no longer. Not only is his connection with his spiritual creation most intimate, but the steady, regular, self-continuing order of the universe is recognized as his own order, truly expressive of his wisdom and his will. He has not to break into the world, for he is in the world. He needs not to break the order if he would express himself, for the order itself expresses him. He can break the order if he desires, but the assumed need of his doing so for self-expression does not exist. In view of such a vision of God in his world, miracles cannot be as prominent in Christian thought as they were when God was differently conceived. All religious thinking at present is subject to influences that make miracles seem at once less necessary and less likely to have occurred; and the influences are not illegitimate ones. The modern loss of interest in miracles is not due chiefly to unbelief, as many have feared, but to the great change that has come over the prevailing conception of God. His providence seems to follow other methods. Accordingly it has come to pass that the attitude of apologetical thought toward miracles is radically changed. Christianity was once defended on the ground of its miracles, which were held to be both indispensable and conclusive. But now the miracles are oftener defended on the ground that they are fit accompaniments of so divine a revelation as Christianity brings from God. Christ was once believed in because of the miracles, but now the miracles are believed in because of Christ. So complete a revolution in the method of considering the miracles of the New Testament is profoundly significant, and significant of a very wholesome change in thought. It is far more Christian-like to believe in the miracles because of Christ than to believe in Christ because of the miracles.

Practically, the sum of the matter is that in modern days we are aware of two strong influences bearing upon the question of miracles as an element in the providence of God. On the one hand there is strong influence to make us believe that there are no genuine miracles such as we have defined, and never have been any; that God never departed from the natural order that he has established, and that all supposed miracles have been accounted such through some kind of misconception, which has been both sincere and blameless. Science finds no evidence of departure from the natural order, or any place for it; and there is a growing Christian conviction that the indwelling and informing God is not likely to depart from an order that he himself has established as a worthy permanent expression of his will. And on the other hand there is a strong impulse to believe the opposite, and be sure that the free Omnipotent manifests himself by breaking through his order when he will. The religious heart cries out for clear signs of the great presence, and declares that the God of its trust is no silent force but a wonder-working Friend. Whether either of these influences will ever consent to be silenced by the other, it is difficult now to tell; but there are some things that we may fairly say about the two positions.

If miracles have never occurred, God's providence is complete without them. For on the one hand the natural order of the world is not an alien and godless thing, but is God's own order. He is in it and works through it, and it is in its own field an expression of himself. He has no need to interrupt or destroy it if he desires to be manifest in the world. On the other hand there is open to God the entire field of direct spiritual operation, or influence upon souls. As we have said, some give to such works of God the name of miracles: the Christian life is said to be a miraculous life, and Christ himself to be the greatest of miracles in his spiritual character and work. This is not the clearest and most helpful way of using terms, and we do better if we keep the name miracles to its narrower meaning. The conversableness of God with men, as the Puritan divine, John Howe, has named it, is as much a part of the natural order of life for us as our conversableness with one another, and we extend it in our thoughts instead of restricting it, when we take it out of the class of the miraculous. The whole world of spiritual intercourse and influence is open to God, and this is enough to constitute his operation among men a providence. With an unbroken natural method and an unbounded spiritual freedom of access to men, God is intelligibly the Lord of providence.

If there are miracles, however, God's providence includes them and gives them meaning. In any case they are not detached events, but occupy a place in the significant purpose of God. Such events as we have defined miracles to be,

being events in the material world, cannot be ultimate: they
are only means to an end. They are means to the end of
God's providence, which is the training of souls. God's
providence is in general the administration of a settled and
trustworthy world. His method is based in part upon what
we call the uniformity of nature, which in the large is a blessing to mankind. If God works miracles in the world, still
we may be sure that he will not make them so frequent and
numerous as to weaken his children's confidence in the
stability of their life. They will not be so plentiful as to
dominate the character of human affairs. That would not
be like the God who has established the world. They will
serve some special ends in his providence that could not
otherwise be served so well. They may well be ministrant
to his great design of grace unto salvation. They will be
signs of God: not sole signs, as if God were otherwise unex-
pressed, or even as if he could be most worthily expressed by
exceptional works, and yet real signs of God, helpful to the
faith of such among his children as need such helps. Jesus
is recorded to have expressly disparaged faith that was
founded upon them, in comparison with faith that was
grounded in spiritual realities, and the Christian doctrine
must always estimate the two forms of confidence in agreement with this mind of the Master. It would be well if popular thinking among Christians were to come into intelligent
unity with Christ in this. Better is the faith that needs no
outward sign, and it is time for theology to take this position
without reserve.

6. SAVIOUR

The glory of Christianity is salvation. The new faith
sprang up, after the departure of its Founder, from the great
experience in which men found peace with God, were morally
transformed, and were born into the hope of perfection.
The new life was a personal possession, and it was more.
It was the crown of individual existence, and it implied the

awakening of a brotherly love and righteousness that would work out into a social salvation. It peopled the kingdom of God with saved souls, and thus created the kingdom of God among men for the fulfilment of God's large purpose. This song of experience and hope is the new song of the Christian faith, and the sound of it has gone forth in all Christian times and places.

Of course salvation is fundamentally an ethical fact, for it contemplates men as involved in sin. It is correct enough, indeed, to speak of men as saved from danger or from punishment, but the Christian vocabulary is richer in meaning. Salvation deals with more than punishment or danger: it is the comprehensive good that men need because of their sinfulness. It includes both ethical change and the practical consequences of such change, but the change is the fundamental element. It includes deliverance from evil both in character and in destiny, and realization of all good possibilities; forgiveness for the past, and successful existence under God's gracious influence in the future. It has effect upon all traits of character, all works of life, and all relations in which men may stand. It is a present gift, and a gift to be completed in another life. It is personal, it is social, it is racial, and so far as its ideal is realized it is universal, since all need it and to all it is adapted.

This salvation has always been ascribed with loyal gratitude to Jesus Christ, adored and loved as the Saviour of the world. He came to seek and to save that which was lost, and his gospel is the power of God unto salvation. It is true that as to the work by which he became the Saviour, and the precise relation that he bears to the accomplishment of the result, no single explanation has ever been universally accepted. There have been many theories of his saving work, but no one of them has ever become the one Christian account of the matter, and happily no Christian authority has ever attempted to dictate a theory to those who put their trust in him. The experience of salvation and the modes of thought in different ages have been so various as to prevent any uniformity of explanation. None the less, however, does salvation stand always associated with Jesus Christ. The writers of the New Testament commemorate him as Saviour and offer him gratitude and love without measure. The creeds of Christendom assign to him the same position, and the hymns of the Church in all ages have sung the praises of the Saviour Christ.

No one has ever supposed, however, that the Jesus whom the Gospels show us was the originator of salvation. The Christian faith and doctrine declare that salvation originated in God. Father and Son being distinguished in thought, it has always been held that salvation originated in the Father. So in the Scriptures. In the synoptical Gospels, Jesus is among men as the messenger of grace and help, doing the Father's will. In the Fourth Gospel he is even more emphatically represented as sent by the Father to give life to men, and as living solely to accomplish that which the Father had given him to do. The Johannine writings are justly represented by the familiar words, "God so loved the world that he gave his only begotten Son" (Jn. iii. 16), and the Pauline writings are no less truly represented by the similar saying, "God commendeth his own love toward us, in that while we were yet sinners Christ died for us" (Rom. v. 8). This truth has always remained in the Christian teaching, though justice has not always been done to it. What Jesus has done for the salvation of the world has been presented as the expression of the eternal heart and counsel of God, from whom as its originator the whole work came. "That your faith and hope may be in God" (1 Pet. i. 21) has been rightly said to be the substance of Christ's message and the purpose of his life and death. We do him wrong if we detach him from the Father here. It is God's love that shines in the face of Jesus Christ and is revealed by his cross, and it is because of this that the Christian confidence in salvation exults in the immovableness of its foundation. Nothing could be firmer than a hope grounded in God.

Here we have the supreme illustration of the truth which lies at the base of the Christian doctrine, that in Jesus Christ we have true revealing of God. This does not mean something technical, as if in Christ we had received a formula concerning the divine nature. It means that Jesus and his life and work constitute a great expression of God and exhibition of his character. It is true, as the Fourth Gospel declares, that Jesus is not alone and does not speak from himself. His word is not his own word, but what he has seen with the Father he speaks to men, and the action of his life is not his own but God's (Jn. viii. 28; xiv. 10). Thus he represents the unseen Father, and sets forth to human knowledge the character of the eternal will. What he does God is doing, and such as he is God is. In him God does that most direct and simple work of revelation—he shows himself as he is. Christ we know as Saviour, and God, we thereby know, is Saviour also. Christ who has lived and died among men, and God whom no man hath seen, are called by this one name. Therefore, if we wish to understand God as Saviour, we look at Christ. In his life and spirit is the authorized interpretation of the divine Saviourhood. What then do we see in Christ the Saviour that illuminates for us God the Saviour?

We have said that Christ was absolutely at the service of God, and now it must be added that he showed it by being absolutely at the service of men. He was in the world to serve God by serving men: the two works were one. We see him living among men, and showing himself day by day as their friend and helper. Unselfish, tender, faithful, he does them good by word and deed. In their sinfulness they need penitence, faith and loyalty to God. He turns their attention to their heavenly Father, and teaches them a religion of sincerity, simplicity and truth. He teaches them, and what is better he shows them, in what spirit to live and how to act toward God and their fellows. He hates their sinfulness unspeakably, and reproves it with burning indignation and patient love. He seeks to show them just what it consists in, and labours to win them away from it into godly life and human fellowship. He is equally the enemy of evil and the friend of man. To the service of men he gives himself utterly. He suffers with them, and he suffers for them. He bears with their hardness, and is patient under their indifference and abuse, and believes in them, in spite of all, as worth his gracious seeking. He surrenders himself unto the uttermost, refusing no pain or burden, and freely accepting the death of the cross, that he may be the means of bringing home to men the redemptive love of God.

This on his own part was the attitude of Jesus as Saviour, and this is the life in which we are to see the Father. In our present study we are concerned with the doctrine of salvation only as far as it is a part of the doctrine of God, and we are interested in this attitude and work of Jesus because it was the saving heart of God that he was expressing, and the saving will of God that he was working out. "If ye had known me, ye would have known my Father also" (Jn. viii. 19). Neither in the words of Jesus nor in his attitude toward either God or men is there any intimation whatever that his Father needed or desired any transaction, directed to himself, in order that it might be possible for him to be a Saviour and for men to be saved. Rather, according to the Christian revelation, Jesus as Saviour is for men the expression and equivalent of God as Saviour. God was in Christ reconciling the world unto himself. In what Jesus did we see what God was doing. The words "I and the Father are one" (Jn. x. 30) relate to the work of salvation, and assert that the sheep of the Son's flock are the sheep of the Father's flock also, since Father and Son are one in Saviourhood. "The Father sent the Son to be the Saviour of the world" (1 Jn. iv. 14), not because the Father was not the Saviour, but because he was.

It is our privilege therefore to read in our doctrine of God the Saviourhood which Jesus has manifested in this world. When we thus follow the revealing Christian light, we approach the central truth of the gospel. God is no longer in obscurity: his position toward sinful men has been made plain. As is Christ, so is God.

God, like Jesus, holds himself at the service of sinful men for their spiritual good. It is evident that at the outset God thinks of men as worth saving from sin, and as capable of being saved. Next to his redemptive character of holiness and love, God's belief in the salvability of mankind is the greatest hopeful fact that lies back of the Christian revelation. By the revealing light of Christ we see that God regards men, and has always regarded them, notwithstanding the depth of their sinfulness, as within the reach of his holy help. Seeing men thus as capable of salvation, God is at their service. This is the spirit of Saviourhood; and we behold this spirit wrought out in action through the mission of Christ. In spirit, the mission of the Son was the coming of the Father, to seek and to save that which was lost. It is God that seeks. The matchless expression of Godlike character in human life was God's own expression of his own character, made that men might come from sin into fellowship with such love and purity. The teaching that Jesus gave concerning simple, sincere religion, with direct access to God, was God's own offer of himself and appeal to the men whose loyalty he desired. The luminous counsel of Jesus concerning duty of man to man was God's own instruction to his unbrotherly children. The love that would die for men was God's love. Beholding Jesus, we behold God.

With regard to sin, when Jesus expressed in his life his deep abhorrence of it, he was doing what he had seen with his Father. God's abhorrence of sin was expressed in him. Jesus so hated sin as to desire to deliver men from it, and so does God. Jesus' hatred of sin amounted to an irresistible impulse to be a Saviour; and this is like God: it is like God, too, that Jesus was inwardly constrained to go all lengths and make all sacrifices in order to save. God is here revealed as the great enemy of human evil, who spares himself no cost that he may save men from it. In Jesus we see how hatred of sin and love for the sinful need no reconciling with each other, but are inseparable aspects of one affection, which partakes equally of the nature of holiness and love.   Through Jesus we see this truth dwelling in God, that hatred of sin and desire to put it away are equal.   Under the quick and powerful impulse of this two-sided affection, we see Jesus untiring in his endeavour, patient, steadfast, consecrated without reserve to love's endeavour, gladly dying for men's good.   This is revelation, for this is expressive of God, who commendeth his own love toward us, not merely that of Jesus, in that while we were yet sinners Christ died for us (Rom. v. 8).   As Jesus was grieved by sin, which beat upon his purity in daily contact and continually prevented the satisfaction of his love, so is God grieved and pained by the sin of the world, which daily does despite to his love and offends his holiness.   In his own grief, Jesus opens for us a living vision of the heart of God, and gives us more than a glimpse of the divine sorrow over sin, which is a perpetual reality. From Jesus we learn that God is always bearing the sin of the world in the pain that it gives him, and in the constant endeavour of seeking the lost which it entails; and Jesus is our evidence that God willingly bears the sin of the world, because of his perfect and persistent grace.   For the joy that was set before him Jesus endured the cross, despising shame (Heb. xii. 2); and so does God.   If he should cease to bear the sins of the world and endure the cross, there could be no salvation; but God has in himself the perpetual fount of mercy, and is perpetually doing the work of redemptive holiness.   Jesus is able to save unto the uttermost because God is willing to save unto the uttermost.

This revelation does not merely concern some times and seasons.   The heart of it is that what is manifested in Christ goes on eternally in God.   Jesus really reveals God: that is, he reveals him not as he is in some special circumstances or relations, or toward some special group of his creatures, but as he really is in himself, by virtue of his nature.   He gives us to know the actual God, the only God that ever has been or will be, and shows us that God as Saviour. That Jesus Christ the Saviour is the revealer of God has always been held by Christians, and yet the essential Saviourhood of God, which is necessarily involved in that belief, has been a very slow lesson for Christendom to learn. It is doubted, and even denied, among Christians. Nevertheless, the lesson is the fundamental gift of Christ. If it were not for the essential and eternal Saviourhood of God, there would be no Christendom, and no Christ, and no salvation. But it is true that God, whom no one has ever seen, is truly manifested by the Son, whereby we know that it is his nature to do for his creation such work of holy love and sacrifice as Jesus did among men.

God's motive and impulse toward salvation we can understand from human analogies, however imperfect. Some deadly but fascinating practice has invaded a school and is spreading among the pupils. It will ruin them if it is not checked. The master, a high-minded and faithful man, knows what is going on, and is unspeakably grieved at the evil and indignant at the welcome that it receives. He hates it for itself and for the harm that it is doing: he sees it as at once a vile and a blameworthy thing. He is moved with compassion toward those who are yielding to temptation; moved, too, with eager desire to save the tempters from their deeper sin. He feels the grief of righteousness and the wrath of love, blending in the intolerable desire to save. So with his purity, his righteousness, his grief, his anger and his love mingling in one overmastering passion, he rises in his might to put away the evil and save his pupils. The labour is long and hard and wearisome, but he will not remit an endeavour or avoid a sacrifice: nothing will satisfy him but that at whatever cost he may become an actual saviour. He is happy only in the work. If he could be satisfied without interposing with all his might, he would not be worthy to be entrusted with the care of youth. But he is both worthy and competent, the plague is stayed, and the perishing are saved.

"If ye then, being evil," are not incapable of such a passion, "how much more shall your Father who is in heaven," all-good, be a Saviour?

It has often been held that God, who might save or not as he chose, by his own will became a Saviour to a certain selected part of mankind—as if to a certain class in the school. It is often represented that God in Christ is a Saviour, while God out of Christ is no Saviour. In various ways it has been represented that Christ made God to be a Saviour, or enabled him to act as one, and that Christ in the effect of his work is necessary in order to his continuing to be one. But the Christian doctrine is that Christ reveals God as he really and permanently is; and this means that with reference to salvation the distinction between God in Christ and God out of Christ is not a true distinction. According to the Christian light, there is no God out of Christ, unlike the God whom in Christ we find revealed. The God who is in Christ is the only God there is. And that God of whom Christ is the expression is not one who becomes a Saviour by decree, or makes special selection of those upon whom his Saviourhood may successfully go forth. When God is a Saviour he is simply himself, for his heart is a Saviour's heart. The one God who, as Paul insists, is the same in heart toward Jews and Gentiles is the same toward all creatures. Toward all spirits he holds one attitude as Creator, Father, Friend; and toward all who are sinful he holds the attitude of a God who hates their evil and seeks their good.

This doctrine makes of the Christian gospel, embodied in Jesus Christ, not an exception in the history of the world, or a contrast to God's character, or a contradiction of his method elsewhere, but the crown and culmination of his characteristic work, the supreme expression of his real life. Christian faith has rightly so described it, though Christian thought has often wrongly represented Christianity as a kind of exception. The divine Saviourhood is a necessary part of the true doctrine of monotheism: over against his creation the only God stands as well-wisher and helper for spiritual good, that is, as Saviour.

This statement is true of the entire sum of created being, and of course it is true of the human world. It is not weakened by the fact that men are variously related to him, or that his action toward them all is not the same. Men differ in regard to him, but he himself is not altered by differences in them. We cannot think that God is more a Saviour because men accept him, or less because they ignore him or hate him or have never heard of him. He is the same, he changes not. His servant Augustine was first an infant in a godly mother's arms, then a boy bright but thoughtless, a youth wicked and reckless, a man doubting and faithless, a soul awakened to know the depth of sin, a new-born witness to the eternal love, a Christian learning the way of God, a saint rising to ecstasy in Christ, a brother and friend to many in godliness, an imperfect child of God growing toward perfection. But at every moment of this career God was the same toward him, the Father of his spirit, the Master of the moral order in which he sinned and was perishing, the Saviour who never left or forsook him because of his sin, who delighted to have mercy upon him, and who bore with all his faults while he was leading him to full salvation. This God also was the God of all. Toward all the men of Augustine's day he was at heart the same holy Lord and Saviour, whether they were pagans or Christians, bad or good. They saw him with various eyes, or not at all, but he was One and unchangeable. And so, whatever stages of moral existence humanity or any part of it may at any time be passing through, God is the same always and toward all, Master of the moral order and God with a Saviour's heart. What he does for men must necessarily vary with their condition, but in himself he never changes. His Saviourhood, like his character of Moral Governor, is grounded in his very being.

In this unchanging Saviourhood God bears the sin of the world, in the spirit of redemptive and suffering love. To us, even a little of the evil of the world seems intolerable, when once we feel it for a moment somewhat as it is. But God, knowing it all, bears it all in infinite patience, because of the love in which he seeks to save. On abstract grounds it has been doubted whether God can suffer. Even on such grounds the doubt is needless; but when we learn of Jesus we clearly see how God suffers because of sin. From Jesus we learn, too, that redemptive suffering is the highest bliss. If the objects of one's love can be redeemed from evil only by his suffering for them, there would be no bliss for him except in suffering. Jesus would not have been happy if he had withheld himself from suffering in behalf of those whom he loved; and if we think of God as living in perfect bliss while he is not bearing in love the burdens of his sinful creatures, we are not thinking of the God and Father of Jesus Christ. His eternal bliss is not destroyed by his perpetual suffering for sin, for it is redemptive suffering, and it is as a Saviour that he is bearing it. Since there is sin, Saviourhood with all that it involves is essential to the joy of God.

The fact of Saviourhood stands in harmonious relation with other facts that we know concerning God. The doctrine of a gracious and paternal providence finds solid foundation in this disposition of God, and the idea of a serious and solemn moral government blends harmoniously with that of redemptive love. The darkest doctrine of sin is implied most certainly in the brightest doctrine of salvation; for God's estimate of sin is revealed in his punishing, but still more in his suffering in order to save. The cross of Christ has always been the great revealer of the dreadfulness of sin; and when it appears that the cross of Christ is the cross of God, the revelation stands as ultimate. Sin burdens the heart of the Eternal Goodness, and evokes the redemptive self-sacrifice of God. The fact of essential Saviourhood, too, throws its light upon the entire administration of the world. It implies that God's administration of the life of the human race is a gracious administration. Since he is Saviour, there is redemptive significance in the life of the world. Not looking for it, Christians have not always found it, or believed in it, but it is there. It is no mystery that he could be merciful to men before the death of Christ, for he was then doing in himself the saving work which Christ revealed; nor is it a mystery that he can be merciful now to all men everywhere. He is merciful everywhere and always because he is God: Christ has taught us that this is so.

It is true that we do not know how the Saviourhood, dear to God, has been active and effective toward men in the infantile periods of the race, or how it is operative now where moral and religious perception is very dim or sadly perverted. Of course, we know that all human prayers, to whomsoever addressed, have been heard by one God, and by no other, and that all religious observances, however unworthy of God or man, have gone on in his presence. It is common to think that he regards misdirected prayers and degrading observances with righteous indignation, and that pagan worshippers can obtain from his existence no benefit in connection with their religion. But when we know God through Christ we know that a Saviour's heart has always heard the prayers of men. Humanity, frail as well as sinful, has always been embraced in a redemptive affection. In a good being, even righteous indignation is always attended by compassion and desire to help. So we may be sure that the misdirection of prayers does not shut out the sins of humanity from God's merciful consideration, and that in some manner his saving impulse has found its way into all human life. We are unable to think of any state or stage of humanity as lying outside the realm of his Saviourhood. What Christ has taught us is that in all ages and all worlds God is Saviour, bearing the sins of the universe, and devoted to the producing of goodness where there is sin.

It was the work of Jesus Christ to express the Saviourhood of God, by living it out in a human career of life and death, in order that men might know it, trust it, and be saved. It was in this character, as revealer and bringer of God's salvation, that Jesus was found adorable by the early church. Paul adored the exalted Christ, not because of supernatural signs in the visible world, but because in his face he saw the glory of redeeming love. Here he beheld the genuine supernatural and divine. In this it is our privilege to follow Paul. We, too, know that God was in the person and work of Jesus, not so much because of miraculous signs or special declarations, as because in him we discover and meet the actual God our Saviour. Like the early church we find God in Christ, and therefore we are sure that he is there. The truest spiritual likeness of God that was ever seen by human eyes or hearts is before us in the face of Jesus Christ. In the Saviourhood is the brightness of his glory and the express image of his person. This inward light of God shines out through Jesus, and without this no external certifications of divinity could lead us to adore him. We should mistake, and depend upon inferior evidence, if we rested our recognition of the divinity of Christ upon anything more external than characteristic work. It is in the holy Saviourhood of Jesus that God shines forth. The mystery of God in Christ is not a physical one, as of birth, or a metaphysical, as of the blending of natures: it is a spiritual mystery. The wonder is that in the human Jesus the Saviour God was so revealingly expressed, and the divine heart and will went forth so powerfully in characteristic action. The Saviourhood revealed in Jesus' holiness, love, sin-bearing and transforming power is no other than the Saviourhood of God, and in the unique Saviourhood we find the unique divinity. The divine in Jesus was the God who in him was reconciling the world unto himself. In him, for bodily manifestation, dwelt all the fulness of the Godhead.

In this direction, and not in the opposite, did the reasoning of the early faith proceed. The Church did not infer the divineness of the salvation from the divinity of the Saviour, as modern Christians often think that they must do: it inferred the divinity of the Saviour from the divineness of the salvation. Neither did it argue that God must be found in Jesus because he is there: it inferred that God is in Jesus because he is there so gloriously found. We prove the divinity of Christ:

they beheld it. We have fallen back on intellectual methods:
they built on spiritual experience. We have to own that the
early method was in better keeping with the nature of the
subject than the later. We may argue on metaphysical
grounds that God is in Christ, and we may know the same on
practical religious grounds; and the latter is the more appropriate way of knowing such truth as we are dealing with.
For good cause Jesus Christ has been adored in all human
ages as the human manifestation of God. In him God is at
hand for us men, bringing his whole self near to us. He is
God's way to us and our way to God. When a sinful soul
finds God in Christ, winning, condemning, loving, pardoning,
transforming, he is entering into the true evangelical knowledge of the person of Jesus. Thus so far as any key is in
our hands, Saviourhood is the key to the mystery of the person
of Christ. Doctrinal statements have sought to solve the
mystery; but we should deceive ourselves if we were to suppose that any doctrinal explanation has ever made the matter
plain, and certainly the explanations have often called us
away from the spiritual to the metaphysical interest. Language easily becomes too clear, analysis is too definite, and
the mystery eludes us. Our hope is rather in large and
mystical views of the most vital of experiences. It is God
as a living and loving Spirit that Christ makes known, and it
is in the gracious work for men that we behold him. When
we look at Jesus we remember that human nature was created
receptive of God, and can receive him into itself in any
degree of fulness that he may will, but that we shall never
know in detail the manner of his indwelling; and we perceive
that in Jesus, for the good of men, God is present in such
fulness as we find nowhere else, so that he stands revealed as
the God that he really is. Not by analysis, but by discernment of God, may we hope to gain some resolution of the
mystery of the person of Christ.

Not in Jesus alone is the Christian expression of God as
Saviour found, but in the Holy Spirit also. Our conception of

God as Saviour would not be complete, or even Christian, if it did not recognize that gracious and powerful indwelling which the early Church celebrated with the deepest reverence and joy. He who in Jesus came seeking to save prosecutes his endeavour in the Spirit who bears the divine message and puts forth the divine power within the living soul. This Spirit is himself, God within. It is thus that the divine Saviour carries his desired work to actual effect in the individual and in the race. The work of the Spirit brings in all holy renewing influence, the fruit of the Spirit consists in all that belongs to worthy character and life, and it is in the production of such character and life that salvation consists. It is an ethical salvation, as the salvation of such a God must be. Rightly is the Spirit who fulfils it called the Holy Spirit, for it is a holy ethical work, placing good where evil was, in the entire life of man. God, through Christ, by the Holy Spirit, is normalizing men, bringing his children to the proper life and character of sons. The work of Christ and the Spirit has its natural place in the order of the world, since God's Saviourhood is a natural and appropriate part of his relation to his human creatures.

The Christian doctrine proclaims Saviourhood in God, and declares it to be an essential fact in his nature. Of necessity therefore it proclaims that he is eternally a Saviour. He changes never. In the light of Christ we perceive that he stands toward his universe the same from everlasting to everlasting, a hater of sin and a holy helper of his creatures. When we see the Saviourhood located so to speak in his very self, we see that it can be no function of a passing period, but abides forever. When we discern him thus in the Christian light, we wonder whether he will ever perfectly accomplish the desire of heart. We long to know whether, as we have supposed, there are causes in his universe from which there can come disappointment to the infinite love, or whether Saviourhood will perfectly have its way in the abolishment of sin and the bringing of all souls to their worthy destiny.

This question is always current in the world of thoughtful men. Often it is thought to have been decided, by revelation, or by reason, or by unconquerable moral convictions, but it opens itself again, and we cannot long neglect it.

As free children of God we certainly are not forbidden to entertain the question of final destinies, but much as it has been discussed we do not find ourselves in a position to dogmatize upon it. The problem has been both enlarged and altered for us by our enlarged acquaintance with mankind, and by the clarifying and exalting of our conceptions of God. But in the relation between God and human life there are some essential elements that we do not fully understand. Sometimes it seems beyond doubt that God in his marvellous gift of freedom has bestowed upon man the power to wreck himself beyond recovery; and sometimes again we are scarcely able to doubt that the faithful Creator has kept in his own good hands the ultimate spiritual power over the destiny of his creation. Direct evidence as to the lodgment of such final control we do not possess. The breadth of our hope is due to what we know of God, and the depth of our fear to what we know of man. The human world looks dark with fear, and the divine reality bright with hope. It is natural and right that such hope should gradually rise above such fear; but the hope, if it is worthy, depends not upon tangible evidence, but upon spiritual faith alone. We trust the world to God, who is at once the righteous Lord and the everlasting Saviour.

7. TRINITY

Although it has not been so done, there appears to be conclusive reason for considering the doctrine of the Trinity here, under the head of the relations of God with men. The reason is that it is a doctrine of religion. Its foundations were laid in the relation that God sustains to men as their Saviour, and it was in connection with the divine Saviourhood that the doctrine received its later development and has had its age-long vitality. In its origin and history the doctrine of the

Trinity has its vital connections almost solely with the doctrine and experience of salvation. In fact, it might fairly be
treated as a development of the doctrine of God as Saviour.
If we are to give it its right position as a religious doctrine
concerning God, it is necessary to view it in the region where
it arose and has had its significance and efficiency.

The doctrine may be approached through one of the earliest
expressions that suggest it. At the end of his second letter
to the Corinthians Paul wrote, "The grace of the Lord Jesus
Christ, and the love of God, and the communion of the Holy
Spirit, be with you all" (2 Cor. xiii. 14).

The genuineness of this prayer in the apostle's soul is beyond question. He was speaking out of experience, and in-
voking the gifts that were characteristic of the Christian life.
His prayer unfolded and interpreted the experience that he
and his readers had in Christ. The grace of the Lord Jesus
Christ, in whose cross he gloried and whose heavenly gifts
were making all things new, had opened to him and them the
infinite riches of the love of God, and introduced them to the
unspeakably precious communion of the Holy Spirit. This
indeed was the Christian experience—Christ bringing home
to his people God's love and the Spirit's fellowship; and Paul
was praying for his readers that in them this work of blessing
might go on. In this prayer he invoked Christianity upon
them. It is all here, and here is the supreme work of God in
religion. The grace that is in Christ does bring to glorious
effect in men the love of God and the communion of the Spirit,
and the best good of life is the result. This, too, is the characteristic order of Christianity: first Christ the revealer, then
God revealed in his love, then the Spirit, whose home is the soul.

This prayer, so truly Christian, seems certainly to have
sprung from experience. The light that it gives upon
Christian truth comes to us as a revelation through life. It
is to be noticed how perfectly informal it is. It has none of
the qualities of a doctrinal formula, and it does not seem to
imply any formula of the Trinity present in the author's

mind. It does not appear to be based upon what we call the baptismal formula, "Baptizing them into the name of the Father, and of the Son, and of the Holy Spirit" (Mt. xxviii. 19). The names do not correspond, for instead of the Father we here have God, and instead of the Son we have the Lord Jesus Christ. Nor does the order correspond, for here the Second of the baptismal formula stands first, and the First stands second. Moreover, the titles that are given to the Second instead of Son—namely, Jesus, Christ and Lord—are not derived from relations in the Godhead, but all come from his human history and relations. If the baptismal formula, bearing the Master's authority, had been present as a trinitarian norm of new doctrine in the apostle's mind, it is difficult to see how his thought and language could have been so flexible and variant from the standard. The free form and experimental character of this epoch-making benediction make us sure that it sprang forth original from the apostle's mind, as a prayer that amounted to an epitome of the Christian faith. Thus he had learned the Christian grace, and thus he now invoked it.

Here, we scarcely need to say, there are recalled three relations of God to men—revealing, revealed and abiding. The relations are not abstract but practical: in these three ways writer and readers were having to do with God. They had to do with Christ revealing God, with God as Christ revealed him, and with God as Christ had brought them home to him. These three were not only relations of one and the same God, but they were relations that concerned the saving of men, and were known through the experience of salvation. Grace in Christ, love in God, communion of the Spirit—in these salvation dwelt, and one Saviour was in them all.

This benediction fairly represents the early Christian records, for Christ, God and the Spirit appear in essentially the same light throughout. The names applied to them are indeed varied in many ways. The names Father and Son are freely used. Father is a frequent name for God, and he is recorded as Father both to Christ and to men. Jesus, known from his lifetime as the Son of God, is now adored, especially in Paul's enraptured vision, as the Son of God in the heavenly glory. The divine Spirit indwelling and sanctifying is the joy of the Church. But in all its variety the vision of God is practical. All thought of Father, Son and Spirit moves within the circle of salvation. It is in the experience of salvation that Christians know the Father and the Spirit, and that experience has been entered through fellowship with the Son. Very significant is the fact that the name given to the Spirit contains the adjective holy—the Holy Spirit. The Spirit existing in the eternal Godhead no one would ever dream of calling holy: that epithet requires the atmosphere of an unholy world to be born in. It is a name due to the experience of sin. Throughout the Epistles Christ is Lord in heavenly glory and in present life, God is Father to Christ and to men, and the Spirit is the cleansing and comforting God within. These three stand forth as one in redemptive work and grace toward men. There is no mystery about their oneness, and no attempt to show that there are three in one, or even a statement that the three are one. The word Trinity is never used, and there is no indication that the idea of Trinity had taken form. It has long been a common practice to read the New Testament as if the ideas of a later age upon this subject were in it, but they are not. In the days of the apostles the doctrine of the Trinity was yet to be created. But the materials for it were already there, and the occasion for the growth of the doctrine was sure to arise. The Christian people were adoring God, and Christ, and the Holy Spirit, not at first in identical manner, yet really, and from the heart. Of course, therefore, the time would come when this threefold adoration must be explained and justified. Not less certainly would the time come when so familiar and heartfelt a reality as this threefold adoration must take effect upon the doctrinal structure of Christian thought.

When that time came, after the lapse of three or four centuries, there was wrought out a doctrine of the Trinity which

became, after a period of conflict, the accepted belief of the
Christian people. This historic doctrine differed widely from
the simplicity of the early faith. It moved in a new region,
it employed new methods, and it required a new kind of
belief, for it was now a metaphysical doctrine concerning
the interior nature and life of God. But it must not be forgotten that in the framing of this deep doctrine the aim was still
practical. Doubtless the love of dialectical discussion grew
keen about it, but in the forming of the doctrine there was no
seeking of abstractions for their own sake. Even in its most
difficult forms the doctrine of the Trinity always held true
rank as a doctrine of religion. Its existence was due to the
fact that the Church was still endeavouring to understand and
justify her Christian experience. It is too often forgotten,
but it is true, that the motive in the construction of the historical doctrine of the Trinity was the desire of the Church to
justify her adoration of her Saviour, and to ground his salvation in the eternal reality of God. The resulting doctrine
carried its positive affirmations far into the mystery of the
Godhead, and often appeared to lose connection with human
interests, but the separation was only apparent. In the
entire endeavour the Church was seeking eternal foundations
for her most precious faith.

In theological construction the starting-point in the doctrine of the Trinity is usually the Father, but in history the
starting-point was the Son. Christ, glorious with the light of
divine love and holiness, known on earth and adored in
heaven as Son of God, was so full of grace and truth that men
not only learned the Father from him but beheld the Father
in him. How did the fulness of the Godhead dwell thus in
him, to be discovered there by men? and by what endowment could he be the bringer of very God to men for their
salvation? The answer was that God was in him really, and
not in some secondary sense: the very essence of the Godhead
was a constituent of his personality. Just as truly as human
nature was in him, so truly was divine. Divine nature and
human were not thought to be alike, but both were equally in

Jesus.   Not indeed, the doctrine said, that incarnation into humanity is possible to God absolute and unconditioned.   Humanity could not contain him, nor would the position of one incarnate be congruous with his relations or his nature.   But there exists forever in the Godhead a Son, identified with the Word that was declared to have become flesh and dwelt among us.   His relation to the Father is somewhat analogous to that of man, and he is in some sense akin to humanity, which was created in his likeness.   The Son is incarnable, and he has entered into closest union with human nature in the person of Jesus.   Therefore it is that Jesus is inherently worthy to receive such honour as the Church gives him, and that his salvation is the very salvation of God.   He is worthy to be adored, and mighty to save, because God the Son is an element in the constitution of his person.   Thus the Christian faith is justified, and an eternal foundation is placed underneath the Christian experience.

From the starting-point in the Son, interpretative thought reached out in both directions.   On the one hand it made its affirmations concerning the Father.   As the titles indicate, the Father was recognized as the source of the Son, though in a manner higher than that of creation.   The Son was uncreated, of the Father's very self, mysteriously and eternally generated from his being.   The Father was God original, eternally self-manifesting through the Son alone, expressed by the Son in humanity.   In the Father first was all that belongs to divine being, and all that was brought by the Son to men.   Thus the salvation that had been received through Christ was grounded beyond Christ, and beyond the eternal Son, in God the Father, source of all.   And on the other hand interpretative thought took hold upon the divine Spirit, the third known form of Godhead.   Experience of indwelling God was as real as evidence of incarnate God.   The Spirit, the abiding agent in salvation, must be as divine as the Father, and it was only natural that the Spirit should be recognized within the Godhead, as the Son was.   It is true that the relation of the Spirit in the Godhead was never so clearly expounded as that of the Son, for it was not a relation that was capable of such exposition; and yet the Spirit was firmly held to be the Third with the Father and the Son in the eternal Being. The forthcoming God in Christ corresponded to one eternal distinction in the Godhead, and the abiding and restoring God the Spirit corresponded to another. Thus the daily experience of the Christian life, as well as the work of grace in Christ, was grounded in eternal reality.

The doctrine that was thus formed retained the name that had been growing into use, and was called the doctrine of the Trinity. But the name was never a true one. That which was adopted in the fifth century was not a doctrine of Trinity, but of Triunity. It was not merely the existence of the eternal Three that was affirmed: it was affirmed that the Three eternally constituted the unity of God. In the one God there existed Father, Son and Spirit, which three were declared necessary to the making up of that unity wherein God is forever perfect. It is plain that in such a doctrine the element of unity was as essential as that of trinity: indeed, it was the element of unity alone that gave it standing as a Christian doctrine. Trinity without unity would have been explicit tritheism, which would have been polytheism; and by no possibility could plain tritheism have been admitted among the ideas of Christianity. As a matter of fact, the historic doctrine absolutely repudiated all charges of tritheism, and made the strongest affirmation of the unity of the God in whom trinity inhered. How much truer to fact it would have been if the accepted doctrine had been called the doctrine of Triunity, and how many misunderstandings and confusions might thus have been avoided! One practical testimony to the propriety of such nomenclature is at hand. Agelong though the use of the word Trinity has been, no one has ever ventured to be so consistent in the use of terms as to speak of the trine God. But adoration of the triune God has been perpetual.

It is evident that there must be difficulty in defining and defending a doctrine of genuine triunity in God, and the difficulty has never been unfelt. There is no difficulty about preserving the threeness, when once it has been admitted to thought, but there is great difficulty in preserving along with it the unity. The danger of tritheism is very great, and probably at all stages of the history the popular belief in the Trinity has approached nearer to a tritheistic belief than the teachers and preachers knew. From the early days of the doctrine until now, the Three in the Godhead have been called Persons, the doctrine affirming three Persons in one God. The name was helpful in the ancient time when it bore a looser and more flexible meaning; but at present, amid the more clear-cut conceptions of personality that are current now, to speak and sing of "God in three Persons" is to give distinct encouragement to tritheistic belief. It must be confessed that there has been too much in the history of Christian teaching to encourage such belief. The Three have often been represented as consulting together, sometimes in "the council-chamber of the Trinity," as making mutual covenants among themselves, and as exerting influence upon one another, in ways that necessarily implied separate wills and sometimes involved differences in character. When a covenant is posited between members of the Trinity, or one exerts influence upon another with reference to the salvation of men, it is impossible to keep a clear and vital sense of the unity of God. Nor has the doctrine been used in such a manner as to free it from its difficulties. For ages this most abstract of the doctrines has been held as the test of orthodoxy, and this has inevitably led to a preciseness in defining that is not justified by the nature of the subject. Moreover, since the unity of God is naturally easier to hold and the trinity more difficult, there has been a tendency to insist more upon the threeness than upon the oneness, lest it should be less esteemed than it deserves. There has been little stress placed upon the unity of God, in comparison with the labour that has been given to defence and exposition of the Trinity.

Nevertheless no remembrance of the difficulties in theory or in practice should be allowed to make us unmindful of the great religious significance of the doctrine. Though speculation has often lost itself in the mystery of God, the doctrine has had abundant vitality in the region of God's relations with men and their salvation. It has been held as the indispensable and sufficient key for explaining the unique divineness of all that pertains to Jesus Christ in his person, his work and his salvation. Despite its mysteriousness, it has made God seem more intelligible to men, and has helped to bring him nearer to the hearts of his children. By its declaration of the real entrance of God into humanity and the taking of manhood up into God, it has placed a crown of glory upon human nature, and has helped in giving practical effect to the dignity and freedom of man. This is its glory, that it has stood as a foundation that sustained the faith of ages and supported a worthy life.

Accordingly it is here and only here, in the field of divine-human relations, that the doctrine of the Trinity has been a strongly vital doctrine. It has been a vital doctrine, powerful even when perplexing, tenacious in its hold upon the heart, in so far as it served as a means of understanding the gospel and justifying the faith in which is salvation; but beyond this field it has not been the prominent element in theology that we might expect it to be. Christian theology has treated it as a specialty of the Christian religion, maintaining that the triunity of God, though groped after in thought by the nations of the world, could never have been known if it had not been for the Christian revelation. There are various departments of Christian thought in which it has no place. Natural Theology has never discovered it. In our Apologetics and general Theism we rejoice that we can claim that God is personal, but we are satisfied with that, and do not undertake to show that he is tripersonal. The doctrine does not appear, and could not well be made use of, in the consideration of Omnipresence, Omniscience or Omnipotence, of Sovereignty, Moral Government or Providence. It has usually been allowed no more than a remote connection with the doctrine of the general

Fatherhood of God towards men. It bears no part in the doctrine of Holiness. It has sometimes been offered as a means of showing how God is Love eternally in himself, apart from all relations and without depending upon creation for an object of his love. But the idea of an internally social God, having within himself an interchange of love, has not very widely commended itself as reconcilable with an intelligible unity; for if we think of two as loving each other, we must soon find it hard to feel that they are one. Triunity has sometimes been proposed as a key to the understanding of self-consciousness in God; Father, Son and Spirit corresponding to subject, object and their unity, which are thought to be facts constituent of self-consciousness in man. But the suggestion has not proved clear and vital enough to establish for itself a permanent place in Christian Theism, and probably has no better future. The agency of the eternal Son in creation, suggested by what is said of the Logos in Jn. i. 3, and by similar passages, has generally been formally accepted on the authority of those statements; but it has not rendered the doctrine of creation more intelligible or more vital than the first words of the Bible make it. Thus the doctrine of the Trinity is absent from large regions of Christian thought. It is only when it is employed as an interpretation of the Christian experience and a justification of the Christian faith on the ground of eternal reality that the doctrine of the Trinity stands forth as a doctrine of living power. This is its sphere of life; and no sublimer tribute to the greatness of salvation could be paid than this, that the very conception of God was reconsidered and reconstructed to establish it upon an adequate foundation.

We desire to know what view of God with reference to Triunity best corresponds at the present time to the revelation that we owe to Jesus Christ. We can easily ascertain what has formerly been thought, but we shall be glad if we can discover what we ought now to think. On this subject as on others it may be that we ought to preserve ancient doctrine, and it may be that we ought to modify it. In what direction does the Christian light lead us now?

One thing is certain. The Christian light and the light of modern knowledge agree perfectly in leading us to a genuine and unalterable monotheism. The Hebrew prophets declared that the one God is the God of all, and Christianity took up their proclamation with a broader sense of its meaning. There was monotheistic thought in the world outside of early Christianity, but it was in the spirit of religion and at the same time of growing intelligence that Christianity proclaimed the soleness and universality of God. With the Christian faith all polytheism, even though it be no more than tritheism, is absolutely inconsistent. It scarcely needs to be said that to the same monotheistic belief the light of modern knowledge leads. The universe is one, and God is one. One God, one mind, one will—this is the only form in which any belief in God whatever is possible in the world as we know it now. Many think, indeed, that no belief in God at all is possible at present; but the Christian faith rises to the recognition of one mind and will, adequate to the operation and control of the entire system of existence. Thus old faith and new knowledge agree that by the existence of God can be meant nothing else than the existence of a single mind, with one all-embracing consciousness and a single will. If there is any God, he is such a God as this. For this we argue in our Apologetics, and to this we must be faithful in our doctrine. As to the personality of the one God, as we have said already, it is the perfection of that personal type of being which has begun to be developed in mankind. He is the complete person, in whom the powers that are essential to our human personality exist in perfection. This we say, although how far this personal description of God after the likeness of men falls short of the reality we do not know. Yet the highest that we do know is that God is personal; and when we have said this we have said that in the modern sense of the term God is one person, and not more than one. Of this there can be no doubt. The three Persons of the Trinity are Persons in an ancient sense of the word, but not in the modern sense. And what we affirm of God is that the one divine Person sustains one all-comprehensive relation to all existence that is not himself, and is absolutely competent to the fulfilling of that relation in all its forms. This is monotheism, and this is the only possible theism. In early Christianity such broad monotheism was beginning to be proclaimed as a conclusion from the Christian revelation: it is now affirmed both in the light of the Christian revelation and as a necessity of all theistic thought.

The recognition of such a God—a single mind and will, competent to all activities that the universe can require—must inevitably modify doctrines that were formed when the conception of God was not so broad and simple. The competence of the one mind to all purposes, of the one heart to all needs, and of the one will to all works, may be expected, when once accepted, to clarify and simplify our ideas of God's operation toward his creatures. When we behold one personal Mind adequate to all works, some of our doctrines will change their form. What might thus be expected is in fact coming to pass. The changes in modern theology are due to this broadening and simplifying of the thought of God, and to more Christian conceptions of his character. What is taking place in other fields of doctrine is occurring also with respect to the doctrine of the Trinity. The existing tendency has not yet come to formulation, but the movement is going on, and must be recognized in a study of the doctrine of God. The modern conception of God is providing in other forms what was provided in the days of a different theism by the doctrine of an eternal Trinity in the Godhead; which is as much as to say that the Christian Theism of the present time is absorbing the doctrine of the Trinity into itself, and making provision for its beneficent work in ways of its own. The doctrine of the Trinity is not destroyed but fulfilled by the doctrine of God which is succeeding to its place. Without the necessity of differentiations in his

Being, the one divine Mind and Will is capable of doing all that has been accounted for by the doctrine of Triunity.

If we begin to confirm this statement by considering the doctrine of the Father, there is but little that needs to be said. No great change is involved in the taking up of the trinitarian doctrine of the Father into the general doctrine of God. It has not been held that only a certain part or element in God was the Father in the Trinity, or that there was need of differentiation within the Godhead in order that God might be adapted to that which the name Father denotes. In the Trinity, according to the ancient doctrine, the Father is God himself, original, complete, unmodified, possessed of all powers and qualities that can be affirmed of God. The whole God is there, anterior, in our way of speaking, to those differentiations of his being which are suited to the works of incarnation and indwelling. According to the doctrine, the Son and the Spirit add nothing to the fulness which the Father has eternally in himself: rather are they expressions or unfoldings of that infinite fulness. If we could set forth all that the historic doctrine attributes to the Father, we should be setting forth all that is conceived to be true of God; and the doctrine simply affirms that his fulness is developed as it were, or brought into relations and modes of action, in the Son and the Spirit. So if we say, in the manner of more modern thought, that God himself is the Father, and is able to do directly all that the Father has been declared to do, we are not departing from the ancient doctrine, but are only repeating its testimony. There is no need to show by what changes of thought the doctrine of the Father in the Trinity is taken up into the general doctrine of God, for in this instance there scarcely are changes. The two conceptions are already one.

The doctrine of the Trinity, or rather of the Triunity, was formed, however, as we have seen, not for explanation of God, or for the establishment of the doctrine of the Father, but for interpretation of Christ and vindication of the faith in him. Triunity in God was received as the ground of the reverence which the Church felt herself justified in giving, and constrained to give, to her exalted Saviour. The underlying question was a practical one. Experience bore witness that God was in Christ reconciling the world unto himself. Christ's work was God's work, his Saviourhood the very Saviourhood of God. The glory of Jesus as men beheld him, full of grace and truth, was divine glory, and was as the glory of one only-begotten from a Father (Jn. i. 14). He was known as the forthshining of God's glory and the express image of his substance (Heb. i. 3): in him dwelt all the fulness of the Godhead bodily (Col. ii. 9), and he that had seen him had seen the Father (Jn. xiv. 9). God, in fact, was manifested through him in nobler and dearer characters than had been known before, and in Jesus men found themselves actually becoming acquainted with him. Thus real and definite was the evidence of God in Christ to the Christian heart. But how was this possible? How came God to be so really in Jesus as the Christians were finding him to be? For Jesus was human, too, born of a woman, brother to man, subject to death. It was as a man living among men that he had been known, and it was in his human life that God had been so marvellously revealed.

The Church accepted the true answer, to the effect that both elements were real, the divine and the human, and neither was a fiction. God was actually in and with the human nature, and was revealed where men had read the revelation. At the same time Jesus was really and truly human, not a mere shadow or seeming of humanity, as some Christians felt that reverence for his divinity required them to believe. The Church was right in discerning in him the presence of divine and human, God and man, both manifest in a single person. The evidence that both are there is found not so much by reasoning or analysis, or in special claims concerning him or declarations as to what he is, as in the experimental fact that in all Christian ages God and man have both been discovered in him. In him manhood is glorified, and in him God revealed shines forth, visible as nowhere else in the beauty of love and holiness.

Explanation of this glorious revealing mystery was undertaken under the silent influence of two presuppositions, apart from which the resulting belief cannot be justly estimated. One was that the personality of Jesus was to be understood by the aid of analysis, searching into his being and discerning the elements of which it was composed. The other was that the essence of divine nature and of human are profoundly unlike each other. Under the influence of these ideas two differing natures were believed to be in the one person Jesus; and this meant that there were present in him the two spiritual substances or essences in which the two natures were held to consist. The method of analysis resulted thus. As for definition of these two natures, the essence of his humanity needed not to be specially defined; for however mysterious it may be, human nature is so familiar that it was enough to describe him as possessing the humanity that is common to the race. But the divine element needed more defining. It was not the Father, but the eternal Son, or the Word expressive and revelatory, that was adapted to entrance into humanity and identification with a human person. He entered into the person Jesus, or became united in him with human nature, and thus brought the substance of Deity to coexist in him with the substance of humanity. Of course so materialistic a word as substance does partial injustice to the thought; but the teaching was that the spiritual reality by virtue of which God is God and the spiritual reality by virtue of which man is man were present, and united, in Jesus. How the two natures blended, being so profoundly unlike, no one could tell; but the mystery of the person was accepted as a part of the mystery of God, and has enhanced rather than diminished the reverence that was given to Christ.

One effect of modern study has been to give new light upon these two presuppositions. The first of them relates to the manner in which personality is to be searched out and understood, and leads, in the case of Jesus, to reliance upon analysis of the personal constitution. But no one now seeks to understand personality by seeking to know of what stuff or substance it is composed. No one knows, so as to describe or define it, anything about that which is the substratum of personality, the material, so to speak, in which the personal life is grounded. It is perceived that personality is not to be understood by analysis of what it consists in. We know nothing about the essence of spiritual being, human or divine, and cannot depend upon definitions that are made in terms of it. There is a more excellent way, more intelligible and more effective. Personality is now understood by means of its expressions, and it is well recognized that through these we are to learn about it all that we can know. Not the constitution of the person, but the manifestation of the person, convinces us of what he is. We do not argue that a man is a man because he is humanly constituted: we know that he is a man because he acts humanly. We do not conclude that God is personal because we can tell what is the essence of his personality, but because we behold works of God that imply self-consciousness and self-direction. Thus we obtain our conception of a personal being not from what he is composed of, but from what he does. His self-expressions are our evidence.

Under this influence, when we approach Jesus we are led to speak of his person in view not of the essence of his being, but of his expression of himself. If we really find anything unique in the person of Jesus, we shall find it in his self-expressions, the manifestations of his inward being It is in life and character that we are to learn what the person is. If God is to be expressed in him, God, we know, will be expressed in character and the work of character. So it comes to pass that we seek the divine in Jesus not in the metaphysical constitution of his being, upon which we can never obtain clear light, but in character worthy of God, in evidence of fellowship or moral unity with God, in purpose, standard of life, holiness, love, righteousness, redemptive aim; for in these the divine can normally find expression in the human, God in man. If we do not find God thus practically revealed in Jesus, a doctrine of his divinity built upon a metaphysical analysis of his person will not be a spiritual or religious doctrine. But in this field of moral, spiritual, practical manifestation we not only seek but find the divine in Jesus. God is there. The long testimony of ages is true, that in seeing him men have seen the Father.

The second of the two presuppositions assumes a deep unlikeness between human nature and divine. In the ancient doctrine the two were held to be so profoundly different that they could only exist side by side in the person of Jesus—or if they blended, it was in a manner essentially mysterious to the human mind. But it has come to pass in these later days that believers in God do not affirm this deep unlikeness in nature between him and men. It is very true that in the abstract or metaphysical realm we are not competent to dogmatize as to the hidden nature of either. But even here we have come to the conviction that spirit must be essentially like unto spirit everywhere; and it is certain that the spirit that we find expressed in the universe is of a nature kindred to our own. Meanwhile, under the influence of Jesus himself, religious thought has come to the definite conviction that in spiritual nature God and man are much more alike than men have supposed. "Forasmuch as we are the offspring of God" it is in no unreal sense that we are said to bear his likeness. In the Christian light the idea of essential contrast and incompatibility between the divine and the human has gradually faded away. Jesus has impressed the world that incarnation, or real entrance of God into humanity, of which many peoples have dreamed, is no mere dream, but is something of which God and man are capable; and if it proves true that incarnation is not a matter for close defining, that is only because the truth involved is too large and mystical for definition, and makes no difference in the strength of the conviction that Jesus has imparted. Any degree of possession or inhabitation of human nature by God is within his normal field of working. And human and divine are not so unlike each other that they must flow like parallel streams through a single life. Each is capable of receiving and expressing the other.

In the light of these considerations we look at Jesus—not at his person, technically regarded, but at himself. We are prepared to see divine and human expressed in one person and life, and it is in view of what the personality has done that we expect to judge of what nature it is. As a matter of fact, we find in Jesus a manifestation of God so great and clear that from him men have learned what God invisible must be like; and the conception of God that he has imparted has commended itself to the best faith and love and judgment of mankind. This is the best evidence that God was in him and was working in him for the good of men—evidence better than either miracles or metaphysics could give. We cannot define what in him is divine and what is human, which indeed no one has ever been able to do, but in the manifestation of the personality we read the personality: in the human expression we read the man, and in the manifestation of God we see God. God is there, and we know it because he has spoken and acted there: he has looked out through the eyes of Jesus, beaming his own character upon the world. He has expressed his own purity, his tenderness toward his creatures, and his redemptive grace. He has shown us his sorrow over our sins, his love for our souls, and his patient will to save. God was in Christ visible, audible and knowable, and we have seen and heard and known him there.

What we know of God reminds us that there was here no need of limitation or differentiation of his being, save as he always limits himself in dealing with his worlds. It is God himself who can make humanity his temple. God who has made man in his own likeness can fill him with his own fullness. It is God who can incarnate himself. He is capable of all relations with his universe for which its needs may call, and his relation to human nature in the person of Jesus is no exception. God himself, whose personality, in our sense of the word, is a single personality is sufficient to account for all that we have seen, and justify all our adoration, of God in Christ. It is in this manner that the present doctrine of God, sole, single and all-competent, takes up or absorbs into itself this part of the ancient doctrine of the Triunity.

When we come to speak of the doctrine of the Holy Spirit as taken up likewise into the general doctrine of God, there is no need of many words. Time was when God was regarded as transcendent in his greatness and purity, and it was not easy to think of him as in closest intimacy with sinful men. The helpful indwelling Spirit was a messenger of God; and when this sanctifying Friend was accounted to be of the Godhead, he was regarded as not the Father or the Son, but a Third, coördinate with these and acting in the line of their redemptive purpose. Very naturally then the Spirit was spoken of as sent forth from God, and as coming from him to men. The long-familiar figurative language tells of the mission of the Spirit, the coming of the Spirit, the outpouring of the Spirit, and the Spirit as representing the Father and the Son. These expressions, consecrated by long use, have outlasted the modes of Theism under the influence of which they were born. At present we have a clearer and diviner thought. Though we may still speak of God as sending his Spirit to us, we are well aware that the language is inherited from a bygone mode of picturing divine realities, and not the language of our present Christian life. God is not afar that he should send to us, any more than he is overhead that he should pour his Spirit out upon us. There is no need that he should be represented in our souls. "God is not so far away as even to be near." It is a vital truth in our doctrine that God himself is the indweller. He himself moves upon the souls that he has created, and abides in the very secret of their life. The profoundest and most inseparable indwelling with men best consummates the relation in which he and they exist. This perfect inhabitation of human souls by himself is what he is seeking to bring to pass: all that he has done through Christ is one long endeavour to this end. And our Christian faith rises to meet Christ's revelation, that God himself is adequate to all the indwelling that his creatures can ever receive. God himself does all that has ever been attributed to the eternal Spirit, for God himself is the Spirit. Gracious and redemptive inhabitation of human life is natural to him who is Creator, Father, Saviour, Lord. There is not less divine indwelling than the ancient doctrine has affirmed, but more, but it is indwelling of God. "I will dwell in them" (2 Cor. vi. 16) is a true word, without diminution.

We have reason to welcome this truth, for the divine Spirit has always offered the point of greatest difficulty in the historic doctrine. Father and Son in God have been found distinguishable, but it has proved difficult to tell what the eternal Spirit is, in equality and correlation with them, and bound with them into the perfect unity. So hard is the problem that it has been considered especially important to insist especially upon the personality of the Spirit, lest it should be lost sight of. But the difficulty would not now arise. With our present conception we can say that what Christians have called the Holy Spirit is God in his people, working in them more freely and richly because of the fresh means of influence that he has provided for himself in Christ. It is his nature to inhabit the human soul, and it is normal for the human soul to be inhabited by him, and as the Holy Spirit God always holds communion with mankind. God is the Holy Spirit. The Holy Spirit is not merely God's influence, but God himself, and his personality is the personality of God. In this manner this part also of the doctrine of the Trinity is taken up into the doctrine of God which the present age is finding clear and precious. For all works God suffices. God himself is the Father, God himself is the divine in Jesus Christ, and God himself is the Holy Spirit.

In this change the substance of the ancient conception of Three in One does not perish, although its form is altered.

The Christian experience from which the doctrine of the Trinity sprang is the same in its essential nature now as at first. We know the three relations of God to men, and have the whole God in them all. Still do we meet upon our way that grace of the Lord Jesus Christ by means of which we learn the love of God and find the communion of the Holy Spirit. Christ brings us the grace that ministers salvation, we live at home in our Father's redeeming love, and the friendship of the Spirit is our comfort and joy. Amid all variations, this is a true account of that Christian experience which has found sublime interpretation in the doctrine of the Trinity, and from this character the Christian experience will never depart. God self-manifesting will still make known his own eternal love and give his present helpful fellowship. We still have God as Father, we still have God in Christ, and we still have God the Holy Spirit.

There are three types of religion that correspond in a measure to the Three of the historic doctrine. There is natural religion, or the religion of God as he is known in the order of the world. There is historical religion, or religion that finds its support in the historical manifestations of God in events of time. And there is personal religion, spiritual, experimental, mystical, that knows God in the soul. "The heavens declare the glory of God" (Ps. xix. 1): "God was in Christ reconciling the world unto himself" (2 Cor. v. 19): "The Spirit beareth witness with our spirit, that we are children of God" (Rom. viii. 16). Many religions have known something of this variety, but these expressions represent the forms in which it is known to the Christian experience. The types when really separate are very unlike each other, and the unity in this variety has not always been plain. An adorer of God in nature may not feel the need of historical revelations or conscious experiences to confirm his faith. One who rests upon historical certainties may feel that nature is insufficient and experience untrustworthy. One who glories in the inward light of God may consider himself independent both of natural and of historical revealing. Doubtless this variety will continue in some measure, while men are as varied as they are, but the all-embracing harmony needs to be more deeply felt. The Christian testimony declares that these three types of religion are one. In each there is true revelation. God is forthshining in the universe, God is self-revealing in the historical work of holy love, and God is self-imparting in the inward life of men. In all these God is one, though variously manifested; and the worthiest religion will not set one form against another, but will learn to delight itself in the one glory thrice revealed, and to be lovingly content while others rejoice in the visions that are less dear to one's own soul. Such comprehensive faith in the real Triunity, comes as the gift of grace and the growth of time.

In this view of the Trinity, it is good to see the two Fatherhoods melting into each other. According to the common doctrine, when we sing, "Praise Father, Son and Holy Ghost," and pray, "Our Father who art in heaven," we really speak of two Fatherhoods, not of one; for in the doctrine of the Trinity the Father is God original, back of all revealing, while in the Lord's Prayer he is God with us and within us, who knows our wants, hears our prayer and forgives our sins. One Fatherhood belongs to God remotest from us, and the other to God nearest to us—an anomaly that has often been perplexing. We cannot help trusting the most intimate use of the name as right, for we owe it to the Son who alone has such knowledge of the Father as to be able to reveal him; (Mt. xi. 27) and as our Father he has revealed him. Most gladly, therefore, may we welcome the dawning of a single Fatherhood. In the Christian light as we behold it now, God is Father to the unique Son who makes him known, Father to those who have entered the conscious fellowship of his spiritual family, and Father to all spirits, in natural relation and in faithful heart.

8. GOD IN HUMAN LIFE

Our view of God in relations with men must not close without mention of God as he is manifested in actual human life, inner and outer, personal and collective. We must show how men have to do with him in whatever life they live.

God the communicating Spirit always has to do with the inner life of men. What has been said already may be recalled—that moral requirements in the soul represent God and his claim of right and duty; that the moral judgment is his witness within; that the voice of conscience self-judging with approval or condemnation is his voice; and that all ethical instructions, when they enter the soul, come as part of his discipline, weighted with his authority and the seriousness that he gives to life. In this contact with the inner life God is strict and holy, and at the same time gracious and helpful. He who is manifested in the gospel as delighting to pardon does delight to pardon, and has always pardoned when the gift could be received. God in the universal inner life is the holy friend of man.

It is difficult, however, to think broadly enough of God. Sometimes we seem to assume that he is altogether a religious being, and is interested only, or mainly, in the part of our affairs that we call religious; or if the ethical realm is added to his field, still it is apt to be regarded as a special region, a section in life, and morality is merely added to religion in making up the sum of that in us which is interesting to God. It is an old assumption that religion and morals constitute the field in which we have to do with him. But the truth is broader. The interest of God in our life is as broad as life itself. In every part of it we have to do with him, and he is always uttering himself to us.

The principle, already stated, is so simple as to be often overlooked. In that which God has given a man, God speaks to him as long as he possesses the gift, and appeals to him to use it worthily. The demand for right and worthy use, which comes with every occasion for using a power or principle, is an appeal of God himself. Men may not know it, but it is so, and the learning of this constitutes a great part of learning the significance of life. For example, it was God, creating him in his own likeness, that made man a rational being and made his rational nature the key to his destiny. Therefore it is right to say that all genuine and worthy suggestions of this destiny-making rationality are from God. The man may hear them without discerning the voice of God, but that is where he misunderstands himself. Every rational suggestion comes not only from our own nature, but from God who gave it.

There are as many illustrations here as there are aspects of human nature. A man is a social being also, and God made him so. A thousand relations with others press upon him; and in them all he is receiving God's perpetual suggestion that he act as a social being ought, suppressing lower motives, and raising conscience and unselfishness to the supreme place. A man is a being of æsthetic endowments: he loves beauty, he has imitative and constructive ability, he has a true creative power, within limits, to produce the beautiful. He has poetic insight. All the fine arts are outgrowths of his nature, and by them he strikes into a wonderful harmony with the order of nature about him, and acts upon the very principles whereby God made the beauty of the universe. God made him thus, and gave him his æsthetic faculties as a part of his own likeness. In these faculties God speaks to him still, appealing to him to prize the gift, to train it normally, and to use it in harmony with the highest good. A man loves pleasure, and God made him so. In all pleasure, and in all appeals of pleasure, God addresses him, urging him to enjoy the pleasure in purity and worthiness, to judge its worth correctly, to keep it in its right place, and make it servant to his higher powers. A man is an active being, with capacities for work, and a nature that cannot prosper without it. He is an aspiring being, with ambitions that reach out for better things, constitutionally discontented with his lot and seeking an upward way. He is a truth-lover, all too unworthily and yet really and forever, perpetually inquiring, longing to see things as they are, clamouring at the gates of mystery beyond which he is sure that reality may be found. He is a worshipper, with eyes turned upward to superior powers, seeking for his soul a fellowship above the human. God made him thus active, aspiring, truth-loving, adoring, and through the possession of these qualities God is constantly in communication with him. In this manner God is in communication with the inner life of every man, no matter where or in what human period, always suggesting through the power the normal use of the power, and calling upon the man to be himself. And when temptations come, urging the man to destroy the balance of his nature, to put pleasure first, to trample down his fellows, to be ambitious for himself alone, to forget God, to enthrone the brute and not the soul, with these also he may hear the voice of God, warning him not thus to defeat his own being, and bidding him rise upon this opportunity of evil to a new assertion, encouragement and strengthening of his better part.

By such means God is in the inner life of men—not of a few men specially privileged, but of all whom he has created human. A God who has placed within a race a growing soul is always in communication with that race through the presence of that soul. With the growth of the soul the moral element in life becomes larger and the religious element more full of meaning, and through conscience and religious aspiration God becomes yet more deeply and closely present in the inner life. Men have known it, too—dimly and gropingly indeed, and without knowing how much it means, and yet so well as to be aware that all their life has moral meaning, and to retain the impression that it has to do with God.

This universal intimacy with men stands not at the end of God's gracious operation but at the beginning. It is a proper part of life. Perfectly normal to humanity, and to be desired by all spirits, is the indwelling of God. Perfectly normal is that sweet and strong indwelling which is set forth in the New Testament under the name of the Spirit (Rom. viii. 9). Other names are used: we read of "God in you" (1 Cor. xiv. 25), and "Christ in you" (Jn. xv. 2), and these three forms of speech have essentially one meaning. But the representation most characteristic of the gospel is the one that gives to the indwelling God the name of the Spirit, often spoken of as the Holy Spirit. Here the high spiritual and practical relation that Christianity contemplates between God and man is fitly represented by a pure ethical doctrine of God in the inner life. According to the New Testament, God has been manifested in Christ for the saving of men, and now the indwelling Spirit brings the revelation home to the soul, that God may accomplish his purpose. God dwells in man to complete his own creative and redemptive work. It is not too much to call this the noblest practical view of divine influence upon the experience of mankind that has ever been known. The full account of it belongs to the doctrine of the Christian life, but the doctrine of God would not be complete without some unfolding of this intimacy of his with men, as the New Testament sets it forth.

To God the Spirit, operative within, is attributed the awakening of that new life which consists in spiritual fellowship with himself. The Spirit regenerates. He bears inward witness to the sonship of the man to God, confirming from the divine side the certainty of the human that such sonship is a fact. As a Spirit of adoption he evokes the cry, "Father," from the child: that is, he develops the free and joyful filial life, and establishes it as the conscious life of the man. He suggests prayer so great and deep as to be beyond expression: that is, he awakens the longings of the soul after the highest good and keeps them stretching forth with untold eagerness, not merely as desires, but as prayers to the Father's love. He thus helps the weakness of those in whom he dwells, stirring the noblest in them to lofty flights of aspiration (Rom. viii. 15-27). He has all sweet and holy traits of character and works of life for the results of his presence, so that "the fruit of the Spirit" includes (Gal. v. 22) all the worthiest things that are known to men. He is the comforter in trouble, the sustainer in reproach, the author of fraternal grace and forgiveness, the inspirer of brotherly love and usefulness. He makes divine realities known to the soul that can discern them, revealing the very deeps of God. He makes Christ ever better known and more richly appreciated. He brings in deep and strong convictions concerning sin and righteousness and God's eternal judgment of the difference between them. He reminds the soul of forgotten truth, and guides on toward ever fuller understanding of what God reveals. He is the very Spirit of truth, who makes truth dear to all who know him. He makes the soul wise with a heavenly wisdom, such as this world untaught by him can never master. He is the inspirer of holy and spiritual hope, both for this life and the life that is to come, and his presence with the soul is the pledge of an inheritance in life eternal. He opposes and defeats the inferior being, sets the soul at liberty, and is the inspiration of the victorious life, wherein hope is fulfilled and the will of God is done.

No more characteristic or convincing picture of the good God could be drawn than is sketched in these descriptions of the work that he delights to perform in every soul that is open to his indwelling. What manner of God the Christian doctrine sets forth, we see clearly in the service that he loves to render to all who will receive it at his hands. This picture of what he does in the Christian life and character is confirmed by experience; or rather, it was out of experience that our accounts of it were written. If Christian souls had not known him in this manner, we should never have read thus of his character and his gracious help. This picture of his influence in the inner life shows how good a God he is, and commends him to the faith of all who hear his name.

In all the thoughtful religions as well as in Christianity the question has arisen whether in the inner life God is known directly or not. Does the soul have immediate cognizance of him, and commune with him face to face in perfect consciousness that he is there? or does the soul know God only mediately, through his truth, through the suggestions of its own spiritual powers inspired by him, and by faith believing that he is there though not distinctly seen? Both answers are given. The mystic is sure that he has immediate touch of God upon his soul: he sees God with the inner eye and is sure of the vision: he hears the voice and knows whose voice it is. That another has no such consciousness is to him no disproof or cause for doubting: he knows for himself, and rises to sublime heights of holy joy in the beatific vision. Who can disprove his claim? and who would do it if he could? The universal Church endorses it by the voice of its hymns, which often sing out the rapture of face-to-face communion with God. Yet many another Christian, no less conscientious and God-loving than the mystic, is aware of no such immediate touch of his God upon his soul, or if he knows it at all it is only in rare moments long desired and long remembered. There are many whose vision of God is all of it consciously a vision of faith alone. That another has seen God face to face in the inner temple does not help these to have immediate vision of him there, but they love him in the dark as sincerely as others in the light, and serve him as loyally in the daily life.

We cannot tell beforehand by theory which view of the matter will be right. We cannot foresee how God in the inner life will manifest himself, but are shut up to the testimony of experience if we wish to know. But experience bears various testimony, as we see: moreover, it is always open to us to question whether experience understands itself aright. Perhaps the vision of God in the dark is more direct than the soul knows, and perhaps the touch that seems most gloriously direct is in some sense mediated, without the soul's knowing it. Or perhaps both reporters may be right, each for himself. But the variety need not trouble us. What can be more natural than that God should have many ways with men? His greatness would lead us to look for this, and so would the variety in human nature. To one it may be given to discern God in one way, and to another in another. He to whose greatness all modes are open is not certain to confine himself to one, and the humanity that has so many forms of inner life can scarcely expect that all its members will recognize in one manner the indwelling God. We must let God be great, and the inner knowledge of him be various. Even in one lifetime there may be many possibilities. A clear vision attained to-day may not be retained to-morrow, and may be remembered with regret and longing till it comes again. It is comforting to learn that "God fulfils himself in many ways" to the secret soul, as well as to the great world.

From considering God in the inner life, we turn to think of God in the open life, and especially in the common life of mankind. It is an old misunderstanding of Christianity to suppose it a religion of the individual alone. There is a passage in Augustine, in which an inquirer for truth is asked what it is that he desires and prays to know; and he declares that it is "God and the soul." "Nothing more?" his companion asks, and "Nothing whatever" is the answer. That religion is a matter between God and the soul alone has never been a doctrine of Christianity, but it has been a frequent impression among Christians, fostered by much true but partial teaching. But if one wishes to see God in the light of Jesus, it is not enough to look above and within: one must look also without and around. God, the soul, and the men with whom we live form a triad not to be diminished if we desire to know any one of the three aright. So the doctrine of God in relations with men is not completed by viewing it as doctrine of God in the inner life. God must be found and recognized in the common life, or the life of men together, no less than in the interior life of the soul.

The starting-point for this part of the doctrine is not a new one, but has been already indicated. That nature of man through which God is always speaking to him includes his social nature. As we have seen, man is not himself, and would never have come to be himself, but for the social relations in which he is placed.   If we say that God permanently appeals to man through the nature that he has given him, of course it is implied that the appeals of his social nature are appeals of God.   The word of God is in the life of man. The opportunity to live according to righteousness with his fellows is a word of God to him, bringing counsel, illumination and appeal.   So is the opportunity to live according to love and in the spirit of helpful fellowship.   The language of natural affection utters in the heart a word of God.   The cry of misery and want brings the sound of two voices, the voice of the wretched and the voice of God.   All appeals of sudden occasion or of steady need, to which a man may make answer with help both warm and wise, are God's appeals. All suggestions arising in the course of history, when common wrong has brought forth misery and human beings are losing their value through the common fault, are God's authoritative suggestions for promotion of a better social righteousness. Not only is God speaking through all awakenings of the public conscience and agitations for better conduct: he is speaking through all the crises in public affairs that bring such awakening of conscience, and through those that ought to bring it but do not.   In all the burning evils of the common life God is speaking, often with a voice of thunder, calling men to better things.   In all the moral aspects of the life of men together, God is giving voice to his own moral nature, that men may learn; and all the life of men together is moral, so that God is working through it at every point, perpetually revealing himself, and giving counsel, reproof and higher instruction.   As in the inner life, so in the common life, men may not know that God is there, and may miss his call or misinterpret his counsel; but none the less is God there, with his living word for them to hear.

These statements are not to be understood as applying to Christian lands and times alone. This work of God comes to pass by no special revelation; it comes in the course of nature. That we have not discerned it does not destroy it.   God has made men so that this instruction from him comes to them by their very nature. Through the moral nature of their social life, as well as of their inner life, God keeps in administrative communication, so to speak, with all human beings. His authority is upon them in their social duties. It was so from the first hour when there were social duties that men could intelligently perceive. To many Christians it has been an obscure question how God could have and hold such connection, righteously, with "dusky tribes and twilight centuries," where he was unknown in his true character and called by wrong names. In these facts the question is answered. He gave men their personal powers and social relations, and thus placed them under duty, where they could never escape its claims; and of necessity he who thus constituted their life was the one who would hold authority and judgment over it. There has never been a human being who did not have to do with God in the duties that he owed to the men who lived about him. There is no proud structure of social order that does not stand approved or condemned in God's own presence, according as it does right or wrong toward the human beings whose destinies are committed to its care. Through the relations and attendant duties that he has constituted throughout humanity, God stands in authority over all men, and their relations to one another form an element in their relation to him.

This is the same as to say that no man and no society can fulfil duty toward God by considering God alone. Human relations enter into religion. Duty toward men is part of duty toward God, and the two can never be separated. It is in the very constitution of nature that God must be served by serving men. Not by this alone is he to be served, but without this never to the full; and God, being the God that he is, could not have appointed it to be otherwise.

When we come to that clearer manifestation of God which is made in Jesus Christ, we find this provision of nature reaffirmed with perfect distinctness. From Jesus we hear that the supreme requirements in religion are two, not one. They are alike, he says, but they are two. "Thou shalt love the Lord thy God with all thy heart" is one, and "Thou shalt love thy neighbour as thyself" is the other (Mt. xxii. 37–39). They are alike, in that both are calls for love. Each requires the placing of self where self belongs but does not always wish to go, and the choosing and honouring of another object. Here is the triad that was mentioned a little while ago—God, the self and the neighbour—and all three are included in the scope of religion. The God of the first commandment is the God of the second, and men cannot expect that he will be satisfied with obedience to the first while the second is disregarded—even if such obedience were possible. The claim of God is just as truly present in the second as in the first, and a man deals with God in dealing with his neighbour, just as truly as in dealing directly with God himself. There is an impact of God upon the soul in every contact with the neighbour, and the thing that ought to be done toward the neighbour is a thing in which God is revealed in his authority and his character to the man who ought to do it.

Other words to the same effect fell from the lips of Jesus. He told the man who was ready in the temple with an offering to God to leave his gift at the altar and go and be reconciled to the brother who had something against him, before he should offer his gift (Mt. v. 23–24). God did not wish to be served with a service that ignored a moral claim of man, and took the place of what ought to be done to an injured brother. God thus associates man with himself, so to speak, and declines to be honoured when man is wronged. A more radical word, or one more profoundly true, Jesus never uttered. Some of the most terrible of the reproofs that he administered to the Pharisees were reproofs for thinking that they could combine the wronging of men with the service of God. They claimed much devoutness, but they wronged the poor. In the parable of the Good Samaritan Jesus showed, in reality, how both the great commands were to be honoured. The parable was framed in answer to the question, "Who is my neighbour?" but that the Samaritan in serving the suffering neighbour was doing the will of his God is obvious upon the very face of this splendid utterance. The priest and the Levite were of the temple but not of God: the Samaritan, thought to be outside God's fold, did God's will in serving his human brother. All through the New Testament the same principle rules. It is true that the large social applications of the Christian spirit are not unfolded upon those pages, the time for them not having fully come, but the principle is there. Consider the brother; look not to your own interests but also to those of others; no man liveth to himself; I seek not yours, but you. The First Epistle of John works a *reductio ad absurdum* upon the claim that a man loves God while he does not love his neighbour (iv. 20): it is impossible; one who does not love close at hand in actual life, where there is tangible opportunity to test the love, cannot love in the unseen region where it is so easy to mistake an abstraction for an affection. Thus the Christian revelation repeats and reinforces that law of nature according to which the human claim is a divine claim also, and the cry of the neighbour is the call of God. How vivid is the picture in the parable of Judgment—"Inasmuch as ye did it unto one of the least of these my brethren, ye did it unto me" (Mt. xxv. 40)!

In the very centre of Christianity this law is again expressed in supreme power and beauty. Jesus is the finest illustration that we know of love to God. All the signs of love—the confidence, the devotion, the delight—appear in him. To God he was absolutely loyal, and in his love he performed God's will with an understanding of it most profoundly true. When we ask how he showed this most loyal and intelligent love to God, and how he satisfied his own heart in doing the Father's will, the answer is ready. He showed his love to God in the service that he performed for men. He loved his neighbour as himself, and better, as our hearts cry when we behold his cross, and it was in such love that he expressed his love and wrought out his loyalty to God. In life and death, Jesus is the supreme illustration of the truth that God is served in serving men.

This truth has sometimes been accounted mysterious, but it is quite plain as soon as we remember what God is doing for men. It has often been asked in sincere reverence whether man, in his littleness, can bring to God any real service. We instinctively approve what some one has said, that there cannot be any such thing as mere court-service to God, a service of external form and deference, in which nothing important is really done; but if something really serviceable to God is called for, what is there that a man can render? Light upon the question does not come, so long as we think of God as reigning afar, and absorbed in purposes that are beyond our comprehension. But we ought to know by this time that God is steadily devoted to promoting the welfare of the human race which he created. The course of its history is the course of God's training of its life and development of its destiny. This is no new doctrine: it is as old as the doctrine of a good God; and yet it comes almost as if it were new, for illumination upon our question. Any work of man that helps humanity furthers the desire and purpose of God. Certainly he must be really served by any work that tends to promote the end that he is seeking. Any work that promotes high and pure religion, or sound intelligence, or righteousness between man and man, or justice and helpfulness in the social order, or better opportunities for successful life, or the development of the human faculties, or the lessening of any evil that represses and spoils human beings, is real service to God, for it promotes his purpose and tends toward the completing of his creative design. There is no need of wondering how we can offer to God a service of real value, for the world is full of opportunities, since it is a fact that God is to be served by serving men.

This truth offers itself to the Christian doctrine of God as a descriptive statement. God is a Being who can be served by serving men. More—he is a God who must be served by serving men, if service to him is to be of the kind that will please him best. Service to him consists in contributing to the accomplishment of his purpose; and his purpose, which we call his will, includes worthy and successful life, both for the person who serves and for the common humanity to which he belongs. So a man may serve God by seeking to fulfil his own true destiny, and by helping others to fulfil theirs. Service that is not gathered under one of these two heads is mere formality or court-service. It may take some approved and acceptable form, but it accomplishes nothing beyond itself, and contributes nothing to the doing of the will of God.

Here we meet again the ancient conception of the Kingdom of God, and here we can best understand it in relation to the present time. Whatever else the kingdom of God was expected to be, it was to include a multitude of men, who would have to do with one another and with God. It was not to be a fact in the field of individualism, but an institution of the common life, a social fact.

The kingdom of God, we know, was expected to be a renewed and glorified kingdom of Israel. We often condemn the Jews for what we call an earthly hope, but we are only partly right. To them the glorious Israel of the past was the Israel of David's kingdom, and the typical and glorious Israel of the future was a kingdom also, the kingdom of God. Whether with or without a vicegerent of his power, God would be the king. Of course, there could be no single picture of that coming time as imagination foresaw it, and the pictures that were drawn varied widely. But to all it was the good time coming, all the faithful of Israel would have part in it, wrongs would be righted, right would be done, righteousness would bring peace, the people of the kingdom would prosper and be joyful under their divine King. In favourable conditions it might have been expected that the existing Israel would develop through faith and righteousness into such a kingdom, but conditions grew unfavourable to such a hope. The national organization was lost and failed to be restored, and the national virtue did not rise to so high a quality as the hope required. But the hope could not die: instead, it changed its tone, and became a hope of miraculous transformations. The kingdom would not belong to the present order of the world. All would be changed, the conditions of life would be altered, the faithful dead would come forth from their graves, the kingdom would be manifested in a flash of divine power, various marvels would attend upon the happy life within its bounds, the world outside would perish in its sins, and the full glory of God would be manifested in his reigning over a righteous people.

When Jesus appeared in Israel, it was announced that the kingdom of God was at hand. Expectations varied, and just what was to be looked for this proclamation did not make entirely plain. It has been much discussed how Jesus himself understood the kingdom of God; whether he looked for a kingdom of miraculous transformations, in new heavens and earth, or for the gradual introduction of a holy spiritual dominion of God in the existing world. But the question is not important to the present purpose, which leads us to be concerned only with the actual historical development. We wish to know what kingdom of God there is, that we can see coming forth from the work of Jesus and advancing through the Christian period. If we can rightly identify such a kingdom of God, we shall be able to judge what light the Christian doctrine of God receives from this ancient conception.

On this point the light is clear. We know what manner of kingdom of God came forth. The miraculous transformation did not occur, and no kingdom of radically new and unearthly type was initiated. The world went on. The kingdom of God that was really at hand when Jesus appeared has been developed in the existing order of this world's life. At present we can read the past plainly enough to see that this was the only right and possible method. There was nothing in the work of Jesus that tended to bring upon the world a miraculous catastrophe, and nothing in his influence for good that would have had its characteristic promotion in such an event. From the result it does not appear that he came to produce new heavens and a new earth, except as any place is new wherein dwells righteousness. In the normal successions of human history his work was wrought out in accordance with its nature. The appropriate result of a work like his was the long unfolding of the grace of God in the world. The kingdom of God that came in with Jesus was the practical dominion of God in the life that men live together—a kingdom that came, and is still coming, and has yet to come.

In the highest religion, the kingly idea retires in great measure into the fatherly, to the great enriching of our thoughts of God. In the Epistles of the New Testament, where the new life in Christ is an experience, the kingdom of God is but very slightly mentioned, while Fatherhood and Saviourhood are at the front. But the ethical conception which the ancient idea of the kingdom sends down with power into the modern time is not destroyed or weakened by this change. It is a conception not of formal royalty, but of ethical sovereignty and practical sway, and its field is that of the general life, socially considered. Bringing the biblical idea to present application, by the kingdom of God we mean God's moral government of social life on Christian principles. The kingdom of God is a very different thing from a body of people, to be enumerated in a census, and from a visible institution with its organization and official corps. No man has ever seen it. It is not the Church, as has often been sup-posed. The Church is one of its agencies, but the kingdom itself is that which the Church is intended to promote. It is not a domain but a dominion. It is a divine pervasion of human facts. It is an influence, a searching and controlling Christian force, taking effect upon the life that men live together. We cannot put it into an exhaustive definition; but when the kingdom has come, the eternal goodness loving in wisdom will have human goodness loving in wisdom for its counterpart on earth. When the kingdom has come, the relations of man with man, of man with woman, of parent with child, of neighbour with neighbour, of individual with society, of class with class, of trade with trade, of citizen with state, of strong with weak, of nation with nation, of race with race, will be determined and pervaded by the mind of Christ, which is the will of God. In so far as these relations are thus determined and God does have his way, the kingdom of God has come, and his will is done on earth as it is in heaven. In so far as this is not yet true, the kingdom has yet to come, and may be promoted by any man's endeavour.

The Christian doctrine of God in his relations with men is not complete until he has been presented as a God who has such a kingdom as this in the world, and is seeking to make it perfect. He seeks to permeate the large life of mankind with the principles that correspond to his character. This endeavour is the natural fulfilment of his creative purpose, and of his redeeming love revealed in Christ. All that opposes or resists this endeavour is hateful to him, and not less because he is patient, bearing with it till it can be overcome. All social good is his, in all the world: all social wrong, injustice, frivolity, falseness, greed, base passion, unbrotherliness, he hates. His reign is not solely in the personal life, nor is the saving of individuals the whole of his gracious work. He is intent upon putting away the evils that afflict and corrupt humanity in groups and masses. From the many hells of this life he is seeking to save. He is the God of social righteousness and brotherhood, of justice and love among men. Demands for these are his demands, sin against these is sin against him, and service to these is his service. The extension of the mind of Christ is his means of answering the prayer, "Thy will be done." Any church that would represent him worthily must devote itself alike to the saving of individuals and the promotion of the social kingdom. To neglect either object is to fall out of his fellowship. This quick and powerful conception of the God of universal morality is just as essential to the Christian doctrine as any view of him that may be accounted more doctrinal or more technically religious, for in this manner God is in human life, seeking actually to become the Lord of all men and all their doings.

III. GOD AND THE UNIVERSE

1. MONOTHEISM

In accordance with the principle already laid down, we now proceed from the circle of human relations to the vaster concentric circle of relations between God and the universe. Of course it is true that man is a part of the universe, and has to do with God in the relations that are yet to be considered. To this extent the classification may be criticised; nevertheless, the distinction is a proper one, and a helpful one also. It is in human life that we know God as Father, Saviour, Friend: it is in his relation to universal existence that we contemplate him as Self-existent, Transcendent, Omnipresent. Following the order that corresponds to the nature of Christianity, we proceed from that which our own life has taught us, to that larger sphere in which our own life, with all other being, is embraced. This method is reasonable, for we begin with what we know best, and advance to that which is less known. We begin also with what is most surely interpretative; for character gives more light upon universal relations than universal relations give upon character, and in the relations of God with men character is the determinative element. So our first study provides us with light for our second.

Although the method is sometimes distrusted, it is really a great advantage to Christianity as a teacher of Theism that its doctrine of God has a basis in the familiar region of vital and serious experience. Under the Christian influence we learn to think of God as rational, moral, spiritual, personal; and thinking thus of him we go out to study him in universal relations. There are many who feel on scientific grounds that they must search the universe for God without having personality and moral significance first in mind. But we are thankful not to feel thus, for certainly in searching the universe for the Supreme Mind we are entitled to start from the highest ground that human experience has reached. The Christian doctrine puts the right things first, and leads on with all the confidence that religion imparts. We need not distrust our method, but may be thankful that when we go forth searching for knowledge of God in the regions beyond, the Founder of Christianity leads us out from the Father's house, where we have begun to be acquainted with him for whom we seek.

In this region the soleness or singleness of God is the first fact with which we have to deal. The Christian doctrine of God as it is offered to us to-day is the purest and broadest Monotheism. Islam has claimed to be the most genuine monotheism in the world, and has founded its claim of superiority to Christianity in this respect mainly upon its understanding of the Christian doctrine of the Trinity; but the Christian faith holds a richer and truer monotheism by far. Only by misunderstanding is it supposed to hold doctrine inconsistent with a positive and uncompromising spiritual monotheism. No other religion has ever risen to such affirmation of the unity and soleness of God, in terms suited to any and every stage of human knowledge. Monotheism is the natural doctrine when the natural order is well understood, and it is the Christian doctrine.

That which monotheism supersedes and renders impossible is polytheism. Monotheism affirms one divine Being, will and administration: polytheism believes in many superhuman wills, acting in many limited administrations of affairs. Polytheism came naturally into the world in the early days of humanity. It is no wonder that the powers of nature, so real and seemingly so distinct, were idealized into personality and deified in popular religion, or that natural objects, as the sun and moon, were worshipped. Nor is it surprising that legends of greatness gathered around famous men, so that in course of time they were regarded as more than human. By such processes superhuman beings and forces came to be present in great numbers to human wonder and reverence, and the impulse to worship was called out by innumerable objects. The processes were long and persistent, and the array of gods tended ever to increase. Every place and thing and practice may come to have its deity.

Yet polytheism is not the most natural form of religion, nor is it certain that it was the earliest. That which first evoked religious feeling in infant humanity may not have been some separate power of nature, or some wonderful object, as the heavens or the sun. It is quite as probable that the sense of something more than human in the world as a whole was borne in upon the observing spirit, before any separate part was recognized as fit to receive worship. The total effect of the sum of things observed, the sense of finding himself in a world mysterious and greater than himself, may well have been the provocative that stirred man to religion. This seems the more natural order. It is more probable that polytheism came by differentiation of broad religious feeling than that it was the earliest method in religion.

It might seem that polytheism in any form must necessarily break up all religious unity, and be fatal to all sense of singleness in religion and in the world. But so it has not proved. Beneath the endless variety of polytheism there has often been a deep sense of the singleness and unity of the divine. Doubtless this conception of oneness has been rather intellectual than religious, and has taken effect in an underlying sense of things rather than in modes of worship; nevertheless polytheism is not justly interpreted without recognition of this tendency to be aware of an underlying divine unity. One divine, many times and ways expressed—this has been the thought. So it is in India, where the vastest polytheism that the world has known is accompanied by a profound philosophy of unity. There is no reason why these companion-ideas, of unity in the divine and multiplicity in its expression, should not be strong together. Both are natural. The recognition of unity is so natural as to look out through all the multiplicity of the polytheism.

But the unity, when the two are combined, is not that of monotheism. The tendency is rather to a pantheistic conception of oneness. One might suppose that the personal element so prominent in the polytheistic idea of gods was sure to dominate, so that monotheism would be reached, by the exaltation of one personal deity and the elimination of the many. But the tendency to a pantheistic view seems more natural. In polytheism the demand for personality seems to be satisfied in the acknowledgement of the many deities. In these there is personality enough and to spare, and the underlying divine, expressed in these many, tends to be regarded as impersonal. What indeed can that divine be, which is expressed in so many personal deities, except a quality, or some impersonal kind of being? The hope that polytheistic religion will work out by its own impulse into a vital monotheistic faith has never yet been realized, and seems likely never to come true. The natural tendencies in the other direction are too strong.

The Hebrew doctrine of God grew up out of polytheism, for the fathers had their many gods. It was not a philosophical doctrine, but an outgrowth of moral and religious life. It appears to have passed through the henotheistic stage, affirming one God for Israel while there were other gods for other peoples; but under the influence of the prophets it became a doctrine of genuine monotheism, affirming one God alone existing. It was not merely an ordinary development from the polytheism of early days, but was rather a reaction against it. It came from those deep and inspiring insights of the best men that so well deserve the name of revelation. The living God was manifesting himself to men who could discern him. It was in the ethical life and the life of religion that the conviction of the divine unity was borne in. God was conceived as bearing the qualities that we call personal, and as having such character as to command a reverence and loyalty such as no deity had ever obtained. He was conceived as living, knowing, loving, desiring, purposing, directing his own action, and influential upon the affairs of men. It was a doctrine of divine unity that stood in contrast to everything pantheistic: it was a true monotheism, a doctrine of one personal God. Monotheism is contrasted with polytheism in affirming the unity of the divine, and with pantheism in affirming the personality. The Hebrew doctrine proclaimed both.

The Christian doctrine continued the life of the Hebrew. From the beginning it assumed, with no effort to prove it, the reality of God as absolutely sole and alone, filling the whole conception covered by the name, with no other God actual, possible or conceivable in the field of being. All that God can be, its one God is. His relation as God is a relation to absolutely all existence that is not himself. All that he is, whether in character, in power or in actual relations, he is through the entire range of existence, whether spatial or temporal. This statement, though couched in terms that early Christian utterance did not know, well represents God as early Christian faith and thought discerned him.

Such a monotheistic conception as this is evidently expansible, and is naturally destined to be expanded as human knowledge is enlarged. It is suited to any conception of the extent of existence. With any enlargement in the range of knowledge it does not change its character, but only its extent. When knowledge was practically limited to the heavens and the earth as the eye beholds them, monotheism affirmed, as in the first chapter of Genesis, that one intelligent and creative God sustained one relation to all that heavens and earth were, and all that they contained. However the conception of the extent of existence might become enlarged, monotheism continued the same declaration. When modern modes of discovery extended the range of known existence immeasurably beyond all human power of imagining, and revealed besides a fulness and variety that renders every part as wonderful as the whole, still monotheism uttered the same great word, and that word sufficed. Monotheism affirms to-day that one conscious and intelligent Being holds the place and relation of God toward all existence, is all that God can be, and signifies all that God can signify. This the Christian doctrine has always asserted, and this it now asserts.

Such monotheism is the only theism that can exist in power where the Christian faith has done its work. It is needless to say that the influence of Jesus is fatal to all polytheism, when once it has its way. It is true that in Christian history pagan ideas inherited from older time were long in dying, and results from ancient polytheism were long lingering in the common mind. Not even yet is all such influence extinct. But the spiritual world of Christian faith really has place for the One who is God alone, and for no other. As Christian thought advances toward completeness and consistency, whatever is out of harmony with pure monotheism, and the broadest monotheism that can be conceived, must retire, never to return. This statement is not less true in connection with the ethical dualism which the moral perplexities of life have suggested. The divided field and the bitter conflict of good and evil have often been accounted for by belief in rival powers, sometimes regarded as equal, sometimes as almost equal but with preponderance of the good. The suggestion of such a dualism was natural once, but is impossible now in the Christian light. The Christian monotheism is too strong. However great the moral difficulties in the doctrine of one God, they are not to be removed by denying the sound and final conviction of universal unity. Though clouds and darkness be around him, God is one. There is deeper darkness in denying it.

It is equally true that such monotheism is the only theism that is possible in the world where modern knowledge is influential in religious thought. The oneness of the world has expanded into the oneness of the universe, and the unity of the vaster whole is far plainer and more impressive than the unity of the lesser whole ever was. No thought of division is ever to enter hereafter. The unity of the universe dictates belief in the singleness of the power that controls it. **If any God is to be believed in, it must be one God in all.** Here the Christian doctrine is finely in harmony with modern knowledge. Jesus has given us a living confidence in God as One, and is for all ages a powerful sustainer of monotheistic faith. The religious inspiration that we owe to him enables us to maintain the divine oneness in the face of the immensity of the universe, and of its moral perplexities as well. Christianity dooms all polytheism, and all practical dualism, to banishment from its field, for it is a living faith in one only God. But while this faith has been coming toward maturity, modern thought has been maturing also, and has reached a conception of the universe that confirms the Christian claim. The present view of the unity of the universe is monotheistic to the core. In its earlier stages it may be suggestive of pantheism, but the facts that support it are premises for a monotheistic conclusion and for no other, and in its maturity the modern view of existence is sure to proclaim the one God alone.

It has always been easy to make monotheism too much a negative doctrine. "There is only one God," is the form in which the claim is often made, and the great assertion still sounds too much like a polemic against polytheism. But a negative or defensive monotheism is not the doctrine of power, and is not the full Christian doctrine. Power awaits the assertion of the positive monotheism with all its meaning. "There is one God, in all and over all: there is One, who to all the universe is all that God can be: there is One God, whom it is life to know"—this is the monotheism that the Christian doctrine embodies. Sound Theism not only denies the existence of the many, but insists upon the reality of the One; and this part of its teaching should be at the front.

2. THE TWO UNITS OF EXISTENCE

The one God is not alone. We have no occasion to speak or think of him in a solitary existence, for though we may talk of him thus, we have no power to conceive of God existing by himself, and we should mislead ourselves if we imagined that we could form clear thoughts or valid judgments in that region. We know that in fact God is not alone, but is accompanied in existence by an immense mass of being which we call the universe.

Here, as often happens, we must own that we are using language that we cannot well define. For us mystery runs back to the uttermost. What we mean by reality, or even by existence, we may not be able to make entirely clear. What it is for anything to exist we may not be able to tell in unambiguous terms, and of the manner or sense in which the universe exists we may offer various expositions. But the broad popular statement that the universe exists is not to be set aside as useless or misleading because our theories of existence are conflicting or uncertain. The statement is true. The one eternal Being is not alone, but is accompanied in existence by something that must be distinguished from himself.

If we attempt to give account of that which accompanies God in existence, we can say some things confidently, at least in popular language. The universe is partly material, as we understand the word, and partly spiritual: in part it is unconscious, and in part conscious. It is vaster than we can know, and complex beyond all our imagining. In proportion to our mental capacity, it seems infinite. Whether it actually is infinite in extent, or has limits, we may never know, though both observation and reasoning are always tempting us toward a conclusion. Probably physicists are more of the opinion that it is finite, and philosophers that it is infinite. It includes what we know as matter, energy, life and spirit, all in amount that far transcends our power to conceive. It is a system, as we have good reason to think, and its methods and operations, so far as our observation has gone, prove intelligible to human rational powers.

According to the Christian conception, the universe stands in existence over against God, and God over against the universe. In existence there are two, God and that which is not God. The two are not identical, and the two names are not names for one reality. God is one, and the universe is another. Its entire body of vastness and complexity forms the second unit of existence. Of ultimate units of existence there are two, and no more. There cannot be more, but there are two—God and that which is not God, or God and the universe.

This has been implied all along, in what has been said of God. He has been represented as a Spirit possessed of a completeness corresponding to the constitution that we know as personal. We are compelled to attribute to him a self-consciousness and a self-determination. But if he possesses these, he is thereby a Being who is not identical with anything outside his self-consciousness and self-determination. If he produces something, or brings something into existence, or something exists because of his existence and activity, that something may be ever so closely associated with himself, but it will not be himself. The Being in whom will, character and power inhere cannot well be the universe, nor can the universe be he, or a part of him. The God of whom the Christian doctrine speaks, and all clear theism with it, must be one unit of existence, and the universe must be another.

Upon this distinction between God and the universe, or the existence not only of God but of that which is not God, the Christian doctrine has always strongly insisted, and must continue to insist. The relation between the two may be defined in whatever terms the knowledge of an age may make most true and tenable, but the distinction itself belongs to the foundation of the Christian faith. Pantheistic thought identifies God and the universe. It recognizes only a single unit of existence, or one substance, of which the universe is the expression. Consequently all the God that it recognizes is the sum of existence, viewed with reference to its order and significance; the universe in its higher meaning. Such a doctrine of course finds no personality in God, and no distinctness: it gives him no separate existence, but binds him in with the universe. In fact, it knows him only as an inference from what we know of the universe. Christianity has always held a radically different view of God from this. The ancient ethical conception handed on by Jesus and embodied in the Christian doctrine presents a God who is not the world, and a world that is not God. The whole system of religion for which Christianity stands implies a God with whom the universe cannot be identified. It conceives of God in terms of personality: it assumes in him a consciousness, a will and a heart: it addresses him as One with whom man can hold genuine converse, and whose will man can do or reject. This is a most vital point in the nature of Christianity, not only in its historic forms but in its substance and its claims for the future. The Christian faith cannot abandon the conviction that God is himself, and that in a true sense the universe is other than he.

Nevertheless, the distinction and difference between the two units of existence is by no means all that we must affirm. We have to confess that clear language here, if we yield to the necessity of using it, is too clear to do justice to the reality. It sounds as if we were disclaiming the vagueness that attends the essential mystery. But in truth the relation between God and the universe can never be clearly defined. Through some divine process that we shall never understand, the second unit is perpetually deriving from the first its existence, its order and its significance. On the other hand, to God the universe is an organ for perpetual self-expression. In it he lives his forthgoing and self-manifesting life. No illustration can ever set all this forth; but if we were to say that God is the soul and the universe is to him as a body, we should be doing far better justice to the truth than if we spoke of the two as distinct and different from each other, making no attempt to illustrate their connection. The union of the thinking spirit with the body which is its organ of expression comes nearer than anything else that we know to illustrating the indescribable relation between God and the universe. It is no more explainable than the infinite mystery, but it is familiar to us, and helpful by its familiarity. In and through that which is not himself God is always exercising his power, love and wisdom. In it he is always maintaining life from his own inexhaustible fulness. For the realization of his will he is always putting it to use. No part of it is ever uninfluenced by his will or his affection. The universe is not himself, but it is so closely and deeply united to himself as to be the organ by which he goes forth to the action that is characteristic of his nature.

It is in some such way as this that the Christian doctrine does justice to the conditions that have so often suggested Pantheism. It keeps in sight the union—not the identity—of the universe with God. While it distinguishes between God and the universe, it beholds them existing together in so indistinguishable a union that one cannot tell where is the line between, any more than one can find the union-point of soul and body. It is true that Christianity has not yet worked through its problem of dealing with pantheistic thought, and its statements on the subject must represent unfinished work. Pantheistic thought has often offered itself temptingly within the field of Christianity itself. Sometimes it has entered by way of reaction. Christian teaching has unjustly represented the world as essentially evil, and uninhabitable by God, and has often portrayed God as practically outside the world. Its affirmation of its own truth of Omnipresence has often been only formal and ineffective. So sometimes there has been a feeling that pantheism brings the divine nearer than Christian thought, and makes it actually more available, even though the personal conception be wanting. Living pantheistic thought in India, with which Christianity is just becoming acquainted, considers the doctrine of a personal God inferior to its own, less inspiring and less consoling. Yet the Christian doctrine brings God as near to man as does the doctrine that makes man a part of him, and offers the blessing of a living Father, which pantheism knows not. It offers the wealth of divine personality and the glory of holiness and love, and fully equals pantheism in its assertion of the greatness, fulness and nearness of the divine. This breadth and richness of the Christian doctrine must be insisted upon. No narrow or provincial view of God under the Christian name can displace the pantheistic impressions that come so easily. Pantheism challenges Christianity to make the most of its monotheism. This is the strength and glory of the Christian faith, that its monotheism is a gospel. Its monotheism is the universal dominion of the One, and the One is he whom the Christian vision beholds in the light of Jesus Christ. In the confidence and joy that the divine character inspires, Christianity proclaims the one living God as the hope of the universe.

3. "GOD IS A SPIRIT"

One of the two units of existence is a Spirit. The other includes spirits innumerable, and has a spiritual movement and end, but is not a spirit itself. That God is a Spirit is one of the ancient words of the Christian religion, always held fast in its doctrine and precious in its life. As we have said elsewhere, it is not probable that this word in the New Testament was intended to describe God in contrast with matter: it was rather designed to present him in his availableness to the human spirit, as a Father to be worshipped in spirit and truth, and found wherever the human spirit sought him (Jn. iv. 21–24). In this region lies the richness and value of the Christian idea of God as a Spirit, and from this point all Christian use of the idea proceeds. In unfolding the Christian doctrine it is no part of our task to explain the difference between matter and spirit, and show in what metaphysical sense the name spirit belongs to God. For this we may be thankful, for at present no one can define matter and spirit: that definition is for the future, if indeed it lies within human reach at all. If it turn out, as it may, that matter is only a form or manifestation of what we know as spirit, then all the more needless will discussion of the difference be in the doctrine of God. Nevertheless what is commonly meant by spirit, and by a spirit, differs radically from what is commonly meant by matter, and the difference is permanent; and the Christian doctrine affirms that one of the two units of existence is a Being whom spiritual beings known to us resemble.

We do well to note how humanly intelligible is this word concerning God. What we know of the nature of a spirit we know from ourselves. Here again in our knowledge of God we profit by the fact that we were created in his likeness, and we should not fear to claim the benefit of this enlightenment. We pass by all shadowy conceptions of what a spirit is, and say at once that the word denotes in God, as in us, a being possessed of intelligence, will and affection. A spirit is a self-directing actor. When the Christian doctrine calls God a Spirit, it means that he is a God who knows and understands, a God who acts, putting himself forth in endless and varied working, and a God of character. God the Spirit is the living God of rational and spiritual powers, conscious, active, affectional, ethical. Into this definition, in fact, enters all that was said in the first part of this book concerning God, in respect of personality and character. His personality and character have been illustrated in his relations with men, and now they must be affirmed again in those comprehensive relations that are as wide as all existence that is not himself.

Christianity does not borrow this conception of God as a Spirit from science or philosophy, or learn it first by study in their fields. The idea finds confirmation there, but did not there originate, for it is older than science or philosophy. Nor is it peculiar to the Christian doctrine. It is a characteristic conception of religion, and as a fruit of religious discernment it enters into Christian thought. From the very beginning it has been of the common stock of religious convictions.

That the invisible divine is of the nature of a spirit, with thought, will, action and character, is the certainty with which religion began. Whether the divine be one or many, it has will and character and stands in living relations with men—this is the very starting-point of religion, and religion has never lost this indispensable conviction. Indispensable it is, and religion loses its quality if it fades away Religion advancing to its height and fulness is simply growing clearer and more worthy in its use of this first truth. Christianity affirms this truth in its utmost greatness, declaring that there is One, and only One, in whom are perfect mind, will, affection, action, character. The vastness of this utterance, and of the field in which it must be true if it is true at all, does not deter Christianity from proclaiming it with confidence. Rather is the vastness a proper accompaniment of such a truth, and a commendation of it, not a reason for doubt.

It may perhaps seem necessary to offer some detailed account of the qualities that are ascribed to God when he is said to be a spirit; but the necessity is less than it may appear to be. God is the object of boundless curiosity and consequent inquiry, but satisfaction of the curiosity is not indispensable to the Christian doctrine. Only broad statements are possible, and only what is possible is necessary. We cannot say much more by way of description than that the intellectual action of God as a spirit is that of the perfect mind, the voluntary action is that of the perfect will, and the moral action is that of the perfect character. That we cannot describe what this broad statement contains will give us neither surprise nor dismay, when we are aware of our unchangeable limitations. We cannot expect to know all that our words mean when we speak of the perfect Being, but we need not therefore hesitate to affirm the reality of such a Being. No spirit but himself can comprehend him, but there lives one perfect Spirit, who is God. So says the Christian doctrine.

This Christian affirmation is made as confidently in the present state of knowledge as in any other. At present the great visible fact is the universe, boundless to our imagination even if finite in itself, overwhelming in its vastness, and inconceivable in its variety, ordered by method that seems inflexible, and apparently containing all that its operations require. It is not the function of religion to explore the universe and learn what it contains, and so it may seem presumptuous for religion to say anything at all about the power by which the universe is maintained and directed. In the realm where religion is at home, theism and the reign of spiritual forces might seem reasonable enough as interpretation of human affairs, but theism and the reign of spiritual forces in the universal sweep of existence may seem beyond the right of religion to affirm. Nevertheless, exactly this the Christian doctrine does affirm. In proclaiming the one God who is a spirit it proclaims a universal doctrine. It declares that all operations of the universe are spiritual in their source, quality and direction; that all that seems material is serving the ends of spirit; that the one Spirit pervades, sustains, animates and directs the whole. On the part of Christianity this is first a religious conviction and certainty. In the religious realm it finds good reason to believe in God; and believing in God it can neither assert anything less than this universal sway, nor doubt the truth of the assertion. It does not claim to have explored the universal field and found its affirmation proven by the facts observed, and there are many who think that until this has been done it is folly to say that the source and force are spiritual and the God of all is a spirit. But the Christian doctrine does say just this, and offers it as a conclusion from facts known in the field of religion; and it waits for science and philosophy to confirm what its own faith and insight declare to be true.

The undying curiosity concerning God includes a deep desire to know in what manner the one living Spirit puts forth his action upon other existence. How the supreme spirit sends forth energy and organizing power upon the unfree material creation is one question: how the infinite spirit acts in mysterious relations with finite spirits, free but limited, like our own, is another. The first question commands eager intellectual interest, and the second presses hard upon us when we wish to solve the mysteries of our own life. But we cannot answer them. It is entirely correct to say that we cannot answer because the action of the perfect mind lies beyond our experience, and so beyond our understanding. Yet we do not need this refuge for our inability, for we have one nearer home. Just how any mind acts upon anything that is not itself we do not know. Spiritual action itself, the transfer of energy, the embodying of idea in act, is in its own nature a mystery to us, and one that we are not likely to solve. Doubly then are we exempt from the need of embarrassment in our inability to describe the action of God the spirit upon other existence, and not for a moment need we hesitate to affirm the fact because we cannot give account of its method.

That which most impresses us when we reflect upon the action of God, the perfect spirit, is the inconceivable vastness and variety of it. Even we as spirits find much to think of and carry upon our hearts, and now and then we obtain swift and astonishing glimpses of the greatness of human affairs. Yet that which is too great for us is only a drop in the ocean of existence. We are hopelessly unable to comprehend what it must be for a spirit to bear all existence within his thought; yet that is no reason why we should question the welcome fact that it is done. If we think the Christian thought concerning God we think that to him, the perfect spirit, all existence is one great enterprise, borne upon his mind and heart, understood, directed. If this language sounds anthropomorphic, none the less does it express the truth.

Along with the action of the perfect spirit goes of course his character. When the Christian doctrine affirms that the scope of God's spiritual action is wide as the universe, it equally affirms the universal scope and activity of his character. Concerning the character that enters into the operation of God the spirit, the Christian doctrine speaks with the utmost clearness and confidence, and its testimony relates to the entire field of divine activity. It is here that we reach that magnificent conception of God which Christianity is offering the world, to be welcomed into the bosom of universal thought, which waits the glory that it will impart. On the plane of human life, where alone men could observe it, Christianity has learned through its Founder and through other teachings the character of God. It has learned that forever and everywhere God is holy, God is righteous, God is love, worthy of the perfect confidence and affection of all beings who have power to love, trust and be loyal. With unspeakable joy Christian faith has received this revelation as true, and placed it in the Christian doctrine as the revelation of a truth not partial or temporary but universal and eternal. It holds that Jesus Christ simply revealed realities as they are, and showed God to men as he really is. The God who is imperfectly but rightly known to men in the experience that Christ inspires is the living God, the universal Spirit, in whom all live and move and have their being. Wherever he may exist and be manifested in his working, such he is. The One Spirit may be discovered in any and every part of existence, working in infinite variety of ways, thinking, acting, willing, controlling, but the character that is borne by this one and only God is everywhere and always that character of love, holiness and wisdom which the Christian doctrine ascribes to him. That vastly extended spiritual working which is discovered through enlargement of our knowledge of the universe is a working not only of power but of character, and of this character. Throughout the universe and throughout eternity, the one spirit who pervades, sustains and orders all is the same right and trustworthy Being, working in goodness, perfectly deserving the confidence and love of all moral beings. This is the Christian doctrine.

That this claim of a perfect ethical Spirit operative in all existence must be tested by comparison with facts, the Christion doctrine does not forget, neither does it ignore the greatness of this undertaking. Just as we might expect, the difficulties that attend so high a claim are commensurate with its greatness. We are not in the region of small issues here, but of vast ones, where all questions are great. To demonstrate the reality of the One Spirit, first of the two units of existence, is impossible; but it is quite another question whether we may not find good reason for believing in it. The Christian faith is a rational impulse, while the Christian doctrine is a rational teaching; and the impulse is as sound as the teaching. Impulse and teaching alike are confident in proclaiming the reality of the one personal Spirit, perfectly good, as the supreme fact of existence, and in offering this belief to all as worthy to be received. This is not the place to show the reasons for this claim, but only to set it forth in its due position in the Christian doctrine. Before we come to the commendation of it by evidence, it will already have commended itself by its harmony with the best that we know.

4. GOD THE SOURCE

The relation between the two units of existence is made plain when it is said that one is the source of the other. The second is dependent upon the first, and is due to the causative or productive energy of it; or, more definitely still, the existence of the second is due to the will of the first. God is the first, and the universe is the second, and the existence of the universe is due to the energy and will of God. All will is as mysterious as it is familiar, but here we meet an element of mystery that we do not encounter in ourselves. Human volition makes use of energy, but never originates it, and human control over modes and expressions of energy, though real, is closely limited. But the infinite One differs from us mysteriously in this, that he can put forth productive energy: in him it originates, and from him proceeds. His will is a creative will, accompanied by perfect power. Moreover, it moves in the realm of comprehensive and balanced intelligence, which is wisdom, and acts out the suggestions of the perfect character. At all stages of its life the Christian doctrine has taught that God, by voluntary action of this sovereign and perfect kind, has caused, and still causes, the universe to exist. God is the original, the source of all existence that is not himself.

The usual expression of this truth is, that God is the Creator of the universe. The words create, creator and creation are ancient and familiar, and have this peculiarity, that they usually suggest rather definite ideas as to the manner in which God has produced other existence, and even as to the time at which that work was done. Creation has been conceived as absolute origination of something when before there had been nothing, and as occurring at some definite time. "To create out of nothing" is a familiar phrase, which has only too often represented a kind of impression that God created something, with nothing as the material out of which it was made. If the phrase were used, of course it ought to mean only that after nothing had been, something was caused to be; but the language is misleading and unhelpful, and it would be well if it were forgotten. But apart from this mode of speech, creation has been conceived as an absolute origination of existence after nothing had existed, and as occurring at some particular moment of time. Such an event of course must work a change inconceivably great. God was alone in existence until a given time, and then brought the universe into being. Thus regarded, creation was a temporal act, and one that altered the life of God, changing it from solitude to a state in which he was accompanied by a vast and complex total of existence. Still further, until recently Christian thought has generally regarded the time of creation as pretty definitely known: when this earth was created all besides came into being—except that angels were assumed to exist already, and to rejoice in the creation—and that the creation of all occurred at a date indicated by the chronology of the book of Genesis, a few thousand years ago. Through eternity to that date, or to the creation of angels, God was alone: since then he has been accompanied in existence.

Some parts of his created work, being of spiritual nature, will continue to exist forever, but the material part, it has been predicted, will go out of existence again. In company with these conceptions it has very naturally been thought that God's work of origination was attended by work of invention and construction, somewhat resembling the operations by which men become makers of things. Probably the work of creation has been more thoroughly anthropomorphized than any other work or relation attributed to God.

Changes, however, have invaded this field of thought, and creation can no longer be conceived in so pictorial and external a manner. Better understanding of the Old Testament removes it from among the witnesses regarding times and dates, and gives us imaginative representation in place of literal description. Better knowledge of the method of the world renders the old view of creation untenable. The anthropomorphic picture was too clear: we knew too much. We cannot draw so clear a picture. The mode of God's activity toward other existence must remain mysterious to us, and how the infinite One brings anything into being we shall never know. But we have knowledge enough to make us sure that we must make room for other ideas of creation than those that have usually borne the Christian name. If we cannot attain to clear description, we may be thankful that much is to be gained by opening our minds to large and flexible conceptions. It is in order to assert only the central fact and avoid unhelpful associations that the present section is entitled God the Source, instead of God the Creator.

For this is all that the Christian doctrine has occasion to affirm concerning this original relation. It does assert that the existence of God is necessary to that of the universe, while the existence of the universe is not necessary to that of God. One of the two is self-existent and the other is not, and the one is the source of the other. Because of the will and work of God the universe exists. The Christian doctrine does not insist upon any account or description of God's creative activity, or any theory of the manner in which power went forth, or goes forth, from him to act upon that which is not himself. On these points it has no objection to agnosticism, for it has no means of knowing what to proclaim. The method of fiat is the natural one to be represented in an anthropomorphic picture. The everlasting truth of divine origination was best represented, in such an atmosphere, by the sublime formula, "God said, Let there be light, and there was light" (Gen. i. 3). When something more philosophical was desired, emanation was proposed as the method in which the universe came forth from God. At present it is common to speak of processes, or of one comprehensive process, through which the universe came into existence. But all accounts that can be given of processes tell only of organization, for they imply existing material upon which the organizing process works. Origination they do not touch. No doctrine of creation tells anything about the nature of the divine creative movement itself, and no doctrine or theory will ever describe that movement. It lies beyond us, in a region of which we can never have clear knowledge. The recognition of this indescribableness in the creative work is indispensable if we are to think rightly of it. Of course we can obtain much knowledge of the great process by which the existing universe came to be such a universe as it now is, and we may understand more of God by learning it. Christian thought may accept in this region anything that may be established as true; but the heart of creative action is unsearchable.

As the Christian doctrine decides nothing as to the manner of creation, so it is indifferent concerning all questions of date and time. It will never again be held that the date of creation can be ascertained by reckoning up the generations of a human genealogy, or that man and the universe were created at the same time. We know too much of both man and the universe to imagine that. The real question is larger far: it is, whether the universe was brought into being at some given time, after God had existed alone from eternity, or whether God has always been accompanied in existence by a universe dependent upon himself. This question must be decided, if it can be decided at all, by evidence if there is evidence available, and upon grounds of rational probability if there is not. It may never be really decided. But the Christian doctrine is in no way affected, either by the question or by the decision. That doctrine affirms only that the universe exists because God exists and will have it so, and because he puts forth will, wisdom and power to make it exist. It goes no farther. It is no part of Christian doctrine that all that is not God had a day of absolute beginning, before which God was alone, or on the contrary that the existence of the universe is eternal. Either may be true.

Nevertheless, although we are not called by the Christian doctrine to choose between these two conceptions, we are very likely to find ourselves judging and choosing between them, each in his own way. Different minds judge differently. Doubtless the growing idea at present is that of an eternal universe, or one to which neither beginning nor end can be assigned. The growth of this view is not to be wondered at. The idea of an absolute beginning, before which there was nothing but God, is very easily put into words, but not so easily grasped in thought. The mind staggers at the thought of the universe as we know it, and still more as it really is, as brought into being after nothing had been. It is true that the staggering of the mind is not a final argument; but it is well to remember that when we assert an absolute beginning for the whole we are uttering clear words but an unclear thought, and not to think that we understand the matter better than we do. Nor is it easier to conceive of God as existing alone until a certain time and then calling a universe into existence. Such a change in the life of God it is easy to mention in words, but very difficult really to believe in. It seems in deeper harmony with our best conception of the infinite and eternal One in his unchangeableness and efficiency to think that God is eternally a creator, or an original from which other existence ever proceeds in accordance with his will and wisdom, and that thus he always has about him a universe, or a sum of organized being, into which always flows the fulness of his energy and love. According to this, which seems the nobler and worthier view, the divine will is eternally productive, and God has never been without a creation, and will never be alone. This appears to be the view that has best promise of the future.

It is to be noticed that this is no doctrine of the eternity of matter, as if the universe were something that God found existing together with himself, and had to deal with as an independent entity. The Christian doctrine of God has no place for such a doctrine as that. God alone is independently eternal, and if there is eternally a universe it is because God eternally wills it and makes it to exist. As a whole and in all its parts it depends upon him and without him would have no being; but his creative volition never fails, and the universe responds to his will by existing. Neither is this a doctrine of the indispensableness of the universe to God, as if he could not be God without it. In the Christian view of the matter God is the master, and it is by his will that the universe stands forth in being. Not because he must have a universe to be God, but because being God he will have a universe, he brings it into existence. In this there is no constraint and no dependence. God is supreme, and all else comes at the call of his will and character.

Can we identify the motive of God in creation? If the prevailing conception is that of a sudden act after ages of solitude, the question is, Why, having been so long alone, did God exchange his solitary life for one in which there was other existence? If the other idea be adopted, of a perpetual producing and sustaining of existence that is not himself, the question is, Why does God always desire that there may be existence besides his own? The two questions do not radically differ, but the latter is the easier in the answering. We can understand a perpetual activity better than one long unexercised and then ever afterward in use. If we venture to speak of the motive that leads to creation, we shall find ourselves remembering the impulse to self-expression that is characteristic of conscious life. It is impossible to think of an intelligent and worthy Spirit capable of creation as refraining from the act. Such powers must forth. Utterance is the natural law of life, honoured in God as it is in men, and creation is utterance. Creation is impartation also; and when we come to impartation we come to the field of character. The motive to creation, we may be sure, is not to be found in power, or in inventiveness and constructiveness: it lies deeper, in the moral realm. Self-utterance is self-impartation, and this is the work of love, and God is love. God's desire for being and welfare, for worthy existence and lofty use, for creatures who may have his fellowship and for fellowship with them, for a vast sum of created being in which his worthy character may have its way—this is the motive for creating that we behold in God when we view him in the light of Jesus.

To beget or bear a child is to accept a great responsibility: how much more to call a universe into existence! If God were not all-good and all-great, he would have no moral right to be a creator. If he were not the perfect holiness and love and wisdom, he could not take due care of that which he brings forth, and would wrong it in creating it. But the Christian faith, clear-eyed, sees a God worthy to be Creator of a universe, and such a God the Christian doctrine proclaims. No loftier word concerning him can ever be spoken than this, that he is worthy to be the source of boundless and endless being. Nor is there any vaster or more impressive thought of God than the thought of the creative mind and heart, the intelligence of the universe, the productive and sustaining power, acknowledging that which he has created, and fulfilling in its destinies the purpose of a faithful Creator. In this relation all others are embraced—the good God is the Source of all existence.

5. THE SELF-EXISTENT

The child's question, "Who made God?" is a perfectly natural and proper question, but the true answer is not such as the child expects. God simply is, and always has been, with nothing beyond him in duration or in causation. He is self-existent. The Christian doctrine affirms that God is uncreated, unoriginated, having no beginning and owing his existence to none. He is the great Original, with existence all his own. This has been implied in the doctrine of God as the Source of all. Of the two units of existence, one originates and sustains the other, but the One is itself originated not at all. All that exists consists of Creator and creation: the creation is from the Creator, but the Creator simply is.

It is convenient here to tell in two parts what God's self-existence means. One true statement is that the perfect mind is self-existent, underived, independent. The Original of all being is the perfect mind with all its powers. The first existence, all uncaused, is One who knows, wills, acts, feels, and is capable of standing in relation with other being. Primal being, underived, from which all else proceeds, consists in voluntary power with understanding. It is thought-producing mind, with operative and efficient energy. Another statement, equally true with this, is that in God the perfect character is self-existent. Original being is right, good, perfect. That which is unproduced and from eternity is wisdom, holiness, love: it is the character that deserves approval, admiration, worship, confidence, loyalty, from all intelligent beings that may ever exist. Primal existence has moral perfection. This is the Christian doctrine.

When these two thoughts are combined, we have the entire Christian statement as to that which stands back of all besides, as the uncaused original. It is not enough to say that qualities, whether intellectual or moral, are self-existent. It is not that wisdom, love or power is original and self-existent: this is true, but with a more helpful truth underlying. Wisdom, love and power are personal qualities or endowments, so far as we know them at all, and personal qualities and powers inhere in personality and in nothing else. Thought belongs to mind, and character to person, while power is at least in the habit of being an accompaniment of will. It is God himself that is self-existent, not merely the qualities of God. God the living heart and will, bearing the perfect character, with perfect moral quality, intellectual operation and volitional control, is the One underived and self-existent.

Self-existence is often said to be inconceivable, involving contradictory elements of thought. Our impulse to assign to everything its cause, or causes, is so strong and so necessary to our ordinary thinking that it is accounted impossible for our minds to hold the idea of independent and uncaused existence. But here is a paradox. Whether the idea of self-existence is impossible or not, experience shows it to be an unavoidable conception. Practically all minds entertain it, or at any rate assume it in their thinking. If we do not hold it concerning God, we shall find ourselves holding it concerning the universe. A self-existent universe, indeed, has the first opportunity to be believed in, and a very clear opportunity it is. God we do not see, but we do see the world around us, and then, with larger scope, the universe. The universe was there before we came, or any of our kind, and although we know that it is ever changing, still we know it as an ever-changing sum of existence, which as a total seems stable and everlasting. No sign of its origin is apparent as we look, and the more we know of it, although we may trace present forms to their beginning, the less does a date of absolute origination appear. We may refer its existence back to God, and say that it owes itself to a power and will that lie back of it, and then we may say that this God is self-existent. If we do not do this in some form, we shall inevitably attribute self-existence to the universe itself. We may profess agnosticism on the subject, and declare that we do not know whence the universe is; but this is only another way of saying that so far as we can see the universe exists independently of any known causation, which is practically to call it self-existent. We shall believe either in a self-existing God adequate to the causing of the universe, or in a universe apparently existing of itself. Certainly it is a strange kind of inconceivableness, that belongs to an idea that all minds are sure to hold, and to apply to the greatest object that is known to them. Self-existence is not picturable, or accountable in clearly-defined theory, and the exposition of it may involve contradictory statements, but it is very far from inconceivable. It is nearer the truth to call it an idea that we cannot escape.

It is fair to ask which is the more reasonable to believe in, the universe existing of itself, or God existing of himself and adequate to giving existence to the universe? In some aspects the universe may seem sufficient to itself; and yet it is a striking fact that the human mind has steadily entertained the opposite belief. In the agelong common understanding, some adequate mind and power has been posited to account for that which exists. The description of this adequate mind and power has often been childish, and therefore we may proceed to call the entire idea of such a power childish, and declare that we know better now; and yet the question of comparative reasonableness remains to be judged. The truth will be found to be that the only self-existence in which we can rest is the self-existence of a sufficient God.

The present form and state of the universe is a result of processes: this is the great inference from modern observation. By processes things have come to be as they are. The processes are intellectual in their nature, in the sense that they work out intelligible results, and are directed meanwhile by intelligible principles. They are long and steady processes, and the existing results have been brought about only through long and steady operation. The whole sum of processes and results constitutes what we may fairly call a system. The entire system is not visible to us, and can never become so, and yet we are in a position to be sure that there is indeed a system comprehending all. A system is of course an intellectual fact, not a physical. It is a deep misconception to think of what we call the material universe as mainly material in its essential nature. Apart from all questions as to the nature of matter and spirit, and from the present recognition of psychical quality where only matter was but lately supposed to be, the universe as we observe it is one vast working-out of ideas in material forms of expression. The extent of this fact already known is far too vast to be conceived by human thought, and the one thing certain about future knowledge is that this extent will still be indefinitely enlarged. All science takes for granted the universal scope and sway of ideas, and is never disappointed in so doing. Rational quality pervades the universe, and more and more it is destined to be known as a universe of ideas in action.

Then the question is, which is more reasonably regarded as self-existent, an infinitely vast body of ideas in operation without a mind to originate and operate them, or a mind originating the ideas and holding them in operation? We may ask ourselves whether we are capable of judging upon such a question, because our range is so limited and there is so much that we cannot know. But we must judge by such light as we have, and such light as we have gives us all our science; and in such light as we have it is impossible to judge otherwise than that a mind is farther back than an idea, and more original. We know nothing of an idea except as the act and product of a mind. To affirm that a mass of ideas in effective operation, constituting a universal system, exists of itself is far less reasonable than to say that there exists of itself a mind, to which the ideas owe their existence and operative power. The self-existence of God is the doctrine that was first suggested, and the doctrine that will stand.

The Christian doctrine offers no apology to science for affirming the self-existence of God. The conviction was reached, it is true, not so much through speculative thought as through religion; for religion, which is an experience, is a confidence in One who alone is God, and rests in the absolute independence of his being. Its God simply is. This conviction Christian faith is well entitled to hold, without objection from the scientific point of view. Modern science has been observing facts, and has naturally been agnostic, for the time, as to origins, with the result that the universe was easily thought to be sufficient to itself, and science came to be counted as a witness to its independence. But the agnostic conclusion is only negative, and only tentative, and is by no means sure to be final on the part of science; and science with its method is by no means the only authorized explorer in the wide realm of being. In its own field religion may discover sound reason for believing in a God who can be no other than the source of all, existent by his own nature. If such discovery is made, it is quite legitimate for the report of it to be welcomed by all who are seeking to know whence all things come, and adopted as the truth that best gives rational unity to the whole.

The self-existence of the God of perfect character is even more profoundly significant than the self-existence of the God of mind and power. Practical inferences from it are drawn in the same manner, but they come home to us more closely. Since the God of power is self-existent and the source of all, we know that all manifestations of power that we observe are secondary and contingent, and all power in finite beings is derived; and the all-comprehensive and unborrowed power stands back of all. Again, since the God of mind is self-existent, all human intellect and mental work is derived and secondary, while back of all is the uncreated mind, source and type of all intelligence, upon which the created mind may rest for confidence in its own trustworthiness. Now in the same strain we add, that since the God of perfect character is self-existent, all human morality is secondary and derived, the entire conception and sphere of morals in this world is embraced in something infinitely greater than itself, and underneath the whole lies a primary, independent and original foundation for ethical life and meaning. And further, since the eternal goodness is self-existent, religion has immovable ground for existence, throughout the universe and forever the reasons for it are the same, and the highest reach of purity in religion comes nearest to the truth. This is what God's self-existence means to us.

Perhaps we cannot prove that there can be only one self-existent—unless by some technical arguing that is too small for the subject. But the probability to that effect is equal to certainty. The Christian doctrine assigns to God a sole self-existence when it says that of the two units one is the source of the other, for it accounts for everything else by referring it to him, and sets all in the rank of the dependent; and this is a reasonable position. Certainly there is one self-existent, and only one. We may well be thankful that concerning the cause of self-existence, or the method of it, there can be no argument. That lies beyond all arguing and explaining. But there can be no more joyful and reassuring word than this, that the Being whom we know in our best religion is the underived and self-existent God, believing in whom we build our faith and our doctrine upon ultimate foundations.

6. THE ETERNAL.

The Christian doctrine always proclaims an eternal God. "Now unto the King eternal, immortal, invisible, the only God, be honour and glory for ever and ever" (1 Tim. i. 17), is the song that it sings. By the eternal God is meant in common speech the God whose existence has neither beginning nor end: the God who by his nature has ever been and must forever be. Such a God the Christian doctrine affirms.

In this sense, to be self-existent is to be eternal. To be self-existent is to be without beginning, and by natural implication it is to be without end. Self-existence is simply existence wholly independent. As nothing initiated it, so nothing can terminate it. It is essentially eternal, without limits upon its duration. As perhaps we cannot prove that there can be only one self-existent, so perhaps we cannot prove that there can exist only one Being whose nature it is to be eternal; but here again the probability is overwhelming, and may be taken as equal to certainty. When Christianity speaks of the eternal God, it means that the one Spirit, who alone is God, is alone possessed of independent being that never began and can never end. The Christian doctrine proclaims a theism, and a monotheism, for eternity past and eternity to come. The intelligence, power and perfect goodness that belong to the only God are from everlasting to everlasting—or to speak more correctly, that eternal God in whom these qualities inhere is without beginning and without end of life. Whatever may change, he exists forever.

Here again we affirm what we cannot portray, but that is no reason against our affirming it. Existence without beginning or end is beyond our power to comprehend, but notwithstanding this it stands as a necessary element in our thought. It is no more unthinkable than its opposite. If we try to conceive of all existence as confined within certain limits of duration, we shall be compelled to abandon the endeavour because of its sheer absurdity; while the effort to grasp eternal being conquers us only by its greatness. Eternity of being is beyond our range of thought, but contains no element of absurdity. It is rational to believe in the eternal God.

The word eternal, however, conveys another idea besides that of duration without beginning or end. It is a secondary meaning, into which the first is naturally developed. If we try to think of existence whose duration is unlimited, and to conceive in any measure what it must be, we shall find ourselves thinking of an existence superior to all temporal conditions, and unaffected by them. It is a mistake to think of existence that we call eternal as exempt from the influence of duration merely with reference to beginning and ending. Such existence is exempt from the control of duration throughout its boundless extent. The word does more than deny termini for existence: it affirms or implies an abiding quality in the existence which it thus represents as limitless. The absence of limits of time opens the way for a quality that can have no place in our time-measured life, save as it enters through fellowship with the Eternal. That quality is superiority to time, freedom from the effects of the method of succession. It is a quality that we are compelled to set forth in negative form, because the positive nature of it lies beyond our experience. We may wish for a better word, but we cannot go farther than to describe the eternal life of God as a timeless life. Eternity differs from time not merely in length, but in freedom from the limitations that time imposes upon intelligent existence.

Various illustrations of this idea will meet us as we go on through the doctrine of God: at present we must only endeavour to see in general what it means. Our minds are controlled and limited by succession. Duration takes this form in its influence upon us—it sets one thing before and another after, and prevents us from experiencing them except in their order. To us yesterday is yesterday, not to-day, and to-morrow is to-morrow. We live exclusively in an ever-moving moment, with the past behind it and the future before it. Nothing could be briefer than the fragment of time that is actually present. We have indeed a personal continuity, which is one of the most mysterious things about our life; but this does not make it the less true that yesterday is ours only in its results, and to-morrow only in expectation. This is so thoroughly a part of our natural mode of living as often to be taken for a necessary mode of rational existence; and under this impression eternity is taken to be merely a prolongation of time, with the element of temporal succession forever unmodified. But this subjection to succession is no necessary part of rational life. Our bondage to succession is one of our limitations. Even now we should often be glad if we could transcend it and live on a larger scale. Broader mental operations are perfectly conceivable to us, and we know that they would not be abnormal in rational existence, but would bring a noble and worthy enlargement. If there exists a perfect mind, we are sure that it must be free from this limitation; for our dependence upon succession, with its consequences, though it be a part of ourselves, is an imperfection in rational life. If God is the perfect mind, he is superior to time: he lives a timeless life, governed by no limitations from duration with its series of successions. His life is eternal: it is not merely of boundless length, but is full of that infinite largeness and richness which must accompany superiority to time and all its influences.

Of this life above time we can at least see that it must be a life all-comprehensive. To the perfect mind thus living, the whole range and sum of existence, whether his own or that of other being, must be perpetually present. Of course he must be aware of succession, or he would not know things as they are, but it is also true that he knows all from above succession, and independently of it. He does not learn by experience, or obtain his knowledge of things by seeing them come and pass, as we do. To him all is present, and all enters always into his life. And so his life does not depend for its worth and interest upon the changes, the surprises, the quick developments, upon which we count so much, and which constitute so large a part of the charm of our limited existence. We are dependent upon "the chances and changes of this mortal life" for much of the interest and value of our experience; but all this has no place with God. He is superior to all such dependence, and lives forever a life whose glory is in itself. From everlasting to everlasting he is God. As the perfect Being he has the entire fulness of his own unmeasured life always in mind and heart, and has no need of those uncertainties and surprises, bound in with our kind of life, with which time diversifies and renders piquant our experience. The divine perfection, purpose and work are always with him in their completeness, and all the workings of his goodness are always with him in their preciousness. The life of God that is eternal contains the secret of perpetual satisfaction, for the divine fulness is in it, and it is worth living not merely for what will come of it, but for its own sake.

Along with this superiority to control from time, denoted

by the word eternal, there must go a like superiority to control from the limitations of space. This idea belongs in company with the other, though strictly it is not indicated by the word eternal. We are even more closely limited in space than we are in time, for we have no spatial faculty that corresponds to memory, or to imagination. But through all places as well as through all times the life of the eternal Spirit ranges free, and all parts of the universe as well as all moments of duration are present to him. Thus the life of God as eternal is the largest life, and the fullest, that can possibly exist. To call it the largest and fullest that can be conceived is to fall far below the reality.

This qualitative meaning in the word eternal is quite as important to sound Christian thought concerning God as the meaning that relates to duration. But it has been much less considered, and there is great need that it be taken up with fresh interest and appreciation. By most Christians it would not be mentioned at all in a definition of the term: they would define eternity simply as a word of duration. Doubtless the idea of infinite length of duration is impressive, but in itself it has no spiritual quality whatever: that must be imparted to it by the connection in which it is used. And yet when once it is seriously considered the temporal or durational sense does imply a superiority to time-conditions that must impart to existence a quality and character of its own; and this fact, though scarcely recognized, has certainly influenced the popular conception of the eternity of God. The popular conception is certainly richer than the durational definition commonly accepted could ever make it. Probably at present more of helpful spiritual truth concerning God is to be learned by meditation upon this rich qualitative sense of his eternity than can be drawn from thinking of it as infinite duration. It is by way of this second meaning that the adjective eternal passes over to objects other than God. The eternal life that is set forth in the New Testament is not merely life that has no end, any more than it is life that has no beginning. The durational sense of the word cannot apply in its fulness to anything human or finite: strictly, there is only one Eternal. Moreover, mere existence without end cannot be offered as a boon, for the value of such a gift must be determined by its quality. The "eternal life" of the gospel is an unending life that partakes in the eternity of God: life of God's own children, above time and its changes: life worth living in itself and for its own sake: life whose everlastingness is precious by reason of its worth in fellowship with him who is eternal. The obscuring of this element in our conception of the eternal must mean impoverishment to all our Christian thought, and ultimately to our Christian life, while by means of it we may rise to the highest conceptions both of God and of human destiny of which our minds are capable.

Under the conception of his eternity, then, the Christian doctrine affirms that God has always existed and will always exist, possessed of all the qualities that make up his being and character; that through eternal duration he always lives a life of eternal quality and fulness, superior to time and independent of succession, into which all its elements always enter at once and abide together; and that this eternal life of God is a life in which existence for its own sake is perfectly worthy of the perfect Being.

7. THE INFINITE

The word infinite has long been a familiar and favourite word in statements of the Christian doctrine of God. The word itself, meaning simply without bounds, or unlimited, is perfectly colourless and unsuggestive, entirely devoid of spiritual quality; and yet in Christian thought and devotion it has proved to be a word of vast suggestiveness and power, expansive for the mind and uplifting for the heart. Doubtless the thought of God has done far more to enrich the word than the word has done to define or clarify the thought of God. But the Christian doctrine needs the word, and insists upon the thought which it expresses.

The idea of infinity, strictly speaking, is an abstract idea that belongs rather to philosophy than to religion. Yet it is in the field of religion that the idea first became impressive, and it is thence that it passed as an influential idea into philosophy. Religion does not concern itself with the distinction between the infinite and the finite, but it does impel the soul to stand in awe before a Being who impresses it as infinite. From the point of view of the living soul, infinity is not a quality defined, nor is the mention of it the affirming of a comparison between it and the finite: it is simply an unmeasured and immeasurable greatness. In religion, infinity is not reasoned out, it is felt. Man stands before it, feels himself surrounded by it, and responds to it with reverence and humility. It wins upon him, impresses him, makes him a worshipper, long before he has grasped it as a metaphysical conception, or thought of defining it. It is by standing awed before an indefinite divine greatness that man has come to think of what he afterward names the infinite.

In this practical light, which is the historical, infinity is of course a relative conception, variable in the extent of its meaning. Long before worshipping man is capable of thinking what vastness such a word would cover, he may be impressed by the sense of infinity in the object of his worship, and may begin to use the word, with but a narrow significance. The infinite is the Being who seems great beyond all conception, to whose greatness no limits can be imagined. The essential sense of the infinite may be present while the range of recognized greatness is but small, since infinity is not at first a matter of measurements but of sensations. As the human powers grow and the spiritual susceptibilities are deepened, the meaning is enlarged. By and by philosophical reflection enters, and analysis of working ideas begins, and then man inquires what he understands by the infinite. He has long been setting it over against his own littleness, but now he begins to distinguish in thought between infinite and finite. He comes to have a doctrine. But very likely he has no more sense of the infinite than he had before. He may have less. The religious content and effect of the infinite for the soul is independent of the clearness with which the intellectual conception is apprehended. The infinite is too great for man; but that may mean perplexity for the intellect, while it means rapture for the heart. A man may think upon the infinite, unmoved; but he may be deeply moved by an infinite of which he knows not how to think. The utmost that a man can hope is that he may possess a worthy and ever-growing sense of the inconceivable greatness of God, and think with some justice of its meaning.

Very naturally, it is the religious and practical meaning of the infinity of God that has place in the Christian doctrine. Yet there is good reason why the idea of infinity as applied to him should be made as clear as possible.

Ourselves we call finite, by which we mean that on every side our powers and our relations reach their limit. We are not universal in our range, and we are not adequate to all the possibilities that lie within the range that is actually ours. We are limited by relations of time and space. We can act only now and here. Such limits of relation are enough to constitute close restriction upon our possibilities. As for our actual powers, we have never seen them by themselves, and they have never been tested to the full extent, so that we do not precisely know how much they are capable of; but we know beyond a doubt that limitation is an unremovable part of our being. The limitation is not merely in our relations, but also in ourselves. A being that can act only here and now can never become able to do all that corresponds to the nature of spiritual powers; and we can act only here and now—or if there be any modification to be made to this statement it is too slight to discredit it. We are thus limited not by circumstances merely, but by our nature—we were made so. By our very nature some possibilities of spiritual activity are shut out from us. Some things we can do, and some we cannot, and from this condition we shall never escape. Our powers will grow, but our essential rank and description as limited beings will never be altered. This is what it is to be finite.

When we say that God is infinite, we reverse the affirmations and denials that we have made concerning ourselves. We say that his powers are such as never to reach the limit of their possibilities, and that he is in universal and perfect relation with all other existence. He is infinite or unbounded in himself, and infinite or unrestrained in the freedom and opportunity of action that his perfect relation to other existence opens to him. If we think of him by himself, then in himself all powers are of unlimited greatness and sufficiency. If we think of him in connection with other being, then those powers are in perfect relation to it all, so that to him all normal action is freely possible. This is what it is to be infinite.

In trying to think somewhat definitely of the infinity of God, we often assert the infinity of his separate powers. "Infinite in all his attributes" is a common form of speech. His power is infinite: upon his ability to act, and to do whatever is normal to him, there are no limits, either in his own nature or in his relations to other existence. In a like sense his knowledge is infinite, or unbounded and complete. His presence is infinite: from no place is he excluded, but in all space, as in all duration, he exists in the fulness of his being. These may be taken as true descriptions of the infinity of God in certain aspects or operations of his nature. We often speak also of infinity in his moral attributes, and tell of his infinite holiness and infinite love. Here the language is often used loosely and popularly, and perhaps the grouping of infinity with a moral trait does not yield itself to precise expression. But the names serve a useful purpose. Infinite holiness and love are the moral characteristics of the Being in whom all powers are perfect, unlimited, adequate: they are holiness and love perfect in quality, boundless in range, sovereign in action. So if we subdivide, and speak of infinite righteousness or infinite mercy, the adjective will denote the immeasurable greatness, fulness, efficiency, of the quality that it describes. It is right thus to represent the moral qualities as infinite, if we remember that we are speaking in the religious sphere, rather than in the philosophical.

Yet the full wealth of the word infinite is not opened when we speak of infinite power and knowledge, or even of infinite holiness and love. That these are infinite is not the central Christian truth concerning infinity. The central truth is that God is infinite—not the qualities and powers, but the Being to whom they belong. We ascribe infinity to God himself, possessed of will and mind and heart and character in unlimited perfection, from whom every work that is normal to such a Being goes forth unrestrained. This is the glorious reality which the Christian doctrine proclaims. No wonder that in Christian use the word infinite has passed over from negative significance to positive, and been redeemed from colourlessness to spiritual beauty.

Christianity always speaks of God as a spirit, meaning by a spirit a personal being, and at the same time it speaks of him as infinite. It thus affirms a combination that knows no parallel. We need not wonder that it is questioned. Finite spirits we know, and our conception of them has their finitude for a constituent element, but now we tell of a spirit beyond all finitude, an infinite spirit. In common use the word spirit is a more variable word than infinite, and in this combination the more flexible noun tends to yield to the more exacting adjective, and take on a shadowy meaning. Its connotation of personal quality may easily fade away, and the phrase infinite spirit may turn to the service of a pantheistic cast of thought. Many think it must do so. Personality fades out in infinity, and it sometimes almost seems that by insisting upon his infinity we may be in danger of losing our living God.

But the Christian doctrine does not yield to this suggestion. It does not shrink from the great paradox that appears when God is presented as both personal and infinite. It makes bold to affirm the infinite Person. For this it is charged with folly, since infinity and personality are accounted exclusive of each other. Since personality is limited and the infinite is unlimited, the two are incompatible: the personal cannot be infinite, or the infinite personal. By this dilemma the question of a personal God is often thought to be settled once for all in the negative. Nevertheless Christianity holds fast that the infinite Spirit is a personal Spirit, and that in this there is no absurdity. We have already spoken of the Personality of God, and beginning from the human have sought to show that from our limited personality we may legitimately look up to the perfect personality in God alone. At present we approach the question from the other side: we begin from above, and endeavour to tell what we mean by the infinite personal Spirit.

When God is called the infinite Being, it is meant that upon his powers and qualities there are no limitations. Then we naturally ask what are the powers upon which we are declaring that there is no limitation. We turn at first to the quarter where signs of greatness are most apparent and familiar, and look for God in as much of the vast and various universe as we can behold. If there is any power or quality that is manifest everywhere, it is intelligence; equally clear is activity directed by intelligence; while implied in both is relatedness of the efficient intelligence to other being. If any Being whatever is expressed in the universe that we behold, these are his qualities. The universal frame is one vast expression of intelligence and activity, standing in relation with that upon which they work. But these, we have only to repeat, are the constituent elements of personality. What makes us persons is self-consciousness, or intelligence, and self-determination, or intelligent activity, and relatedness to other beings. We do not behold these elements gathered up into a person when we look abroad upon the world, but neither do we behold that in observing men. Everywhere we learn personality from its expressions. If there exists an intelligence adequate to those vast works in which we in our measure can discern it, an intelligence so great that we name it infinite, surely it is only the most natural of observations to look upon that intelligence as self-conscious. Can we think it knows so much and does not know itself? And if there is so great activity ordered by intelligence, all that we know of intelligence and activity tells us that the Actor must be self-directing in the operation that so intelligently controls the universe. And if there is a Being who thus acts upon the universe, there belongs to him that relatedness which we account a mark of operative personality. Thus the very elements that make up personality in us are clearly traceable in him whom we call infinite, and they seem there to be sufficiently at home, with nothing absurd in their association with the greatness of God.

As soon as we go a step farther and recognize in the infinite anything of character, we are still more plainly in the realm of personality. If we think of the infinite Being as holy, or righteous, or gracious, or if we should go to the opposite extreme and look upon the infinite movement as the work of one great cruelty and wrong, all this is to attribute to the infinite the acts of personality. It is only by personification that a storm can be called cruel or an earthquake unjust, for it is only to a real person that we can properly attribute either cruelty and injustice or righteousness and love. If the infinite Being has character, the infinite Being is personal; and if we have anything to do with an infinite Being at all, we have to do with a Being who is possessed of character. Whatever our speculative difficulties may be, we are practically compelled to attribute infinity and personality to the same Being. The difficulties may remain, but confidence in the Infinite Person will remain also.

The relation between the infinite and the finite offers a problem that has often proved troublesome, and unfavourable to religious confidence. The finite, it is said, must of necessity be included in the infinite; for if it is not, the infinite belies its name, and is only another finite, since it is not all-comprehensive, but leaves something outside of itself. But if the finite is included in the infinite, it must be a part of the infinite; and if the infinite is God, man, being finite, must be a part of God: pantheism is the outcome, and human responsibility with moral significance in life is gone.

Perhaps the whole question is due to ambiguity in terms. Infinity seems here to be thought of in a kind of numerical fashion, and an infinite as the sum-total of all that is of its kind. If this were right, and the infinite mind were the sum of all mind, so that there would be room for nothing else of that nature, then of course the pantheistic conclusion would be justified. There could be no finite, and God would be alone. But that is not the idea of infinity with which we have to deal. It is not with "the infinite" that our existence is concerned; it is with the infinite Being, God. The infinity which the Christian doctrine attributes to him is not of such nature as to extinguish or absorb finite beings. We speak of an infinite presence, but the infinity of his presence does not absorb into himself that which it embosoms, nor does the infinity of his knowledge destroy the separate existence of that which he knows. The infinite God is different from an infinite number, embracing all numbers in itself; different too from an infinite universe, in which by the very definition all existing things would be included. The Christian doctrine does not regard him as the sum of existence. In the Christian light, the real question concerns the relation between beings of limited powers and the Being whose powers are all unlimited. God's infinity is his superiority to all limitations in all the powers and qualities of his being: it is the measureless amplitude of the powers that make up his living personality: it is the boundlessness of his intelligence, his power, his moral excellence, and his sufficiency for the fulfilling of all relations. A kind of infinity that would leave no room for the finite may be conceivable to us, but it has no existence in him. His being is all-comprehensive, but not destructive of what it comprehends: he embraces all, but does not identify it with himself.

When we think as well as we may of the infinite personality, or of the free and unhindered heart and mind and will, reaching with his infinity far beyond the needs of all his creatures, it does not naturally occur to us that his infinity absorbs our personality. Rather does it seem likely to promote and favour separateness in us. If self-conscious and self-determining life is the type set for all other spiritual existence by his nature, surely the infinity of such life in him will be the pledge of the integrity of such life in us. The infinite personality is the sure hope of the finite personality in the universe of God. The great Person who has brought forth other persons will surely give their personality its due place and honour, and preserve it sacred as the finite likeness of his own. The infinite Spirit is personal in the full and typical sense, and his personal nature is the guaranty of ours. Finite spirits bearing the likeness of God are selves, to whose personal distinctness the infinite One is not a destroyer but a friend. At the same time it is true in a sense beyond our explaining that his being embraces theirs—a mysterious fact which has its practical value in this, that God does not have to go out of himself to find them, or they to go out of themselves to dwell in the secret of his presence. The spheres of finite and infinite so blend that "spirit with Spirit can meet."

To this effect experience bears testimony. In our misunderstanding of infinity we may fear that we shall find ourselves only unresponsible parts of one infinite substance: but experience bears witness that we are not. Our relation to the infinite is no other than a personal relation. The distinctness of man from God is certified by the facts of moral responsibility and significance that belong to our life. We can consent to God, or we can resist him and refuse him his place. The long story of wills is in part a story of accord with God, and in part a story of resistance, only too often positive and determined. Our independence makes the glory and tragedy of our career, and alike in the glory and in the tragedy it is the sign of our personal separateness from God. And because we are separate, it is our privilege to adore the Infinite.

In the only sense in which Christian Theology needs to dwell upon the term, the infinite God is the Absolute. The

absolute is the ultimate in thought and in relations: it is that
in which all relations have their ground, and beyond which
thought has neither power nor need to go. This is precisely
what the Christian doctrine declares God to be. With
reference to relations, God is the ground of the world, the
One whose existence is the indispensable condition for the
existence of anything else, the ultimate source from which
all proceeds. On the bosom of the infinite reposes the finite
with all its relations and affairs. With reference to thought
which explores all things conceivable, God is the One beyond
whom thought cannot go, and has no need of going. Both
in thought and in fact, he is the first and the last, the original
and the farthest, beyond whom there is no reason to search
for more. He exists of himself, and is the uttermost than can
be found by searching, in this world or in any other. Since
his existence with his character and powers is sufficient to
account for all else that exists, he is the uttermost that we
need to find. There are mysteries for us in the universe, but
the hope for solution of them resides in his nature. He is
the ground of truth. He is the ground of right. He is the
original source of all true ideals of spiritual existence. He is
the sole fount of intellectual power and spiritual aspiration,
and the great Original of holiness and righteousness and
love. Beyond him is nothing, from him is all. This is the
view of God that Christian thought has always held, now
more dimly and now more clearly, but it still awaits larger
exposition and worthier appreciation than it has ever yet
received. It is a view that is naturally involved in all clear
theism, and is of the very substance of all that deserves the
name of monotheism. The Christian faith and doctrine
ascribe all glory to the infinite holy and gracious Spirit, the
Alpha and the Omega, the beginning and the ending, in
whom all live and move and have their being, the one God
of all.

8. THE UNCHANGEABLE

The unchangeableness of God needs no separate proof, after we have recognized his self-existence and eternity. The One who is self-existent and eternal cannot change, but is ever the same. The universe in itself is mutable, for it has no independent existence, but hangs upon a will that is not its own. Power works through it, not from it. It has no wisdom of its own, but may become this or that, according to the wisdom and will of that Other whose dependent companion it is. But that Other is immutable. There is nothing that has power to affect him with change. His independent, self-existent being is beyond the reach of alteration, and from eternity to eternity he is the same. So the best Hebrew faith discerned, and so the Christian doctrine has always set him forth.

The unchangeableness of God is not in his methods, but in himself. It is often spoken of as if it were in his methods, and were sufficiently well illustrated by such a fact as the uniformity of nature. The one God, it is virtually assumed, will always do everything in the same way. His unchangeableness is sometimes conceived as a kind of rigidity or immobility, an unalterableness of method that in human affairs we should associate with littleness rather than with greatness. We are acquainted with a changelessness which is really a form of helplessness, and the divine immutability has sometimes been set forth in terms almost suggestive of this. But very unlike this is the quality of which we are thinking. The unchangeableness of God in himself is that finality and unalterableness in powers and character which belongs to eternal being. Self-existence is once for all, with all that it contains. As manifested in his action, God's unchangeableness is that steady operation which expresses always the working of one mind and heart. It is the quality in God by virtue of which the universe through its whole duration is truly one and continuous, a single outworking from one source. It is the ground in God of his own consistency, intellectual, moral and practical, and of the consistency of his perpetual and abiding operation.

Evidently such an unchangeableness as this has nothing in common with immobility. It suggests no singleness in mode of working, but rather has in it all the breadth and fulness of infinity. It is entirely consistent with endless variety in operation. It does not prevent God from working differently in different conditions, or employing whatever method may suit his purpose best. The greatness of God is an infinite versatility, rendering natural to him an infinite variety of action, adapted to the infinite variety of needs and occasions. We understand the liberty of the versatile and exercise it ourselves, within our limits: surely then we should welcome it among our thoughts of God. In fact, we do make use of it there. We say that in forgiving a sinner the attitude of God toward the man is changed, and yet no one understands this change to be inconsistent with his immutability. Rather is it required by his immutablity; for God is unalterable in the quality that will bless the needy and deliver the sinful at every opportunity. The change is not in God, but in the man, and in the moral situation that conditions God's attitude toward the man. Versatility in action is no sign of feebleness of will or fickleness of purpose: it may be a sign of firmness of will and inflexibility of purpose. We know very well that a determined man, holding a settled purpose, will change his method of action, as often as steadfastness in his purpose requires the change. He is certain to employ means after means and method after method, if only he is unchangeably determined to accomplish an important purpose that sweeps through long time and varying conditions. The very immutability of the purpose, and of him who holds it, leads to the use of as many means and methods as the case may demand. On this familiar principle the unchangeableness of God prescribes no enforced uniformity for his methods, and is attended by nothing of that persistent immobility which in men is so often a sign of weakness. Just because he is unchangeably the same, "God fulfils himself in many ways."

The unchangeableness upon which the Christian doctrine has most occasion to dwell is of course in the realm of character. It is when the divine character is perceived as it is shown in Christ that immutability becomes the theme of joy. It means that God has always been and will always be the holy, righteous and gracious God, who is absolutely worthy of all confidence and love. His goodness has not been developed, and will never be altered: from everlasting to everlasting he is the same, with character unchangeable. Such immutability is the hope of the universe. The dependent and mutable rests upon the bosom of the self-existent and changeless, and finds there its stability and hope. In the spiritual life of men, the unchangeableness of God is ground for complete and unalterable confidence. Both in the Old Testament and in the New, the spirit of his word, "I change not" (Mal. iii. 8), brings the inspiration of undying hope to all that is good. It seems pathetic that in the long course of religion the God who is always the same has been so variously conceived by men. Amid the incessant variations of thought concerning him it has often seemed as if there could be no sure and unalterable reality for men to discover. But the variableness has been in human knowledge, not in that which men were seeking to know. Within the darkness stands the One whom we seek, himself always desiring not only to be sought but to be found, and welcoming every eye that looks to him, and every gain in trueness of vision. The assurance given in Christ that God is the same forever comes with reassuring power to every heart that discerns him in the Christian light.

9. TRANSCENDENCE

We have spoken of the two units of existence, or of God and the universe, and have thus distinguished all that exists or ever can exist into two parts that differ profoundly from each other. However unable we may be to define satisfactorily, there stands an immeasurable difference between God and all that is not God. But when we have affirmed this great distinction, it is natural to inquire how these two units of existence are related to each other. We wish to judge them justly in their relative magnitude, and we desire if possible to obtain some conception of the manner in which they are practically related. Which is the greater of the two, and what do we mean when we say that one is greater than the other? This is one of our questions, and another is, How intimate is their mutual interaction, or the action of one upon the other? In our present study these inquiries are undertaken not so much from a speculative interest in the result as from the desire to know God more truly by viewing him in his relation to that which is not himself.

In comparatively recent times two words, Immanence and Transcendence, have come into common use for setting forth the relation between God and the universe. They are not new words, and still less are they expressive of new ideas, but of late they have apparently found a new usefulness, appealing helpfully to the needs of religious thought. Whether they will always remain as acceptable and helpful as they appear to be at present is a question that we have no need to answer, but for the service of present-day thought they are useful words, and they are well adapted to the statement of truth that is now in hand. In the word Transcendence comparison is affirmed between the two units of existence, while the companion-word Immanence tells of the closeness of their mutual relation. The first asserts that the one unit transcends or exceeds the other; the second, that the greater inhabits and pervades the less. Great as they are, these appear to be simple and obvious statements, properly implied in any monotheism. Yet there is need of a certain amount of definition, for there are more senses than one in which God may be conceived as immanent and as transcendent. The clearness and strength of our doctrine of God will depend somewhat upon the nature of our conclusions upon these two aspects of his being.

At present we speak of Transcendence, endeavouring to answer the question what we mean when we say that God is transcendent in his relation to the universe. It is necessary first to remove some ambiguity, by pointing out a sense in which Transcendence is not to be understood. We have said that the word transcendence institutes the great comparison between God and the universe, and asserts the superiority of God. But this superiority or transcendence of God has sometimes been interpreted in ways that are impossible in the light of our present knowledge. Under a variety of influences it has come to pass that the transcendent God was represented as a God outside the world and above it, separated from an order so inferior as to be unworthy of his immediate presence.

Perhaps this way of thinking had its starting-point in the thoughts of primitive man. When the earth was supposed to be flat and motionless, it was not unnatural to conceive of the Supreme as locally higher than man. The overarching heaven was regarded as the abode of God, and worship was directed to One who was directly overhead. Hence men looked up in worship, or else bowed in reverence before that which was high. The habit of placing God physically above us has outlived its usefulness without losing its power. By great multitudes of Christians, inheriting from the ancient past, he is still imagined as overhead and far away. General antiquity has bequeathed even to us the conception of a distant God.

When reflection had entered the field, the world came to be regarded as material; and then it followed that God was set in contrast with it in his quality as a Spirit. Spirit is of a higher order than matter, it was said, and God is the greatest Spirit, contrasted with matter in the highest degree. His attitude toward the material world must be determined by his superiority and by his consciousness of it. The one pure Spirit must certainly be removed from contact with the material world and order. He dwells apart, untouched by that which is so profoundly in contrast with his nature.

This conception of transcendence is confirmed and intensified when to the obvious difference between matter and spirit is added the doctrine, long held, that matter is the seat of evil, and is itself corrupt. The human body has been taken to be the seat and provoking cause of sin; and from this starting-point it has been thought that matter in all its forms is contaminated by evil, or else is so suggestive of evil to the spirit as to be condemnable. Then once more it naturally follows that the high and pure God can have nothing to do with a material world. It has been held that he cannot have created matter by direct action, but must have brought it into existence through intermediate agencies. Between the purity of God and the production of so corrupt a thing there must have been a line of mediators, gradually descending in moral quality as distance from the holy source increased, until at length there was a being far enough removed from the divine perfection to create the material world with all its corruptness. With such an idea of the beginning, and often without the help of such an idea, it has been held that God must always communicate with the world through mediating agencies. Revelation as well as creation must needs be mediated, since God's greatness and purity really detach him from human affairs. There must be messengers sent to bring his word to men, and they must be supernaturally certified as the genuine representatives of him in whose name they come. Angels owe very much of their prominence in the history of religion to this conception of the absence of God on account of the unworthiness of the world: there are spirits who dwell with him, and they can come forth to bear his messages. Prophets, apostles or preachers have been deemed essential for divine communication, and where no human messenger could be found it has been very difficult for Christians to believe that God had any means of spiritual communication with men. Some of these ideas, once powerful, have passed away from the place of accepted doctrine, but they have left their influence behind them, even until now. The transcendence of God, by whatever name it might be called, has meant not only his superiority, but his dwelling apart from that which was unworthy of his presence.

Conscience has been a ready witness in support of this doctrine. All serious consciousness of sin has brought a new sense of the remoteness of God. It was the sense of human sinfulness that suggested the moral corruptness of the material world, but still more forcibly did it suggest the necessary separation between God and the sinful humanity. That a pure God can have nothing directly to do with sinful men is a conviction very ancient, perpetually supported by the testimony of guilty conscience. Conscience approves of the separation, too, declaring that God ought not to dwell with sinners—so deeply does guilty conscience misunderstand the highest virtue of God. All temples of God shut away in holy solitude, and all organized priesthoods with their indispensable mediation, bear witness to the same effect. The withdrawal of God is taken as the sign of his worthiness and the unworthiness of men.

Thus various influences have conspired to fix an unhappy definition of transcendence. The ethereality of spirit in contrast with the grossness of matter, the purity of God as against the vileness of sin, the justice of God as against the guilt of sin, and the ancient association of excellence with elevation, have all helped to identify transcendence with separation.

If the word transcendence could not be detached from such associations, it would be necessary to drop it from use in Christian Theology. Such conceptions of the remoteness of God were natural once, but modern knowledge conspires with the spirit of Christ to condemn them as unworthy of even a waning influence. All condemnation of matter as corrupt or contaminating belongs to the dead ages. Whatever it is, matter is innocent. The idea that for any reason matter and spirit are so incompatible that spirit must hold itself aloof is antiquated and can never renew its youth. Whatever the difference between matter and spirit may be, it is no difference that calls for separation. On the contrary, the spiritual or psychical quality is now discovered in the mysterious depths of what we have called dead matter, and the growing doctrine is that the universe is pervaded through and through by the quality that we name spiritual. When we come to religious meanings the case is not less strong. Upon the idea that because of his superiority God can have no contact with an evil world, the Christian revelation puts an absolute negative. This is an ancient thought of ignorance and error, misjudging God, as sinfulness is sure to do, and it is not too much to say that the Christianity of Jesus is an organized denial and refutation of it. The Christian doctrine proclaims God loving the sinful world, seeking moral entrance to its deepest life, and not content till he has drawn it into his own holy fellowship. That he is withdrawn or shut away from the universe by his superiority to it, the Christian doctrine absolutely denies. His very superiority is of a kind that renders that impossible.

The true idea of transcendence is before us as soon as we consistently treat the term as a word of comparison between God and all that is not God. The comparison is not between this lower world and his dwelling-place above, and the term conveys no suggestions as to the manner in which God communicates with his works. It is God that is transcendent, not his abode or his method, and the transcendence is not local, or quantitative in any sense, or occasioned by the moral condition of the world, or established by any special will of God. The point is simply that of the two units of existence one transcends, exceeds, excels the other, and the difference is a real difference in the objects that are compared. God is greater than all besides, and in every sense superior. The universe stands over against him, but not as his equal: he stands over against the universe, but as One who surpasses it: and there are qualities in which we can distinctly understand that his superiority consists. And it is when we fix our eyes upon these surpassing glories of God that we come nearest to seeing him as he is.

In order to see what these qualities of transcendence are,

we have only to recall what has lately been before us in our study. It may be said with truth that our entire study of God thus far has been a preparation for the assertion and defining of his transcendence. If we compare the God whom we have been considering with the universe, or with all that is not himself, we see at once wherein his superiority consists.

God is a Spirit, a conscious and self-directing Being. He knows, and he loves. He gives himself, and is a communicating Spirit toward all. He is a Spirit so great that he has to do with all, and all have to do with him. All the personal qualities are his in that fulness which must belong to the typical and perfect person. But the universe is not a spirit. It is full of the evidences of spiritual activity, and contains innumerable spirits within itself, but in itself it is neither communicating nor conscious. As a whole it has neither knowledge, will, nor character. The spirits that it contains, precious as their being is, are but infants in personality, in comparison with the perfect Person. We often say that any one of them has value that transcends the entire non-spiritual part of the universe, and in a sense this is true; but when we think of him who is the perfect type of all these minor personalities, no thought can do justice to the superiority of this one Spirit of an infinite majesty who is one of the two units of existence. Since one unit is a Spirit and the other is not, and the one Spirit is perfect while all other spirits are but children, we begin to see the meaning of his transcendence. It is the transcendence first of Life, and then of the perfect Life.

This is not the whole of his transcendence. We have already looked upon God as the source, or Creator, of that with which he must be compared. We have seen that he and he alone exists in and of himself, independently and without source or origin, while the universe, his sole companion in existence, exists simply and solely because of him. He is the Creator, it is the creature. His is the will, and the universe is the response. In self-existence and creatorhood he stands transcendent. If we wish to bring him into comparison, we can only compare him with his own work, which without him could have no being. When we look beyond this practical relation, so to call it, with the kind of transcendence which it implies, we behold him in his self-existence as the Eternal; not only without beginning and without end of being, but as having in himself and in his life the eternal quality, timeless, all-inclusive, raised above all contingencies, evermore unchangeable yet infinitely versatile, with life worth living for its own sake. Contrasted with him stands the universe, dependent, contingent, variable, in perpetual bondage to succession, unfolding, developing, rising and falling in perpetual change, unaware of itself as a whole, nowhere containing a comprehensive knowledge of its own end and way, incapable of ever understanding itself. God excels the universe in the nature of his being. And in all in which he excels he is infinite, absolutely unlimited and free in the exercise of his powers, while in contrast the universe is finite, limited in all its powers and acts and possibilities. If we venture to guess that it is infinite in extent or duration, still even then we shall call it infinite only in some minor aspects of being, while God is infinite in infinitely higher respects. Infinite ability to know and act infinitely excels infinite extent or number or duration, being an infinity in the nobler realm of the spirit; and God has the whole of a spirit's possible infinity.

In this manner does God transcend the universe, and yet the crowning word still remains to be spoken. When we pass from the universe to him with whom we are comparing it, we come for the first time to the glory of the perfect character. Over against the sum of secondary existence stands the great primal One, whose goodness is his glory. The material universe has no character, of course: the spiritual universe contains developing characters, good and bad: but God stands over against the whole as the eternal goodness loving in wisdom. All that is worthy to be glorified in character is glorious in him, and he is the transcendent One as being the One in whom all that ought to exist in character exists without imperfection and beyond degree. The perfect character is the most transcendent of facts.

With such an idea of transcendence in mind, we may recall an objection that is sometimes felt. It is sometimes thought absurd for us to speak of God as greater than the universe, when the universe itself is immeasurably greater than we can think. So it might be, we must confess, if the greatness that we were attributing to God were of the same kind with that of the universe. But it is not. We have been attributing to God greatness of a kind that is his alone. When we speak of a greatness that includes, besides eternal self-existence and perfect character, the ability to conceive, to produce, to sustain, to love and to rule the universe, we set forth a genuine transcendence, not in size or extent, but in nature, of which it is perfectly legitimate for us to speak.

It is finally to be added, completing the definition of transcendence, that God is adequate to his universe, and more. Such a God does not need to put forth all that he is in producing it and maintaining its existence. He is not exhausted by its demands, nor can he ever be. If it were vaster than it is, still it could not be too vast for him. Beyond all requirements that may be made by that which is not himself, there remains in him a fulness and power, a reserve as we should say if we were speaking of human affairs, a surplus of being, sufficient for more than the universe can demand. Such language represents God after the manner of men, but the representation is a true one, for which there is no need to apologize. Pantheistic and semi-pantheistic conceptions place God within the universe and make him equal to it, the mere life of it, and not greater. All that he is it expresses, or will at some time express. But the Christian religion has no place for such a doctrine, or for any of its results. It beholds God so infinitely superior in rank and quality to all that is not himself as to be more than equal to all that its existence requires of him. As a man is greater than his works, so, much more, is God. Upon him as the greater

One all other existence is absolutely dependent, but he is not dependent upon it, since he is of a higher order of being. All glories of the universe are but broken lights of him, and if it should attain to such perfection as belongs to its nature, still its glory would fall immeasurably short of his, and he would be holding his perfected work in the larger embrace of his transcendent power and love.

Thus the doctrine of transcendence simply affirms the superiority, independence and super-sufficiency of God. It declares that which worship has always recognized with humble joy. It is an essential element in the Christian doctrine, and the God of the Christian faith is such a God as it sets forth. As a matter of experience, we know that our conception of God's greatness grows with our knowledge of the universe: the great word all, indefinitely expansible, has been immensely enlarged already in our thoughts and is growing every day, and the thought of God constantly expands with it and beyond it. We see God greater than his works on every side. We may think of this enlargement of our thought of God as a result of our advancing knowledge; but while it is that it is also more—it is a constant approximation to the truth. God really is greater than all, in his relation to all and in the quality of his being, and this is his transcendence. Therefore it is that we may reasonably trust, adore and worship him, counting him to be "able to do exceeding abundantly above all that we ask or think," not only now but evermore. In his transcendence God is inexhaustible: this is the glory and comfort of our Christian faith.

10. IMMANENCE

That great reality which is the counterpart to the Transcendence of God is usually called Immanence, in modern times. It is true that there are objections to the name. It savours of philosophy rather than of religion, for in this use it is distinctly a modern term, and has not yet had time to win its religious associations. Moreover, it is not without ambiguity, it seems to promise more of definiteness than it really brings to the subject, and in actual usage it has often brought a suggestion of pantheism. For such reasons one could wish that some other word might be found to take its place. But no more satisfactory word is at hand. A term of strict precision would not correspond to the meaning that is to be expressed: the suggestion of pantheism does not belong in the word: and what we know of God will in due time bring in the religious significance that we may feel to be lacking. If we use the name without being bound to it, it will serve us well.

The Christian thought that meets us here is as simple as it is great and satisfying. We have thought of God as transcendent, superior, dominant, in comparison with all that is not himself; and now we are to add that the God who transcends all is present with all—he inhabits, pervades, moves, inspires, the universe. Of the two units of existence the One, infinitely excelling the other in grade and quality of being, maintains and ministers to the other by intimate inward operation. The Self-existent sustains the contingent, the Creator abides with the creation, the eternal Goodness loving in wisdom is with all that is not himself.

It is sometimes thought that transcendence and immanence are opposite conceptions, inconsistent with each other. Often they have been suspiciously set over against each other, as if we should need to make our choice between them. But that was because of that false idea of transcendence, according to which God's superiority removed him from contact with the world. Between the actual transcendence of God over the universe and his real indwelling there is no shadow of incompatibility. If God is transcendent as the self-existent and creative Spirit who is love, nothing can be more certain than that he will stand in intimate relation with that which he creates. The two facts are natural counterparts, and the true doctrine of God embraces both.

We need have no doubt as to the order in which the two should enter into our doctrine of God. Transcendence is first. When we consider the two units of existence in their relation to each other, it is right that we should begin with the original and the greater. It is the transcendence that gives the immanence its meaning, and its reality too. The Christian thought is not so much that the immanent God is transcendent, as it is that the transcendent God is immanent. We sing the praise of the all-excelling God who abides with all. We might attempt the opposite order, and say that he who abides with all surpasses all: he who inhabits the creation surpasses the creation. In that case we should be undertaking an argument, and assuming a burden of proof. But when we infer immanence from transcendence, God's indwelling from his greatness, we are simply drawing a natural conclusion. What we speak of under the name of immanence is a real presence, with all that the presence of such a God must mean; and such a presence needs no proof, when once we have first in mind the greatness, power and character of which the word transcendence tells.

Indeed, instead of needing special proof of it, we find such a real pervading presence urged upon us from so many quarters that recognition of it cannot be escaped.

For one thing, we are reaping here the benefit that is involved in the recent enlargement of the universe in our thought. When the created universe was conceived as small, it was natural and easy to localize God in a dwelling-place beyond its limits. But at present we have no power of imagining anything beyond the universe, and localizing of God beyond the limit of his works has become impossible. It is true that many hymns and prayers still represent the sky as his abode, but this is well known to be only the survival of old forms of thought that could not now arise. Besides what it owes to the enrichment of the conception of God himself, religion is indebted also to changes that have occurred in the conception of the universe. All opportunity to think of an infinitely distant home of God is crowded out, and it is by a practical necessity that we look

upon him as a pervading presence. If we are to think of him
as anywhere, we are compelled to think of him as everywhere.

We are indebted also to the change that has come upon the
manner of conceiving the method of the universe. When
God was pictured as outside and afar, there had been little
observation upon the manner in which the world was conducted, and it was easily assumed that God governed it
from without. The ideas of divine administration that were
generally characteristic of Deism were by no means out of
the question. But at present it is apparent that the universe
operates, or is operated, from within. The forces that are
found at work are resident forces, existing and acting within
the system. It is not to be assumed that this is all that we
can know about them, but this we do know. The universe
has the appearance of a self-working system. Not only its
vastness, but its internal self-sufficiency, forbids us to think
of it as controlled from without. If God is the operant force
of the great system, and it is operated from within, then
certainly he is within, with his operative will and energy.
Thus by the modern judgment as to the actual method we
are bidden welcome God into his world, and look upon him
as governing that which is not himself by a most intimate
and efficient presence.

These conclusions from the modern knowledge fall in with
what we know of God in the Christian light. Under the
Christian influence we are sure that his character is determi-
nant of his relation with other being. We cannot minutely
describe the relation in which his character will place him
with his universe, but we may safely be sure that the God of
the Christian faith will hold himself intimately near to his
creatures. If he has given existence, he is not a God who
will be aloof from it. In Christ he is known as a self-imparting God, ever seeking the closest intimacy with men. That
is his nature. In creation he has revealed his mind, in his
Son he has manifested himself among men, and as the
Holy Spirit he dwells with the soul in the intimacy of spiritual
fellowship; and this closest fellowship of all is the one that

fulfils his intention for mankind. His gospel shows him **near** to his world, seeking to be known in his nearness. When his will is fully done, God will be all in all—everything to every one. To any who are not at home with the Christian view and feeling this ground of confidence in the divine indwelling may not appeal; but to the Christian heart it is the most certain of realities that God is near to his creation, bearing upon his bosom that which he has called into being, ever serving the 'universe of which he is Father. The necessities of modern knowledge require us to believe in such a God if we believe in any God at all, and this is the God whom we already know in the Christian gospel. He is an abiding, indwelling God, concealed in that which reveals him, manifest without in the results of invisible operation within.

Thus the greatness of the universe, the method of its operation, the character of God and the nature of his gospel all conspire to give us a doctrine of real indwelling. By all these ways we are led again to the conviction with which we began, that the transcendent God is immanent also. We are sure that the greater unit of existence will be with the less: the life of God will blend mysteriously with the life that he has caused to be.

This real presence of God has long been known to faith, and has been commemorated in Theology under the name of Omnipresence. The omnipresence of God, familiar in doctrine, is of course included in that which is meant by the newer name Immanence. The older name has not been deemed sufficient for the later thought, and yet it is a noble name when its full meaning is perceived. It may be that under the title The Real Presence all that it is necessary to say of Immanence might be said. At any rate this last title will be helpful to our thought.

It is common to count the omnipresence of God among the natural attributes, in distinction from the moral attributes that constitute the divine character. The distinction is correct, for the fact of presence is in itself a natural and not a moral fact, and universality of presence is the divine mode of a natural relation. But the reckoning of omnipresence as a non-moral attribute does not do it justice. That of which we speak is not merely a presence—it is the presence of God, and the mention of it carries with it all the meaning that the name of God implies. Doubtless it is true that the presence or absence of a friend is purely a physical fact, yet friendship is scarcely satisfied with that estimation of it. The presence of the friend is the presence of the heart that loves and is loved, and of the character that justifies the friendship. By the medium of the natural attribute, omnipresence, there is represented to us the real and universal presence of all that we mean by God—of all the fulness of character and wealth of relations and versatility of energy of which God is possessed. Omnipresence is the natural mode of being by virtue of which all the moral worth of God is everywhere available.

This conception of omnipresence comes to us out of real life. The Christian doctrine has always affirmed the omnipresence of God, and has proclaimed it primarily as a truth of religion. Naturally there are speculative inquiries about so great a fact, but, just as it ought, the religious interest has far exceeded the philosophical. The presence of the living God is the most vital of realities, and ought to command an interest that is not curious but practical. A presence must be felt: it cannot have its due effect by being reasoned about. The divine omnipresence becomes effective upon men, and becomes even a noticeable reality, only in that experience which is religion. It is in the record of experience that we find it acknowledged. Psalm cxxxix gives classical expression to the conviction that there is no possibility of putting distance between a soul and God: "Thou hast beset me behind and before. . . . Whither shall I flee from thy presence?" To the psalmist this is a solemn thing, for it is the presence of a God who knows his words and understands his thoughts, and is sure to search out all his sins. But it also brings him unspeakable joy and rest, since he is sure that wherever he may go it will be to him a friendly and sustaining presence.

> "If I take the wings of the morning,
>   And dwell in the uttermost parts of the sea,
> Even there shall thy hand lead me,
>   And thy right hand shall hold me."

With equal awe and gladness he celebrates God's omnipresence as a fact inevitable, and as the invaluable support of his religious confidence.

> "How precious also are thy thoughts unto me, O God!
>   How great is the sum of them!
> When I awake, I am still with thee."

This conviction of God's universal and unfailing nearness runs increasingly through the Bible. There is no difficulty in making allowance for the anthropomorphic localizing of God, or the representation that in his majesty he comes from afar to reward or punish. Such representations were so natural in their time that we could not expect the Scriptures to be free from them. In its day such language was the language of power, and we must confess that something of its old power still attends it. But in the Bible as a whole such views of God form a gradually retiring element, and the entering and growing thought is that of universal presence. Naturally it is so, for the Bible is a history of the growth and deepening of religion, and the deepening of religion and the sense of God are inseparable companions.

The religious quality of our doctrine of omnipresence, however, does not prevent our inquiring about the manner of it. The metaphysics of the divine presence cannot cease to be interesting. But we shall be disappointed if we expect any clear answering of our questions. According to our observation a presence involves an occupying of space; and naturally we inquire whether, or in what sense, the present God occupies space, as familiar objects seem to us to do.

We may be led to speak of the essence of God, and to imagine that it must be everywhere. But what may be meant by the essence of God we can never tell. We say that God is immaterial: what then can we mean by his essence, regarded as something that occupies space? If we begin with inquiries of this kind we shall not get beyond thinking of God somewhat as we think of an atmosphere, far-spread and thinly-diffused, a conception devoid of spiritual quality. This is not the best way to approach the subject. We shall do better if we follow in the direction in which religion leads us. The psalmist is a better guide here than the scientist can be. His tribute to the Omnipresent is a tribute to a living God, whose knowledge, will and friendly care he commemorates. We predicate omnipresence of the Possessor of the powers of a living Spirit. Religion proclaims not an omnipresent essence, but an omnipresent God: "Lo, God is here!" It is the Father, Saviour, Lord, who is everywhere: "underneath are the everlasting arms" (Dt. xxxiii. 27) of sustaining personality and spiritual strength. Faith celebrates the real presence of the eternal righteousness and love, characteristic of the infinite Mind to whom they belong. The natural presence glows with the spiritual perfections, and is best described in terms of them.

With the moral perfections of course we include in our thought the inexhaustible fount of action. The will of God is everywhere. For him to live is to work: "My Father worketh even until now" (Jn. v. 17). When we affirm the omnipresence of God we mean that God is free from all limitations of space in his activities, and can do everywhere all that he can do anywhere. All that he is, is everywhere available for action at all times. He never needs to move in order to be at any place in which he wills to work. All the energy that goes forth from his wisdom, love and holiness, or is summoned by his purpose, works everywhere at once in equal perfection. To say this is to affirm that he himself works everywhere at once, and is present everywhere. The acting God is omnipresent. How energy goes forth from him no one knows, but from him it does everywhere go forth. If we cannot say much more than this about the manner of his omnipresence we need not be troubled, for this conception is at once the clearest and the most helpful. A metaphysical conception of omnipresence, if we could form it, would be spiritually barren. We are influenced by the idea of omnipresence when we feel it as the real presence of God's character, heart and moral energy; and it is from confidence in this that we come to have vital belief in such presence as is sufficient for ends that are not moral. Though we cannot mentally picture such a presence, a personal sense of it is possible to every soul without a mental picture.

How truly such a real presence is implied in all satisfactory religion we know. All our best religious acts and hopes depend upon it. The doctrine of omnipresence is simply a form of the doctrine of monotheism. Omnipresence is unipresence. All strong religion says, "God is here." Although the practice of praying to a God far off in heaven has outlived its time and survived till now, the happy inconsistency of faith helps to correct the error. More or less clearly and powerfully, men feel the presence of God when they pray. Jesus never spoke of omnipresence, but he assumed that the Father was always within reach. All living sense of God is sense of a present God. All faith in providence implies faith in universal presence. A living trust in God implies that wherever one may go, he is there, and wherever he is needed he is. If we had to say, "The Lord is in this place and I knew it not," because we thought we had passed the limits of his country, we should be only on the threshold of religion. If we are to believe in a future life that is worthy of the soul, we must believe that wherever the soul may find itself hereafter, God is there, with power and character adequate to its destinies. Thus "God with us" is the life of our religion, and in him we rest. Wherever a man may be, the God of holiness and love, the Creator and Judge of men, the Father of Jesus, is present, with all his character and power. In the spirit of the psalmist, who gave us our classic of omnipresence (Ps. cxxxix), we may cultivate that "practice of the presence of God" by which life is advanced to its highest dignity and worth.

When we pass from Omnipresence to Immanence, it is important that we learn how far and in what sense we are passing into a new region. Immanence is presence, and omnipresence, but the entrance of the newer name seems to indicate that modern thought desired to express something more concerning God than the doctrine of omnipresence has been understood to affirm. The idea of immanence is constantly represented to be a new idea in theology, and one that introduces a new element to our thought of God. Precisely what that additional something is, is a question that is always arising. If we speak of immanence, we are sure to be asked, "Exactly what do you mean by it?" and a clear answer is desired. It is true that vagueness here is no crime, for this is no region for formulas; and yet if we speak of immanence at all we wish to know what under this name is added to our doctrine of God. Is anything really added? In studying immanence, are we on old ground, or on new?

The question is answered by clearing it of its ambiguity. If by omnipresence we mean simply what is commonly included under the definition of that word, immanence includes something that the older term does not cover. But if omnipresence be allowed all the fulness of meaning that belongs to it when it is the omnipresence of God, then all that immanence means is included in it. To omnipresence itself, a fact of the divine being, immanence, which is also a fact of the divine being, adds nothing. An omnipresent God is immanent. But to the human doctrine of omnipresence, which is only an interpretation of the fact, the human doctrine of immanence does contribute an addition, and one that we can define.

To the doctrine of omnipresence, the doctrine of immanence adds the endeavour to expound the relation between the omnipresent God and the universe with which he is present. It not only affirms that God is present, but attempts to suggest something as to what he effects by virtue of his presence, and how the universe is affected by it. The doctrine of immanence is nothing more than an endeavour to interpret the fact of God's universal presence, and tell what that presence signifies, or accomplishes. What does the real presence of the sole transcendent Being, bearing all the power and character of God, mean to the universe, material and spiritual? In what manner of contact with it does he stand? Wherein is the universe different because he is in it from what it would be if he were governing it from without? What is it receiving or becoming, in consequence of its immediate contact with all the fulness of God? To these far-reaching questions the doctrine of immanence would fain propose some helpful answers. Whatever the answers may be, it is plain that the effort is only an endeavour to interpret God's presence with all his creatures, and show what it means to them. The doctrine of omnipresence affirms that God is everywhere: the doctrine of immanence affirms what it means that God is everywhere. The indwelling of God which is affirmed as omnipresence is expounded under the name of immanence, but under whatever name the presence is the same. Omnipresence is immanence. So the two doctrines differ in their scope, but the reality with which they deal is one and the same.

In view of this distinction between the great reality and the two doctrines concerning it, it appears that the old religious doctrine of omnipresence is not superseded by the newer doctrine of immanence, and that the two doctrines stand in no sort of contrast to each other. In both we contemplate only the one relation of the living God to his universe. In our study of immanence we simply read the fulness of the significance of God into the announcement of his universal presence. We can never do this perfectly, and therefore our doctrine of immanence will always be incomplete. But the effort is a worthy one, and we shall conceive more truly both of God and of the world for making it.

It is a fact so fundamental that it must never be forgotten

that the presence of God with his universe is a presence that involves or constitutes a relation. It is not an identity, but a presence of One with another. That with which God abides stands in an actual relation to him, in which one party is just as real as the other. The universe is not a part of God, and God does not hold the universe absorbed into himself, or come to be himself by means of it. The Christian doctrine knows no such thought. God is in and with the universe, but that very statement means that he and it are two, not one, however wondrously in union. God is marvellously united to that which is not himself, but he is not the universe, nor is the universe he.

The significance of the universal presence must be read first of all in the light of the fact that it is the presence of the self-communicating God. Forthgoing and self-expression belong to his eternal nature. That rational forthgoing character in God which in the Fourth Gospel (Jn. i. 1–18) is called the Logos is in his very life: it was with God and was God from the beginning, and will be forever. This means that God is eternally self-uttering and self-imparting. He does not live unto himself. He does not dwell in his universe statically and self-contained. Action is his life, and his life is everywhere. This means that the real presence is a creative presence. Creation is the fruit of the forthgoing. Without the Logos was not anything made that hath been made. Creation is not a work wrought upon the world from beyond, or bespoken from afar, but a work of self-uttering volition wrought from within. Whether creation has beginning or end we do not know, but we do know that in past, present or future it proceeds from the inward impulse of the present God. We remember also that creation and sustaining are not two works but one. The impulse that creates sustains and orders also, and the work of God in his universe is one work from first to last. And this single work of creating, sustaining and ordering is a work of his presence, going forth to action in virtue of his quality as Logos. What comes to the universe, because he is present, is that the universe exists, and is maintained in being, ordered in its movement, and directed to its end.   This is that effect of God's omnipresence which the doctrine of immanence endeavours to set forth. Because the self-uttering God is present there is a universe brought forth and kept in significant existence.

When God is spoken of as creating, he is popularly thought of as creating the material universe; and when he is said to be immanent, it is in the material universe that his immanence is first located.   This is unfortunate, but not surprising. The venerable narrative of the creation sums all up in the creation of the heavens and the earth.   It is in the school of science that we have lately learned most about the universe, and it is no wonder that it is regarded too exclusively in its physical aspects.   It is easy to think of the universe as virtually identical with that which is seen or suggested in the starry heavens on a cloudless night: the worlds compose it, and the telescope and the microscope together, with perfect power, might reveal it to us.   We ourselves as spiritual beings, and the dwellers in Mars, if such there are, are often regarded as denizens of the universe but scarcely as a part of it.   It is in this universe of matter that God is often represented as immanent, putting forth energy, holding the worlds together by gravitation, maintaining the universal order.   So naturally has this idea of immanence come in that some Christians have incautiously assented to it, and accepted or declined the doctrine with this understanding of what it means.

It is right to recognize the presence of God in the material universe, and to call him immanent there.   It is true that he has not made his presence discernible by the sight of the eye or the hearing of the ear, and that we do not know how his work is done.   But it is right to say that the immeasurable energy that goes forth in the material universe proceeds from him, and that all signs of mind, intelligence, rational understanding in the material universe are signs of God and expressions of his being.   Signs of power and signs of mind are expressive, too, not only of God, but of the present God.   It is true that the forces of the material universe are resident forces, as the scientists say, and that the intelligence is resident intelligence. The forces and intelligence are resident because God is resident. All suggestions of a godless world, or a world so orderly as to need no God, are due to observation of results of divine indwelling, without recognition of their source. If it has ever seemed that the order of the world was automatic, that was because the invisible God has done so well the work of his indwelling. The boundless energy and intelligence that the universe displays simply fill out the second term of Paul's great ascription, "From him, and through him, and unto him, are all things" (Rom. xi. 36). That which came from him and turns to him is sustained and ordered also by his presence.

Such divine indwelling is the foundation of what we are wont to call the order, or the uniformity, of nature. The order of nature is often spoken of almost as if it were an independent entity, of which God himself must take account in his governance of the world, to observe it or to violate it. But apart from God there is no such thing as an order of nature, or as nature itself. His influence upon the world is not an inreaching, to affect nature: it is rather an inspiration, constituting nature. The order of the world is his own order, and he himself, working within, maintains it. As for our belief in the uniformity of nature, it is founded in experience, not in theory: it is a lesson learned from what God has done. The order of nature is commended to us by our observation, as the expression of a rational mind.

The God whose method is nature is not incapable of departing from his method. He is a free Spirit, and the very fact that he has a method is to us an evidence that he is not in bondage to it. In the fullest sense of the word, he may work miracles, if he will. But his indwelling enables us to put a new estimate upon miracles if they occur. If he should depart from his order and work miracles, they would not be so unlike his other works as we have thought. It is not true that he enters the world through the door of the miraculous, for he is in the world already, and a miracle would be nothing more than a variant act of his ever-present will. Discerning the real presence, we can never again imagine that nothing but a miracle is a direct work of his. Not chiefly in flashes of God, but in a steady world, is the divine reality revealed. The present God warrants the settled confidence. Accordingly, our trust in God becomes a trust in a beneficent steadiness in the operation of the world. The firm order in which we have come to rest has beneath it the solidity of God, and we trust in the faithfulness of nature because it is a form of his own faithfulness. He may depart from his order, but he will not vary it so much as to break up our confidence in the order that serves as the security of our life.

But the vital part of the doctrine of immanence is not found in any doctrine of the material universe. Those who look no farther may find an immanence that serves as a theistic key to universal physics, and a confirmation of teleology, but the full glory of the real presence is not here to be perceived. The material universe is not the whole, or the chief part, of that in which God dwells. The universe in which he dwells includes all living spirits; for the mind that thinks of the sun is a part of the universe as truly as the sun. The God who is immanent in the universe is immanent in the spiritual order of which our spirits and their life form a part. "In him we live, and move, and have our being" (Acts xvii. 28) —we, whose being does not belong altogether to this world which we behold. Not until we have said this have we opened the heart of our doctrine. More important is the real presence with the soul than the real presence with the stars. Here lie the deepest questions about the divine indwelling, and here shine its chief glories.

There is a name that we can give to the immanent self-communicating God, when we think of him in his relation to spiritual beings. Toward them he must be the creative God, the Father of spirits. He is, they become. Here creation is more characteristic of him than it can be elsewhere, for it is reproduction of his own likeness. This spiritual creativeness of God was in action in the world long before men were men, for it was due to his nature that life, once initiated in the world by him, advanced and expanded into life that was human. Because God self-communicating was in the world, life was trained up to humanity. Thus by process, but as really as if by a stroke, God creates his like in the human race. The eternal Mind wills it, and in due time there are minds. The eternal Goodness wills it, and beings to whom goodness is possible appear. The perfect Person wills it, and man stands forth a person. Thus living spirits in likeness to God rise in answer to his energizing action, and live thenceforth, sustained by the present power that created them.

With the spirits into whom the living God has thus breathed the breath of life, their creative Father sustains a most intimate relation. Everywhere and forever, he is as near to them as they are to themselves, and yet he and they are not the same. Here most evidently does immanence exclude the idea of identity, for it is a real indwelling of Spirit with spirit, and one that implies the real existence of both the spirits. There is no shadow of pantheism in any true doctrine of divine immanence. On the contrary, that which the self-communicating God has brought into existence is an innumerable multitude of persons, whom he sustains in life and embraces in his presence. In their personality they bear his likeness: his likeness is in little, but it is real. The personality in which his likeness resides he in his dealings with them respects. He is associated with them in an indescribable intimacy of presence, the mystery of which they can never solve, but he does not absorb them into himself, or by any means supersede the distinctness of their being. Rather is his personality the pledge of theirs. Because he lives they live also, and shall live and be themselves. In the relation that is denoted by the real presence individuality is perfectly itself, and the individual man, unchanged, is simply embraced in the all-encompassing reality of the present God. Man is a genuine moral being, whose dignity and responsibility are never neutralized by any absorption into God or annulling of his personality. Life in God retains forever all the ethical significance that God himself has given it.

We are always wishing that we could describe the relation between the divine will and the human, in the unseen region where the two most closely meet. But here we shall always be compelled to acknowledge mystery. That God should have set off the human will in a real separateness is itself a most wonderful thing. How far the divine is from abolishing the human that has been thus made separate we see in the amazing fact that with all his nearness God does not prevent man from acting in opposition to his will. That a spirit gifted with godlike power of will and borne upon the very bosom of divine being should act against the God whose presence is his life is surely the most tragic of things. But human separateness appears in this awful gift of power. Our separateness is proved by the fact of our sinning. This fact is enough to show that the touch of the divine presence is not of a compelling kind. The whole of the divine character is here, and yet man is allowed to be himself. It is the character that makes sin most dreadful, and at the same time it is the character that keeps the hope of holiness at hand. Every sinful soul is in perpetual contact with holy divine judgment, and also with holy redemptive love.

It is in the life of spirits akin to himself that God's self-communicating nature appears in greatest significance. We use the truest of images when we say that in his spiritual world God is light (1 Jn. i. 5). It is the nature of light to shine, and it is the nature of God to impart himself. In his spiritual indwelling God is the true light that lighteth every man. Such is his relation to souls that he is always shining into their life, or giving them influence for illumination and guidance. It is not that there exists a true light provided and sent forth, intervening between God and men, representing him and blessing them. God himself, present and self-imparting, is the true light that lightens all men (Jn. i. 9). Men may darken this light for themselves, so far as their own highest benefit is concerned, but since the light is God himself they cannot extinguish it or banish it from their sphere. All men have to do with the enlightening God, and a dark soul is a soul dark in the midst of light.

If we ask what this means, and what action corresponds to this description of God as the light of men, we shall find the answer in the fact that God has imparted to man an intellectual nature, a moral nature, and a religious nature. From his own being he has given forth to men the qualities that these names represent. The answer is completed in this other fact, that he who has given man such a nature acts toward him as a faithful Creator and a ministering Father, mindful of that which he has made. He does not forsake the work of his own hands. The present God is always in the attitude of one who remembers his offspring and nourishes the nature that he has given.

In consequence of this all-embracing faithfulness, there is a genuine inspiration of God in the growing life and thought of mankind. When men are receptive of his best gifts, he dwells with them in rich self-impartation: "I dwell in the high and holy place, with him also that is of a humble and contrite spirit" (Isa. lvii. 15). But even when divine indwelling cannot be thus fruitful, man is never alone, alone though he may seem to be. In the aspirations of religion there is no such thing as the unaided heart of man, and in the endeavour of duty there is no such thing as the unaided human conscience. God is with the thinking mind, the trusting heart and the struggling will. Through this insistent helpful presence it comes to pass that there is a serious and solemn law in human life. The present God is the eternal right, and his indwelling keeps the law of right in human life as a perfectly inevitable thing, as urgent as it is beneficent. The law of the good in life is from God, and is the law of the present God. When men are good, they are responding to him whether they know it or not. When they are evil, still it is God within who ministers to them that inward good by comparison with which they are so evil and condemned. This all-penetrating moral relation to God belongs not to some special men privileged to be aware of it, but to men as spirits and offspring of God, and to all souls, in whatever realm of existence they may be. This is the method of the living God toward all the living.

Not that God is recognized in all this work of his, or that men usually even suspect the real presence in its fulness of meaning. It is far otherwise, even apart from the fact of moral indifference in men. In vast activities God is hidden behind the processes. There is much that man considers all his own, or else anonymous and devoid of character, but God is in it all. The universe, observed, has provided abundant instruction for the intellect and material for knowledge. How inexhaustible is that harvest we well know. Nothing could appear more anonymous than these gifts of knowledge: did they not lie there in the field, waiting to be gathered up? But the presence and value of these lessons, and their availableness to men, were not accidental. The unseen teacher who taught men knowledge was God self-uttering, manifested in his world. Moreover, life has always been a school of ethics, in which sound principles of living have been learned; but there being no visible teacher, this has often been taken to be a bare fact of history and human nature, sufficiently dealt with in being recorded. But the teacher of morals is God indwelling. Through that social order which comes of his creative wisdom, and through experience in his world, he himself has been slowly bearing in upon men moral lessons that correspond to his character. That men have learned the lessons only in part, and have often misused them, is nothing against the teaching, which is the fundamental ethical fact of history. In like manner religion, one of the most ancient and honourable possessions of the race, has often been regarded as an ungiven gift, a possession wholly unaccounted for, except that it belonged to human nature and was found in life. A superficial search could indeed yield nothing more than this. But in truth the religious possibility was the gift of the Creator who made man for himself, and the religious development was the response of the living man to the living God. These are instances of the effect of immanence, God uttering himself to man, and sending his wholesome influence into the human intelligence and experience.

In the light of God's immanence we obtain a double view of the universe. We contemplate it as it is by itself to our senses and our thoughts, and at the same time we behold it with the present God shining through it. On the one hand we may examine the world and life in scientific fashion, and learn to read and classify the facts that we observe; and on the other we may contemplate the whole universe and all its parts as filled, animated, maintained, inspired, by the inworking of the present God. These views are not successive but simultaneous, and they do not relate at the same time to different parts of the universe. We do not find nature in some things and God in others: that division of things belongs to the past. It was tenable when God was judged to be separate from his works, but now we know that he is "not so far away as even to be near." In all parts of his universe, in ways differing according to the quality of that which he has created, God works always in, with and through that which is not himself. So we take scientific cognizance of "earth and every common bush," and at the same time are aware that

> "Earth's crammed with heaven,
> And every common bush alive with God."

This is the meaning of immanence.

This truth of the transcendent God immanent in his universe helps us to see what is really meant by the distinction, familiar but not easily defined, between the natural and the supernatural.

The distinction is insisted upon in ordinary Christian discourse as positively as if it were perfectly understood, and few who speak easily of the supernatural have any idea how difficult of definition it is. But those who have seriously tried to define it know. Before we can clearly tell what is supernatural we must know how much is included in nature;

for until we have drawn the upper limit of the natural we cannot tell on what principle we are to say of anything that it is above that limit, or supernatural. But here lies the difficulty. Nature is a very ambiguous and uncertain word, and it inevitably imparts its uncertainty to its companion-word. As a matter of fact, the line between natural and supernatural has been drawn, or attempted, at many different points. Sometimes it is drawn between that which is caused in the ordinary manner and that which is not. Popularly, the supernatural is taken to mean scarcely more than the extraordinary or the unknown. Sometimes the line is drawn between the rational and personal and the irrational and impersonal, ranking the spirit of man with God as supernatural; and sometimes the supernatural is conceived as an order existing beyond this world, but occasionally breaking in upon the order that we know here. The result of all the defining is that no definition has proved satisfactory enough to be rewarded by general acceptance, and the old obscurity continues. The distinction is felt to be both real and important, but just how is it to be made?

The trouble is that the dividing line has been drawn too low. It has been assumed that the universe, the creation of God, could be divided into two parts, of which one could intelligibly be called natural and the other supernatural. There being such a thing as nature, and God himself being above it, it has been taken for granted that some part of his creation shared in his superiority. Just how much of his creation was to be enthroned above nature with God it has been hard to show, and we cannot wonder. It is impossible to define the natural by division of the world. There is no place at which the created universe can be thus bisected. In no tolerable sense is it true that some part of God's creation possesses supernaturalness together with God. There is no place to draw such a line through the sum-total of existence, except between what we have called the two units, the universe and God. God is alone in his superiority to all besides, and all that is below him forms a single class. What is really meant by the supernatural is God himself, and by the natural that which he does or produces. The natural is the universe and what it contains, in its manifold aspects of dependent existence. The supernatural is God who alone is greater.

If God in his transcendence were beyond the universe, as he was once thought to be, the supernatural, thus defined, would be manifest to men in the form of exceptional occurrences, or incursions into the accustomed order. But he is not. We can conceive of no union more intimate than that in which the two units of existence stand. God lives in the universe and the universe lives in God. The common order is animated by the living will. That is to say, the natural and the supernatural exist together, not only in the same world but in the same events and objects. The natural implies and reveals the supernatural, and is absolutely dependent upon it. The sole supernatural is that creative, quickening, inspiring life which is God himself, and the natural includes anything and everything in which the living will is expressed. The act or product is in nature, but God is the supernatural agent who is essential to its being. So the event or work which lies within the order of the world is at the same time a self-expression of him who is above all. A leaf, we say, is a product of nature, and an illustration of nature's method. So it is, but it is just as truly a product of supernature and an expression of God. The tree that bears it is rooted in the ground, and is rooted in God. In the natural leaf, which is one of the vehicles of the infinite energizing will, the supernatural shines forth. What is true of a leaf is true in like manner of a bird in the air, a child in the cradle, and a saint in heaven. Nature and supernature appear in them all. That which lies back of the ever-present mystery of nature is the only God, the sole fount of power, the true and only supernatural. In his transcendence he is above nature, and by his immanence makes nature what it is.

Thus it comes to pass that we have to go no farther from home to find the supernatural than to meet the natural. Nor have we to wait for some startling moment when the supernatural shall break through the daily order of our life and appear to us. It is here. Nature does not exclude it, but expresses it. One is of God, and the other is God. The variety of the ways in which God is both hidden and revealed in the order of the world must not blind us to his real presence, for it is true that the world in which we live is both natural and supernatural at once. But whether the ancient terms, nature and the supernatural, are best adapted to the expression of this truth, or whether we need them, we are quite free to doubt. Probably at present the words do more toward perpetuating confusion than toward strengthening the hold of spiritual truth. But the distinction between God and the world is everlasting, and this is the distinction which the familiar terms have endeavoured to set forth.

A truth so central as the immanence of the transcendent God cannot fail to dictate throughout the entire field of doctrine. By its own nature it presses in to the definitions that belong alike to theology and to the common thoughts of men. Where it is not influential to-day it is certain to be to-morrow. In view of it, creation was not a work of days, undertaken, performed and finished, followed by cessation and rest. Creation is the productive outflow of the divine energy, normal to God, limitless in time, conditioned only by his nature and will. Providence is not a series of interpositions in which God's world is touched and retouched by his special power in order to better the work of the general method. Providence is the perpetual governance of the indwelling Lord and Friend, no part of whose world is ever without his presence and care. Revelation is not a special work in a special field, mediated by messengers, attended by attesting miracles, limited to a certain time, completed and not to be renewed. Revelation equally includes the continuous, infinitely varied and endless manifestation of the transcendent God through his indwelling, and all more special expressions of himself that he may make. Salvation is not an exceptional gift of grace from afar, but the characteristic working-out of the eternal divinity of God, and the communion of the Holy Spirit is the fulfilment of the ideal of existence.

11. OMNISCIENCE

Coming to Omniscience, we might say that it is a companion-fact to Omnipresence; but it would be truer to call it a part of Omnipresence, and an essential element in Immanence. In Omnipresence, God with all his power of action is present to all and absent from nothing—present therefore with all his power of knowing. The perfect mind cannot be present without knowing that to which he is present, and cannot be omnipresent without knowing all. In that Psalm cxxxix, in which both attributes are celebrated with such reverent gladness, this practical identity of the two is taken for granted. In the esteem of the Psalmist, God knows all because he is everywhere. If one cannot escape from his knowledge, it is because one cannot flee from his presence.

Omnipresence is unipresence, the presence of the one and only God; and in like manner omniscience is uniscience, a single and all-comprehensive knowledge. It is thus a form of the divine unity, and the doctrine of it is one of the assertions of monotheism. It simply affirms that one knowing mind pervades and embraces all. When we say that God has perfect knowledge of the universe, we declare that one of the two units of existence has perfect knowledge of the other. And yet even this is not all that the doctrine of omniscience affirms. God has greater knowledge than this, for besides knowing the universe, he knows himself. One of the two units of existence has perfect knowledge not of the other only, but of both. Literally and absolutely, God has perfect knowledge of all.

Concerning the knowledge that the Christian doctrine thus attributes to God we are able to make some descriptive statements that will have some value. Of course we may simply say that it is what we know as knowledge—God really knows.

And we may add that it is knowledge of any and every worthy kind, except such as may imply the limitations of finitude. By its very title it is complete knowledge; but this plain statement includes two meanings. The presence of one knowing God in all the universe implies the perception and understanding of each and every part, and of the whole. It is a complete detailed knowledge, and at the same time a complete comprehensive knowledge. We may also say that while it is a complete knowledge in both these modes, it is also a correct knowledge. As nothing escapes it, so nothing is misknown by it. All is known in its real nature, relations, significance and possibilities. With such a knowledge the universe is thought through, and known with perfect understanding through its whole extent. Every item and element in it is understood, and the universe itself is understood in its real significance as a unit of existence. The comprehensive and perfect knowledge that could be attributed to God by men when the world seemed small is still attributed to him by the Christian doctrine when the universe appears practically infinite. And this divine knowledge has moral value to us as ground for confidence in the sanity of existence, in the fact that God also perfectly knows himself, and knows all other being in its relation to himself.

As between the two aspects of omniscience that have just been mentioned, it is quite natural that the main emphasis should often fall upon the completeness of God's knowledge in detail. Very impressive is the fact that nothing is hidden from him, and nothing is too minute or insignificant for him to discern. "Thou God seest me" (Gen. xvi. 13) was a word of grateful acknowledgment in the ancient story, and in the confession, "There is not a word in my tongue, but lo, O Lord, thou knowest it altogether" (Ps. cxxxix. 4), the psalmist noted how great a meaning omniscience brings into common life. From the human side, whether in the light of guilty conscience or of filial trust, it is natural to put emphasis on the fact that God knows everything. So this is the first and abiding popular form of the doctrine. Nevertheless, the other aspect of omniscience, that God knows all, or knows the whole, is quite as important, both for thought and for faith. Experience teaches us that details can be rightly understood only in their place in the whole of which they form a part. It follows that all human knowledge is imperfect. Human beings do not understand anything completely, not even the least thing or the most familiar, because they do not perfectly understand the whole to which each thing belongs. God himself would be like us in this imperfection, if his knowledge were only detailed knowledge of the items of existence. But in reality his omniscience takes in the entire mass of particulars, and holds them all in their true place in the universal total, which as a total he perfectly understands. Thus while the Christian doctrine bears testimony that God knows everything, it best awakens confidence by its assurance that God knows all. Faith takes hold upon the completeness of his perception and understanding, and rests upon that as an immovable foundation.

Sometimes we suspect that it is vain for us to think of omniscience, and presumptuous to speak as if we had any clear idea of it. Omniscience must be unlike all knowledge that is possible to us, and our experience gives us little aid in comprehending it. The difference in range and extent between our knowledge and that of an omniscient mind is of course unimaginably great. All our knowledge seems almost blank ignorance and folly in comparison. Yet this is not the only difference. Our knowledge is acquired, gained gradually, and always capable of improvement both in quantity and in quality; but the knowledge of the omniscient mind is not acquired or improvable. This impassable difference in method seems to put omniscience forever out of the reach of our understanding, and we may sometimes wonder whether our statements about so great a matter are anything more than words. But our suspicion is needless. Omniscience is of course beyond us, for it is the knowledge of the perfect mind. But it is the knowledge of a mind, and even we in our remoteness from perfection are not without some real and true suggestions of what it is. It is not true that between our minds and an omniscient mind there is no community. Methods of knowing differ immeasurably, but at the heart of it the fact of knowing is the same to all intelligences. Degrees of knowing differ immeasurably, too, but without altering the identity of the thing itself. God, as the only independent and perfect Being, knows perfectly: in him is the ideal and perfection of knowledge, both in manner and in result. We bear his likeness, but his likeness diminished and within the bounds of finitude. Our littleness and limitations do not forbid us to believe in his greatness, or prevent us from forming some idea of what it is.

We shall conceive more truly of omniscience if we remember that it is a double knowledge: it includes knowledge of two kinds, one of which is beyond our experience, while the other is not. Omniscience means simultaneous knowledge of all things, past, present, future and everywhere; and it none the less means awareness of succession and knowledge of events as they occur. With the latter way of knowing we are familiar, for our finitude shuts us up to it; but with the former we are not, for our finitude shuts us out from it. In the simultaneity of universal knowledge God stands alone, but we share in his power of knowing in succession. Knowledge in succession has often been thought to be no part of omniscience, and no possession of God. It has been said that all his knowledge was timeless, and that the "eternal now" was so real to him as to allow him no power of knowing succession. But this cannot be true, for succession is essential to the significance of events in time, and if God had no knowledge of it he could not understand events, or the history that is composed of them, or the life of his children. He has both kinds of knowledge: he eternally knows all things at once, and is also aware of them as they become realized in time and space; and in the perfect mind there is no inconsistency between these two modes. Our finite nature limits us to the narrower way of knowing, but we can well see that the perfect mind is not so limited, nor is it shut out from the successional manner. Omniscience includes at once the simultaneous and universal knowledge that corresponds to the timelessness of the eternal God, and the successive knowing that corresponds to the nature and movement of the created universe.

From the human point of view, God's knowledge of the events of time appears as foreknowledge. If in the beginning of the gospel, for example, he knew how wide would be its influence to-day, we say that he foreknew it. When we have said this, we begin to wonder whether his foreknowing an event does not foreordain it, or render it absolutely certain to occur. Surely it cannot be otherwise than as he knows it, we say, and so his knowledge unchangeably fastens the event. But in this judgment there is some mistaking of the real nature of omniscience. In that omniscience in which God stands alone, nothing in his creatures resembling it, God does not foreknow: he knows. It is only in the human successional view of things that we speak of foreknowledge: in the fundamental quality of God's omniscience there is none. With him all knowledge is simultaneous, save in that second aspect of his omniscience, according to which he is aware of events as they occur in order. Foreknowledge is a human name, to which in the essential quality of God there is nothing that corresponds. He knows, he does not foreknow, the date of his child's death or of the downfall of a nation.

In proportion as we discern this divine method of knowing, foreknowledge will cease to perplex us. In this light it does not differ from knowledge. But we cannot conceive that knowledge of events has any power to determine the events. Not even God's knowledge has that effect. It is not reasonable, or even intelligible, that his knowledge should be the determining condition of occurrences. There are efficient forces of God's creating, whether we can define them well or not, and there are real conditions. Divine knowledge embraces all these, but is not itself a force or a condition. It is not omniscience that determines the movement of the tides, or the rise and fall of nations. No one acts as if it were, and what has troubled so many is a catch in argument, rather than a stumbling-block in the field of fact. From the doctrine of omniscience thus misconceived and misapplied there has been drawn a doctrine of human helplessness; but that which ought rather to be inferred from it is rather an intelligent childlike confidence in the all-knowing One.

Omniscience is more than perception and awareness of things. We have described it as a true knowledge of things as they really are, discernment and understanding of that which really is. The contents of the universe, past, present and future, it knows correctly and without error, not merely as separate facts but in their relation to one another, to the whole, and to God himself. The one unit of existence not only is aware of the other, but understands it. God understands the universe. This we can easily say, and believe, and yet there are hard questions involved in it. Full understanding implies full knowledge of the possibilities of things, not only of what they actually are, but of what they might have been. It seems to imply ability to compare that which is with what would have been under conditions that never existed. Comparison of possible universes seems essential to the wise creation of one. But how such knowledge is possible we can scarcely see; and if anything is by its very nature essentially unknowable, of course it is not to be supposed that omniscience knows it. It is difficult, or perhaps impossible, for us to imagine how God can know all alternatives—for example, what would have occurred in America if the slave-trade had never reached its shores, or what human history would have been if Mohammed had been slain by robbers in his first caravan journey. To us it seems as if the action of free wills were not knowable in advance, and still more unknowable seems the action that would have occurred in conditions that never came into being. Nevertheless, we must say that the genuine understanding of the universe which is certainly included in omniscience does imply knowledge of alternatives, and we cannot think of God as fulfilling his relation to other existence without such knowledge. Greater difficulties would beset our thinking if we were to deny it.

The very thought of understanding the universe is too great for us, and yet we can identify some of its contents. Understanding of the universe must imply knowledge of all changes and tendencies, all movements by which things fulfil their nature, and all nature of things from which characteristic changes proceed. It includes ability to estimate all such changes and tendencies for exactly what they are, and to judge their importance in the universal scheme. For the understanding of the universe implies that the universe can be understood. If one perfect mind can grasp it all, that means that there is a scheme of things, an intelligible wholeness. The omniscient God knows what end his universe is designed to serve, how each part of it is adapted to serve that end, and how well each part is filling its place. It is by perfect comprehension of the whole that he is able to hold a true and righteous estimate of every part.

We thus reach the fact that in omniscience there is a moral quality—a fact that has not received due attention in Christian thought. By a sad mistake, God's omniscience has often been represented as scarcely more than the perception and judgment of the perfect intellect. If it is conceived more ethically, still the recognition of the moral element is apt to be one-sided and incomplete. The truth is simply that the Being who has the knowledge is the Being who has the character, and the entire character of God conditions all his knowing. No knowledge of moral beings is possible to God that is not the knowledge of a perfect moral judge, estimating good and evil as they are. Universal knowledge involves universal judgment, and universal judgment on the part of the all-knowing God is omnipresent and perpetual. This aspect of omniscience has often been recognized, and men aware of their sinfulness have felt themselves enveloped in a searching and condemnatory presence as unescapable as the atmosphere, and the present holy God has seemed to them as dreadful as a consuming fire. But while it is true that omniscience means universal judgment, it is equally true that omniscience means universal compassion. The omniscient God is not only Judge but Saviour. God is love. We do him deep injustice if we contemplate his omniscience without remembering that his knowledge is pervaded by the sympathetic quality. That which he knows so well he accounts his own, and is bearing on his heart. The souls that his knowledge searches he also understands: they are his spiritual offspring, capable of fellowship with him, and he knows them with the insight of love. He knows their evil and their good, their strength and weakness, and embraces them all in the sympathetic understanding of the Saviour-God. The judgment that his omniscience implies is the judgment at once of righteousness and of compassion. The troubles of the world God knows with a heart of sympathy. If it were not so, it would be happier for men to blot out their belief in his omniscience; for a Being who knew this present world only as a Judge and not as a sympathetic Friend would be no God for us. But his knowledge of all human sorrow is the knowledge of One who is afflicted in all the afflictions of his creatures. He who knows all is the God and Father of Jesus Christ, who views all in the light of his perfect holiness, his fatherly compassion and his redemptive love.

Knowing all with such a holy, righteous, condemnatory, sympathetic, friendly, helpful knowledge, the one God is omnipresent and eternal. His whole universe is upon his heart as well as his mind, and thus his omniscience becomes a foundation for rich and satisfactory religion. He who knows is he who can be trusted. That any object within the field of omniscience will ever be misknown or misjudged by the omniscient One no being need ever suspect or fear. He is the holy and trustworthy One, whose knowledge will never be unfairly used against any. So his omniscience is a blessing to his universe, not a cloud over it, or a reason for trembling. The psalmist was right in esteeming it a privilege to stand embraced behind and before in the knowledge from which no darkness could hide him and no distance remove. All the surer and more blessed is our confidence, because God's knowledge of all his works is grounded deep in knowledge of himself, and in his own sense of his perfect goodness and perfect sufficiency to all existence.

13. OMNIPOTENCE

Companion to omnipresence and omniscience is Omnipotence. As in those attributes, so in this, the unity and soleness of God is asserted, and the doctrine is that of monotheism; for omnipotence is no other than unipotence, the adequacy and control of the One, in relation to all that is not himself. Of the two units of existence the One is master of the other. God is master of the universe, and holds it in control. He is able, or adequate, or sufficient. He is the Almighty, competent to the work.

The Christian doctrine of God, like the Hebrew, has always affirmed the divine omnipotence, by which has been meant complete and perfect power, or ability to do all things that he would. Probably the most prominent element in the doctrine has been the simple idea of power. In the Scriptures, however, the starting-point is not the abstract conception of power, so much as it is the more concrete idea of control, or mastery. The Almighty is not merely the All-Strong, but rather the All-Master, the strong Lord of all. In his mastership is of course implied power sufficient for such a relation, yet apparently the sufficiency of power was inferred from the universal control, rather than the universal control from the sufficiency of power. The Almighty of the Scriptures is the All-Sovereign, rather than merely the possessor of immeasurable energy.

Evidently this is the more religious conception of omnipotence, or at least the more worthily religious. It is a worthy act of worship to adore the Lord of all, who possesses with other qualities the power that corresponds to universal lordship. But in power itself there is nothing to worship, though there may be much to admire and wonder at. If mere power is worshipped, as too often it has been, it makes a religion of fear as men look toward God, and cruelty or indifference as they look upon their fellows. If, in a farther stage, the doctrine of power becomes prominent, and the idea of omnipotence rules in the realm of thought, then it proves that the intellectual conception of power is not competent to command the best religious feeling. The general thought of the Bible is best, according to which omnipotence is a concrete and practical fact, not power, but a universal control in which power sufficient is implied. We need not fear that our conception of the power of God will be diminished if it takes this form. On the contrary it is much more likely to be a living truth to us, and thus be really great. An abstract conception of boundless might is far less effective in its greatness than recognition of the living God as acting upon all as Master, and using all power that his work upon so vast a universe requires.

So omnipotence, in the Christian doctrine, is adequate ability. It is the sufficiency of God. This brief definition declares first that God is equal in power to all possible demands of his universe upon him. Taken in connection with what we perceive of the divine transcendence, it says more than this. God is greater than his universe, and the whole of his power is not exhausted or required by its demands. He is adequate to more than he is doing. God is All-Master, and competent to be Master of more. Thus our idea of omnipotence is extended beyond all reach of words or imagining. God is mighty even beyond all demands of that universe which so far exceeds our power of thought.

In this large view, the doctrine of omnipotence at once rises above puzzles as to whether God can do this or that particular thing. If we were to start with defining omnipotence as absolutely unlimited ability, such puzzles would lie directly before us, and have to be considered. Perplexity as to whether God can do certain special things that look impossible has done much to dim the glory of omnipotence for Christian faith. But the definition that has now been given leaves such questions aside. We need not inquire whether God could create a world in which two and two make five. The doctrine of omnipotence does not imply that God can do everything that can be mentioned. It does not even suggest the question whether he can do things that imply some essential contradiction or contain some irremovable absurdity. There are two units of existence, God and the universe; and the doctrine of omnipotence declares that God can do all that is required by either of them. He can do all that his own nature and character call for, and all that his universe demands. The one field of existence which is not God is inhabited and controlled by God, the one Being who is able to do the work of it, and to do in it whatever manner corresponds to what he himself is. He is thus adequate to his universe because he is more and greater than his universe; and this sufficiency or adequacy to his universe and to himself is his omnipotence. This doctrine suggests unanswerable questions, but it suggests no absurdities or fruitless puzzles.

According to popular thought, omnipotence is exhibited chiefly in the material universe on the one hand, and on the other in the ordering of events and securing of results in human affairs. It is shown in that immense sum of energy which we wonderingly observe in the operations of the universe: this is the power of God, and it is boundless. It is shown also in that general providential control by which God is able to overrule events and bring out of them his own intended issue: this also is the power of God, and it is sufficient.

As for the former of these fields of omnipotence, we can only say that we observe in actual operation an amount of energy that is perfectly overwhelming to contemplate. This is a fact that suggests agnosticism, for a genuine clear conception of the source and origin of all this energy seems hopelessly beyond our reach. We accept it as a fact existing, but how can we go farther and account for it? Origins of energy are in any case beyond our human experience, and beyond our understanding. The Christian doctrine offers no explanation in detail: it only proclaims God, and declares that he is the source of all power. It is by reason of his omnipotence that the universe is full of organized and operative energy. This is the only alternative to agnosticism on the subject: we must say that God is the source of energy, or else that energy is here and we know not whence it is. But the affirmation of an almighty God is all that the Christian doctrine has to offer. It has no theory of the manner in which God's power goes forth in the forms in which we discover power at work, and Christian thought would suffer no surprise or discomfiture if no further knowledge of this mystery were ever to be had.

In the latter of these fields of omnipotence, the providential and practical, we come to the region in which moral agents are to be dealt with, and existence is full of moral significance. Here, if omnipotence is to have any meaning, we must define it in other terms than those of physical power. Thus we are at once introduced to the higher meaning of the doctrine. We wrong the idea of omnipotence if we picture it mainly as power effective in the physical realm, and as bearing a character such as physical energy suggests. We must not allow Samson or Hercules to stand as type of the power of God, or think of gravitation as a sufficient symbol of his mighty working. An omnipotence that is not operative in the field that corresponds to his character cannot be the omnipotence of the God of Jesus Christ. Physical omnipotence is but the ground on which we build the nobler idea of moral omnipotence.

The Christian doctrine affirms that while God is adequate to the universe in respect of its physical being, he is morally and spiritually adequate to the universe also. This is what is meant by moral omnipotence. He is able to pour into the universe the power which its physical necessities require, and he is able also to pour into the universe the moral and spiritual energy by which the work that corresponds to his character shall be accomplished in its existence. In this he is adequate to himself, able to do justice to his own moral nature, and thus to do justice to the moral nature of that which he has created. He is as capable of supplying the moral and spiritual needs of his universe as he is of filling it with physical energy. His fulness of spiritual power for the use of spiritual beings is as inexhaustible as his infinity of power for physical purposes. In all moral and spiritual relations God is the sufficient One, adequate to himself, greater than the universe and free in action toward it, equal to its needs, and equal to more if its needs were greater.

This affirmation of moral omnipotence is the heart of the Christian doctrine of the omnipotence of God. It is evident at a glance that if this were omitted omnipotence would be nothing but strength, and worship of the Almighty would be only an exaltation of force, degrading to the worshipper and unworthy of God. Without moral omnipotence there could be no sure providential control, and no trustworthy ability to turn human movements to divine purpose. Moral power indeed is all that makes the doctrine of omnipotence a religious doctrine. The Almighty whom we can worship must be almighty in the realm of the spirit. We cannot rest without the confidence that in that realm he is not only potent but omnipotent, able to do all that his own nature and the needs of his universe require.

What the moral omnipotence of God means for the universe we can forecast only in the vision of faith. By natural interpretation the meaning of it is that God is able in his own time to bring to pass the perfect doing of his own worthy will by his creatures, and bring all spiritual beings into moral fellowship with himself—not of course by compulsion, for that would be neither worthy of him nor possible, but by effective moral means. If God is able to accomplish this result, there is no need to show that he is willing, or to argue that it will be done.   But here we meet our own limitations. We cannot forecast such an outcome on the ground of anything that we have seen as yet, for though God's work is great, the signs of a victory that can be called universal are not visible to us.   Probably in this world they cannot be; for we can see that if God is to do a work that corresponds to moral omnipotence he must have at his command a far vaster sweep of time than our human powers can even imagine. Clouds and darkness indeed are round about him still.   How even God can overcome the resistances we cannot see.   But while we acknowledge our littleness, and humbly accept the consequences of our narrow range of view, it is necessary to insist that moral omnipotence must not be denied to God, or left in abeyance in our thinking because we know so little. The right way out of our difficulties is never by diminishing our conception of God.   Moral omnipotence is one of the fixed points of Christian faith, and must be held as the joy and crown of moral existence, and allowed to put forth its uplifting power upon our life.   For even though we made no inquiry about the destinies of a universe, a morally omnipotent God is necessary for the peace and comfort of a single soul.

IV. EVIDENCE

1. THE QUESTION AND THE EVIDENCE

Is the Christian doctrine of God true? In other words,
Is there such a living God as that doctrine proclaims?

The time for considering this question is after the doctrine
has been set forth. Thus far in the present work there has
been no effort to prove the doctrine true: now comes the
great inquiry whether the view of God that has been presented
will stand. It is true that the opposite order has frequently
been followed. Christian Theology has often begun its
work with the endeavour to prove the existence of God, and
has thus undertaken to defend the most vital of its doctrines
before it had been formulated. But it is not best to try to
establish the existence of God until we have shown what
we mean by God. In that way lie ambiguity in the argument
and uncertainty in the conclusion. Doubtless in presenting
and defining the doctrine there must be some attempt at
proof, but the attempt is only incidental. Proof comes at
the end. Doubtless also the very presentation contains an
element of proof, for a worthy conception of God has genuine
self-evidencing power. The doubt concerning him which
is always possible is less easy when his character and relations
with men are seen in their Christian simplicity and natural-
ness. Nevertheless, the time comes when we must assert
that the Christian doctrine of God is true, and consider
whether the proposition is tenable.

It is important to note that the whole question comes up
at once, in all its greatness. We do not encounter it in parts.
We do not first seek to show that there exists a God, afterward
to be defined; nor do we build our argument up in successive

stages. Our search for evidence concerning God does not follow the line of history, or of philosophical development. We do not begin with natural religion, and ascend through a rising scale of evidences, and watch the conception while it clear itself of primitive errors, and finally discover in Christ the material for making a satisfactory doctrine complete. This would be a legitimate process, but it is not the process that is now required. In our construction of the Christian doctrine we have already come to know what we mean when we speak of God, and the meaning that we have thus obtained is now to be judged as a whole. We are now to inquire whether there is reason to believe that this God, or God thus conceived, is a reality. Under the influence of Jesus Christ we have learned to think of God as the personal Spirit, perfectly good, who in holy love creates, sustains and orders all. Now we take at once this vast conception, and inquire whether there exists a reality to which it corresponds. This is the great and only question, in which all minor questions are wrapped up.

The question thus raised is a question of fact, or of reality. The Christian doctrine proclaims one only God, and declares that the gracious and holy Father of Jesus Christ is he; and nothing can be more thoroughly a question of fact than the question whether this is so. It deals not with mere theory or abstraction, but with reality of the most practical and decisive kind. On the one hand, it is concerning a reality that we inquire; for we ask, Is it right for us to interpret our life in the light of such a Being? are we safe in committing ourselves to him? is he there when we trust him? and does the world mean what such a God would make it mean? Belief in such a God would give a solid foundation for all virtue, righteousness and hope—and is there such a foundation? On the other hand, it is in the world of concrete reality that our question is to be answered. The truth of the Christian doctrine is to be judged as other questions of fact are judged, in the light of such knowledge as experience has brought to living men. Its affirmation is to be tested by comparison with the large experience of mankind, and the facts with which men are acquainted. Its appeal is made to the human faculties of perception and judgment. There is no external requirement that we shall believe in God, nor is there any such thing as believing in him at the command of authority. We have to discover whether belief in the Christian God is possible. We must pass judgment, in the light of all that we know, whether the Christian affirmation concerning him will stand. This judgment must be formed in this present world of concrete reality. The question of God is every man's question, in the sense that every man is interested in it, and must pass upon it for himself; in the sense also that every man lives in the world where it is to be answered, and has in his own life the facts that are most decisive of the solution. Not in the difficult region of abstract thought is the main work to be done, and not in the mysterious depths of divine being is the chief material for conclusions to be found. It is in the common world that the argument proceeds. Just here, where we all know and are ignorant and our rational being is put to the test of life; just here, where we struggle with the moral problem and obey or sin against the best that we know; just here, where life with all its mysteries and possibilities is upon us and we must solve its problem if we can—just here is the question of God to be anwered, as other questions of reality are answered, in the light of common knowledge.

It should be added that the Christian doctrine requires to be received as other conclusions concerning questions of fact should be received. It requires practical acceptance. A theoretical acceptance of fact may indeed suffice if the fact is far away from real life, but not if it is near, practical and important. In that case good acceptance implies putting the fact to use. The Christian belief in God is more than assent to his existence: it is personal conviction and confidence, with loyalty and devotion, into which a man enters with the best energy of his entire being. Though he profess a belief and suppose that he holds it, he has not done justice to the case in hand until he has accepted the fact of God as a fact to live by. This urgent practical quality in Christian belief corresponds perfectly to the nature of the question of God as a question of fact.

The question of fact concerning the reality of God may be presented with one or another of its elements at the front. The conception is many-sided. Proclaiming the God whom he discovers, a student of nature may set one aspect of the divine being at the front, and a student of life another, while within each of these fields there may be emphasis upon any one of various elements. The Christian doctrine has its own point of view and special emphasis. No one doubts what it is, though the fact discerned by all has not been fully put to its helpful use.

The specialty of the Christian doctrine resides in the character which it attributes to God, and the relations with men in which his character is expressed. It is first a doctrine in the realm of morality and religion. It has visions of infinite holiness and love, and declares that these qualities determine what God is to other beings. Its emphasis falls upon perfect goodness. Attributes that are not moral in themselves it includes in its predication, but in him they cease to be non-moral. It calls him omnipotent and omniscient, for example, but even these attributes it beholds suffused with character. Even his creatorship is important to the Christian doctrine chiefly because it is the primary fact in his practical relation with men. For its central substance the Christian doctrine has the inherent goodness of God, and the expression of that goodness in his relations with his creatures. Holiness and love expressed in Fatherhood and Saviourhood as these are revealed in Christ—that is the heart of the matter. Hence in our inquiry as to the truth of the doctrine the primary question is the question of character. We ask whether we can hold that there exists a Being worthy to be called God, and filling the place of God to all other existence, who is the eternal holiness and love, and is related to all other being as holiness and love must be related, in moral government and spiritual grace. The inquiry touches the whole sphere of the Godhead, but here falls the emphasis. Is the good God a reality?

It must be added at once that all doctrine of character implies an equally clear and positive doctrine of rationality. Rationality and character may be distinguished in thought, but are never separate in fact. Each implies the other. None but a reasonable being can be a moral being. A good God therefore must be a Being of rational powers; and the perfect goodness can be attributed only to the Being in whom dwells the perfect reason. Hence all evidence of the rationality of the universal order, and of the Mind which it represents, falls readily into its place in support of the Christian doctrine. That doctrine affirms the perfectness of the divine mind as well as the eternal goodness of the divine heart, and welcomes all evidence of the rationality of the universe in which the divine mind has expressed itself. It would be a mistake to suppose that because Christianity is a religion, evidence for its doctrine of God must be found exclusively in religious experience. In that region lies its specialty, indeed, but the heavens may still declare the glory of God, and the earth be full of his wisdom. Without evidence from this field the proof of God would be incomplete. Hence we must look not only at moral and religious reasons for belief in him, but at rational grounds as well.

Some helpful light may be obtained in advance upon the kind of evidence by which the Christian doctrine of God is to be supported. The principle is very simple. Obviously the broad fact is that the nature of the evidence, in order to be valuable, must correspond to the nature of the doctrine. This one fact will help us draw the line between various kinds of evidence that are offered for our use.

If the manner of proof must correspond to the nature of the doctrine, one of our first certainties will be that we cannot have demonstration. Not by strict logical process is the Christian doctrine of God to be established. There is an ancient prejudice in favour of demonstration, or at least an impression that it is far the most desirable kind of proof, —as indeed it is, in its own field. But it has often been tacitly assumed that whatever cannot be proved in this strictest sense is not certainly to be known as true. Accordingly it has been supposed that there must be some straight and unmistakable road of argument to the great conclusion concerning God, a road of syllogistic reasoning, so constructed that any sane mind must follow it and acknowledge the result. Much labour has been spent upon such arguments, in hope that conclusive demonstration might be obtained. But the results are disappointing. We must say without reserve that strict demonstration of the Christian doctrine of God is impossible.

To show this impossibility it might be enough to allege the greatness of the subject. The conclusion that is sought is too vast to be embraced in the premises of a syllogism. Whether or not some parts or elements of the Christian doctrine of God may be demonstrable, certainly the doctrine as a whole is too vast and comprehensive to be contained in the premises of any syllogism that can be devised.

Yet this reason for the impossibility, good though it is, is a formal and external one, dealing with the dimensions of the subject rather than with the subject itself. Our view of the doctrine thus far has been of little use if it has not shown us that it lies in a region where belief comes by other means than logic. What is it that we affirm of God? We affirm that he is one, the God of all; that he inhabits his creation, and is in spiritual communication with spiritual beings who bear his likeness; that he is worthy of the love and confidence of all who live, since he is the perfect holiness and love; that he is rightful Lord of all, and Friend and Saviour to the sinful and needy; that he has made us for himself, and our heart is restless until it rests in him. Shall we attempt to demonstrate this? Can we hope to do so? Is there any such thing as proving such a God, in such manner that no right mind can depart from the path by which we lead to our conclusion? No. The conclusion and the method do not correspond. Our affirmations are not of a kind to stand at the end of a logical process. The Christian belief in God is a great conviction, attained through reasoning, experience, and faith, a conviction to which the soul is led by the various influences of life, the universe and God, in which a man rests because its foundations are deep and broad and eternal. It is a conviction that carries with it the affections of the heart and the devotion of the will, as well as the assent of the intellect. Such a conviction must be reached by other means than argument. Demonstration is of the intellect alone. It is a true saying that there is no necessary love between the soul and the last step in a logical process. Belief in God is larger and more profound. The character of the invisible Spirit cannot be demonstrated, neither can even his existence or his relation to us men; and if they could, still the demonstration would not introduce the right kind of belief in realities so high and spiritual. The Christian doctrine of God moves in a realm where spiritual discernment dwells and love is at home, and not outside that realm is the chief evidence of God to be found.

This is to say that the Christian belief in God cannot be reached by any process that is the same for all minds. One must come to it by one road and another by another, for it is at once too large and too spiritual for logical uniformity. Arguments of many kinds are helpful to it, but out of the boundless field of existence and the fruitful soil of experience, evidence in endless variety in support of it must come. Plainly then the evidence cannot be of uniform character or force, or equally convincing to all persons. There is no overmastering proof that can put belief in God beyond the possibility of doubt. There can be no formula for the Christian belief. The great conviction must come as it can. There may indeed be a formal belief, produced by formal proof. Men may call themselves believers in God because they have followed a line of proof that satisfies them.

Such belief is not to be despised, for it has its value, and fulfils important uses in the history of religion; but it is not such belief as the significance of the living God demands and the Christian doctrine contemplates. To that larger and richer conviction there exists no single road.

This impossibility of demonstration is not to be regretted. That ancient impression, amounting almost to a superstition, that demonstration is the only sure way to sound knowledge, has been renewed in modified form in our time under the influence of science. But it is a superstition that ought to die. There are other sound ways of knowing besides the logical way. Only the lesser part of truth has come by demonstration. The strictly inductive method of learning is immensely valuable, but it is a mistake to suspect that it is the only road to truth. The Christian doctrine of God employs it, but it makes use of other approaches too.

Christian Theology has long experience with arguments for the existence of God. There is a well-known group of arguments, long venerable, that may be called the ancient contribution of philosophy to theism. The Cosmological argument has inferred from the existence of the world a sufficient cause therefor. The Teleological argument has inferred from adaptations in the world an intending Mind. The Moral or Anthropological argument has inferred from the ethical nature of man a moral source and ground of existence. The Ontological argument has inferred the existence of an infinite and perfect Being from the necessary ideas of the human mind. All these arguments have been cast and recast in syllogistic form, and turned to the various use of changing generations. They are justly venerated, for they represent strong thought upon the profoundest problems of existence. The material that they have handled is of permanent value and cannot be lost to theology: it is certain to be used in substance, though forms may change. But at present the ancient arguments in their familiar forms are retiring from their old prominence, because it is felt that they do not now accomplish what they originally proposed. Probably they will never again be largely used, in the forms in which they have come to us from the past. Knowledge and thought have changed so much that the ancient arguments do not meet the test—they do not correspond to the nature of the question as it now exists. Now, as in other ages, great changes in knowledge and thought require that the evidence concerning God be cast in new forms, and be welcomed from new quarters.

It might seem that an argument once good must be good forever. But the fact is that no argument upon a vital theme can be estimated by itself, or be effective without regard to the manner in which it fits in with known truth around it. To be convincing, an argument must move in the same realm and live in the same world with the men who are to be convinced. To be valid with a given generation, it must have the same large presuppositions that underlie the thought of that generation. It must not imply presuppositions that no longer exist. Just as reasoning that implied the Ptolemaic view of the solar system was of no effect when the Copernican view had been established, so any reasoning that implies philosophical or scientific conceptions that have been superseded needs at least to be recast before it can be effective, and may prove to have no place at all in the later time. Genuine truth that has been maintained upon one ground must be maintained upon some other when the presuppositions of thought have changed. This is no hardship or misfortune: it is a necessary part in human progress, affecting all departments of thought alike. It is as important in chemistry as in theology. Of necessity it affects the standing of arguments concerning the existence of God. Here, as everywhere, arguments that depend upon principles or mental methods now abandoned, or require a view of facts that cannot now be held, cannot now be effective, and must not be relied upon. To wield them with power is impossible, since our age like any other must be governed by the views of reality that have entered into its life. To whatever extent the venerable arguments for the existence of God fail to meet this test, to that extent they are unavailable for present use, and must at least be modified before they can be used with power. Yet they do not perish, but only pass their value on, to be as great as ever in the later time.

The Ontological argument illustrates the effect of a deep change in the current presuppositions. It endeavours to deduce from the necessary modes of human thought the necessary existence of a perfect Being. It has been variously constructed, but always with this one object, and it has always been felt that to argue toward this end could not be all in vain. Yet to the modern mind the argument is not successful. It does not go farther than to establish the reasonableness of its conclusion, it does not establish the conclusion itself. This is doubtless a useful service to thought, but it is not proof: if it had not been confounded with proof the argument might have better standing now. It was once regarded as proof, but that was when presuppositions were different. It was once assumed that to prove an abstract proposition was to establish a fact. There was full belief in the reality of abstract conceptions; and upon the basis of such belief greater value was attributed to abstract argument than it could have on any other ground. But the ancient doctrine of realism has long ago departed from philosophy, and consequently abstract reasoning has ceased to be regarded as concrete proof. Interest in abstract thought will never cease, as the undying interest in philosophy gives assurance, and abstract thinking will always have its place in theology. But it is no longer taken for granted that such thinking will yield definite proof of concrete realities; and with this change in presuppositions the ontological argument for the existence of God has lost its convincing force.

Perhaps it may seem that this is a movement in the wrong direction, and interest in abstract proof ought to revive. There is an old impression that there is somehow an affinity between abstract reasoning and spiritual affairs—an impression that has penetrated even into popular thought about religion. But the affinity, such as there is, is not so essential as to be of permanent effect. The retirement of interest in abstract proofs is a part of the modern interest in facts, which implies its own presuppositions and point of view. It is a right and valuable interest, and one that will not be superseded. The question of God is a question of fact, or of reality, and it is not the nature of a fact that it can be established by abstract reasoning. By such means it may be shown to be reasonable, or even morally necessary, but not by such means can it be proved to be a fact. The question of the existence of the good God is like other questions of fact in this respect—it is by the testimony of other facts, or realities, reasonably interpreted, that the existence and character of God must be established. The subject is one for the newer method to work upon, and the ancient emphasis will never again be placed upon the abstract arguments.

The Christian doctrine has nothing to fear from this shifting of interest from the abstract to the concrete. It has been helped by abstract reasonings, and will be helped by them still, but it was never founded upon them. The Christian conception of God was grounded in experience, and has always had its strength in the region of concrete reality. The doctrine is first a doctrine of life, and it will be strengthened, not weakened, by the deepening of interest in the field in which its greatest vitality has always been shown. For confirmation it now looks not to syllogistic constructions, and not first to argument at all, but to the facts of nature and life, to the significance of the universe, to rational meanings, to ethical relations, to spiritual experiences, to a fair understanding of things that are.

The Teleological argument for the existence of God brings another illustration of the effect of change in presuppositions. No confirmation of belief in God is older or more natural or more impressive than that which is discovered in adaptations and the seeking of ends. That end-seeking is the work of a mind, no one naturally doubts: experience has laid firm foundations for that conviction. It has always been natural for men to say that if there are unquestionable adaptations and end-seekings in the order of nature they were introduced there by an intelligent and powerful mind, a creator who understood his work. And if beyond all special adaptations there seemed to be discovered one great increasing purpose in the world as a whole, all the more impressive was the evidence of a designing mind. The Old Testament looks abroad in this spirit, though more in adoration than in argument, and thus the Psalm is sung: "O Lord, how manifold are thy works! in wisdom hast thou made them all." (Ps. civ. 24.) When the modern age of investigation opened, innumerable adaptations in the world were noticed, and the fitness of things to serve their purpose was read as evidence of God. Every period of serious thought in Theism has turned this reasoning to the account of faith, and with good reason. An argument so ready everywhere, so straightforward in its movement and supported by so great an array of facts, is not the work of folly. It is of the kindred of truth, and cannot be lost out of use as worthless. There is at least a strong presumption in favour of its being valid as long as the world stands.

But not in any one form. The argument makes use of facts in nature and life, many of which are brought to its hand by Science, and it is necessary that the facts be rightly known. In order to serve an argument from design, they must be correctly reported, and seen in their true relations in the order of nature: otherwise inferences from them will be untrustworthy. At the beginning of the nineteenth century Paley wrought out the argument from design for the existence of God. He traced the teleological aspect of the world through many instances, and exhibited the purposeful God in nature and life in a manner exceedingly impressive. He popularized the doctrine, and enabled it to serve as a strong support for faith. But his argument no longer stands in the books on Theism. It has retired. A student of modern mind, however well convinced concerning design, will not use Paley's proofs of it; and coincidently there has come a great loss of confidence in arguments from design in general.

For the change there may be various reasons, but one sufficient reason is that the science of the early nineteenth century has become antiquated. The facts are better known at present, and many of them are not as Paley supposed. Not only are single facts differently reported, but his general view of the manner in which facts in nature are related among themselves and bound into unity has passed away. With the knowledge of his time his reasoning was in accord, but not so well with the knowledge of ours. This is reason enough why his argument has fallen out of vogue: present knowledge does not support it. Arguments that consist in interpretation of facts must depend for their validity upon the correctness with which the facts are known. If a radical change or a great enlargement of knowledge comes, such arguments must at least be reconsidered, and may have to be given up. This is nothing to be complained of, for it is only the common lot of thought in an advancing world. "Our little systems have their day," and their day ends as soon as larger knowledge makes a better day possible.

The Paleyan construction of the argument from design has lapsed with the lapsing of the science which it represented, and a host of men have been ready to accept the change as the passing of argument from design altogether. But such a reaction is excessive. Teleology is not dead. If certain adaptations are not as they were thought to be, it does not follow that the world is purposeless. Instead of that, the whole question remains, to be judged on its merits. The fact and scope of purpose in the world have not been disproved, but must still be estimated in that more recent light which has disproved some old opinions. For all that the lapsing of the old argument shows, the world may be far more purposeful than Paley ever supposed. Probably it will be found that teleology is only driven from smaller fields to greater by the change. Certainly there is vast room for purpose in the universe to which we now lift up our eyes. But we have to approach the new field of inquiry in new methods, and study out the problem of purpose in view of our own presuppositions, in the world with which we are now acquainted.

Of the two other famous arguments for the existence of God similar things may be said. Both make use of essential and permanent truth, and both use it in the light of presuppositions of thought that are necessarily passing, not permanent. Both deal with truth that concerns the relation between God and his creation. The Cosmological argument infers God as ground of the existence of the universe and cause of its changes: the Moral or Anthropological infers God as the Original of man and the source of morality. Both conclusions are true, and are obtainable by legitimate process in every age. But it is evident that the form of these arguments must change if there comes some decided change in our knowledge of the universe and its mode of being, and in our conceptions of the constitution and spiritual relations of man. Such changes have come. The very thing that has occurred in the thinking of recent time is a reconstruction of our ideas of the universe and the human race. The reconstruction is far from complete as yet, and we are not called upon to deal with it as with a finished thing, but it is well begun, the principle of it is plain, and it will not be discontinued. It is in the world as now conceived that we have to think of the human race and the relation of God to his universe. It is in the world as now conceived that we have to become convinced that the good God of Jesus Christ is the living God. Our Cosmological and Anthropological arguments—for we shall have them, though we shall not name them so—will have to take their form from our conceptions of the cosmos and the anthropos, not from those of our fathers. They will stand as part of our interpretation of existence as it appears to us. They will be constructed, too, in the more recent method of reasoning on universal themes. We shall not frame syllogisms, so much as seek meanings. We shall not expect to make ourselves sure of God by demonstration, so much as we hope to understand that which lies before us, and discover him wherever he is expressed. Our reasonings will not be altogether like those which we inherit, because they are our own, growths of our own age, rooted in the soil of our own presuppositions.

As to these presuppositions which newly condition all thought concerning God, they lie in the two great fields, which by man himself are bound together as one. They lie in the material universe and in the spiritual universe. Only the barest hint of them can be given here, but the hint may not be in vain. The universe, practically unbounded, is one vast system, interrelated through its whole extent, and held in unity by one operation and a single method; the universe, so far as we can judge, is operated from within, by forces in itself, rather than by some power that acts upon it from beyond itself; change everywhere is incessant, each state unfolding out of that which preceded it, as if the whole were advancing in one mighty growth. As for this human race to which we belong, it is part and parcel of the universe, for it has grown up out of the life that is below it on the earth; its present condition is the outgrowth of all its immeasurable past; it has been very long upon the earth, its higher powers have begun to open and are slowly opening still, and its destiny lies ahead; it does not understand itself, and yet is dimly groping forward. It is in a world thus conceived that we are to inquire whether God is real. We contemplate not a late-born race planted from the outside in a little world, but an ancient race that is of one substance with the universe, while its true life is in the powers of the spirit that reach out to that which is above. It is plain that in such a field of existence we cannot think of God, if he exists at all, except as universal in his relations. All provincialism, partialism, specialism, narrowness, must go out of our thoughts of him: he must be one God, related equally to all souls, and to all existence. We seek to know whether there is evidence in the universal field that the one good God is real. Can we say that the universe is the creation and the home of such a God? and if we answer, Yes, on what grounds do we venture the affirmation?

If the field of inquiry is of this kind, one thing is certain. It is by evidence rather than by proof that the Christian doctrine of God will be confirmed; and the evidence will be found in large meanings. We shall not prove our doctrine, but we may find reason for being sure that it is true; and this we shall find not so much in single facts or special fields of inquiry as in significances that appear in the most meaningful realms of being. To speak of universal meanings may perhaps be deemed presumptuous, for what are we that we should talk of understanding what is universal? But we may be allowed to speak of large meanings, discovered in that realm of existence where meaning goes deepest; and these large meanings we may consult more confidently than any minor witnesses to God. We shall not do well to attend chiefly to incidental proofs of him. Single facts and special evidences may bear their testimony, but they bring less than we seek. We are seeking not so much for evidences as for evidence, universally and forever valid; and to the broadest and most significant fields of existence we must go to find it. The most convincing evidence is that of great and indispensable meaning. If a truth fits into the frame of truth, it cannot be removed: if it is the keystone of the arch of truth, it will remain forever. If we find that God is the necessary counterpart of all that we know to be most real, we shall count him real. And we need not fear that this counsel to explore large meanings will lead us out into some wilderness of universality, where the soul cannot be at home. What is great in the universe is great in the soul, and that which is great with God is great with man. Large meanings are meanings that the soul can read. This is the glory and wonder of man the earth-born, that the child of time can read in the light of eternity. So we turn to the large meanings, and seek by interpretation of existence in its highest significance to learn whether God is there.

The great meanings are only two: a rational meaning and a spiritual meaning. We are acquainted with these two aspects of existence, and in the significance of existence from these two points of view we find the supreme evidence of the reality of God. It is true that these two terms are not free from ambiguity, and yet the sense in which they are employed for the present purpose can be made sufficiently plain. It is a most interesting and suggestive fact that there is no separate line of physical evidence for the existence of God. Innumerable facts in the material universe bear their testimony to him, but all consideration of signs of God in the material order falls at once under one or both of the other heads: it cannot be kept separate. It is the rationality of the material order, or else the spirituality of its significance, that we find ourselves considering, whenever we trace God in the physical universe. This is a true sign of the greatness and universality of the higher sense in all existence. So we turn to the rational and the spiritual interpretation of life and the world, asking what we can learn in these quarters about God; and we shall find that each field in its own manner yields impressive and convincing evidence in support of the Christian doctrine.

It is plain that we are entering upon a field of evidence that can never be fully explored. No age or generation can have command of the knowledge that would be required to complete the inquiry. If life and the world do really bear the testimony to God that we claim for them, additional confirmations of the claim will always be coming in: if not, the deepening spiritual poverty of life will be an ever-strengthening refutation. There is no hope of saying on these pages all that ought to be said in the present light by way of evidence for the Christian view of God. It is intended only to indicate what evidence there is in the great meanings, in the fields where evidence is most real and convincing. It will be enough if it is shown that the most fundamental qualities of existence point surely to the reality of such a God as Jesus teaches us to trust.

There is a widespread impression that the present conditions of knowledge are unfavourable to the obtaining of good evidence of the reality of God.   The ancient arguments for his existence are more or less discredited, it is agreed that demonstration of God is impossible, and it is claimed that the new presuppositions in the general thought leave no place for such a Being.   Some doubt, and some deny, that the modern view of the world allows belief in God.   Meanwhile the modes of religion have so changed as to make many suspect that religion itself is destined to leave the field.   Moral difficulties in actual life, now clearly noticed and keenly felt, are often supposed to render Christian Theism, the doctrine of the good Father, hopeless.   It may be possible, many think, to construct a beautiful idea of God, inspired by the best that we know, but there was never a time when it was so impossible to affirm that the lovely picture is a true one.   Fancy may worship it, but facts condemn it.

But the case is not thus hopeless.   It is very true that belief in God has its difficulties peculiar to the present age, but this is not the first time that such an experience has befallen it.   It is true also that the vastness of the new conceptions involves difficulties suddenly brought on and new in kind.   But it is not true that modern knowledge deprives the Christian doctrine of its opportunity of evidence concerning God.   Conditions are not such as to drive Christian Theism from the field, or to shadow the central Christian doctrine with doubt.   Are we told that the type of satisfactory evidence has changed ?   Most willingly do we cease to rely upon evidence that does not correspond to present knowledge, but in turn we call upon all students of the subject to attend to the evidence that does correspond to present knowledge.   The truth is that there has never been a time when a simple and sufficient confirmation of belief in the living and good God could be better obtained than now.   The large realities that tell of such a God are the very ones that stand clearest and firmest in the modern light, and the special difficulties that come with modern thought are destined to be relieved in the further movement of the thought that has encountered them. So we look out into the world and life, well assured that we cannot look thither with right vision without beholding God.

Although the specialty of the Christian doctrine lies in the spiritual and moral sphere, it is necessary to look first at the evidence that arises from the facts of rational existence.

2. EVIDENCE FROM THE RATIONAL

The largest is the simplest, and the argument from the rational for the reality of God, if it may be called an argument, is a very simple one. From a rational humanity and a rational universe, constituting one rational system, we infer a rational God. No other inference is justified by the facts, and we should stand condemned by the facts if we did not draw this inference; for of so rational a system the existence of a rational God is the only rational explanation. How true this simple statement is the present chapter is intended to show.

The first requirement upon one who would unfold this statement is that he make plain what is meant by rational. The word stands for a quality that belongs to normal intellectual operations. All thoughtful men have some good impression of its nature, and yet to point out its differentiating quality may not be easy. Analytical definitions of it may differ, but there is a practical definition ready to our hand that may serve a better purpose than a more philosophical one. At least it offers the best starting-point. If we are to define the rational we must define it as it appears where we find it; and we find it where at least we know it on the practical side. The rational we discover in ourselves. It is the normal method of humanity. Though we were to enumerate its processes, this reference to its home in ourselves tells us more about it than would our specifications. This mental method exists in all men. It exists in all degrees of fulness and power, but no sane human being is without it. In partial degree it exists in the animal world below the grade of man. All mind is rational, and rudimental mind is rudimentally rational. Yet though it is present in lower life, rationality is rightly regarded as the distinctive trait and quality of man. It is not merely the reasoning process so called: it includes the entire normal method and process of the human mind. In man the rational element becomes conscious and organized: it is adequate to the needs and undertakings of human life: it trains itself, and sets itself to use: in the highest of men it is brought by experience to systematic method and high efficiency. Thus it is in ourselves and our kind that we become acquainted with the rational. Self-knowledge exhibits it to us. The rational is the self-like, the man-like.

As soon as the rational has thus been defined as the human, it may be objected that our argument concerning God takes its start from man, and we are expressly preparing to present the divine in terms of the human. To this the answer is that of course it is true. The argument does start from man, as it ought. Objection to this is sometimes made, as if the process which it introduces must be a subjective process, bound to end in constructing a doctrine of God formed on human models, and therefore untrustworthy. But the objection misconceives the case. If we are to search for truth about God, we ought to start from man. In all existence that is known to us the personal human being is the highest form of being that we discover, and the rational nature is the highest nature that we have ever met. From this highest point in the world of human experience we certainly ought to set out, if we propose either to interpret what is below it or to explore what is above it. Any evidence concerning God that does not start from man is scarcely more than preparatory to that which does, and finds its true place and meaning only within the field of this more direct and valid operation. Instead of apologizing for setting out from man and his rational life when we wish to rise to knowledge of God or show that he is real, it is right to claim that this is the only right and hopeful way. So great a fact as the rational nature in mankind is the one from which to make our beginning when we seek to know that which is above mankind.

The practical standing of the rational is beyond question. All men trust it. They assume its validity as a guide to reality outside themselves. Even animals do the same, so far as they act upon reasons. They do not know that they are assuming the validity of the rational process, but they are, whenever they act upon mental suggestions, however rudimentary. The farthest intellectual advance of humanity is made by acting upon the same assumption. Without claiming that the rational element in our personal case or anywhere else among men is perfect, still we always treat it as a trustworthy quality of mankind, the operation of which will lead to sound results. In fact we cannot do otherwise than trust it. As we are compelled to trust our sight and hearing though we know that they lack something of perfection, so we are compelled to trust our rational powers though we are aware of their defects. The activities of life would cease if we did not. But the point is not that we are compelled to trust our rational powers: it is that they are trustworthy. We have reasonable confidence in them as leading us aright. A trustworthy faculty or power is one that corresponds to that upon which it has to act. It is capable of discerning reality and acting upon it: it perceives that which is, and deals with it according to its nature. This is what we mean when we call our bodily senses trustworthy: we can count upon them to perceive things as they are, at least so far as to make them generally safe guides for us to follow. In the same manner our rational powers are trustworthy: they take hold of reality in objects with which they have to do. That it is the nature of our rational powers to lead us to truth no sane mind thinks of doubting, for of this the long and fruitful history of the mind is evidence enough. Despite all human imperfection, it is ages too late for us to need to argue that humanity is justified in trusting its own rationality to lead it into truth.

From this universal, ever-used, ever-trusted human faculty we take our start when we search for evidence of God. Indeed we might as well say that we take our start from human nature. The rational powers, organized in self-consciousness and directed according to their nature, constitute the very substance of the human; so that we are not proceeding from some minor part or incident of humanity, but from humanity itself. Beginning at man, we set forth to find God.

We have first to do with origins. Whence came the rational in man? It is the wise old way in religion to refer it back to God the creator. That way is still as wise and right as ever, and to it we shall come; but at present we are inquiring about God, not making affirmations as to what he has done. Besides, the question that is now to be considered relates not so much to original causation as to method of development. By our question we mean, By what kind of process did man come to be the rational being that he is? How did his rationality come to pass?

We used to answer promptly that the rational in human kind was created by God, at a stroke. God said, "Let us make man," and man was made, with the rational powers that he possesses all complete; or else, as in the other narrative, into a lifeless body formed from the dust of the ground God breathed the breath of life, so that man became a living soul (Gen. i. 26–27; ii. 7). The rational nature of man had thus an instantaneous beginning: out of non-existence it sprang up at once through the act of God. A momentary event made man a rational being, where there was no being at all before. But later knowledge has displaced this picture of the human beginning, and set in its place another far more wonderful. The rational nature of man was not instantaneously created: it was developed in the developing of the world. Instead of standing out as a solitary thing in sharp contrast with other existence, it appears as a part of a larger whole, developed, trained, supported, by the world, or rather by the universe, in which it lives.

The rational quality is a quality or function of life. The human is the highest instance of the living that this world contains, and it is as a living being that man is rational. He is not the only living being, or the only rational being, in the world, though he is the most rational. Life is inconceivably ancient, and has borne innumerable forms, but all life is one. It has one essential nature, and tends to one character. Life tends to rationality. Not that all life is rational in the human manner, or will ever become so, but life is naturally a basis for rationality, and life as life has the rational quality for its proper crown. When life first came into existence the seed of the harvest of rationality was already sown. From that beginning it was natural that this end should be reached.

When life began to exist in this world we do not know, nor do we know the manner of its origin. Neither do we know its inner nature; but we do know in some measure how it works and to what it tends. It tends at once to sensibility. Probably the very beginning of life was the beginning of sensation. If we define life as correlation of what is within with what is without, or in any other reasonable way, our definition will imply such dependence of the living upon the external world as to require sensation or something akin thereto, to constitute the working connection between the two correlated elements. Life would naturally need to possess sensation, as the means of its appropriating that upon which it depends. Even the lowliest life must have this need. By sensation we human beings mean so much, because of our rich group of senses, that we can scarcely do justice in our thoughts to the lowest perceptions that can bear the name; yet we know that these are real, and are as serviceable to lower life in proportion to its needs as ours to us. It would seem that the essential functions of life necessarily imply the presence of sensation; and certainly all development of life implies the development of sensation to higher forms.

Sensation is a most suggestive thing, for it brings experience of pleasure and pain. It cannot proceed without introducing these to the living subject. All life must know something of them. Probably the flower must in some manner feel the dew on its petals by night, and the enlivening touch of the sun by day, and have something akin to pleasure in the wholesome gifts that they bring. We may fairly suspect that the tree suffers when it is girdled and the healthful flow of its sap is stopped and fatal disease results. As soon as we pass from vegetable life to animal, the presence of pleasure and pain in consequence of sensation is too manifest to need proof, or even illustration. All animate existence has perpetual sensation, with the inevitable results. All life, for example, must be nourished, and there is pleasure in receiving the benefit of nourishment, and pain in the lack of it. Even in the lowest life this must be true. And so on—all experience of life involves sensation, and sensation renders it certain that life will always have pain and pleasure for its characteristics, proportioned in degree to its own intensity.

But pleasure and pain, existing as characteristics of life, are enough to render life rational. Sensation, with the sensations pleasant and unpleasant that come on, suffices to introduce rationality as an element in the living being. For whatever is conscious of good and bad sensations is able to compare them—or they would not be known as good or bad at all—and to have impressions as to their relative desirableness, and to be led to act in view of the comparison thus made. Not only is this possible, it is sure to occur. Pain and pleasure do not long exist uncompared. Judgment between them arises, and choice between them follows, and effort to obtain what is chosen is the result. Life sends tendrils toward the light, and roots toward the water. Life sends animals seeking food and drink. Life compels man to judge what he wants most, and impels him to obtain it. All this is rational, in higher degree or lower. The rationality that sends the root down for water is rationality of low degree; but it is the result of sensation and of want, and is of the same kind

at heart with the rationality that makes a young man seek
an education because he feels his ignorance and unreadiness
for the coming years. It is of the very nature of life to put
forth rational endeavour.

To this it is no objection that so much of the rationality is
only in its rudiments. Of course it is not meant that all
living beings are philosophers. All degrees of rationality
must be counted upon, from the least to the greatest. We
have the habit of regarding rationality as confined to man, and
drawing a deep distinction between it and instinct, attributed
to all lower animals. Though we have learned that the distinction will not hold, the effect of it still remains with us.
But instinct also is a rational thing. Instinct had rudimentary reason for its starting-point, but, reason not having developed beyond a certain point, the advantageous results of
certain reasonable action became solidified into heredity.
The existence of such results from rudimentary reasoning
are just as truly parts of a reasonable world as are the rational
acts of men. The rational element in life has not been
everywhere developed; in some regions its progress seems to
have ceased, and in some it may have retrograded; only in
the human field has it attained to the human quality, and even
here it is incomplete. Nevertheless it is the nature of life
with its sensations to become a rational experience, and this
nature has been realized more or less in all living beings, and
most in man.

In this it is implied that the experience of life serves for the
training of rationality. Life has its organism, which is necessarily used for acting out the choices that result from perception and judgment. Like any other power, the rational
power is trained through its activities. As organisms grow
higher and more largely effective, opportunity for training in
rationality grows more abundant. Already, before life had
reached the grade of the human, its rational powers were thus
trained by use, and all such reason as belongs to lower life
had been developed. The movement was cumulative. The
well-grown mind grows most normally. When mind and

organism and experience all were human, life trained rationality to new grades, and for the first time revealed its higher quality. The human reason is the normal fruit of the tree of universal life.

Thus the realm of life, in which we are looking for evidence of God, is a realm of rational powers in actual operation; not of promise but of genuine performance, from the very beginning of life till now. Mind was born when life was born, though both were in feeblest infancy, and the entire career of life has meant training, development, and use for the powers of mind. This is the region concerning which we are inquiring whether it is expressive of a rational mind above itself. Here at any rate are rational powers produced. From some source the living world has been sown full of the seeds of reason; and surely a world so full of rationality must be the expression of a mind to which its own best quality is akin. The rationality of life is undying evidence of the rationality of God.

But this is not the whole of the matter, for we have still to consider that world, or universe, in which life was produced and in which it has been trained. Life with its inherent rationality has had its quality developed under the influence of the universe in which it was placed. This universe bears, as truly as life itself, the marks of rationality. It is common to speak of man as mind and the universe as matter, to locate the rational in the human and exclude from that category the mass of non-human existence. But when we consider the relation of the universe to the rational in man, we may be able to set this manner of thinking aside, in favour of a truer one. The universe is not a reasoner, but in its own differing way it has the rational quality bound in as a vital element in its being.

In tracing the rational in that universe which is the home of life we must begin far back, and observe that life itself appears to be a product of the universal order. Life was the germ of rationality, and the universe was one in which this

wonderful germ could be brought forth.   There is no reason
for supposing that when life first appeared it was created by
an act that did not belong to the order of the world.   The only
fact that may seem to require such a belief is that we cannot
understand or conceive how so marvellous a thing as life, so
unlike all that was before it, could possibly be brought forth
by any process whatever.   The introduction of life was a
work that required a God.   So it was; it required a God, and
a living God; but what if the God was already in the order?
Our alarm at the suggestion that life might have been produced without an exceptional creative act was natural, but
only because we were accustomed to think of God as striking
through the order from above when great work was to be
done, and not as "working hitherto" in and through the
order itself.   But when we look for actual reasons, there is
no constraining reason against the idea that life blossomed
in due time upon the ancient stock of the universe.   That the
process is too wonderful for us is nothing against it, but rather
in its favour.   Probably it is true that the order of the
world brought forth life when the time had come.   Probably the stock of the universe is not rightly appreciated
until it is regarded as a stock upon which this flower might
bloom.

If we have looked upon this as a process inferior and un-
divine, we have misjudged it.   The glory of the significance
of life cannot be overestimated.   The first movement of life
was the presage of rationality, the promise of man, and the
pledge of spiritual destiny, and the coming of life brought
the due significance to the world into which it came.   If the
universe could bring it forth—that is, if it was a universe in
whose career there should come a crisis out of which life
was born—then it can be understood and estimated only in
the light of this amazing fact.   Only from a stock of rational
existence could the flower of rational promise open.   It is
quite right to say that life, so rational a thing, could not come
forth from the universe if the universe were irrational.   The
common saying that all the living comes from the living is

right and true.   But if life was born of the universe, life was somehow already in the universe or working through it; and if life was so rational a thing, pledge of reason and all its high possibilities, the life that was working in the universe was of high rational quality.   A rational system the universe must have been, if life and rationality were outcomes of its movement.   In this doctrine there is no bringing of life down to the grade and quality of a brute universe: there is bringing of the universe up to the grade of a system through which life, reason and the spirit could be brought forth.

When man had come, his powers were such as to make of him a rational observer, able to take note of things about him and to read their meaning.   Observation and interpretation were crude processes, and much that was noticed was inevitably misjudged.   But acceleration of growth in knowledge and judgment went on apace, and human powers more and more took in and utilized the facts that were observable. This advancing process has established beyond the possibility of doubt the common rationality of man and the universe in which he dwells.   Man has proved himself a rational being, and the universe has proved itself a rational universe, one as truly as the other.

The common rationality of man and the universe is sufficiently shown by the fact that man finds the universe intelligible.   The world is a book, and man is the reader.   Read it he can, and does.   He has full confidence that he could read it all if it were all laid open before him.   He has often misread, partly because his powers were insufficiently developed, and partly because he knew too little to understand his book. His eager desire to know cannot wait either for training adequate to the task or for the opening of facts enough to render judgment sure.   It is by reading that man learns to read. It is the swift rushing on to know that trains the powers and discovers facts that will rectify premature judgment.   That he will not find facts if he seeks for them, or that what he finds will not be rational, he never imagines.   The book is open, and sure to be still wider open, and the reader is intent upon his reading. The rational within meets the rational without, and recognizes it, and cannot rest without laying hands upon it. The world is so like man that man can lay upon it the intelligent grasp of his rational understanding.

Confirmatory of the common rationality of the world and man is the fact that the surrounding world, or universe, has always been, and still is, the educator of the rational humanity. Powers are developed within, but educated from without. We have said elsewhere that a child would never become a genuine person if he were not in social contact with other persons. In like manner we may doubt whether the race would have been a rational race if it had not been living in a rational world. Development comes by response of the inner to the outer. Response to a rational environment has trained human life to its normal rationality. Living in an intelligible world has developed observation, judgment and constructive interpretation. Living in an orderly world has trained the human mind to orderliness in thought. Living in a world that calls for reason in conduct builds up reason in the mind. The surrounding world has always trained life in this manner, and man most of all. That means that it is full of the rational quality.

The amount of reason legible to man in the universe is so great as to be a theme of perpetual wonder. It is found in the ordinary matters that lie open for all to see: it is found equally in the immeasurably great, and not less in the inconceivably small. The common world shows it, the telescope reveals it, and the microscope opens views of it perhaps the most marvellous of all. The latest glimpses into the infinitesimal discover there a fulness of rational meaning so disproportionate to the dimensions of the field as to bring overwhelming surprise. Theories, like the atomic theory, have been formed for interpretation, tracing one organizing idea through infinitesimal and infinite; then new facts are discovered that discredit the theories and suggest some other organizing idea and method. But it is always an idea that is posited there. The whole is known to be a system, and a rational system—for there is no system that is not rational. The reign of the rational is always assumed to be co-extensive with the universe. This assumption can never be verified by exhaustive examination; but it is doubtful whether exhaustive examination would render the scientific mind more certain than it now is that the entire universe is bound together by a rational quality which it possesses in common with us men. One who does not believe in God assumes the rational character of existing things as readily as a Christian.

It is worth while to look at some most familiar facts that show how largely and efficiently the universe does the work of an intellectual system. Science, Philosophy, Poetry and Art exist because man has the powers that he has, but equally because the surrounding universe is one vast storehouse of material for science, philosophy, poetry and art. Each of these four is a separate evidence of the intellectual or rational character of the existing universe. Each of them is stronger proof than any constructed argument could be, of that quality which bears witness to God.

In the universe about us there exists that rational order which renders Science possible. Surrounding facts are observable by human powers, estimable by human judgment, and amenable to scientific treatment. When they have been observed and weighed, that is not the end, for facts prove to have a method in them. They are not only discoverable, but classifiable. By inward affinities they fall into groups, which prove to be systems. Facts in animal life or the life of plants, for example, have an internal unity that man discovers but did not invent. This responsiveness of facts to human reason was unsuspected, of course, when the study of nature was begun, but it was there in the facts, and men could not long study them without finding it. Because facts of various kinds fall into groups of internal solidarity, the universe, examined, yields sciences. Its broad reasonableness renders science possible, and science results in sciences when the field is divided into its natural parts. The world is found in itself capable of receiving true scientific analysis and classification. It is a systematic world.

This systematic or scientific quality extends wherever observation reaches, and no one doubts that it is universal. All facts that are contemporaneous with one another have it, and, what is quite as impressive, the same quality sweeps also through time as well as space. Facts follow one another in a rational order, from the first, if there be a first, to the last, if there be a last. There is orderly movement as well as orderly grouping. Out of one state the next unfolds, on intelligible principles. This, long known as the manner in which flowers grow in the garden, is now perceived to be the way in which all things have their being. Thus progress, or rational movement, is characteristic of all that we observe, and doubtless of the universe as a whole. Such is the nature of things that every fact falls under the head of its science, or its sciences, and a universal science has nothing against it but human limitations. A science of all things is unattainable, but the idea of it is perfectly reasonable and in the direction of it all actual science moves. This is the kind of universe it is—a universe scientifically knowable. All the human sciences are simply approximate descriptions of its actual contents.

In the universe there exists also that rational significance which renders Philosophy possible. Philosophy advances beyond science, endeavouring to interpret the orderly world that Science discovers and describes. It seeks to find the meanings that run through it, and if possible the meaning that belongs to it as a whole. But why should there be such a thing as meaning? If science proved possible, still what suggested something more? What set the human mind upon the task of interpretation? From what cause should philosophy be born? To these questions there can be but one answer. The universe itself is responsible for philosophy. It was the universe itself that suggested to man, its kinsman, that it was the bearer of a meaning. Experience long ago convinced mankind that the universe must be interpreted not merely in terms like light and heat, gravitation and chemical affinity, but also in terms like will and purpose and character. The early thinking of men about the world moved more in the realm of philosophy than of science, for the desire to understand facts arose much earlier than desire to know them precisely. Myths made for explanation of things all move in the region of will and purpose, and seek to set forth meanings. From such beginnings philosophy has come to be the broadest movement of the mind, but it has never been anything else than a response of man to the universe, felt to be meaningful and offering itself to be understood. It is no wonder that successful interpretation comes but slowly, and that endeavour after endeavour proves insufficient. It is no reproach to philosophy that its work is yet unfinished, for the task is great, and new knowledge is constantly adding to the problem. Thought is still struggling with its task, and will never surrender it. It is true that agnosticism enters this field as well as that of religion, and doubt arises whether the universe is a field for philosophical interpretation; but this is only a passing mood and cannot last. It comes on when the vastness and complexity of the universe makes the human mind aware of its own littleness, or when conflicting elements in the problem appear. But the universe which has inspired all the philosophy that mankind has thus far known will continue to inspire philosophy as long as it and the human mind exist together, simply because it is what it is, a system full of meaning.

Still further, there exists in the universe that rational suggestiveness which renders Poetry possible. No less significant is this quality for the present purpose than those that are responsible for philosophy and science. The poetic quality may be almost undefinable, but it is no obscure or doubtful thing, neither is it a modern discovery. From its early days the human mind has been poetic. Perhaps man began as poet. His early observation of things about him was very far from being exact, but it was suggestive, and much of his primitive philosophy was nothing but poetry.

There was good reason. The mind has been poetic just as it has been scientific and philosophical, because its environment contained influences that trained it to be so. The universe was the first great poet, or man would have been none. When the eye has looked upon an object it has not seen it all. Senses cannot find the whole, nor can the whole be told by science or philosophy. Any given thing means more than in itself it appears to mean, and carries the suggestion of something larger and of finer quality. Analogies run through existence and wait to be discovered. Instructive fables from nature have occurred to men from the earliest times. Parables are possible, for nature and common affairs suggest lessons in the higher life of the spirit. For that higher world nature is boundlessly suggestive. Now and then, indeed, some one maintains that Peter Bell was right when

> "A primrose by the river's brim
> A yellow primrose was to him,
> And it was nothing more,"

because he saw precisely what was there. But he saw only a small part of what was there. When a poet looked upon a flower he said:

> "Flower in the crannied wall,
> I pluck you out of the crannies,
> Hold you here, root and all, in my hand.
> Little flower—but *if* I could understand
> What you are, root and all, and all in all,
> I should know what God and man is."

His insight is true, for this is a world in which suggestiveness has no limits. Both in nature and in life poets have perceived beauty and truth beyond all that language could express. Language, indeed, has been made what it is through the ministrations of the poetic element in the world and life. Not only its finest uses, but most of its really expressive ordinary forms, are outgrowths of analogy and utterances of the spirit of poetry. Language is a perpetual witness to the suggestiveness of all things, but even language has proved too feeble an instrument for voicing the poetry that is in the world. No poet has ever had an eye for a tithe of the possibilities, nor have all poets together gone so far. Poetic significance belongs to all existence, and doubtless to existence as a whole, if only we could read its universal meaning. Experience with epics is enough to assure us that there must be possible an epic of the mighty whole. The universe is a poetic universe.

And yet, again, there exists in the universe that rational æsthetic quality which renders Art possible. This quality is akin to the suggestiveness that gives rise to poetry, and in their development the two have been closely allied, but they are not the same. In animals and men there is a surplus of energy, which, not being required for the labours of life, expresses itself in play. With all his work, sportive movements fill out the measure of man's activity. Out of sportiveness comes gracefulness, first half-consciously assumed, then cultivated. To grace of form is added charm of colour, and step by step out of the play of man is developed what we know as art. Man in his sportive moods never suspects that his play is anything more than play, and when he begins to turn the pleasuring impulse into the rudiments of artistic expression he has no idea that he is doing anything of large significance. Not until art has grown, and brought forth noble works, and been subjected to analysis, is the secret understood. But at length it becomes known that in this development from his play man has struck into the great system of principles respecting colour, form and beauty, that runs through the universe. All unconsciously, he has become an interpreter of nature and a reproducer of her methods. In being a player for his own pleasure he has become an actor in a natural realm of whose existence he never dreamed. The universe was about him, ready as soon as he could receive it to reveal to him the everlasting law which he had so unconsciously been obeying. That æsthetic law, too, is rational, like the rest of the world, or man would never have laid hold of it. The æsthetic nature of the world, and the poetic also, blends with the scientific and the philosophical in rational harmony. No one is out of keeping with the others, or is complete without them. The universe could not be æsthetic if it were not orderly, meaningful and suggestive. Such a universe it is, sounding with this harmony of qualities, expressive of rational mind.

Thus Science, Philosophy, Poetry, Art, have come through response of man to qualities manifested by the universe in his presence. Living in the universe has trained him to respond to these qualities indwelling in it, until now the response has become the very body of his intellectual life. The response in lower forms began before man appeared. The universe received life into its bosom at its lowest beginnings, and has trained it up to this. It is an educative universe, capable of this high service. It is the school in which man has become scientist, philosopher, poet and artist, and which has more to teach him yet.

Certainly the testimony of the universe to its own rational character is clear and convincing, and certainly we human beings have no reason to doubt its word or complain of it for deceiving us. To us it has always been an honest world, where that which is within and that which is without correspond each to the other. Our nature compels us to trust the world, and the world has earned our confidence. If it testifies to its own rationality we can believe it, and if it bears witness to God its voice is worthy to be heard.

Of all that has been said in this chapter, the proper meaning has all the time been plainly in sight, and must now be distinctly brought forward. A very few words, however, will suffice to express it. It is simply that the universe, thus rational in itself and in its workings, bears witness everywhere to the existence of a rational Mind inspiring it and giving it its character. A system organized and operating on rational principles, bringing forth life which is a rational thing from its birth, training life up to human reasonableness, educating mankind in rationality, and inexhaustible in rational quality to man who explores it—a system that thus has rationality for its supreme trait—is certainly most naturally accounted for by saying that it owes its character to a rational mind. This simple and natural account of the matter the Christian doctrine accepts and proclaims. Thought implies a thinker, rationality implies active reason, and a system implies an organizing knowledge and purpose. Finding the whole scheme of things expressive of thought and organized for the promotion of thought, the Christian doctrine agrees to the explanation, natural to a child and not improved upon by a philosopher, that all this reasonableness and efficiency "cometh from the Lord, who is wonderful in counsel and excellent in working" (Isa. xxviii. 29). It refers rational facts to a rational source, and declares that in discovering a rational universe we discover a rational God.

This, indeed, is very simple. Perhaps it may appear too simple. Nevertheless, this is the Christian doctrine in this part of the field, this and nothing more. The Christian doctrine simply holds that such a world as this bears conclusive witness to the one all-comprehensive mind of God. The doctrine is as comprehensive as it is simple. It is capable of expansion, and yet for its due effect it does not require expansion. Under its main point are included all the arguments for the existence of God that turn upon the intellectual quality of the world. The Christian affirmation itself does not expressly contain all of these: they may be constructed and employed if it is desirable, but that which is essential to the Christian doctrine is merely the central truth that the rational world implies the rational God, and gives us sufficient reason to believe in him. To the simplicity of this we shall not do well to make objection, for if the claim is true the evidence is sufficient, and if the evidence is sufficient, the simpler it is the better.

This theistic explanation of the rationality of the universe is not only the sufficient one: it may further be said that it is the only explanation.

It is fair to say at this stage of history that all materialistic explanations of existing things have lapsed into common failure. Although some of them still have a certain vogue, we need not dwell upon them now. At the end, no one of them really explains anything: they may try to describe processes, but the resort to matter and energy really provides no explanation at all. It has come to be entirely plain that the only alternative to the doctrine of eternal and perfect mind is Agnosticism. If we do not account for the rational character of the universe by referring it to God, we shall not account for it at all, but say that we know not whence it came. We shall recognize it, and make use of it as constantly as if we could account for it, but shall simply say that we do live in a rational world, we know not how or why. Either the theistic explanation of the reasonable world stands true, or we have none. Of the pantheistic view of the world it may suffice to say that pantheism does not account for the world: it identifies the world and God, but gives no light upon origins or original causation. Our judgment in respect of accounting for the world must lie between Theism and Agnosticism: we believe in God, or else we do not know.

Why not Agnosticism? What is the objection to falling back upon our ignorance and saying that we do not know, and cannot know, how the universe ought to be interpreted? Agnosticism is not to be condemned as always evil, for in its place it is good; but we have to judge whether in the present case it is the reasonable attitude for us to hold.

One relevant fact certainly is that agnosticism is unreasonable where it is avoidable. It is reasonable to trace things to their causes when we can. Agnosticism in the field of causation may sometimes be unavoidable, but it is natural for us to hope that in any important case it may be only a temporary thing. We are always glad to pass beyond it, and account it a normal act to do so. When we consider the possibility of accounting for the rational order that we behold, it seems right to say that hopeless ignorance here is not something to be welcomed, or regarded as likely to be our normal lot. It would seem probable that in a world so rational as this world proves to be, the key to a right general understanding of things would be within our reach. It scarcely seems probable that men will be compelled permanently to say that they do not know how the world came to be a reasonable order. We ought not to accept an explanation without evidence, merely to please or satisfy ourselves, but if a fair way out of agnosticism appears, we should hail it as a gift in harmony with our nature and a sign of our destiny. And now the Christian doctrine declares that the rationality of the world is due to a rational mind producing the world with its high quality. If we accept this, we shall be tracing rationality back to its kind, and attributing an observed quality to the congenial action of a kindred power. We shall say that rationality in the universe, which we cannot regard as conscious, was imparted by a conscious and mighty Agent to whom the quality belonged. The Christian doctrine offers this as the reasonable explanation of what would otherwise be unexplained. When there is so good a case of reason as this, surely we may claim that it is not our duty to leave ourselves in agnosticism. It is right to pass over from sense of ignorance to sense of conviction, and let it stand for certain that the reasonable world is the offspring of a reasonable Mind capable of producing it.

If we take this step, we shall be moving along with the common judgment of mankind in one important matter. The Christian doctrine joins with the common judgment, founded in experience, that thought implies a thinker; that an idea has its origin in a mind. Agnosticism declines, or does not venture, to apply this principle to the interpretation of the rationality of the world: it suspects that we are not justified in such an act. But the Christian doctrine affirms that the rational fact comes forth from the rational power. Great, far-reaching ideas expressed throughout the universal order it regards as thoughts of a creative mind. In this it passes over from an ignorance that is exceptional in the methods of human thought to a conviction that accords with those methods. In this the Christian doctrine seems to have reason on its side.

But further, the claim for agnosticism as a matter of necessity and duty breaks down. Experience does not support it.

When we find ourselves drawing conclusions about the universe and God, it is not surprising if we pause and ask ourselves whether such themes are not beyond our powers. How dare we? What do we know about the sum of things? and what are we that we should draw inferences about the total of existence and the origin of the universe? We are often told that nothing becomes us but a confession of ignorance, and of inability, too: we do not know, and what is more, we cannot know: we have no right to be anything but agnostics in the field of the universal.

A healthy sense of ignorance is a true friend of wisdom, and it is wholesome to ask again whether affirmation of the rational universe and the rational God is not beyond our powers. We should not inquire concerning God without remembering the limits which we cannot pass. But in the present case we have something to remember besides our own limitations: we have to consider the real significance of the call for agnosticism. What is now demanded is that we refrain from judgment about things universal because they are too great for us. Such is our inability to know, that agnosticism is our only reasonable attitude. It is necessary that we consider what this means.

Inability to know is a very exacting master, that requires complete loyalty. After we have avowed our agnosticism, we must be faithful to it. If we are to be agnostics, agnostics we must be, confining our judgments to matters that are within our scope. Concerning things universal we cannot affirm, neither can we deny. If one act is beyond us, so is the other. If we cannot affirm theism, neither can we affirm atheism. This agnosticism is incurable, too, for it is grounded in our very nature. We must not quietly slip over into denial of the eternal Reason, as many a professed agnostic has done: such a man is as false to his principles as one who relapses from agnosticism into religion. Agnosticism grounded in our necessary limitations is necessarily complete and final. Not only does it disqualify us for judging whether God is real, but, by the same token, for judging whether the universe is really a rational system. Both judgments are beyond our range: we can form no opinion that ought to command our confidence, and our only course is to refrain from judging.

But such agnosticism is impossible. It cannot be sincere enough to last. If we profess it in words, still we shall not even try to live up to it, for we cannot. Some affirmations about things universal lie beyond our range, but not the affirmation that we live in an all-comprehensive rational order, or that the reasonable account of such an order is found in the existence of God. No power to judge whether we live in a rational universe? There is no day when we do not pass such judgment. The conception of a universal rational order is the underlying thought in all our thoughts and works. Our living consists in the use of that idea. Every personal life is grounded in it, and so is the entire intelligent career of mankind. All social relations imply the universal reason, all mental growth implies it, and all hopes for the future assume the permanence as well as the universality of its sway. The campaign of science, the endeavour of philosophy, the flight of poetry, the insight of art, all consist in the utilizing of the rational quality about us. All our activities assume the all-pervading rationality, as breathing assumes the air. It is not open to us to say that the rationality may be only a local fact, existing where we discover it, but not necessarily elsewhere. In the present state of knowledge there is no such thing to be thought of as a limited or local rationality, or a reasonable method that is less than universal. Once it might have been possible to think of a rational method prevailing in this world of ours, while yet we did not know whether it extended further. It was somewhat as when the early navigators fancied that different laws might prevail in seas which their ships had not yet entered.

They found at length that nature was the same in all seas; and we have learned that the rational order is one in all worlds. We do not have to visit all the suns to learn whether the spectrum will open to us their secrets, nor do we even have to inquire: we know it will. The universe is not made up of separate districts, some of which may be rational while others are not: rational here, it is known to be rational everywhere. The modern light is the very light in which we cannot decline to judge whether the great whole is a rational system. Doubt of our ability to answer that question is behind the age, even though it be urged upon us by men who are accounted leaders of our time: it belongs to the same period with polytheism, the ages before unity.

The littleness of the human mind and knowledge is pleaded as the ground for agnosticism as to the meaning of the universe and the being of God. The appeal is plausible, but unsound. The limitations are real, but justify a very different inference from this. On the contrary, when we take note of the character of our own knowledge, it is incredible that there does not exist a knowledge radically different from it in character and scope.

We cannot doubt that our rational process is a valid way of knowing, but neither can we imagine that it can ever lead us to perfect knowledge. The method of our knowing settles that. For all that we know we are absolutely dependent upon the method of observation and experience. All our knowledge is empirical. What we know we have learned, and what we are yet to know we have yet to learn. Each of us began with nothing. Our acquiring has been limited, and must always be, by our opportunities to learn, and these are never complete, or even well-proportioned. An element that we call chance helps to determine them. We cannot know the future, and hence our interpretation of the past can be only tentative, while of the past itself we can know only a minor part. Full comprehensive knowledge of any single fact is impossible to us, even though it be a fact of our own most intimate experience. Thus all our knowledge is fragmentary and imperfect, and cannot be otherwise. It is all secondary, not primary—knowledge of that which existed before we knew it. The field of science lay there with all its contents before science was born. We originate nothing of what we know, save in so far as we originate our actions. We are born to be explorers, observers, learners, in realms already full of matter to be learned; and all that is human is like us in this respect.

Indeed, all finite knowledge is alike; and by finite knowledge is meant all knowledge that exists within the universe. There may be knowledge far wider and deeper than ours, more accurate and more adequate, but in whatever finite mind it may exist, and in whatever age or world it may have come into existence, it has been acquired. It is secondary knowledge, not primary, obtained like ours by observation and experience, and, like ours, fragmentary and incomplete. No finite mind can think anything completely through, or know the whole of anything. If the loftiest of intelligences, with the utmost of opportunity, had occupied himself for ages in learning, still there would be inconceivable amounts that he did not know, and nothing that he knew to perfection. Our limitations are not special or temporary, or even exclusively human: the very structure and position of the finite forbid perfect knowledge, and an endless future will not make it otherwise.

If we think there is no God, we shall be compelled to think that no knowledge radically unlike this of ours exists or can exist: that all knowledge is secondary, experimental, fragmentary: that the universe has never been thought through or held as a whole in any mind, neither has any single thing been grasped and understood in all its relations. If there is no mind greater and more primary than the minds that are part of the universe, then there is no mind capable of understanding all things, or of fully understanding anything. All knowledge is like ours, greater, perhaps, but not essentially different, if there is no God. And yet all the material for all the secondary and experimental knowledge that exists was in existence, no one knows how or whence, ready to be known as soon as there were minds to know it. This is the view of the universe that is true if no place is found for God. If we are atheists, we shall affirm this: if we are agnostics, we shall simply say that we have no means of knowing whether this view of the universe is true or not.

To state the position fairly is to refute it. A good deal about the universe we do know, and what we know teaches a different doctrine from this. If the sum of existence contained no signs of intellect, and had never nourished a mind, if it were a dull and senseless mass, dead matter and brute force, without movement or meaning, then, perhaps, we might think that no mind had ever thought it through— which would be the largest thought about it that had ever been entertained. But of the universe that exists we can imagine no such thing. It has structure and order, and method is its prime characteristic. It is so full of ideas in operation that all human study has only begun to find them out. It has provided material for all the systematic knowledge that men possess, and suggestion for all their finer thought. Nay, it has brought forth man himself, and trained him to his present rationality, and is training him still. And shall we now call such a universe an unthought thing? or shall we say that we can form no judgment as to whether it has ever been embraced in a perfect comprehension? By all progress in science and philosophy and all vitality in poetry and art, by the significance of life and the effectiveness of experience as an instructor, the world commends itself to us as a world known before we knew it, and understood better than we can ever understand it. The facts are convincing, and we are quite competent to be convinced.

The inference that we ought to draw from our own limitations is that there must be a Mind that is free from them. Our kind of knowledge cannot possibly be the best that exists. There must be a knowledge that is primary, independent, perfect. The eternal Reason, the omniscient Mind, the all-embracing Wisdom, the perfect understanding, the long foresight, the comprehensive purpose, the living God—all these must be real, in contrast to the limited knowledge which we are unable to transcend. The greatness which religion attributes to God is a necessity to all clear thought.

The question that we have thus answered is a serious one in practical light. If we were compelled to affirm that there was no original and comprehensive conception of existence, and the universe had never been thought through, two familiar conceptions of the world would pass away. We might wish to retain them, and cherish arguments in their favour, but in vain.

One of these is the religious or providential view of the world. The providential idea has been variously expressed —all things work together for good; every man's life a plan of God; one far-off divine event, to which the whole creation moves. It is not a Christian idea alone, for other religions have held it also. Life has been thought to have a meaning that men did not put into it, a meaning ordered and developed by the counsel of God. Of course it is implied that God knows the end from the beginning, and understands the system and order that he has created. In fact, the doctrine of providence is simply the doctrine of the comprehensiveness and perfection of the divine thought. If we cannot affirm a comprehensive and perfect divine thought, all idea of an intended providential and religious meaning in life must vanish. This view of existence, however precious, cannot survive the influence of that agnosticism which we are invited to regard as unavoidable.

The providential or religious view of the world will not vanish alone if it is thus driven out by agnosticism. With it will go the evolutionary view of existence. In evolutionary doctrine it is held that the universe is pervaded by a method rational and intelligible. Conditions are followed by results in a way that our intelligence can grasp and interpret. One vast conception runs through from first to last, from lowest to highest, and all is done in pursuance of one idea, more accurately than human plans are ever followed by human action. The intellectual nature of the movement is affirmed as something that was there before there was man to discover it, inwrought from remotest ages to the system and indispensable to its existence. But this conception of the universe has no better standing-ground than the providential view of life, if there exists no knowledge such as we attribute to God. The evolutionary doctrine implies that the universe has been thought through and made the vehicle of an original purpose, just as truly as does the religious doctrine. Evolution is the scientific providence. If there is no original and originative mind comprehending all, the evolutionary conception of a significant unity in all things is absolutely unsupported. We are trifling with our own intelligence if we say that the rational quality may have come into the great unfolding without a rational mind to put it there. A rational evolution implies a rational God, and the denial of the comprehensive knowledge leaves the evolutionary view of the world without the possibility of sound support.

It is true that there are many believers in the fact of evolution who do not see this to be true. But that is mainly because they have been occupied with other aspects of the subject. The intellectual quality of the universe they have been progressively discovering and establishing, but the theistic bearing of their own work they have not yet considered. Its time is coming. They are establishing the presence of mind in the universe so firmly that the presence of a supreme and perfect Mind cannot much longer be obscure.

The rational order is the real order, original and everlasting, else our first rational convictions are refuted and our intellectual life is put to confusion. We assent with mind and heart to the reality that accounts for sound reason, and bow in worship before the God of infinite knowledge, wisdom and power.

3. EVIDENCE FROM THE SPIRITUAL

Still the argument starts from man. From the rational in man we proceeded to the rational in the universe, and from the great unity of rational being thus discovered to the certainty of a rational source and inspiration for the whole in God. Now from a kindred but still higher quality in man, still farther advanced from mere life, and of even higher significance in the human story, we proceed to such inferences as it may warrant concerning the Being who is above. We still have the advantages that come from a starting-point in humanity. We begin with that which we know, and with the greatest that our known world contains. If we can deal fairly with the materials that are here before us, surely we may hope for truth in our conclusions.

This word spiritual with which we begin may seem too ambiguous for our purpose, for, familiar though it is, it is a word of various use, and perhaps is more suggestive than exact. But we need a single word, and there is none better than this: moreover, it is not so ambiguous as to lose its usefulness. There is a set of powers in man and qualities in life which this term clearly enough describes. The part of human nature to which it applies is not far from the rational element, which, indeed, is included or implied in its connotation. But it includes more. With the rational it includes the moral, and with the moral the religious. When we call man a being of spiritual endowments, we mean that he is possessor of the powers out of which morality and religion have been brought forth, and is open to all the possibilities that rationality, morality and religion imply. By possession of his rational nature he has moral responsibility and religious powers, and is capable of rising to life above sensuous and temporal things, in the fellowship of the eternal. Of this ability he gives proof, in that he actually lives a life of morality and religion, far from the best, but sufficient to show him capable of the best. It is from man as such a being that the present line of evidence for the reality of God proceeds.

The first thing to be mentioned here is the unqualified breadth of this statement concerning man. For the present purpose we must be careful to admit no partial or provincial conception of mankind. We must enlarge our thought to take in, if we are able, absolutely the whole of humanity. When we call man a being of spiritual endowments, it is not enough to be thinking of man as he exists under Christian influences or the influence of other of the higher religions. It is not enough to think of him as he now is, at the present stage of his racial experience, or to learn what he is from the available records of history. We often form our mental picture of mankind in such ways as these, but for the present purpose these modes are too narrow. The true and adequate conception of man as a spiritual being regards humanity as more ancient than we can measure, a race brought forth from lower life, and continuous from its beginning until to-day. What is said of man and his nature is said of this entire race. The point is that ever since man became man he has been gifted with spiritual as well as with rational endowments. Those qualities in humanity to which we look for testimony to God belong to humanity taken as a single whole, and extend through the entire sweep of human existence. This, which is a vital point in our study of the rational in man, is no less vital in our study of the spiritual. What we affirm of the spiritual nature is affirmed of men as men, and of them all.

The coming of man into the world consisted in the coming of the soul into man. The ambiguities in this true statement need not perplex us. We need not be troubled because we cannot define the substance of the soul, or tell exactly at what point of time it might first have been said to be present. We know that it did not spring up all in a moment, but came through gradual development of its faculties in experience.

When certain powers and faculties had reached a certain stage, their possessor was man, and continued to be man thenceforth because he was their possessor. That we cannot define the degree of development that was necessary to make him man is of no importance here. The soul is the differentiating element of the man, and the dawning of the soul was the entering of the human. And the dawning of the soul was the natural development of life, through the experience that was normal to it.

The statement that rationality is only the normal unfolding of life we have already expounded thus: Life has senses, senses bring sensations, sensations must be compared and choice between their values must be made, and thus rational judgment comes into existence from the nature and conditions of life itself. Having entered in its lowest forms to the realm of life, rationality was trained by experience in a rational universe until the human grade was reached: and since man became aware of his rational powers the education has been far more rapid and comprehensive. To this account of the rational in man must now be added a similar account of the spiritual. This, too, the spiritual nature, is a normal development of life. From the rational stage life works on in accordance with its own nature to the spiritual. Both the moral element and the religious belong to man as man, and to all men, because they are thus genuine unfoldings of life itself.

Look first at the life in morals. The entrance of the moral quality to life has seemed mysterious, and has often been accounted so great an event as to be possible only by special creative act of God. It is of God indeed, but it is not so mysterious, nor must it have been due to a sudden stroke of creative power. Man's rational nature is of such a kind that he cannot fail to find himself a moral being also. For man is an actor: he is capable of conscious and intentional action, and it is his nature to be always performing it. He lives not alone, but in relations with other beings, and in those relations his actions proceed. Naturally his actions will sometimes be such as those relations, rightly understood, require, and sometimes such as they would forbid or condemn. Some may be neutral, but many will be of decided character, normal or abnormal in the relations of the doer. But what is normal in one's relations is right, and what is abnormal there is wrong: this is the fundamental definition of right and wrong, which, though manifold interpretations of it are added as life goes on, has never been superseded as incorrect. At the same time it is equally true that for a man to act normally in his relations is to be normal in himself, and to act abnormally there is to sin against himself: these social and personal definitions of right and wrong are parallel and harmonious. So it is plain that since man is always living and acting in relations with his fellows he is always doing right and wrong. It is quite impossible to keep the moral quality out of the active life of a rational being. That quality did not need to be specially created, for it is a natural and inevitable trait of life, when once life has moved on to the grade of rationality.

It must be added that the perception of this quality is as inevitable as the possession of it. It is the nature of a rational being to pass judgment upon whatever comes into his life, and the common power of judgment estimates good and evil, right and wrong, as it estimates other matters of experience. Not that it always estimates them clearly or correctly, for the power of judgment was begun, like the bodily senses, in deep imperfectness; but like them it was capable of training through experience, and certain to receive it. And such is the nature of right and wrong that a rational being must feel himself responsible when he has done the one or the other. This, too, is done imperfectly, but it is done, by the nature of the case, and life becomes solemn in proportion as the sense of responsibility becomes a real thing.

Moral nature thus belongs to man as man. It is a property of that soul whose coming constituted him human. Man himself has been aware of it much longer than he has called it by a name or recorded his reflections upon it. Long before his consciousness of it became distinct and definable he was conducting his life upon a crude but urgent sense of his moral nature. It dates back to his very origin, and can never be eliminated from his constitution.

Look now at the life of man in religion. It is one of the commonplaces of modern knowledge that religion in some form has been practically universal in the human race from earlier times than we have opportunity of observing. Very early in his career man was influenced by religious motives. It is not surprising that he should be, for this too is a natural unfolding of the nature of rational existence, which itself is a natural unfolding of life. The human being exists in a world greater than himself, and is constantly influenced by its forces. Its powers are mysterious to him, its wonders are many. Often he is made to feel his own insignificance, for the world can do him boundless good or harm. Moreover, as soon as he is able to put thoughts together he knows that he did not make himself, but was somehow brought into existence in this powerful and mysterious world. Now it cannot be claimed that out of these primitive sensations any theory of religion could be constructed; but it is quite impossible to think that primitive man could live in such conditions without having the rudimentary experiences of religion. Recognition of a greater power on which he was dependent was a part of the very substance of his early life. Modes and forms of religion were of course determined by various and changing conditions, and so was the prominence of this or that element in the complex conception; but life in a great world of mysterious forces would inevitably suggest to a thinking race the considerations of which religion is composed. This, too, is simply a normal unfolding of the nature of life, when life had become human in a world like this. There was no need of special creation to produce religion in mankind. This is why religion belongs to man as man, and to all men—because it is a true and proper consequence of the relations in which all men find themselves. The relations of man to his fellows brought forth morality: the relations of man to larger existence around him brought forth religion. Both are equally normal and inevitable developments from the nature of life.

We cannot here follow out the growth of the various elements that have entered into the religious life of mankind. But we can say with confidence that primitive religion, as far back as we can trace it, contained all the elements that constitute religion now, whether in its lowest or its highest forms; only they were present in modes that correspond to the childhood of the race. The sense of dependence was present in force, as we have just said, being inspired by the greatness of the nature-powers, and by man's consciousness that he did not originate himself. Then it was the most natural thing in the world that man should think of those tremendous controlling powers as powers to which he might address himself, admiring and adoring them, seeking their help, or begging off from their vengeance; and thus the possibility of communion, of worship, and ultimately of revelation to man, came naturally to be believed in. And when it was thought possible to communicate with the higher powers, it naturally followed that a sense of some duty toward them arose, and a binding authority was attributed to them; and it was inevitable that in the course of time the sanctions of that morality which was developed in human relations should be found in the character and government of the powers above. But we know that the sense of dependence upon God, the sense of obligation to God, and the sense of ability to commune with God, make up the consciousness that constitutes the experience of religion, even in the highest forms that it bears to-day; and all these were present, crude but genuine, in primitive human experience, being naturally suggested by facts with which all men were concerned. Thus all the essential elements of religion came by normal process into the universal experience of the race.

It is a familiar question which of the two elements in life, the moral or the religious, was the earlier, and whether either one may have been the source of the other. All possible answers have been given, but probably the inquiry is unnecessary. Each of the two sprang up by itself, at the suggestion of facts suitable and sufficient to produce it, and the two grew side by side. Not at first did they come together to reinforce each other effectively, but it was a part of the nature of the case that they should thus at length unite, and so they have done, in various degrees of effectiveness. But as a matter of origins, neither was needed to produce the other, each being a true outgrowth from the nature of life itself. This is a sufficient reason why both belong to man as man, and are inalienable elements of his human nature.

The moral and religious elements in life are certainly worthy to be united under a single name, for they belong together. By their quality they are adapted to blend into a noble unity. Through long periods both have been crude and low in grade, neither of them fully appearing for what it is; but it is possible for the two to appear together in high degree and quality. Then religion takes hold upon a worthy superhuman object for its worship and confidence, and morality, with growing discrimination and sense of right and wrong, is glad to draw its motives from sources divine as well as human. Then these two elements in human nature conspire to set their affections on things that are above, and seek the highest ends of existence. This devotion to the highest ends of life, in which religion and morality unite, constitute, both in individuals and in peoples, that noble character which is often called spirituality, and illustrates the ideal of that which in this chapter is meant by the spiritual in man. When the spiritual in man attains to its ideal meaning and fulness, it brings forth this ethico-religious devotion to the most normal ends of existence. This result has appeared in various degrees in various ages the world over. Even when sadly imperfect, it has been worthy of grateful recognition. It is the crown of life, in all lands and times. At any given day it is the noblest crown that life then wears, and at its best it is absolutely the crown of life, than which nothing nobler will ever be possible to men.

We must not be led by our interest in the higher forms of this great gift to undervalue it in its lower stages, neither must we find in those lower stages more than is really there. Either of these errors comes easily. Some students of mankind would define religion only in its higher terms, and consider all religious manifestations below the best as entirely of another class; while others would speak almost as if religion bore a uniform value, whatever its grade. It is needless, however, to fall into either extreme. The spiritual in man has always been precious: relatively to his life and his outfit of powers it has always been his noblest part. Yet it has sadly failed to come to its best, and only through the revelation of God does anything like its full value appear. We rejoice in the spiritual at its worthiest: and yet if we prize the best in morals and religion, our eyes ought to be all the clearer to discern the lower forms of the same great good, and our hearts the more tender to appreciate their preciousness to mankind.

This account of the spiritual in man has been given in order that reasonable inferences may be drawn from its existence. It is to be used as evidence concerning God.

Here we must start from the fact that the spiritual in man cannot be understood if we regard it merely as an inward experience. It is very far from being something self-contained. It is not fully seen till we have looked beyond man himself. Its supreme quality is that it looks and reaches outward, to take hold of some reality existing outside.

This, we are at once reminded, is a quality not peculiar to this element in human powers. All human powers do the same, and so do all powers that are characteristic of life. Life indeed consists, so far as we can define it, in the mysterious ability to seize upon surrounding things and utilize them for its purpose. The lowliest thing that lives, as well as the loftiest, lives by laying hold of that which is beyond itself. The working of this process is life, the end of it is death.

We have already seen how the human powers illustrate this method. The bodily senses could have no existence, because they could be of no use, if it were not for corresponding realities outside. The eye is an organ for utilizing light, the ear for appropriating sound. The rational powers of humanity are powers for utilizing the rational quality in the universe where man has his home. They reach out to the reasonable order around, and by that order they are educated, drawing in knowledge that feeds and strengthens them and serves their purpose. Like all other samples of life, man is an out-reaching being, whose connections are essential to his existence. What is thus true of his other powers is true also of his spiritual element. This, too, implies and assumes something outside of itself, and seizes upon it for its own use. Here in fact is found the most significant illustration of this principle that the study of mankind anywhere affords.

What is that which the spiritual in man has implied, assumed and sought to utilize, in all stages of its existence? The question can be answered, for there is one constant assumption, made in the first primeval spiritual outreach, made by all religions, and made by Jesus Christ himself. All religion assumes that outside the range of human life there exists an unseen higher power, of such character that it is right and well for man to look up to it with reverence and commit himself to it with trust and loyalty. That man is not the highest being; that there exists something or some one superior to him whereon it is both worthy and profitable for him to rely for help; that without this outreach his life is not complete, and that from that unseen region power for good can come to him in answer to seeking—this is the underlying creed in every religion that ever laid its grasp upon the heart of man. In the apprehension of it there are all possible degrees of clearness and grades of moral value, but in this great faith mankind is one; exceptions are only apparent; and the actual process and work of religion in all its forms has been the endeavour of man to seize and utilize this invisible reality in which he has believed. As the eye has turned light to the uses of life, so the spiritual in man has sought to turn to the uses of life this great reality. It has been variously defined, or has remained undefined, but the endeavour to seize it for the due support of an inalienable element in life has been the one endeavour of morality and religion in every age.

In order to complete this simple statement, and see how much it means, we must note how much of the powers of man has been at work in this great activity of outreaching. When light is needed, only one sense out of five goes after it. When reasonable thought is searched for, a larger part of the human energies is concerned. How is it when man reaches out after that which under various modes of naming he calls God? The question cannot be answered completely, but we can at least see how large the answer is.

Both in his personal and in his social character man has reached out after God. Of course, the earliest thought must be personal, the individual taking notice; but the first large spiritual activity seems to have been social, the group uniting to express its need and desire. The family, the clan, the tribe, the nation, long acted upon the spiritual impulse, before the individual came to regard himself as a spiritual fact and centre. But his time came, and continued, though the time of the social spiritual endeavour was not thereby terminated. Both individually and socially mankind has stretched forth its hands to the unseen.

As for the motive to this perpetual endeavour, it has, of course, been various, but like most great and effective motives, it has been mainly emotional in its nature. Reflection is naturally involved in the turning to unseen powers for help, but the call to such action sounded in the emotional region of man's being. Whether the darker or the brighter aspect of religion has had the greater effect, and which was the original, we need not here discuss, but both have been intensely real, and both are natural. Fear was an early motive of tremendous force. Man trembled with good reason before the vast forces of nature. He trembled before the dim and mysterious, which surrounded him on every side. With his animal inheritance had come the timidity of a weaker creature. It was natural for him, himself self-moved by will, to attribute will to the powers of the world around him; and then the dread was still more firmly grounded. When the powers of nature did him injury, it was natural to think that they were offended, and fear was intensified again. With the deepening of the moral sense deeper became the sense of unworthiness in the presence of higher powers. The sense of sin did not need to be intelligent in order to be keen. So, under the motive of a highly complex fear, religion came to be an outreach for safety, full of deprecation against divine anger, labouring to propitiate powers that could destroy or bless. The spiritual in man, trembling, reached out, hoping, as it were, to ward off the lightning.

The intense and painful sincerity of such an outreach is plain at once. Through long ages the upward reach was doubtless little comfort: how gladly then would humanity have ceased from it if it could! But it could not. Even to its own sorrow, humanity has steadily affirmed the reality of a divine power of which it had reason to be afraid.

The brighter aspect is real also. The joyful emotions reach out to that which is above. Sometimes the bright aspect has been the dominant one. Along with dread of the divine powers there is gratitude when they have done their kindly work. The more harm they can do, the brighter is the day when they do good. Whether it be the forces of nature, or a throng of deities, or the only God, that which is above has been credited with gifts of good, and thanksgiving in word and deed has been offered in return. The religion of gratitude recognizes divine operation in daily affairs, and gracious activity directed to the inner life of man. As religion advances to finer spiritual quality, a vital conception of divine providence comes in, and men rejoice to trust in divine guidance, care and protection. Gratitude implies the acknowledgment of life as full of God; and this interpretation is both ancient and modern, Christian and pagan. It is so broad and lasting that we may fairly call it human. The human thanks the divine.

With the advance of moral life comes aspiration, which becomes an additional motive to the great outreaching. Aspiration is a fruit of the spiritual, but a seed-bearing fruit that brings harvest of the spiritual again. When worthy traits of character are believed to belong to the higher power, aspiration lays hold of them with desire, and thus becomes a promoter of that spiritual quality and life which brought it forth. When noble character is recognized in God, a high ethical joy in God comes in. At lower stages the divine has been so conceived that the human gladly sang its praise, but now in higher grades the human is attuned somewhat to the excellence that it discerns in God, and finds the highest joy in contemplating his goodness and seeking to be conformed thereto. Now joyful hope springs up, hope of acceptance with God and full fellowship with him in a life to come. Thus the spiritual is exalted to ever worthier forms by reaching out with worthier estimate of that which is above.

Into this great outreach of the spiritual there have entered a great variety of acts, and many institutions have sprung up to represent it. The characteristic action of the spiritual in man is prayer, and prayer is a universal practice. Through uncounted ages the human race has been in the habit of standing with upturned face, speaking out into the unseen. There it has poured out its joys and sorrows, confessed its sins and sought forgiveness, acknowledged its benefits received, pleaded against the evils that it dreaded, laboured to avert the divine anger, and adored the power and goodness that it believed to be over all. Prayer has varied greatly in its depth and breadth, and doubtless there have always been persons who did not pray at all, but still the practice has been so general and continuous as to be truly characteristic of mankind. It has not waited for any special conceptions or theories of God, but has risen from man as he was to God as he was conceived, and thus has borne the impress of both the virtues and the faults of humanity. The belief that man could talk with the unseen powers has made prayer to be a lifelong habit of the race.

A concrete and vivid form of prayer is sacrifice, in which the various motives of prayer have found tangible expression. Offerings to God have been expressive sometimes of gratitude, sometimes of conscious guilt, sometimes of the sense of friendship. Sometimes they have expressed the conviction that between the divine and the human there existed a living bond of genuine kinship. How positively all these acts of sacrifice assume the invisible divine and lay hold upon it with the strength of human heart and will, it is needless to tell. Out of the practices of prayer and sacrifice have grown up many institutions. There have been forms of prayer, private and public, now simple and now elaborate. There have been songs of worship in every conceivable key. Liturgies have been wild, fanatical, coarse, drunken, brutal, and they have been serious, solemn, spiritual, uplifting, worthy of the good God and of the best in man. There have been places of prayer, with modes of architecture adapted to their purpose, various as the worships that they enshrine. There have been orders of praying men, priesthoods, representing the people in their address to the higher powers, bringing their offerings of gratitude and propitiation, and proclaiming the favour of the deity to his worshippers. There have been organizations for promotion of religious life and service—churches, societies, monasticisms, fraternities. There have been orders of religious teachers—prophets, pastors, guides, to bring messages from God, and unfold the mysteries and show the duties of religion. By all these practical means humanity has given effect to its convictions, and shown how vital and irrepressible is its outreach after divine realities.

Implied in all this group of outreaching activities is the firm belief in the fact of mutual intercourse between human and divine. Moving in one direction this intercourse is worship: in the other it is inspiration. It is much if man can speak to God: it is more if God speaks to man. Belief in both movements has been general in the race. Mankind has believed that the invisible Spirit inspired mortal men and expressed himself through them. One may almost say that under the influence of all religions the divine voice has been heard speaking through the human, and men have exulted in the consciousness of inspiration. That the proceeding has often been coarse and low in its quality is nothing against the fact. Men have believed in such inspiration as they were qualified to welcome, and it has often been unworthy of their best manhood. Even in drunkenness they have thought themselves inspired; and yet, at the other extreme, men have heard the voice of inspiration uttering the highest truth that they had ever known. The point to be noticed is that the spiritual in man has not merely reached out in search of an unseen spiritual, but has firmly believed that it had grasped it and was receiving from it actual communications.

It has already been implied that conscience and the moral sense take part in this great outreaching. For the developing of the moral sense and judgment there are sufficient means, as we have seen, in the social life of men. But when the idea of the divine has become strong and vital, it is not long before morality demonstrates its kinship with religion and appears as a part of the great outreach to that which is above. The moral judgment comes to be regarded as bearing a witness that is more than human, and conscience is felt to be an echo of the voice of God. The divine will becomes a standard of duty, the authority of heaven resides in the demands of righteousness, and the moral quality of life thus stands closely connected with the moral quality in higher being. All peoples and all religions have something of this. The recognized moral precepts may be crude and partly false, and the conception of divine authority may be very imperfect, and yet the call of duty carries a more than human sanction, and morality is believed to be grounded out of sight, in divine realities.

To this corresponds the fact that in early times the laws of many nations were believed to have come as a gift from heaven. All kinds of law have been regarded as ordinances of God. The common rules of social right have in fact been learned from experience, and are commended by their practical worth; nevertheless, they have not been considered sufficiently strong, except as they were proclaimed from heaven. It was social experience that first codified the precept, "Thou shalt not steal," and yet for great parts of mankind the strength of this law has resided in the divine authority that had proclaimed it. "It is God's will that thou steal not" is the form in which the command has been felt to be most binding. Government, an outgrowth of human experience, has often been strongest with the people because of the belief that it was grounded in divine authority. Justice is a human reality, but seeks its foundations in divine righteousness, and commends itself as an endeavour to do here what is required above. Common life is full of institutions and practices that would not be what they are if the moral sense were not seeking support in divine reality. In all these ways does the ethical element in life claim its place beside the religious, and join it in laying hold of that which is above.

The intellect bears its part in the great outreaching of humanity after God. Human thought is far from having been altogether of this world: it has been interested in divine matters as truly as in human, and almost as long. The abundance of early myths of creation is enough to show how naturally thought went out beyond that which is seen. To account for existing things is to enter the realm of theology, and the endeavour to do this has been made by all peoples. Wonder has been the mother of doctrine, and wonder is universal. Every religion has made its efforts to solve the mysteries of existence. The deepest thought has been that of the greatest and most serious religions, but it is the way of human nature to think of these things, and the crudest religions have had their theology, as truly as the best. To reject a current theology is only to make way for another, for no people will be long without one. The finest thought of man has been devoted to the labour of knowing God, and will never cease from the divine quest. No vision can be more impressive than the vision of mankind in a mysterious world, instinctively assuming that there must be an explanation of the mysteries, and reaching into the unknown with eager thought, to find eternal foundations for temporal things. The human intellect has habitually assumed that it is natural, necessary, wise and profitable to seek for God.

Quite as important as any element in the case is the fact that character takes hold upon that which is above, and rises to its best in response to it. Character, with conduct its correlative, is indeed formed by means of the human relations and experiences of this world; but it does not owe itself to these alone. It has been a common understanding that character and conduct ought to conform to standards derived from the invisible world. This is not merely a principle of Hebrew and Christian religion. All religions have made more or less application of it, often poorly enough, but with a sincerity that attested the common belief in the unseen standards of goodness. Even where all seemed most human this divine test has been present. Travellers have now and then reported certain low tribes as having no religion. But when acquaintance had been made, and suspicion and secretiveness had been overcome, it was discovered that the daily conduct of those peoples, so far from being without religious control, was governed by religious considerations, or appeal to the unseen, even down to the minutest details. Their ignorance may be deep, but the work of their life is done in the conscious presence of powers invisible.

In proportion as religion advances toward its best, the transforming power of the invisible divine becomes more effective, and character comes to be touched by quality from the realm of divine purity and righteousness and love. The finest character that humanity has known has rested most directly upon the divine perfection. There is a stage of life at which the ethical and religious elements combine at their worthiest into that which we have called the spiritual, which now appears at its best. When this has occurred, the whole of life is built upon foundations that are out of sight. Man has cast himself upon the reality of divine being and character, assuming God, and putting belief in him to daily use. He adopts eternal considerations, and turns them to the promotion of all that is best in the life of time. The spiritual rises to the Spiritual. It finds its standards, its inspiration, its comfort and its strength in God. It takes hold on immortality. It brings forth the best life that was ever lived. But such life is inspired from above. It depends upon God, and especially upon God as all-good and gracious, the true standard for all beings. It is not merely that such life rests upon conscious faith in such a God, for that statement covers only a part of the case. It rests upon the assumption of God as the foundation of morals and the inspiration of religion, and comes as the large response of life to that unseen reality. The power of such response to elevate character, and to create the highest character when God is conceived as worthiest, is confirmed by long experience, and stands beyond the reach of reasonable doubt.

We have been inquiring how much there is in man that reaches out to take hold upon such unseen reality as we include under the name of God. We find that the human emotional nature has always been acting in view of divine realities, darkening and brightening life by turns; that vast practices in morals, religion and the general life have arisen in response to divine existence, character and relations with men; that moral judgment comes to assume a divine standard of good and evil; that the intellect has taken boundless interest in things that are out of sight, and devoted itself to eternal verities; that character and conduct have responded to the idea of divine will and standards, and character is best when this conception is worthiest. We see that this outreach to divine realities is both ancient and modern, belonging to the infancy of man and to his maturer life; it grows with his growth and is the companion of his greatness; when it is best he is best, and the supreme destiny of the race moves in unison with this high quality.

It must be remembered that this is no mere exhibition of facts in Christian history. To interpret the idea of religion from Christianity alone, though it has often been done, does deep injustice to the human race. What has here been hinted at is the story of mankind. In all its religions and in all its ethical history the human has thus been assuming, directly or indirectly, that the divine is real. If there are apparent exceptions, they only show that the process has not been perfect, or always self-consistent. Buddhism, for example, professes no knowledge of God. Yet in its doctrine of *karma* it recognizes an inflexibly righteous order to which all existence is subject, and this righteous order is the ground on which its peace is built. Faulty and perverted has the process often been, but the instinctive, habitual and undying practice of taking the divine for a fact is a main element in the history of human kind.

The testimony of mankind concerning the nature of that which it assumes may seem hopelessly mixed and contradictory. One religion seems to be assuming one thing and another another. Polytheism, Pantheism, Dualism, Monotheism; nature-forces, deified heroes, gods of mixed character, the God of perfect goodness; out of this what unity can be brought forth? Can we tell what it is that the spiritual in man has taken for true?

Yes, for religion in all religions has always meant one thing. Men have always been acting as if there were some unseen spiritual power to which it was both right and advantageous for them to commit themselves in trust and loyalty. This in fact is exactly what men have done through all their history—they have taken for granted a greatness and goodness on which it was right and good for them to rest. They have felt that reliance upon such a power was a normal part of their life, and accordingly have had religion. The confi-

dence of the soul in something great and good above is the
key to the spiritual history of mankind. Against this the defects of religion in the world, terrible as they are, are no objection. Doubtless the one great assumption about God has
been broken into a multitude of apparently irreconcilable
beliefs. That was because human limitation, ignorance and
sin came in to injure and corrupt the conception of the higher
power. Men were not wise or good enough to discover what
kind of Being God must be, and so they misconceived him in
all possible ways, determining their conceptions of him
through their own littleness, or immaturity, or sinfulness.
Religion has had innumerable forms, and been degraded in
ways without number, all because men were not competent
to have it otherwise. Nevertheless, through all the forms and
modes has sounded the one great affirmation—man is not
the highest being, and there is a power above in which it is
right and good for him to put his trust.

How much this sounds like the Christian doctrine!—only
this is the bare statement, while the Christian doctrine includes the rich unfolding. The Christian word is simply that
there does exist a Being so great and good that all other beings
ought to live in view of him, and are blest only when they do.
The spiritual in mankind has always blindly and gropingly
acted as if this were true, and sometimes more intelligently,
often missing the real character but never giving up the claim
that religion has a worthy ground. The Christian doctrine
confirms the claim and fills out its meaning, by revelation of
the eternal goodness in the living God. It says to all people,
"What therefore ye worship in ignorance, this I set forth
unto you" (Acts xvii. 23). It tells men that their primary
assumption is far more gloriously true than they could dream,
and shows them what their aspirations signify. Setting forth
the spiritual glory of God in Christ, it offers satisfaction to the
longings that have made religion a part of the universal life.

Returning now to the fact that this great assertion of the
worth and rightfulness of religion has been made by the

general race of man, we must ask what is the best explanation of it. Why should this higher element in human nature be always throwing itself out upon higher powers as if they existed? Why has mankind acted as if there were some power above it that could satisfy its deepest needs? If there were no good power above man, religion would be folly; why has it been taken for granted that it is not?

The simple and obvious explanation is that the assumption is true. No other explanation can compare with this in reasonableness: in fact, it may be doubted whether any other can be found that is worthy to be brought into comparison with this at all. The phenomena to be accounted for are too vast to be covered by any special theory or matched by any laboured explanation. Great characteristic movements of mankind have their justification in the simplicity of truth. Special theories of how man became religious may be dispensed with. The seeming realities that have produced religion are realities indeed: religion had to exist, for there was ground for it in the nature of things: reality justifies it and calls it out. That there is a worthy God above is no wild guess, it is a fact, and religion is the response of mankind to it. The spiritual has been right in rising to meet the Spiritual.

We are justified in including the perfect goodness of God in the fact that religion has assumed. The One who exists is not such a being as this or that religion discerned and proclaimed. The fact that men believed in Zeus or Vishnu does not prove that Zeus or Vishnu was in existence. That men have held a Christian doctrine of God does not prove that God is like the doctrine. What religion really implies and has always implied is the existence of One who is absolutely worthy to be addressed as God by all beings, sufficient to satisfy all needs, entitled to all confidence and loyalty. Only the existence of such a God would redeem religion from being false and foolish. The only reasonable explanation of universal religion is that there is such a Being, and mankind has been feeling after him to find him. All races have perceived some truth concerning him, but all have missed him in part, and many have missed him deplorably. Nevertheless, his existence is the true explanation of their upward gaze.

For if this is not so, and there is no such God, then there is a part of the human endowment that has nothing beyond itself to correspond to it. There is no spiritual without to match the spiritual within. There is no superhuman right, and no divine reality. There is no higher authority, power or fellowship. That element in human nature which has persistently made man religious is a false element. It has acted all these ages without just cause, for it has risen to meet that which never existed. The powers that make religion universal evidently belong to the human outfit, and yet there is absolutely nothing to justify religion. Moreover, these powers that have no counterpart constitute no slight or minor part of man. They are the powers in which he has always felt that his chief significance resided. It is in them that he differs most from all that is below him, and has seemed to himself to be one with the infinite above him. In them has arisen his hope of immortality. But in fact they lead him nowhither. There is nothing for them to take hold upon. He has attuned his conscience to a divine standard that did not exist, and shrunk in fear from a divine power that was not. He has prayed when there was no one to hear, and rejoiced in divine inspiration, protection and salvation which had no existence. He has framed the affections, institutions and customs of his life to correspond to a relation that existed only in his own mistaken mind. In a word, he has furnished the earth to match an inhabited heaven, when the heaven was empty from everlasting to everlasting. And this he has done by an abiding impulse of his nature that was as genuine a part of himself as his eyesight or his memory.

This is very difficult to believe. In fact, it is incredible. Various reasons might be given for saying so, but a sufficient reason is that such a condition of things would be utterly unlike everything else that we know. The proposition does not correspond to the character of the world. Everything else proceeds on a different principle. If the spiritual in man is thus astray in its primary assertion, the fact stands as a great contradictory exception in the nature of things: and a great contradictory exception in the nature of things cannot be permanently believed in.

Every other power of human nature has something to correspond to it, and to support and justify its existence. Each bodily sense has its corresponding reality: the eye has light and the ear has sound, and the sense of touch is simply the correspondence of the living man to the environment that touches him. The counterparts are as real as the powers. So our intellect, as we have seen, has its counterpart and support in the intellectual order and method of the universe. The rational man and the rational world fit each other. Steady and trustworthy life is possible because every power of body and mind thus has its true and trusty counterpart in the world. In bodily life, health consists in normal relation to surrounding conditions. In mental life, sanity consists in harmony with the universal reason, and insanity in inability to act in unity with the order of the world.

If there is no good God, so that the moral and religious nature has no trustworthy counterpart or supporting fact, we can only say that the moral and religious part of the human experience is radically unlike all the rest. The recognition of its counterpart by the spiritual in man has been quite as steady, sincere and practical as the recognition of their counterparts by sight and hearing and intelligence. All that we know of the reasonable processes of our life goes to assure us of the validity of all these acts alike, of one as truly as of another. There appears no reason for doubting the moral and religious counterpart, and it is doubtful whether any valid reason for a doubt so radical could exist. It is not rationally possible to rule out the moral and religious part of our being from the method that governs all other parts of our life. This is the strongest reason that we could have for being sure of our primary religious convictions. We might be most unwilling to feel that our moral and religious powers were unsupported and misleading, and yet be aware that our feeling did not settle the question of fact. Many believers in God are precisely in this situation, and are deeply troubled lest their confidence in religion be taken away from them. But the conclusive argument is that the well-tested structure of the world is against any godless supposition. Human experience, ages long, is experience of living among facts; and unless experience in religion is one long contradictory exception, which we cannot hold, the facts that are necessary to religion can be trusted as safely as the facts upon which the other experiences of our life are built. And the first fact essential to religion is a God so great and good that religion is normal, necessary and beneficial to men.

The whole truth, however, is not that the human powers have something to correspond to them in the world around. This even greater thing is true, that the human powers have grown up in response to the realities by which they were surrounded. Senses and mental powers were not the first things to exist: they were developed through contact with corresponding realities that were here before them. There was a world into which life in due time entered. Life is that mysterious something which is able to turn things outside of itself to its own inner uses. It has responded to surrounding realities by utilizing them, but first, and still more wonderfully, by developing means for utilizing them. This is the manner in which science now holds that the working powers of life, the senses and the faculties, came into being. They were developed by life, to meet its own necessities. They are due on the one hand to the marvellous power resident in life itself, and on the other to the equally marvellous material that life had to work upon.

Nothing more wonderful will ever be conceived than the method in which life obtained its effective working organs. The living thing was surrounded on every side by material objects, and life provided it with a sensitive internal structure whereby it could feel its contact with them. Thus, through the sense of touch, life established conscious connections with the world. In the invisible element around there was a certain set of vibrations, resulting in what we know as light; and life proceeded gradually to develop an organ through which those vibrations were utilized for its purposes through vision, without which life could never have made its normal advance. Life, seizing what was about it, turned its own darkness into light. In the same surrounding element there was another set of vibrations, producing what we know as sound; and life went on to form another organ through which these entered into its own habitation to serve the purpose of hearing, without which again it would have been at infinite disadvantage. Thus life dispelled the silence in which it was born. There were qualities exhaling from various objects in the world, and life built up organs whereby they came to serve needs of its own, represented by the names of taste and smell. Thus life ministered to its own nourishment and enjoyment by appropriating qualities that were floating in the air. Words cannot tell how wonderful this is, but this is what has occurred. Light and the eye were not created independently of each other, but the formation of the eye was the response of life to the fact of light.

Here we must recall that the mental powers were developed on the same principle. When life had brought sensation, experience of sensation developed the power of judgment, and set the intellect at work. Intellect as well as sensation was developed in response to kindred qualities in the world around. Our race owes itself intellectually to the intellectual quality inwrought to the world in which it has been reared. The changeless and yet ever-changing order of the starry heavens moving in silent majesty across the night was a main educator of early mankind, and it was the intellectual quality above that trained the same below. As the successful working of our senses is proof of the reality of those elements in the world to which they make response, so the successful operation of our rational powers is proof of the rational quality in the world that educated them. And both these proofs were pledged when life was born; for life was of such nature that it could not have continued without that use of outward things, both material and rational, which serves as proof that the outward things exist.

When life had advanced to the rational stage, its spiritual necessities came on, and life sought satisfaction for them in the same old way. As before, it laid hold upon existing reality outside of itself. The rising powers adapted to morality and religion ascended seeking a worthy object above the human realm. The outreach after God was a third outreach in a natural succession; or rather, it was a third simultaneous with the second. It was just as genuine an expression of the nature of life as the outreach after light and sound, or after reason. When life has come to the stage of man, it reaches out for God: that is its nature and necessity, for man needs God above himself. When life was born, the birth of religion was pledged and certain, just as truly as the life of sensation or of intellect. It came necessarily to pass that men assumed the existence of some Being who could adequately satisfy their spiritual needs, so that life with him would be their highest good.

In the other cases, the object sought by life was there to be seized upon, and there is no reason for doubting that in the last case it was the same. Life has not reached out for support where there was nothing. We have obtained our moral and religious nature through the response of life to the reality of God. According to the analogy of other experience we are entitled to say that the reality of God is implied in the spiritual in man, as the reality of light is implied in vision. Light is as real as the power that seizes upon it, and so is God. He was there, and the soul corresponded to him, wherefore the impulse to trust, worship and communion arose. The idea of goodness and right came into life because goodness and right were already existent in the Being to whom humanity was correlative. Men felt that they were dependent upon a higher power, because they were dependent: they felt that God was expressed in the world, because he was there expressed: they spoke to him, because he was there to be spoken to, and thought he could breathe his spirit into them, because he could. They were impelled to obey him, because the real authority of eternal right was there. They built morality and religion into their life, because God the eternal foundation of morality and religion was the foundation of their life. They sinned, not because there was sin in God, but because they failed to live up to the best they knew. They misjudged God, because of their ignorance, their immaturity and their evil choice, no one of these elements being absent from the case; but even in their ignorance and sin, by which morals and religion were kept low in quality, their life was always an answer, though a poor one, to the reality of God.

The long imperfectness of this process is no argument against it. The eye is adapted to the light, but it was long in becoming adapted, and the adaptation is not perfect yet; but no one questions the adaptation because of the early imperfection of the organ. High and fine rational processes are normal to mankind, and are trustworthy when they come; and no one doubts them because primitive immaturity was capable only of imperfect judgment. So the spiritual life of the race has long been sadly low and poor, and still continues so; but that is no reason for denying that the race was all the time taking hold, though imperfect hold, upon the great divine reality. Nay, the very length and patience of the process, in spite of its own defects, renders the responsive nature of it all the more certain and impressive. Humanity has not grown by adequately understanding the things by which it grew. It took hold of them long before it understood them, and was growing by means of them before it even knew what they were. The imperfectness has been in man, not in God. He has always been the same, and religion in all its stages has been the genuine but partial human answer to the call of his great presence.

We must remember again how great and simple is the truth implied in the religious outreach. If we looked merely at the great variety of religious manifestations, it might appear that humanity had been reaching out uncertainly into the dark, and that by reason of its indefiniteness the outreach signified nothing. But the truth is rather that humanity has always been acting on the principle that religion is justified by the facts. It has assumed that it was worth while to seek an everlasting foundation for the life of the soul. Every religious outreach has assumed not only that there was something in the spiritual realm that could be laid hold of, but that there existed something, real and ultimately attainable by man, in which the spiritual needs and aspirations can find full and worthy satisfaction. Every man needs the whole of God, and all religion implies the whole of God. If religion as a whole is not a delusion, there must exist a living God so great and good that in him all spiritual needs may find full satisfaction. That is to say, in language that has been used already, the evidence from the spiritual in the human race leads to the conclusion that, unless life is a lie, there lives a God of all goodness, adequate to all the spiritual necessities of men. The evidence from the spiritual confirms the testimony of Jesus Christ.

We may still wonder that the good God, if he exists, should leave his children so long in poor and unsatisfactory spiritual life. The vastness of the race, the seriousness of its destinies, and the pitiableness of its long infancy, overwhelm us. It may seem incredible that he created a race to grope after him so long and find him so slowly, if indeed it finds him at all. Can this be the method of a good God? It certainly is the fact that the slow unfolding of religious nature, with all that must attend upon it, is what we have to accept. Like the eye and the hand, the soul has developed slowly. We cannot escape perplexity by denying the facts. If we believe in God we believe that he has always been God, and to him we must attribute the method of the world and life. He has made no great thing except by giving it time to grow, and the spiritual life of his offspring is no exception. Hence, long childhood and long childishness.

The Christian explanation of this mystery rests not on demonstration, but on the conviction to which all the spiritual realities lead. It has been implied already. From the spiritual in man we have drawn the evidence that there exists a Being who is able to do full justice to all spiritual necessities, a God sufficient, so great and good as to satisfy all human needs and possibilities. It is our privilege to accept this great conclusion in its full force and significance. We are perplexed because we do not recognize in the living God that perfect goodness which we ascribe to him. We do not do him justice. A God sufficient to humanity, such as is implied in all spiritual experience of man, is good enough to be trusted with all human affairs and interests whatever. A good God must be good enough to be trusted not merely with the destinies of the well-ripened saints: he must be good enough to be trusted with the destinies of the slowly-ripening world of men, and of all the half-developed souls that such a world has contained. The constitutional outreach of human life implies a God of comprehensive and particularizing goodness, whose tender mercies are over all his works, and who forsakes not the works of his own hands; and such a God lives, from everlasting to everlasting. The living God can be relied upon to do the right and best for the whole of that which he has brought into existence. This is the conclusion from what we know of the spiritual in man, this is true if we live in an honest world, and this is the doctrine that we learn when we sit at the feet of Jesus.

In pursuance of this conviction the Christian doctrine has always held that the good God would certainly reveal himself to his creatures. This is a true utterance of the Christian heart, which bodies forth that principle of faith in the eternal goodness which lies at the heart of all worthy religion. Our faith would confidently affirm it, too, in view of the pathetic spectacle of the worshipping world, a spectacle always under the eye of God. Accordingly the Christian faith has welcomed the Bible with its divine self-revealings, and cherished it as worthy to have come from God. This is what we might expect of the good Being, it has said, that he would reveal himself as he did to Abraham and Moses and the prophets, and above all as he has done in his Son Jesus Christ, expressive of his inmost heart. God and men being what they are, this revelation is the very gift that we might expect.

This is entirely true, and every one who knows the Christian revelation ought to think thus gratefully and loyally of God from whom it came. By the same loyal reasoning more is true, and a conclusion already recorded here meets us again. It is time for Christians to cease to limit God's direct spiritual operation toward men to that which the Bible records. The idea of a self-communicating action of God toward the human race as a race of spirits has never yet taken its due place in Christian thought. At this we must not wonder, for until recently there has been no adequate conception of the human race as a whole, in its age, extent and variety. But at present we know that Abraham was a member of no infant race, that the Hebrew period is far down in the human career, and that a vast part of mankind has never been considered in our estimates of the sufficiency of revelation. People after people has lived and vanished wholly untouched by the revealing God, if his self-imparting action is limited to the Bible, and through the Bible he has influenced only a minor part even of the later race. There exists a relation of the one God to the one humanity; and the argument for the probability of the revelation in the Bible stands equally as an argument for much more. As that revelation might be expected from a good God, so also might a wider work. We should expect such a God to be self-communicating toward all spiritual beings of his own creation, as we have already found reason for believing that he is. Such a God of universal scope is the One in whom the spiritual element in man leads us to believe,—a God to whom human nature makes response because he has created it responsive to himself, and who responds to it in turn when it appeals to him. Such a God of universal scope we discern when we look upon the divine reality in the light of Christ. He is a God who does not leave to itself the spiritual nature that he has created, but stands toward it self-imparting.

When we have uttered such a truth as this, we must be faithful to it. We must freely allow the spiritual in man to teach us its lesson. It stands as a fair conclusion that in all human rationality and moral sense God himself is dealing with men, so that every voice of truth and righteousness that they hear is his, and that in creating man to lift his heart above he has become responsible for a religious outreach which he does not neglect. The true light that lighteth every man is the perpetual gift of God. And we may record with joy that he whose reality is thus taught us by the general human experience is the same God who is known in fuller manifestation as the God and Father of Jesus Christ.

4. THE GREAT OBJECTION

Thus far the Christian doctrine of God has been presented without explicit reference to the great objection that is brought against it. So worthy and self-commending does it appear in itself that it might seem to be a calmly optimistic doctrine, untroubled by oppositions. But it is met by doubt and denial, and even for those who hold it steadfastly and count it their chief joy it is embarrassed by questionings, and the grounds of difficulty are so obvious that they cannot be overlooked. No presentation of the Christian doctrine of God can be satisfactory that does not consider the great objection.

Broadly stated, the objection is that this world which we know is a very hard world in which to believe in the good God whom the Christian doctrine sets forth as the one God of all. Experience, it is said, cries out against the belief. Facts condemn it. The general method of the administration of the world—if there be an administration—does not correspond to the character that is attributed to God in the

Christian doctrine, and there are important special facts that cannot be reconciled with such a character. In the philosophy of pessimism this denial is made at the strongest and pressed to the uttermost, and all the way this side of that extreme are ranged the various denials, doubts and questionings that are suggested by common life. And no one can live in the world without knowing that the difficulties are real, and the objection is not to be attributed entirely to sinful unbelief.

The objection appears in three forms. They cannot be kept entirely distinct from one another, or presented without some anticipation of matters yet to be stated, and yet they are so far distinct as best to be set forth separately.

First stands the broad assertion that the order of the world does not bear the marks of being an order directed by a personal will, certainly not by such a personal will as the Christian doctrine attributes to the God and Father of Jesus. It is not directed by a personal will at all, the modern judgment often declares, in the light of modern knowledge. It is a vast machine, working right on by forces inherent in itself, and bringing forth whatever results are implied in existing antecedents. That any will directs it is declared to be both unprovable, and improbable in the highest degree. If there is any will, it is represented by force, not by character. Impartiality is the law. The system moves on regardless of all, making no exceptions for the sake of any. It never forgives, but exacts to the uttermost the penalty of resistance to its method, whether the act be blameworthy or innocent. It moves on through a great progressive unfolding, in which ascending life proves to be the portion of the few, and decline or defeat the destiny of the many. It has no help for the weak. Its movement is without mercy, abandoning to their fate all who fail to keep up with the pace. To the single life and to the type nature seems alike indifferent. In all this, even if there are signs of will, there are no signs of that tender affection and helpfulness, that brooding care, that righteous oversight, that interest in those who sin and fail, which

Jesus so insistently attributes to the God of all. The system is heartless, and "Where is now thy God?" many an observer of the world-order feels that he has a right to ask. In this indictment there may be misunderstanding and exaggeration, and it may rest upon a partial view of the facts, but it cannot be put out of court as groundless. There is truth in this form of the plea that this is a hard world in which to believe in the good God.

The second form of the objection is perhaps a specification under the first, but its special character gives it a power of its own. It is a protest to which written words can do no justice. The world is full of suffering, and the amount of it is inconceivable. No one escapes it, or can escape. Trouble is everywhere. There is physical pain, and there is mental anguish, both in endless variety. The suffering is not distributed according to desert, for no attention appears to be paid to merit or demerit when it comes. While it is true that sin brings misery to the sinner, it is equally true that it often brings keener misery to the sinner's virtuous friends, and that its agonizing results are scattered at random through the world. Trouble comes by inheritance, where there can be no question of personal desert, and through associations that involve no guilt. The complications of suffering are often so terrible and seemingly unjust as to appear as if they must have been invented by an infinitely ingenious hatred. The astonishing sufferings of human kind have long been the theme of wonder and the text of unbelief, but now comes modern knowledge, extending far the scope of the problem. The race is far older than we thought, and its earlier stages of life, so far as we can see, have been such as to intensify rather than relieve our perplexity. Moreover, it has always been known that our lower companions in life were sharers in our lot of suffering, the animal world being full of pain, with no moral ground so much as suggested for so great a fact—for the old doctrine that animal suffering was inflicted because of human sin was only an intellectual guess, not an ethical suggestion. But now we catch glimpses of an immeasurably long course of animal life before man appeared, and learn that all its ages have been as full of pain as the present time. Ever since it came to be what we call animate existence, life has brought pain as well as pleasure—pleasure, but always pain also. If we say that God is watching over his world, he is watching a world so full of misery that we often think if we were in his place we would annihilate it, if we could not mitigate its agonies. How, we ask, can this be the world of that good God of whom Jesus spoke—Jesus the healer, who had compassion upon the sufferers and forgot himself in the joy of giving them relief?

In this indictment also there may easily be one-sidedness and exaggeration, but all the world knows that behind it there is a dread array of facts. Probably this is the form in which the problem comes tormentingly to the greatest number of persons. Perhaps we may safely guess that even in Christian lands, where there are two persons troubled about believing in God because of sin, there are three troubled because of suffering. This is not to be wondered at, for power to suffer is common to all men, and no spiritual preparation is required for drawing inferences from it.

Nevertheless the most serious form of the objection is the third. The world is a world of sin. The problem of moral evil is very ancient, and very modern, too. As soon as we state the Christian doctrine the problem is upon us. The world, which has no existence apart from God, abounds in opposition to his character and will. That which he hates is done by beings for whose existence he alone is responsible. Instead of the good and harmonious world that would correspond to his holy love and power, we behold a world in which good and evil exist in perpetual struggle. It is no wonder that a genuine dualism, of opposite powers approximately if not absolutely equal, has sometimes been invoked for explanation of the facts. In Christian thought, where the eternal goodness is affirmed, it has still been deemed necessary to believe in an evil spirit, less indeed than God but for the time not badly matched against his omnipotence, in order to account for the conflict. However it may have come to pass, evil gets possession of beings whom God created for himself, and only a minor part of them does he appear to us to be getting back. When we turn from individuals to the course of history, we find that the human career shows a long history of right and wrong, wrong often seeming stronger than right, sin persisting, and evil rising in new forms after defeat. Evil seems far easier than good to perpetuate and increase. The scene is all unlike what we should expect if the one good God were God alone, as the Christian doctrine declares. The better God is claimed to be, the deeper becomes the mystery of evil in his world. Can we believe in him in the face of this? And if we think of men as destined to live beyond the present life, and going from this world to some other with their evil in them, the field of the problem is at once indefinitely enlarged. Out into the unexplored spiritual realm it extends, where it seems to have possession of all the future.

In this complaint again there may be inadequate knowledge of things and faulty interpretation: we may perhaps be under a nightmare of facts that we do not rightly understand. But if so, we still beg to be told why God made such a nightmare possible, and in any case we cannot deny the seriousness of the problem. The fact of evil has darkened the heaven of God for ages, and the cloud is still there.

These three points make up the great moral objection against the Christian doctrine of God. It is hard to believe in the God of Jesus Christ, because the world in which we live is so impersonal and heartless a world, a world of suffering and a world of sin. The objection is not merely an affair of the schools, but is found among the people everywhere and always. To all sorts and conditions of men it sometimes seems that the whole doctrine is refuted by the facts of every day, and left as a beautiful speculation condemned by reality.

The consideration of this problem must begin with frank confession. We must say at once that a full solution of the problem is not to be expected. We may find rest to our souls in its presence, attaining to a confidence that is well-grounded, but a full solution, such that every reasonable mind must accept it, is beyond our power. The question will always be with us and with our successors. Expectation of fully mastering it will quickly pass when we note more precisely what the question really is.

We wish to know whether the existing world can be the work and kingdom of a perfectly good God. The question is not an abstract one, asking what kind of world such a God must make, but a concrete one, asking whether this particular world can be thought to be created and conducted by such a God. Evidently the full answer to a concrete question like this must be obtained, if at all, by interpretation of facts. We must not only know the facts with which the question is concerned, but understand them. How large a work this is a glance will show. We inquire about a world; but we find at once that we are really inquiring about a universe. There is only one empire, in which this world is only a province, and it seems certain that understanding of this part must depend somewhat upon understanding of the whole. Methods are doubtless essentially the same throughout, and there may be aims and ends in view that we could know if we knew the whole, which our vision of the part is too narrow to reveal to us. Until we know something of the place of our world in the vast whole to which it belongs, and of the character of that whole, we may misjudge in our interpretation of facts that affect us here. Periods that seem long to us are but moments in the great day of the universe, and how shall we understand them without first knowing something of the sweep and purpose of that day? But this how shall we learn, so well as to call ourselves sure?

Every part of the problem is in this manner involved in larger issues that are too large for clear reasoning. We wish to understand the significance of suffering; for upon this depends the question whether it can coexist with ruling divine goodness. But, in order to know the significance of suffering, we need to know the significance of souls and their life, the extent of their duration, and the relation of present experience to life and destiny not manifest as yet. Before we can rightly judge suffering, we must know what is good for souls, and what suffering is adapted to do for them, for good or harm. We need to be able to compare the present life of which we complain with a life devoid of suffering, if such a life could be. But how are we to become qualified to pass judgment upon these matters? We wish also to form a clear judgment respecting sin, and whether it can exist in a good God's world. But to this end we need to know much concerning God and men. Before we can solve the mystery of moral opposition to the will of God, we need to know the scope and intention of that will, and the degree of his ability to overcome evil with good among his creatures. We need to know how evil came to exist in men, and what will be its final outcome. Upon these great matters we may obtain some sound convictions, but not in such manner as to make of them a real solution of the problem. And before we can finally judge whether so impersonal and impartial an administration as we seem to discover is worthy of the heavenly Father, we need to know just how impersonal and impartial the actual administration is; and we need to know what should be expected of a heavenly Father, and in what manner a divine care should be expressed in a universal system. Upon these matters we may form good convictions, but as matters for discovery they lie beyond our field. We cannot conclusively justify or condemn sin and suffering in God's universe, or an impartial administration of the world, until we know whether God can make such use of them as to render their existence worthy of him, and bring forth worthy results from the whole enterprise of the universe. In this light it is plain that the full solving of our problem is impossible to men, since the facts necessary for its solving are beyond human knowledge. The moral question of God and the world will always remain more or less a mystery to men. Short solutions of it have abounded, but they are too short and easy. We may escape from bondage to the problem into the liberty of the sons of God, but the problem we shall never wholly solve, for the simple reason that we are finite, and the problem is beyond finite knowledge.

Hence the Christian vindication of God will always, as a matter of proof, be open to the charge of incompleteness. We naturally long for a complete theodicy, and cling to the hope that we may obtain one. A sufficient one we can indeed obtain. We can find rest to our souls, and be able to live in honourable peace and freedom in our Father's world. But our theodicy will always be such vindication of the infinite as is possible to the finite, and nothing more. In the universe of souls the mystery of God is essentially a moral mystery as well as an intellectual, and in the realm of solutions we must be content with what human powers can reach. Yet the human solutions, partial though they are, are worthy of our labour, for we may lay hold of genuine truth, which will help to guide our feet into the way of peace.

Any progress that is to be made toward gaining light on the question whether the present world can be the good God's world must be made by first clearing the question of some of its usual ambiguities, and setting it before us more clearly. The very seriousness of the problem leads often to an inaccurate and unjust statement of the case. We greatly embarrass ourselves by mistaking half-truths for whole truths here, as well as by mistaking half-solutions for whole solutions.

For example, it is common to ask whether a world of sorrow can be the world of the good God. But we need to ask our question more accurately than that. This world is not properly described when it is called a world of sorrow. It is a world of mingled sorrow and joy, pain and pleasure, suffering and satisfaction. What we ought to be inquiring is, whether this familiar world, in which suffering and enjoyment are blended as they are, can be the good God's world. The question commonly arises from hearts that feel the burden and perplexity of the suffering, and so the inquiry is easily made with attention directed mainly, if not entirely, to the darker side. But the world is not all dark, and when we inquire about it, thinking of it simply as a world of sorrow, we are not dealing with the real question.

In like manner we stumble over the impartiality of the universal order, thinking of it as an order that sacrifices the many to the few, and seems not only impersonal but heartless. Can this, we ask, be the method of the Father? But we beg the question when we call the method heartless. Perhaps it is not. There is high authority for referring to a gracious impartiality in which the Father maketh his sun to rise on the evil as well as on the good (Mt. v. 45); and that kind of impartiality is to be traced in the order of the world as truly as the other. The impartial order does other things than those of which we complain. It cannot fairly be judged in the light of one set of results. The method is a vast one, of a universe and not merely of a world, and must be estimated in view of its vastness. Our real question is, whether we can think of the impartial universal order, which seems indispensable to a steadfast universe, which holds all together but works hardship in many a case, as the order of the good God of all. We do the question injustice unless we consider the whole of it at once.

And again, we ask in dismay whether the good God can be conducting a world of sin. Of the evil in the world we cannot doubt, for we know it: it is goodness that we doubt. Evil is so characteristic of the world that we do not scruple to call it a world of sin, and to set it in complete contrast to the good character that we seek to defend in God. But any such statement tells only a part of the truth, and does injustice to the case. This world is not correctly described when it is called a world of evil. It is that, but it is more. It is a world of evil and good, of wrong and right, of sin and goodness. It is of mixed moral quality, and is incorrectly called either a good world or a bad one. The fact that it is constantly called now one and now the other is enough to indicate that each name has some fitness. The problem of evil, dark enough at the best, has been rendered more perplexing than it ought to have been by the overlooking and denial of the existing good and the exaggeration of the relative amount of evil in the world. Christians have often declared that sin constitutes the entire character of man: if there is any goodness at all it is so corrupted as not to count for real goodness: sin has destroyed all virtue. This, strangely enough, has oftenest been held in company with the doctrine that God's sovereign will is done in everything. But this description is not true to the facts. There is sin in the world, and there is also virtue, as all living constantly assumes. Good and evil coexist and are blended. Each modifies the other. It is quite true that all human goodness is corrupted by sin, and it is equally true that all human sin is modified and diminished by the goodness that lives in the same soul with it. Unmixed good and unmixed evil, perfect virtue and perfect sin, are alike unknown in this world, but virtue and sin are known in all experience as blended and diminishing each other. Neither will allow the other to be all that it would. When Paul wrote (Gal. v. 17) "For the flesh lusteth against the Spirit, and the Spirit against the flesh; for these are contrary the one to the other; that ye may not do the things that ye would," he was only describing the higher Christian form of the agelong strife of humanity, evil preventing good, and good preventing evil, from doing its utmost. So the real question is not whether we are to attribute an utterly bad world to the good God and Father, for we do not live in such a world. That question will not encounter us unless we suppose that God's creative enterprise results, through conditions that he has himself established, in the production and final maintenance of an absolutely evil world of spirits beyond this life. Only a final hell of God's own making could force the inquiry upon us in the extreme form which it is too often allowed to take. As long as we deal with experience, the question is whether this well-known world, where good and evil are blended as we find them, can be his.

This clearer defining is not proposed in order to prejudge or limit the answer to the vast question of evil, but because it is necessary, if we are to be right. Here are the facts: viewing one aspect of our life, we must not overlook the other. We must not begin by inquiring about a world of heartless impartiality, for the question remains whether the impartiality is heartless after all. The world about which we inquire is not to be characterized as a world of suffering, for it is a world of suffering and enjoyment blended. Nor are we asking about the relation of the good God to a world of sin, for the existing world is full of mingled sin and virtue, good and evil, right and wrong. Only by keeping the whole case before us can we make a successful inquiry.

Another question must be considered if we are to have the true data before us. As a matter of fact, the world contains these perplexing elements that constitute the perpetual problem. They are here, but how came they here? Where did they come from, and what are their connections? Are they a part of the system that is attributed to God, or are they intruders into that system? Evidently the question is important, for our estimate of these things will differ greatly according as we think they belong in the system where we find them, or have been thrust in upon it as alien elements; and so will our conception of the system itself. Until we have located our perplexing facts, as it were, either as belonging to the system that we ascribe to God or as outside of it, we cannot judge how God is related to them. Are we inquiring how God is related to certain dark and mysterious elements in his own system, or how he is related to certain intrusions made in spite of his will, and for which he has no responsibility? This is a deep and far-reaching question. It is so great that we are often tempted to assume an answer to it without considering the whole case that lies before us. But the Christian doctrine cannot be content with any timid or temporizing approach to so great a question, for the answer must be determinative of much in our thoughts of God. Perhaps the

three perplexing facts may prove to be all alike in this respect—all intruders or all non-intruders—and perhaps not.
At all events we must inquire.

We will begin with suffering; and of this we must say
without hesitation that suffering is no intruder in the world:
it belongs to the system that we are proposing to attribute to
the good God. All observation shows that it is the nature of
the world to contain both pain and pleasure. If this is the
good God's world, then the good God has a world in which
enjoyment and suffering are constantly mingled, through the
operation of the order that he has established.

Suffering in the animal world is no intruder upon nature.
All animal life involves sensation, and there is no way to in-
sure that sensation shall be all pleasant or all painful. If
there are nerves of feeling, and the uses of life are to be
served by them, both pain and pleasure must come in. It is
the very nature of sensitive life to enjoy and suffer. Moreover, the conditions of life render pain inevitable. If God
has ordained them, God has ordained suffering as well as
pleasure. Organisms are liable to injury, and injury involves pain. Organisms have their natural time-limit, so that
dissolution, or death, is sure to come to them; and death
ordinarily involves suffering, more or less. Animals live together; and while their association doubtless enhances their
pleasure, it also offers boundless opportunity for producing
pain. Consequently, in the living world below man physical
enjoyment and suffering have always existed together. Which
has been the greater no one knows or can know. Sometimes
our hearts are almost broken in sympathy with the unutterable agony of the animal world: sometimes they sing for joy
in sympathy with its exuberant life. One element is just as
truly a part of the one system of existence as the other, and
neither may be branded as an intrude. that forced itself in.
The ancient immoral suggestion that animal life was doomed
to suffering in anticipation or punishment of human sin is
now rendered entirely impossible by what we know of the
methods of life, and of the vastness and antiquity of the

animal world. In a system that includes sensitive corporeal life there is no need of any theory to account for suffering. It is a part of the great whole.

When we come to the human race the conditions are the same, except that here there are more ways for pleasure and pain to enter. Here nerves are more sensitive, bringing pleasure and pain more exquisite. Here injury is easy, and death is natural and certain. Here living beings hurt one another, as well as bring one another enjoyment. But here, besides, suffering is mental as well as physical. Man thinks, loves, hates. His thoughts may torment him—witness the effect of this very problem. His affections are his glory and joy, brightening his life beyond description, but the wounding of affection breaks his heart. He loves and loses, and the nobler the love the sorer the bereavement. He hates, too, and hatred is bitter, and anger is painful. The contingencies of life render disappointment certain. It is impossible for pain and pleasure to be distributed according to desert, the misery falling only on the wicked, for obviously the causes are largely independent of character. The old explanation, that human suffering is wholly due to sin, utterly breaks down, and must be entirely abandoned in theology. There is no way to make it credible that sinless life in this world would be free from suffering so long as the natural conditions of life continue as they are. So for men as well as for lower animals it appears that the system of life is one in which pleasure and pain are blended. Neither of the two has been brought in from without. The order of the existing world produces both, and if this is a good God's world, then both exist in the world of a good God. Abnormal doings of men destroy the normal balance of the two, and give sad increase to the pain, but pain as truly as pleasure enters into the scheme of human life.

What the normal balance is we may not be able to tell, nor can we ascertain the actual balance. Is there more pleasure or pain in the total human experience? Who can answer? Enjoyment in its ordinary forms passes unnoticed, but pain does not. If all sensations of body and mind throughout the race could be rightly classified and compared, probably it would appear that mankind lives a life of dominant enjoyment, heavily dashed with suffering. Such probably is that human world which we are seeking to understand.

If suffering is in the scheme of life, it must have some significance in the system. Any doctrine of the world will say that; and any doctrine that takes account of the vast quantity of suffering in the world must allow to it an important significance. Since the universe has evolved suffering as so large an element in its life, suffering must accomplish something. But the meaning of suffering is not hard to find. All who read life can read it. Suffering is educative, and stands forth as a teacher for whose instruction there is no substitute. In lower life it has been a chief means of developing intelligence and turning it to progressive uses. It is doubtful whether, without the discipline of pain, any part of the animal world could have advanced to the possibility of man. "A burnt child dreads the fire" is a wholesome educative law that represents the use of pain in its simplest form; but the simpler the more fundamental, and to this simple principle the growth of intelligence is vastly indebted. When we come to human life, how many out of a deep heart have sung the praises of sorrow as a wise teacher of the soul! There is no need that we repeat the praises in detail: one stanza of the song will suffice. "Our light affliction, which is but for a moment, worketh for us a far more exceeding and eternal weight of glory" (2 Cor. iv. 17). Is that said of Christians? Yes, but it could not be true of Christians if it were not true in principle: this could not be God's way of training Christians if it were not his way of training souls. A power of blessing has been stored in the nature of affliction itself. The general experience bears testimony that it is the true nature of trouble to "yield afterward the peaceable fruit of righteousness" (Heb. xii. 11). That the lesson is often missed is nothing against the reality of the teaching. The world knows that suffering is normally a means of moral education.

We shrink from it, of course, and our dislike of the discipline leads us childishly to ignore its value. But just as we must doubt whether painless life below could ever have brought man into being, so we must doubt whether painless life for man could ever bring into being those sons of God for whose perfecting the Father's affection waits. The upward road runs through regions where pain and pleasure both exist.

If this is true, we need not be so perplexed and troubled because we find suffering in the life that we attribute to the good God. If there is such a God, the training of life is his end in view, and the mingling of pleasure and pain appears to be the best method for that end. The broad fact of suffering would seem thus to be explained, as far as we can expect explanation of it. We may still wonder at the amount and variety of suffering that we meet, and find no explanation of this mystery. The dark facts may still be very dark to us. But we must learn that we are not to obtain relief from our problem by working it out from the details upward. This we might expect at first, but childishly, for the details are too complicated for such a method. Relief can come only by our finding a principle that accounts for suffering and reveals its purpose; and this we find. In the light of experience we may fairly claim a place for pain by the side of pleasure in the system of a good God who is training life toward perfection; and then we may leave the details to a wisdom better than our own.

This leads us on to that impressive and mysterious impartiality, or seemingly impersonal and indifferent operation, of which we have spoken. The system of the world works right on, with interference or modification in behalf of none, bringing to the many far less than to the few, and apparently destitute of interest in any. This seems all unlike a God who loves his creatures each and all, accounts them his own and seeks their good, after the manner of the Father of Jesus. Even in the animal world we wonder at this method, and still more in the human. What does this mean if God is love?

Here we must judge with caution, for we are dealing with something that stretches far beyond our personal scope. The method that we are considering is broader than this world: it is a method of the universe. It is as a province in a vaster realm that this world feels its effect. What we experience in the small we observe in the large, and know to be in the universal. But we must notice that this universality answers our question. The impartial method that we are moved to criticise is evidently a part of the system. By no possibility can we imagine that this element has been brought in through any exceptional operation. This is of God, if there be a God. There can be neither hope nor fear that it will prove otherwise.

This element also, if it is in the system of the world, must have a meaning there; and there is no difficulty in perceiving what the meaning is. This element of steadiness, independence, impartiality, seeming impersonality, is what constitutes it a system. So plain a fact needs only to be mentioned. The regularity of the movement of the world makes hardship often, and the hardship that falls upon us, and still more that which falls upon all, leads us to complain. A more adjustable order, we say, would be more righteous. Yet if the world were made over as we suggest, it would be criticised far more sharply than it is now. If we saw the order modified to help one or punish another, we should exclaim against the favouritism and inequality more urgently than we now do against the grinding of the great machine. If we were imagining a well-ordered world, certainly we should propose that one impartial wisdom govern the whole alike. An order that was not regular and equal, impersonal and calm, we should call unworthy alike of wisdom and of righteousness. The most thoughtful human judgment really approves the impartial method, knowing that there could be no successful world without it.

There is only one condition precedent to the acknowledgment of such a method in the universe of a good God. This condition is not that the method shall work no hardship, or involve no morally perplexing facts. It is that we shall be reasonably able to regard the system as on the whole expressive of the wisdom of God and his good-will toward his creatures. We cannot insist, indeed, that this quality shall be self-evident, or that there shall be no appearances to the contrary. But in any universe that is governed by a good God we are sure that the regular order will be one that on the whole does good service to the universe and to those who inhabit it. This is all that we can ask; and as to the evidence of it that we can expect to receive, of course it will be only such as lies within the range of our ability and our information. We must judge here with caution and humility, because we know so little. We do well to be very cautious about denying the worthiness of the universal order, for how shall we be sure that we understand it well enough to condemn it with confidence? The presumption that our experience warrants is all in favour of the honesty of the scheme to which our life belongs. To condemn it is to cut the ground of rationality from under our own feet. This we will do if we must, but this we will not do unless we must. We will hold rather to the worthiness of the world-order. That it does to a vast extent express wisdom and good-will we know. The method does good service. It is more reasonable to think its seeming contradictions reconcilable in fuller light than to deny the sincerity of the general existence. Our affirmation of the worthiness of the impartial order is not made on the ground of triumphant proof, but it is made in the light of reasonable confidence; and a denial of it cannot be made in the light of either.

It is to be added that no believer in the good God imagines that the impartial order of the world expresses the whole of him. If he seems to hide himself in indifference behind the impersonal order, the Christian doctrine denies the indifference. It declares that whether we discern him or not he is there, the indwelling God, dealing with men in the realm of a spiritual existence that ranks above the order that seems impersonal, caring for all, doing the work of an invisible friend, uttering himself in every instructive voice, communicating with every living soul, providing for destinies as yet unseen. If his creatures seem wronged by the impartial working of his universe, still the deeper truth is that in him they live and move and have their being, and his tender mercies are over all his works (Ps. cxlv. 9). This Christian conception of God himself, though often left out in the consideration of this question, must always be in mind when we interpret divine impartiality. If we are to judge whether the method of the universe is compatible with the reign of the good God, the good God must be defined, as well as the method of the universe. The good God is the more easily definable of the two, and ought never to be so much as mentioned in the discussion without remembrance of his perfect character.

We come now to sin, or moral evil—the existence of so vast a mass of acts and character contrary to the character of the God of the Christian doctrine. Here culminates the ethical objection to the Christian conception of God. We must follow the same order as before, and inquire first whether sin belongs to the system or has been thrust into it—whether human evil is to be treated as a product of the world-order, or as an intruder into its field.

It is an old question, and has been answered by Christian thought in both ways. Consistent Calvinism has always held that sin was a part of the system of the world, being included in the predestinating will of God. Even while it was strenuously denied that God was the author of evil, it has been held that his comprehensive will, foreordaining all that comes to pass, embraced the rise and progress of human sin, and all its developments. On the other hand, this position has been denied as strongly as it has been affirmed. Sin has been declared to be simply an intruder in the world, having no place in the order that God intended. To pronounce him responsible in any sense for its existence has been considered profane and blasphemous. Sin, it is often declared, exists in spite of God, an intruder to his world against his will. It is no wonder that both these positions have been held, for one is a natural inference from God's supremacy, and the other from his character. If, in interpreting the mystery of evil, we start from the sovereignty of God, we shall be likely to conclude that he appointed sin to be, for it exists. If we start from the character of God, we shall be likely to rank sin as an utter alien in his realm, for it is opposite to his character. In either case we shall find deep mystery—how such a God could will such a mass of evil to exist, or else how it could exist against his will. No serious advocate of either view would deny the mystery, or claim that his doctrine solved it.

Apart from what is thought of God, sin is often judged to be no part of the world-system because of its unreasonableness. Moral evil, it is said, is essentially unreasonable: irrationality is its abiding trait: therefore in a rational system it can have no place, and in God's world can only be an intruder. But in this judgment the case has not been fully considered. The irrationality of sin has proved to be no bar to its entrance or its stay, and the question still remains unanswered, why the utterly irrational should be able to establish so strong and permanent a hold within the rational world, whose nature and affinities gave it no welcome.

As usual, it is best to begin with the part of the subject that lies nearest home, and interrogate the available facts. Not by inferences from the divine counsel or character, but by observation of sin and the world-order, can we best judge whether sin entered through the system or in spite of it. It is only human sin that we are called to consider, for this is all the sin that we have clear knowledge of. If we could show that evil was brought into this world from some other, we should find no relief in that: the problem would not be solved, but would only change its place, and even be a larger problem in its vaster field. If we knew of sin existing in other races, still our ignorance of the conditions of their life would forbid our making such examination of it as we can make among men. Our only course is to interrogate the facts of this world, in order to learn whether sin found an open door or could enter only by breaking in.

But sin is not to be considered as if it stood alone. We have already noted that evil is not the only moral quality in the world, for good and evil are not only side by side, but are everywhere mixed and blended. The world-order that we are to examine is not merely one that contains sin, but one that contains sin and goodness, and is peopled by beings who do both right and wrong. This mixed character of the world is not usually considered when the relations of sin are in discussion, but there is no true understanding if this is overlooked.

To the question whether sin is a part of the system or an alien element, there is only one possible answer, in the present state of knowledge. Through its own method the order of the world has produced beings who do right and wrong. Life has developed into good character and bad. Virtue and sin are natural growths in the field of the life of humanity. If there is a good God over all, he is a good God who has himself produced a world of mingled good and evil. It is not difficult to show that this is true.

It has already been shown how naturally the moral element came into the human lot. Sensation belongs to the nature of life, judgment between sensations makes life rational, and choice among judgments and sensations makes life moral. Morality comes as soon as men begin to choose, and consequently to act, either with or against the worthier appeal. Responsibility comes when the choice or act is intelligent enough to be one's own. It is by a perfectly natural movement that life has moved on through these successive stages. The movement was in progress long before man appeared, or he would never have appeared at all. In fact, the progress of this movement, from sensation to morality and religion, constituted the approach of man. In inferior life the mental process is of the same kind as in man, only less advanced, and the moral quality exists, only less developed. When the movement had proceeded so far as to man, there was in him a real though incipient personality, to which incipient responsibility belonged. Man came into existence as a being in whom rationality had grown up, and morality had followed, only one stage behind. Both qualities were inherited from the past, but were inherited as germinant gifts whose significance lay in the future. That the origin of the moral nature of man was of this kind is certain, and we have no right to consider it in any other light.

One inference is plain. Coming thus into existence, it was impossible that mankind should start either good or bad, exclusively. Both good and evil had their beginnings already made and their tendencies established. One was as natural as the other. A career of mingled good and evil, right and wrong, is the career to which the human race was born.

All forward movement of life is movement toward some goal or standard not yet reached: and forward movement of this kind is the normal action of life in all its stages. This fact is plainest when we look at the beginnings of man. The coming of man consisted in what we may rightly call the coming of the soul. Life now at last began to take its highest form, the conscious spiritual. Slowly its powers were now gathered into the personal and responsible. A being was formed who was rationally akin to the structure of the world, and yet was impelled by his higher nature to lay hold of a power above the world. The soul was now the norm, to whose requirements and fitnesses the action of life ought to be conformed. This means that the proper life for man was life in which the purpose looked forward to higher things, the relations were understood and acted upon in the light of reason and religion, and impulses of the lower kind were kept in appropriate subordination. The norm for him to follow was that which had made him man, different from life below. The ascent of life had brought him into being, and now it was normal that life should still ascend, devoting its energies to the perfecting of the best that it had yet brought forth, elevating man toward the kindred spiritual power above. And now that man was a conscious being, looking before and after, with some growing power to perceive what he was and what he might be, it depended upon himself whether or not he was to turn his life to these highest uses. It was his calling to follow his higher nature, and live more and more as a spiritual being, while yet his life had its roots in his animal existence.

But with what powers was he to press on toward the prize of this upward calling? With such as he had, for there was no other way. But the powers that he had were such as the past had bequeathed him and the present was training. The body was old, the soul was new: lower life was ancient, spiritual life incipient. The higher impulses were just struggling into existence: the common life was the soil out of which they must rise, and they had not yet the training that would render them clear and sure. The habits of life, both personal and social, were inherited from periods in which the upward-reaching force was still of inferior grade, reaching up only to the level that had now been attained. Animal impulses were ancient, familiar and powerful: choice and action were adjusted from of old to the methods of the ages before the soul. Meanwhile the early human outreach in religion was only such as it could be, and grasped the unseen more strongly than clearly. The soul planted in man was like the seed in the parable, cast into the midst of thorns. If the thorns did not spring up and choke it altogether, there must have been some good reason why.

There is no doubt what would occur in such a case. Men would do right and do wrong. Right and wrong had been begun, in rudimentary fashion, in the animal world, before man came. If there had not been normal action, which is of the nature of right, man would never have come. When once he had come, with greater intelligence and capable of more various action, it was inevitable that normal conduct and abnormal conduct should be continued. Man would do right. The soul would call him on—for in the order of nature and of God the soul had come to stay, and not only to stay but to grow and to govern. The soul with its rising powers would tell him how he must treat his fellows, what he must make of himself, and how he must ascend to realities above. It would teach him but poorly at first, but it would impel him in the right direction, and not in vain. The power of the spirit is no dream, and it was certain to become effective in man's doing right. And it was equally certain that he would do wrong, for the impulses to do wrong were already present in force. The soul, the heavenly guest, is not most welcome among the earthly powers, and they rise to thwart its endeavours. The inherited impulses are largely selfish—not wholly so but largely—and when they become working material for the human will, they are sure to be transmuted into genuine human selfishness, which is the enemy of the soul. Passions that were normal once may be abnormal when the soul with its higher destinies has come, and yet they are habitual in the life and ingrained in the being of man; and they cannot be prevented from having too much control. Consciousness of power is a fact in animals: when it becomes a more intelligent thing in man with his larger ingenuity and wider range of action, what shall keep him back from violence and oppression? Wherever there is association there is possibility of right and wrong; and man with all his impulses toward good and evil is every moment a social being, sure to seize his innumerable opportunities. The growing soul had to deal with bodily appetites before it could know what domineering enemies they might become. Thus it is unquestionable that human life, coming as it did, must put forth moral activity that is neither all good nor all bad, but both good and bad, in inextricable mingling. The mixed character which the moral life of mankind has always borne was the natural consequence of the manner in which mankind came into existence, and is a genuine part of the system or world-order in which human life is included. Sin cannot be reckoned an intruder in our race, any more than night can be called an alien element in the affairs of our planet.

To say this is not to deny the worth and glory of the good or the genuine badness of sin, or to detract from the solemnity of life. When once the soul has come, life becomes inexpressibly serious, for the question is whether the soul with its godlike possibility is to rule. For the soul to rise to its normal inheritance in God is the best thing that can be: action that helps it is best and worthiest, and action that defeats it is worst. The soul can be defeated only by the bad, and the badness of sin is measured by this worst of tendencies, to drag the soul down from its glory. When we say that the system of life provided for good and evil, we are saying that it opened the door to the very best and the very worst that is possible to spiritual beings.

The conclusion that good and evil have both been brought forth by the operation of the order of the world is not reached by theorizing, but stands as the only reasonable interpretation of the facts. It suggests, however, another important question. Where, then, we shall be asking, rests the responsibility? Who is responsible, according to the Christian doctrine and the facts of life, for the sins, say, of Nero, and the virtues of Socrates? This is the same as asking who is responsible for the mixed moral condition of the world, and for the innumerable instances of good and evil that it presents in bewildering variety?

It is an old assumption, almost held sacred in popular ethics, that the responsibility for any given act must all be concentrated in one place. A strong individualism denies that any one but Nero or Socrates can carry any part of the burden. But if we distinguish things that really differ, we shall say that responsibility, never destroyed, is distributed. The answer to the question of responsibility stands in four parts. For the great world-order, in which good and evil have come into existence according to natural process, God is responsible, and no one else: this he does not wish us to deny. For the accumulated inheritance of good and evil which any given individual, Nero or Socrates, receives in his personal constitution, the human race is responsible—the race, which for good and ill has developed and trained the common nature to the point at which the individual receives it. This racial responsibility is a most real thing. For the acts and choices that make or mar the character and destiny of the man, the individual himself is responsible—the Nero or Socrates who is doing good or evil by his own volition; for the individual in question has not come forth from the humanity that produced him as a spool comes forth from the machine, made and finished, but stands as one more in the long succession of genuine actors, capable of doing real deeds and building up a real character. And for the innumerable influences that affect the individual Nero or Socrates, and help to make his character and conduct right or wrong, the responsibility is distributed among the many persons, past and present, who have done good and evil in the world. Thus among God, humanity, himself, and his various fellows is divided the responsibility of any man's moral condition and conduct. There is no valid way of denying any part of this fourfold assignment. The man can say that God created him so, that humanity produced him so, and that his fellows influenced him so, and yet he must say that he himself, the living person, has acted so, in doing right or wrong.

Since we find moral evil in the system of existence as an element that did not enter by intrusion, shall we inquire, as we did concerning the other perplexing facts, whether we can discover any meaning for it there? This appears to be a hopeless quest, and to propose it may seem to be only an aggravation of the general despair. Sin, we say, is so absolute a contradiction of the divine intent as to be essentially unintelligible: we are sure that no place can be found for it, or any clue to the cause of its being. Nevertheless, the question is forced upon us. When we examine the common life of mankind, we find it bringing forth good and evil side by side. The normal action of such a being as man results in both. Of course it can never appear that sin is normal to man.

By its very nature it is horribly abnormal, and in sound judgment it will always stand as something anomalous in the human world. But the startling significance of this is plain. It is a part of the world-order that something anomalous shall exist in the world, as well as something normal. This fact stands out clearly and is most important: the Mind that conceived and established the system contemplated the presence of an anomalous and abnormal element in his world—that is, of something anomalous and abnormal in relation to the higher ends that he was seeking. He contemplated the doing of something else besides his own will by men. And can we see why? This is the real question concerning evil, and this the real mystery. Why an abnormal element, wrought into the system of God?

We may remember once more that the soul in humanity was not born into peace, but into moral conflict. Its coming and its advancement to responsibility necessarily precipitated moral conflict: so it does in the individual, and so it did in the race. The proper destiny of the human now resided in the soul, and the forward-reaching impulse that is native to life should now normally be a demand for those qualities in which alone the soul could fulfil its nature, namely, for self-command, for high aims, for moral goodness, for divine fellowship. But a destiny, to be fulfilled, must be accepted and wrought out by him to whom it belongs; and the new-born human contained in itself the sure presage of internal conflict as to the acceptance of destiny with the soul. The soul could win its way to dominance only by mastering the divided nature of which it was a part. Thus with the soul came strife between the old and the new, the lower and the higher. It was not between the soul and the body, or between the higher destinies and the animal passions: these are but elements in a larger strife. It was an inward conflict between the past and the future, between what was and what ought to be, between what should be abandoned and what should be attained. It was war for control between these two. The conflict was within, at the seat of the will, and must be there, for it was a strife between impulses that were man's own. The battle must be fought out by his willing and acting now in one way and now in the other, living his divided life, learning by experience, and coming to unity after being first divided against himself. This, whatever we may think of it, and whether we can understand and justify it or not, is the way in which our race was made. From first to last its life is moral conflict.

This view of the facts gives another form to the question of sin and the good God. So to speak, it changes the scene of the inquiry. The question now relates not primarily to the world as we behold it, with all that its life has brought forth, but to the creature who is living the life. We do not inquire first whether God can have originated the actual present-day world, though that may seem to be the obvious question. We ask, Can the good God have originated beings with the fount of good and evil in their nature, whose life is moral conflict, and who are sure to make the world both good and bad? This is what has occurred, for such a race is the race that exists. Can a good God be the source of its being? It is the question of man.

Yet even this is not the question in its ultimate form. Farther back it goes. It is the question not only of man but of life. It is, Can the good God and Father be the originator of life, the embodied life which has existed through uncounted ages in this world? From its first hour life contained all the future, and when it was begun all destinies of the living were launched. A few words of recapitulation will show how true this is. Life, that mysterious something which is to maintain itself by utilizing what surrounds it, implies power of sensation, through which its necessary connections must be made. Experience of sensation, pleasant and painful, brings comparison of sensations, with estimation of them and choice between them; and through such experience life passes into rationality. Rational experience brings judgment as to what will best serve the best ends, and thus life attains a moral quality. All this is done, not in some secret chamber of thought, but in action, and thus the will is always in training, and is always directing the life. The rational and the moral were promised when life began: life had but to do its work, and they would come. The history of embodied life has witnessed the developing of the lower nature first, and the advent of the higher, or of what we call the soul, when the lower was sufficiently developed to serve its uses. When the higher comes, it is born to rational and moral warfare, having to win its place among older powers, and learn to live according to its destiny. What corresponds to the upward, Godward tendency is good and right: what denies or resists that tendency is evil and wrong. In such a case right is done, and wrong is done: good grows in the world, and so does evil. A solid mass of worthy, right and helpful practices, imperfect but good, becomes established in the common life, and so does a dreadful sum and variety of sin and wrong, too terrible for imagination. There is a great stock of common virtues, and a great stock of sin, and the double growth goes on, age after age: this is the world. And all this is only the genuine development from the nature of embodied life. For the explanation of the present conditions of good and evil we must look, not to the beginning of humanity, or to some event in its career, but back to the beginning of life itself. Can the good God have created life? is the question; for life itself contained the secret of sensation, of reason, of morals, of right and wrong, of virtue and sin, and of the present and future glories and terrors of existence.

It is on this primary question that the East and the West are at variance. The East holds that existence is a curse, the West that it is a blessing. In the East, the wonder is that any adequate power was ever so unwise and unkind as to produce conscious life: in the West, even in dark days, the song of gratitude to the Creator has never ceased. Neither view need surprise us, for there are great arguments for both. In the modern beginning of world-wide acquaintance, apparently, the sadness of the East is somewhat sobering the cheerfulness of the West, and the brightness of the West is

tempering the gloom of the East; but these are only beginnings of mutual influence, and the contrast is too deep-seated
to be quickly overcome. Yet all the more because we see
how deep the contrast is, the best that is in us affirms that
the West is right, that creation is worthy of God, and that
life is a good gift. All the weight of the value of moral
reality is on that side. Our trusting of our own souls, our
conviction that the world is an honest world, our sense of the
certainty of utter confusion to our whole being if it were otherwise, all impel us to assert that God was right in creating
life, even though its unfolding brought the evil with the good.

At the element of training through moral conflict which we
find in life we need not be offended, for we know of no other
way in which character was to be formed and the right destiny
of the soul attained. Perhaps we cannot declare it to be the
only way, for perhaps we do not know; but we can say that
it certainly corresponds to human nature. We at least have
seen no other method of attaining to confirmed high character. Moral education must be inward through experience.
Ultimate character, whether good or bad, implies an inward
victory over the opposite. Character untested is insecure. In
men, settled moral character seems to imply personal knowledge of good and evil; not of all possible good and evil, of
course, and not of some specified amount or intensity of strife,
but such acquaintance and such conflict as to make the victory
secure when it has been won. The training of souls to character is a great and exacting work. We often speak as if God
might have ordained it in any way that he liked, and would
have done best if he had chosen an easy way. But we seem
to be justified in saying that the nature of life involves the
present method. If God would have living children like
himself, they must grow up through such experience as life
implies. The discipline of a living race appears to require an
amount and kind of experience that we should never dare to
propose, and only the infinite wisdom could safely dare to
initiate. Such a God as the Father of Jesus is the only God
who can have a right to be the Father of souls. If the train-

ing of children through conflict is not unworthy of him, we cannot blame him for placing his children in a world of mingled good and evil. We can imagine a world that we could not attribute to a perfect God. Perhaps such a world would be one into which so terrible an anomaly as sin had forced its way against the will of the Creator. If it had successfully intruded to his realm and established so vast an empire there in spite of him, certainly we could not attribute to him the supremacy which the perfect goodness must possess. But a world that became a world of good and evil because it was the home of life, and by reason of the advent of the soul that he created for himself, does not seem to be one in which the good God can have had no part.

Of course this view of the matter does not dispel the present darkness. It is not the problem of evil that makes the trouble, it is the evil. Evil is a dreadful thing, for it proposes defeat to God and ruin to man. We may try to comfort ourselves indeed by giving it softer names. We may insist that it is no entity, but only the absence of good, and argue that, as a mere negative, it will by and by disappear. But it is of no use. This is not a true description, and the argument deals with words, not facts. Moral evil is a dreadful thing, and it is here. Sin has entered and has failed to make an exit. Evil stays and grows. It touches everything. It has marvellous power of self-renewal. Belief in immortality only enlarges our conception of its magnitude, for souls full of evil go out into another life. If we speak of evil as an element in the means of training, still we ask ourselves whether it proves to be that, on the whole. Is it accomplishing its end, if the end is this? Does the conflict result in the successful training of mankind? Is evil really of any use? Is it not sheer waste and curse instead, cursing all in vain? No general statement of the relation of good and evil to the world disposes of these facts and questionings. Nevertheless, such a statement is not in vain. It leads us back to origins, and shows us that what we are discussing is really the problem of existence, concerning which we are constrained to affirm the universal goodness. We look back to the origins and find some relief from a part of our perplexities: now if only we could look forward with clear vision to the end! We justly feel that if we are to make a true estimate of the meaning of evil we need to know the outcome. What is to be the end of it? How far is the good God able to utilize for his purpose this darker result of the moral conflict that belongs to life? How much is he able to accomplish, and how much will he accomplish, toward the conquering and eradication of sin? How long will he seek that of his own which is lost? Is the human will so related to the divine that all that is lost can be found and restored by him? and will he find it all? If we could confidently include the vast movement of sin between a Godworthy origin and a Godworthy outcome, we might sadly wonder on the way, but we could rest in hope.

All the doctrine that Christianity has to offer in view of these questions is its doctrine of God. Christianity does not accept the dilemma that if God is love he is not almighty, and if he is almighty he is not love. It believes that he is both. His character is perfect and his power is adequate to his character. It beholds a God so good as to be worthy to be a creator. Jesus has unveiled to us the face of a God who had the right to bring all creatures into being, and who is forever the righteous and holy friend of all existence. This is the supreme fact in the face of which we are to meet all questions and deal with all perplexities. It is true that clouds and darkness are round about him: we cannot solve the questions or see our way through the perplexities, but that does not alter God. It is in his universe that evil exists; and, we must remember also, it is in his eternity that evil has its being. The significance of eternity must never be forgotten here. Evil, since it affects souls of immortal destiny, is a matter of more than earthly scope, and we should be most shortsighted if we were to suppose that any experiences of this world, present or future, could suffice to solve the problem of it. Life in this world is too incomplete for that.

Since departing souls are carrying evil into the unseen world, we cannot fail to see that in that world the question of God's victory over evil must be wrought out. God changes never. In that unseen realm of life he is forever the same as here— or rather, to express the eternal truth more worthily, in this little world he is the same that he forever is in the infinite realms of being—the lover of souls and the enemy of sin. His Saviourhood, which is the expression of his nature, is as eternal as himself. If it were not of wider scope than this present life, we could not possibly think of him as the conqueror of sin, for we know that sin cannot be wholly conquered in this life; but not only "Wide as the world is his command," but "Vast as eternity his love." We are not able to trace out our hopes to their fulfilment or our fears to their extinction, but as Christians we are entitled to leave the problem of evil in the hands of the God and Father of the Lord Jesus Christ, trusting him that, wherever sin has abounded, grace will much more abound.

Evil will remain with us as a problem, however, until the day when the Christian people are possessed heart and soul by the spirit of the cross of Christ. When "the love of Christ constraineth us" we shall find ourselves drawn into fellowship with God's eternal passion for overcoming evil with good. Then evil will not seem less evil, but more, but we shall view it with altered eyes. Now we look at sin, seeking to solve a problem: then we shall look at the sinful, seeking to save. Instead of a problem, we shall have a work; instead of speculation, love; instead of pessimistic doubt, the hope that accompanies holy faith and high endeavour. May that day soon dawn.

5. THE CHRISTIAN BELIEF IN GOD

The doctrine of God is an object of belief, but so, in a more important manner, is the great reality of God himself. It is much to believe the doctrine, knowing what it means, but the characteristic utterance of Christianity has always been, "I believe in God," and that is far more. There is no such thing as faith in a doctrine, but faith in God in the familiar name of the Christian act and attitude. It remains, at the end of our presentation of the Christian doctrine, to give some account of the belief that corresponds to the doctrine, and to the reality which the doctrine sets forth. It is very unfortunate that the word believe is so ambiguous; for when we summon men to believe, as in the name of the gospel we do, they may think we are calling them merely to give assent to our statements, or they may understand that we ask for an act of the whole soul rising to the acceptance of a great conviction. Belief in the doctrine of God may easily be nothing more than assent to testimony or to evidence, acceptance of reasoning, or approval of an intellectual interpretation of the world. But belief in God, of which we are speaking now, is more than assent, more than a work of intellect, more than an understanding of the world. It is greater, and at the same time simpler, than any of these. It is a dealing between the man and God himself. In its effect, it is the flight of the soul to its rest, and the rising of the soul to its strength. It cannot be described in a phrase or two, but some of its qualities may be remembered here.

The Church has always been right in regarding the Christian belief in God as a response to revelation. Naturally it would be so, if there were any God worthy to be believed in. If there is such a God, it must be his good pleasure that men should know him; and if they feel after him and find him, it is because he is not far from every one of us (Acts xvii. 27), and is seeking to be known. The God in whom Christians believe has it for his nature to be self-manifesting, and revelation is not his exceptional work but his everlasting activity. All human belief in God has risen in response to his perpetual self-expression in nature and in man. But the Christian belief is a response to his clearest self-revelation, made in humanity. In the spiritual life of men he has progressively made himself known as the God of righteousness and love, and at length in Jesus Christ he has made the self-expression that taught men more of him than they had ever known before. Those who have learned of Jesus have become acquainted with a God in whom our deepest life can rest and be utterly satisfied: that is to say, they have found the God for whose fellowship man was evidently made. Holy, righteous, gracious, is the Being whom they have come to know; and all their acquaintance with him confirms their certainty that he is the true and living God. But such a God and Father as this was never passively discovered, or found in spite of himself by the mere groping of men. With such a character as he bears, it is absolutely certain that our knowledge of him was obtained not only with his consent, but in pursuance of his active will. God was in Christ self-revealing, and God is in our life self-revealing, and our belief in him is our response. He was beforehand with us in showing us what manner of God he was, and thus it came to pass that we knew.

Put in the more familiar terms, this is simply to say that the Christian belief in God is the child's recognition of the Father—for as Father Jesus reveals him—and it is a matter of course that the Father was there to be recognized, and was showing his face to his child that he might be recognized. The child's gaze into his face is the gaze of confidence deserved forever by his self-imparting goodness.

We do not tell the whole truth, however, when we call the Christian belief a response to the Christian revelation. We should misjudge the greatness and breadth of that belief if we were to think of it as grounded solely in experiences that we are accustomed to call religious, or in any historical revelation. This greatest of our beliefs is a response not only to that which is commonly called revelation, but also to the primary facts of life, and to the realities that encounter us in the general experience. Here, too, we may say if we choose, that we are responding to revelation, for God speaks to us in the order of our life. But it is another set of considerations that here appeals to us, and the response that we make to them when we believe in God is worthy to be mentioned by itself.

When we take for true the reality of the God of the Christian doctrine, we start from the most universal human experiences. It may seem to us that our first step is confidence in the God whom we feel to be worthy of our trust, but it is not. We could have no living confidence in God at all if it were not for certain other confidences that we all hold. Not even upon the authority of revelation could we believe in him, but for certain beliefs that enter into the warp and woof of our daily living. There is a practical substratum, a foundation, without which no belief in God could be trusted to stand fast, or even to arise. It is very true that in the experience of simple and childlike faith this underlying support of our confidence is not recognized and reasoned out: we build upon it without analysis: but none the less do we build upon it, and none the less does it lie firm beneath us.

The Christian confidence in God begins so far back as to include the confidence that we naturally have in ourselves—in our senses, our rational faculties, and our moral powers. It includes confidence in the world as an honest world and the universe as a universe of reality and truth, in which knowledge is trustworthy and religion is not in vain; confidence in the goodness of the good and the badness of the bad; confidence in the worthiness of the searchings of conscience and the inspirations of hope; confidence that the rational order is grounded in the eternal reason and the moral order in the eternal righteousness; confidence that our nature does not search in vain when it seeks divine foundations for human life; confidence, in a word, that the worthiest explanation of existence is the truest, and that that which is bears witness to an eternal interest in that which ought to be. Much of this confidence may be implicit, and as it were instinctive, but all this is included or implied in the Christian belief in God, and if we did not constantly assume these primal realities, we could not attain to that belief. It is on the wings of this comprehensive human confidence that we rise to the simple and all-unifying Christian faith. Indeed, it is in the strength of this primal confidence that we respond to the Christian revelation itself. When we put our trust in the God of Jesus Christ, that which speaks in the voice of faith is the soul claiming its birthright; for such a God is the birthright of man. The soul dares to rise in calm assertion that our nature does not fool us or the world deceive, and that therefore the God who is worthy of our confidence is the God who lives.

In a word, we trust the normal assumption of rational minds, that existence has been fairly and honestly given us, as a blessing and not as a curse. When we assume this, we are moving straight toward the recognition of the God who made us thus; and when we behold the God whom Jesus teaches us to know, we recognize the God in whom our primal confidences have prepared us to believe. Acquaintance with our Father is our birthright, and thus we come to it.

We might make response to revelation and to the common certainties by a belief that was not more than an intellectual assent and conviction. This many do, and perhaps all sometimes do; for no faith is perfect. Such belief, though not the best, is by no means to be condemned or despised. It is a response to evidence, and is at least an honest intellectual acceptance of truth. God who knows our feebleness cannot despise it. But the full Christian belief in God is more than this. It is not merely a reasoned conviction or a free assent: it is also a faith, whose nature and privilege it is to venture out beyond sight and beyond full evidence. In rising to God it rises to the unseen and undemonstrated. It is an assurance of things hoped for, a conviction of things not seen (Heb. xi. 1).

It need not be said that our senses give us no vision of the existence and character of God. Forever is he "God whom no man hath seen or can see" (1 Tim. vi. 16). All belief in him is belief that goes out beyond the field of the senses. It should be so; for belief is a function of the invisible man, and the senses, though they may guide us toward some place of vision, cannot discern the God who is invisible. The soul's transaction of belief both begins and ends where they cannot go. But belief in God lies not only beyond the region of the senses: it lies also beyond the region of demonstration. No one can claim that the existence of God has ever been proved demonstratively. There are good reasons, and great reasons, and sufficient reasons, for believing in it, but if we ask for demonstration we ask in vain, and doubtless it will be so for-ever. The doctrine of God contains truth to which the method of demonstration does not correspond. The intellect must believe in him on the evidence that we possess—and it is great—and the whole man must rise to him in the direction which the evidence warrants, by an act of faith. For it is the nature of faith to go out beyond sight, and to take hold upon that which is not seen or proved. Faith is a rising of the soul to truth. It does not ascend by the mere whim of the mind, for in the best that we know there are good grounds for faith. But the eye of reason does not see the whole height of the ascent of faith: it sees the direction, but not the entire way. Faith is the daring of the soul to go farther than it can see. In it there is sound reason, and hope, and holy courage.

This is what is meant when the Christian act of believing is called, as it often is, the venture of faith. In exercising the Christian belief in God a man must go not only farther, but very much farther, than he can see. The belief to which he rises is that the Source and Lord of all is the eternal goodness loving in wisdom: it is belief in the personal Spirit, perfectly good, who in holy love creates, sustains and orders all. Here the perfect character is believed in, just as distinctly as the eternal existence; and as of the existence, so of the perfect character, we must own that it has never been demonstrated in our presence. Many sincere souls who might believe in a God judge it beyond their power to believe in such a God, in such a world as this. The testimony of innumerable de-tails of dreadful fact agrees that the world in which we live, the only world we know, is an inconceivably hard world in which to believe in a God of perfect goodness. Light upon the dark problem of good and evil in our life is but dim, and it is too much to expect that any investigations of ours will solve the mystery. We are even divided against ourselves; for we feel that the best that is in us requires a different world from this at the hands of a perfect God, and yet the best that is in us feels itself to be built upon the very foundation of the perfect God as the supreme reality. It is plain that if we are to hold the Christian belief in the eternal goodness loving in wisdom, we must hold it by a venture of faith, going out beyond what we can see. We do hold it, and we hold it by such a venture. From the evidence, but beyond the evidence, that our life affords, we follow on to the assertion of God, the living God, absolutely good. From partial proof we rise to the full conclusion. There are doubts and there is darkness, but in faith the soul gathers up its most honourable energies and declares that good is the sun and evil is the cloud, and that the perfect and eternal sun is God. Contrary appearances are plentiful enough, but they are left beneath, while the soul trusts its primal certainties, follows them to their sure conclusion, and proclaims the reality of the eternal goodness loving in wisdom and ruling all.

Nor are we ashamed of the venture of faith. Some would make it a reproach against the Christian faith in God that it thus goes beyond the tangible evidence, and makes affirmations which there are no sufficient inductions to support. The reproach is a natural one coming from the outside, but it is not deserved. The venture of faith is not a wilful act, merely an assertion of something that one wishes to be true: it is the affirmation of something that we have good reason for believing to be true. Faith advances from the best convictions we possess to the only truth that could possibly make them valid, the perfect goodness of God. Such a venture is no foolish or wilful act: it simply sets things in their right order, and gives the best things the best place. Faith acts upon a reasonable judgment, and one that we cannot reject without stultifying our best selves. The venture that it makes, instead of being an unmanly thing, or an escape from untenable ground into a fool's paradise of confidence, is a consistent declaration of the supremacy of all that has a right to be supreme.

This language may sound too much as if faith were mainly a mental act based upon an argument. It is that, to a certain extent, for faith reasons, and reasons soundly; but the crowning element in faith, implied all along and now to be mentioned, shows how much more it is. The Christian faith has for its vitalizing force the element of personal self-commitment. A venture is an act, and an act of the whole man. A belief that God is worthy to be trusted becomes faith when God is trusted. Theoretical belief vanishes, and in faith the soul acts upon the being and the goodness of God. It not only beholds but casts itself upon the God who is good and doeth good, whose tender mercies are over all his works, the faithful Creator, the righteous Father, the holy Saviour. This character of faith is too secret and sacred to be minutely described: it lies in the region of mystery, for the soul itself does not understand it, and sometimes it seems verily to be a leap in the dark. It lies in the region of ecstasy, too, for here the untried is the glorious. Faith is the flight of the soul to its home in the bosom of its Father. Who shall describe it? Who can tell of the waverings and uncertainties before the flight, or of the welcome, the rest and the infinite peace that follow it? Going thus to his own place, a man trusts God for himself and for all creation: all is safe in the Father's hands, and his perfect goodness and redeeming grace are the complete satisfaction of the soul. Plainly, when this has come to pass, God and the soul have come into their right fellowship, and man has entered upon the life for which he was created. This is nature, this is right, and this is everlasting welfare. Who shall separate us from the love of God?

In speaking of the Christian doctrine of God it is only too easy to allow the divine to eclipse the human, instead of illuminating it; and from this account of faith it may seem as if its field and work were in the heavenly world, or else in that secret place of the heart where God and man meet alone in the darkness. But it would be a sad mistake thus to limit the sphere and scope of faith. The true doctrine of faith and works must not be lost sight of through the passing away of the old phraseology. Faith is an ethical force. It rules the life; or rather, it opens the life to God's ruling. It brings the life that now is, in this present world, under the moral inspiration of the heavenly Father. God knows how imperfect our response must be at present, and is more patient with us than we are with one another, or even with ourselves. But the truth is that, to accept God is to accept not only an immortal hope, but a moral standard, valid for the whole of eternity, including to-day. It is also to accept a moral power, and gladly to submit one's self to its working. Whenever an act of faith goes forth, it is a sinful being who betakes himself to God. Hatred of evil on the human side and forgiving grace on the divine are implied in the event. Now, since Father and child are together in the normal life, the Father's goodness is the accepted type of the child's being, and the Father's love is the means of holy transformation to the child. His word to his children is, "Be ye holy, for I am holy," and faith honours the call. In proportion as men believe in God with the Christian faith, there springs up an inspiration of purity, a zeal for righteousness, a fellowship with the spirit of Saviourhood. Not only do there blossom those graces of the Spirit which we are accustomed to group under the name of personal religion: all the social virtues and humane works that the world can need or goodness can inspire spring up and bring forth fruit when the Christian belief in God has free course and is glorified. Committing himself to God, man commits himself to goodness, and to the promotion of goodness, after the likeness of God.

Thus the Christian belief in God is the largest, the most exacting, the most consolatory, and the most inspiring of all the beliefs that are possible to men. No man can rise to the full height of it, nor can all the world do it justice. At the same time, it is a faith for a little child. Nothing can be simpler than to accept as a child the grace that is sufficient for the soul—and from that comes all the rest. Indeed, the Master says that, in order rightly to cherish the Christian faith, a man must become as a little child.

INDEX.

The International
Theological Library

ARRANGEMENT OF VOLUMES AND AUTHORS

THEOLOGICAL ENCYCLOPÆDIA. By CHARLES A. BRIGGS, D.D., D.Litt., sometime Professor of Theological Encyclopædia and Symbolics, Union Theological Seminary, New York.

AN INTRODUCTION TO THE LITERATURE OF THE OLD TESTAMENT. By S. R. DRIVER, D.D., D.Litt., sometime Regius Professor of Hebrew and Canon of Christ Church, Oxford.
[*Revised and Enlarged Edition.*

CANON AND TEXT OF THE OLD TESTAMENT. By the Rev. JOHN SKINNER, D.D., Principal and Professor of Old Testament Language and Literature, College of the Presbyterian Church of England, Cambridge, England, and the Rev. OWEN WHITEHOUSE, B.A., Principal and Professor of Hebrew, Chestnut College, Cambridge, England.

OLD TESTAMENT HISTORY. By HENRY PRESERVED SMITH, D.D., Librarian, Union Theological Seminary, New York. [*Now Ready.*

THEOLOGY OF THE OLD TESTAMENT. By A. B. DAVIDSON, D.D., LL.D., sometime Professor of Hebrew, New College, Edinburgh.
[*Now Ready.*

AN INTRODUCTION TO THE LITERATURE OF THE NEW TESTAMENT. By Rev. JAMES MOFFATT, D.D., D.LITT., Hon. M.A. (Oxon.), Minister United Free Church, Broughty Ferry, Scotland. [*Revised Edition.*

CANON AND TEXT OF THE NEW TESTAMENT. By CASPAR RENÉ GREGORY, D.D., LL.D., sometime Professor of New Testament Exegesis in the University of Leipzig. [*Now Ready.*

The International Theological Library

A HISTORY OF CHRISTIANITY IN THE APOSTOLIC AGE. By ARTHUR C. McGIFFERT, D.D., President Union Theological Seminary, New York. *[Now Ready.*

CONTEMPORARY HISTORY OF THE NEW TESTAMENT. By FRANK C. PORTER, D.D., Professor of Biblical Theology, Yale University, New Haven, Conn.

THEOLOGY OF THE NEW TESTAMENT. By GEORGE B. STEVENS, D.D., sometime Professor of Systematic Theology, Yale University, New Haven, Conn. *[Now Ready.*

BIBLICAL ARCHÆOLOGY. By G. BUCHANAN GRAY, D.D., Professor of Hebrew, Mansfield College, Oxford.

THE ANCIENT CATHOLIC CHURCH. By ROBERT RAINEY, D.D., LL.D., sometime Principal of New College, Edinburgh. *[Now Ready.*

THE LATIN CHURCH IN THE MIDDLE AGES. By ANDRE LAGARDE. *[Now Ready.*

THE GREEK AND EASTERN CHURCHES. By W. F. ADENEY, D.D., Principal of Independent College, Manchester. *[Now Ready.*

THE REFORMATION IN GERMANY. By T. M. LINDSAY, D.D., Principal of the United Free College, Glasgow. *[Now Ready.*

THE REFORMATION IN LANDS BEYOND GERMANY. By T. M. LINDSAY, D.D. *[Now Ready.*

THEOLOGICAL SYMBOLICS. By CHARLES A. BRIGGS, D.D., D.Litt., sometime Professor of Theological Encyclopædia and Symbolics, Union Theological Seminary, New York. *[Now Ready.*

HISTORY OF CHRISTIAN DOCTRINE. By G. P. FISHER, D.D., LL.D., sometime Professor of Ecclesiastical History, Yale University, New Haven, Conn. *[Revised and Enlarged Edition.*

CHRISTIAN INSTITUTIONS. By A. V. G. ALLEN, D.D., sometime Professor of Ecclesiastical History, Protestant Episcopal Divinity School, Cambridge, Mass. *[Now Ready.*

PHILOSOPHY OF RELIGION. By GEORGE GALLOWAY, D.D., Minister of United Free Church, Castle Douglas, Scotland. *[Now Ready.*

HISTORY OF RELIGIONS. I. China, Japan, Egypt, Babylonia, Assyria, India, Persia, Greece, Rome. By GEORGE F. MOORE, D.D., LL.D., Professor in Harvard University. *[Now Ready.*

HISTORY OF RELIGIONS. II. Judaism, Christianity, Mohammedanism. By GEORGE F. MOORE, D.D., LL.D., Professor in Harvard University. *[Now Ready*

APOLOGETICS. By A. B. BRUCE, D.D., sometime Professor of New Testament Exegesis. Free Church College, Glasgow. *[Revised and Enlarged Edition.*

THE CHRISTIAN DOCTRINE OF GOD. By WILLIAM N. CLARKE, D.D., sometime Professor of Systematic Theology, Hamilton Theological Seminary. [*Now Ready.*

THE DOCTRINE OF MAN. By WILLIAM P. PATERSON, D.D., Professor of Divinity, University of Edinburgh.

THE DOCTRINE OF THE PERSON OF JESUS CHRIST. By H. R. MACKINTOSH, Ph.D., D.D., Professor of Theology, New College, Edinburgh. [*Now Ready.*

THE CHRISTIAN DOCTRINE OF SALVATION. By GEORGE B. STEVENS, D.D., sometime Professor of Systematic Theology, Yale University. [*Now Ready.*

THE DOCTRINE OF THE CHRISTIAN LIFE. By WILLIAM ADAMS BROWN, D.D., Professor of Systematic Theology, Union Theological Seminary, New York.

CHRISTIAN! ETHICS. By NEWMAN SMYTH, D.D., Pastor of Congregational Church, New Haven. [*Revised and Enlarged Edition.*

THE CHRISTIAN PASTOR AND THE WORKING CHURCH. By WASHINGTON GLADDEN, D.D., sometime Pastor of Congregational Church, Columbus, Ohio. [*Now Ready.*

THE CHRISTIAN PREACHER. By A. E. GARVIE, D.D., Principal of New College, London, England. [*Now Ready.*

HISTORY OF CHRISTIAN MISSIONS. By CHARLES HENRY ROBINSON, D.D., Hon. Canon of Ripon Cathedral and Editorial Secretary of the Society for the Propagation of the Gospel in Foreign Parts. [*Now Ready.*

The
International Critical Commentary

ARRANGEMENT OF VOLUMES AND AUTHORS

THE OLD TESTAMENT

GENESIS. The Rev. JOHN SKINNER, D.D., Principal and Professor of Old Testament Language and Literature, College of Presbyterian Church of England, Cambridge, England. [*Now Ready.*

EXODUS. The Rev. A. R. S. KENNEDY, D.D., Professor of Hebrew, University of Edinburgh.

LEVITICUS. J. F. STENNING, M.A., Fellow of Wadham College, Oxford.

NUMBERS. The Rev. G. BUCHANAN GRAY, D.D., Professor of Hebrew, Mansfield College, Oxford. [*Now Ready.*

DEUTERONOMY. The Rev. S. R. DRIVER, D.D., D.Litt., sometime Regius Professor of Hebrew, Oxford. [*Now Ready.*

JOSHUA. The Rev. GEORGE ADAM SMITH, D.D., LL.D., Principal of the University of Aberdeen.

JUDGES. The Rev. GEORGE F. MOORE, D.D., LL.D., Professor of Theology, Harvard University, Cambridge, Mass. [*Now Ready.*

SAMUEL. The Rev. H. P. SMITH, D.D., Librarian, Union Theological Seminary, New York. [*Now Ready.*

KINGS. [*Author to be announced.*]

CHRONICLES. The Rev. EDWARD L. CURTIS, D.D., Professor of Hebrew, Yale University, New Haven, Conn. [*Now Ready.*

EZRA AND NEHEMIAH. The Rev. L. W. BATTEN, Ph.D., D.D., Professor of Old Testament Literature, General Theological Seminary, New York City. [*Now Ready.*

PSALMS. The Rev. CHAS. A. BRIGGS, D.D., D.Litt., sometime Graduate Professor of Theological Encyclopædia and Symbolics, Union Theological Seminary, New York. [*2 vols. Now Ready.*

PROVERBS. The Rev. C. H. TOY, D.D., LL.D., Professor of Hebrew, Harvard University, Cambridge, Mass. [*Now Ready.*

JOB. The Rev. G. BUCHANAN GRAY, D.D., Professor of Hebrew, Mansfield College, Oxford, and the Rev. S. R. DRIVER, D.D., D.Litt., sometime Regius Professor of Hebrew, Oxford. [*2 vols. Now Ready.*

ISAIAH. Chaps. I–XXVII. The Rev. G. BUCHANAN GRAY, D.D., Professor of Hebrew, Mansfield College, Oxford. [*Now Ready.*]

ISAIAH. Chaps. XXVIII–XXXIX. The Rev. G. BUCHANAN GRAY, D.D. Chaps. LX–LXVI. The Rev. A. S. PEAKE, M.A., D.D., Dean of the Theological Faculty of the Victoria University and Professor of Biblical Exegesis in the University of Manchester, England.

JEREMIAH. The Rev. A. F. KIRKPATRICK, D.D., Dean of Ely, sometime Regius Professor of Hebrew, Cambridge, England.

EZEKIEL. The Rev. G. A. COOKE, M.A., Oriel Professor of the Interpretation of Holy Scripture, University of Oxford, and the Rev. CHARLES F. BURNEY, D.Litt., Fellow and Lecturer in Hebrew, St. John's College, Oxford.

DANIEL. JAMES A. MONTGOMERY, Ph.D., S.T.D., Professor in the University of Pennsylvania and in the Philadelphia Divinity School.

AMOS AND HOSEA. W. R. HARPER, Ph.D., LL.D., sometime President of the University of Chicago, Illinois. [*Now ready.*]

MICAH, ZEPHANIAH, NAHUM, HABAKKUK, OBADIAH AND JOEL. Prof. JOHN M. P. SMITH, University of Chicago; W. HAYES WARD, D.D., LL.D., New York; Prof. JULIUS A. BEWER, Union Theological Seminary, New York. [*Now ready.*]

HAGGAI, ZECHARIAH, MALACHI AND JONAH. Prof. H. G. MITCHELL, D.D.; Prof. JOHN M. P. SMITH, Ph.D., and Prof. J. A. BEWER, Ph.D. [*Now Ready.*]

ESTHER. The Rev. L. B. PATON, Ph.D., Professor of Hebrew, Hartford Theological Seminary. [*Now Ready.*]

ECCLESIASTES. Prof. GEORGE A. BARTON, Ph.D., Professor of Biblical Literature, Bryn Mawr College, Pa. [*Now Ready.*]

RUTH, SONG OF SONGS AND LAMENTATIONS. Rev. CHARLES A. BRIGGS, D.D., D.Litt., sometime Graduate Professor of Theological Encyclopædia and Symbolics, Union Theological Seminary, New York.

THE NEW TESTAMENT

ST. MATTHEW. The Rev. WILLOUGHBY C. ALLEN, M.A., Fellow and Lecturer in Theology and Hebrew, Exeter College, Oxford. [*Now Ready.*]

ST. MARK. Rev. E. P. GOULD, D.D., sometime Professor of New Testament Literature, P. E. Divinity School, Philadelphia. [*Now Ready.*]

ST. LUKE. The Rev. ALFRED PLUMMER, D.D., late Master of University College, Durham. [*Now Ready.*]

ST. JOHN. The Right Rev. JOHN HENRY BERNARD, D.D., Bishop of Ossory, Ireland.

ACTS. The Rev. C. H. TURNER, D.D., Fellow of Magdalen College, Oxford, and the Rev. H. N. BATE, M.A., Examining Chaplain to the Bishop of London.

ROMANS. The Rev. WILLIAM SANDAY, D.D., LL.D., sometime Lady Margaret Professor of Divinity and Canon of Christ Church, Oxford, and the Rev. A. C. HEADLAM, M.A., D.D., Principal of King's College, London.
[*Now Ready.*

I. CORINTHIANS. The Right Rev. ARCH. ROBERTSON, D.D., LL.D., Lord Bishop of Exeter, and Rev. ALFRED PLUMMER, D.D., late Master of University College, Durham.
[*Now Ready.*

II. CORINTHIANS. The Rev. ALFRED PLUMMER, M.A., D.D., late Master of University College, Durham.
[*Now Ready.*

GALATIANS. The Rev. ERNEST D. BURTON, D.D., President of the University of Chicago.
[*Now Ready.*

EPHESIANS AND COLOSSIANS. The Rev. T. K. ABBOTT, B.D., D.Litt., sometime Professor of Biblical Greek, Trinity College, Dublin, now Librarian of the same.
[*Now Ready.*

PHILIPPIANS AND PHILEMON. The Rev. MARVIN R. VINCENT, D.D., sometime Professor of Biblical Literature, Union Theological Seminary, New York City.
[*Now Ready.*

THESSALONIANS. The Rev. JAMES E. FRAME, M.A., Professor of Biblical Theology, Union Theological Seminary, New York City.
[*Now Ready.*

THE PASTORAL EPISTLES. The Rev. WALTER LOCK, D.D., Professor of Divinity in the University of Oxford and Canon of Christ Church.
[*Now Ready.*

HEBREWS. The Rev. JAMES MOFFATT, D.D., D.Litt., Hon. M.A. (Oxon.), Minister United Free Church, Broughty Ferry, Scotland. [*Now Ready.*

ST. JAMES. The Rev. JAMES H. ROPES, D.D., Bussey Professor of New Testament Criticism in Harvard University.
[*Now Ready.*

PETER AND JUDE. The Rev. CHARLES BIGG, D.D., sometime Regius Professor of Ecclesiastical History and Canon of Christ Church, Oxford.
[*Now Ready.*

THE JOHANNINE EPISTLES. The Rev. E. A. BROOKE, B.D., Fellow and Divinity Lecturer in King's College, Cambridge. [*Now Ready.*

REVELATION. The Rev. ROBERT H. CHARLES, M.A., D.D., sometime Professor of Biblical Greek in the University of Dublin. [2 *vols. Now Ready.*